EL GRINGO

ONCE IN A LIFETIME

JOHN ELLIS

This edition published in Great Britain in 2014 by
MyVoice Publishing
33-34 Mountney Bridge Business Park
Westham
PEVENSEY
BN24 5NJ

ISBN 978-1-909359-42-0

Cover photo: John Ellis in the Arena de Sao Paulo, Brazil

Back cover photos:

Brazilian fans:
Aline Cortes from Porciuncula, living in Copacabana, Rio de Janeiro. Crazy about football and especially Vasco da Gama. Big sports fan and addicted to CrossFit. I love my country!
Jessica Souza from Natal, living in Copacabana, Rio de Janeiro. Vasco da Gama supporter and crazy about the beach. Living with joy in my smile and soul!

View of Rio de Janeiro from Pedra Bonita (Beautiful Rock) Mountain overlooking Copacabana, Ipanema, and favelas nestling in the foothills of Dois Irmaos (Two Brothers) Mountain

Argentina fans:
Sabina Sagripanti from Rosario Passionate about football, motor bikes and lead singer of the Belo Rojo Blues Band
Vanesa Sosa from Cordoba. Football fanatic and especially Argentina
Ana Munoz Bracero from Salta. Huge football fan

Sunrise on Copacabana beach

FOREWORD

This book is a bit of a breakthrough from a writing point of view. It is the first time I am aware of a book being written on an iPhone - a phenomenal task, finger tapping out over 150,000 words. My mind certainly boggles! There is a recent interest in literature written on the mobile phone, but it tends to be flash fiction, poetry, very short works.

Yet this book proves that the phone lends itself perfectly to writing on the go - which is what is required when you have an ardent and engaging witness like John Ellis. Throughout this delightful book, you can really *see* John as he taps in his thoughts on what he is viewing and experiencing. He certainly experienced a lot, from walking round a favela, hiking a mountain, visiting tourist attractions and absorbing the culture as well as the football. Everything is fresh, new, enchanting and 'Oh! There's a different sort of fan, I must go and speak with them!' You cannot help but smile and pick up on his infectious enthusiasm which absolutely permeates this book.

I suspect this book will prove to be a breakthrough in many areas. As well as how to write a diary, it gives a template for attending a World Cup. John narrates his trials and tribulations in arranging tickets, transport and accommodation - there is never a problem with food or drink, though, as he delights in new tastes and cocktails. His attitude is what sets the book apart, and I think that readers will find themselves well rewarded if they emulate this in similar circumstances. Too many people stay aloof, usually from shyness. John doesn't have a shy bone in his body, and the rewards this brings is very evident. He epitomises the benefits to be received from talking and making friends with strangers. This has the very real benefit to the reader of giving so many more stories of Brazil - many of which to be avoided, from love-sick monkeys to zealous portaloo guards.

This is not so much a record of football, as these books tend to be. It is a record of the people, of the fans, the wonderful friendliness of the fan fests where it seems vast numbers of fans end up. It seems to be a purer football experience than being in the heavily controlled stadia of Western Europe, with the personal interaction of the fans from so many different countries. The very idea of segregation appears to have escaped the Brazilians completely, with delightful consequences. The atmosphere in the stadiums would be electric, like a carnival and in the Maracana very special, while the fans could move and intermingle, making friends as they went. It is one long fiesta for John, and I suspect he will find it a life-changing experience.

It is a privilege to join him on his unexpected journey through Brazil and follow not just his travels, but those of the many fans with whom he interacts and cleverly weaves their stories into his book. On reflection, after reading this book, in the way the football brought many nations and cultures together in Brazil, one feels very much at one with the people of this planet.

Rex Sumner, author, publisher and football fan.

EL GRINGO'S ONCE IN A LIFETIME

The experience of the World Cup surprised everybody. First I was thinking about a complete mess, because of the unfinished works and because the people didn't agree with the project and the money spent. But when the games started the society was happy with the many tourists and the tourists were happy with the locals' energy, so the party started! For me it was very interesting because besides meeting people to learn English I learned about other cultures and this makes me more motivated to travel to other countries. I loved the way Brazil was a big party and I am proud to have participated, despite all the problems of my country.

Julia Bomfim Caetano, 19, Rio de Janeiro, Brazil

The World Cup was the greatest event that could happen in Brazil. It gathered together people from all over the world into our country. All celebrating the biggest sport event on the planet in what is known as footballs' home. It brought with it new stadiums and structures but also a new thinking of the game; of the local league and to the event itself but the most important: the hope to see a better social behaviour of the fans, bringing again families to the stadiums. Being a restart point for the game here.

José Roberto Fernandes de Moura Filho, 23,
Recife-Pernambuco, Brazil

CONTENTS

EL GRINGO'S ONCE IN A LIFETIME

PROLOGUE

MONDAY 26TH MAY 2014

The story starts on the evening of the UK Public Holiday, Monday 26th August 2014.

I am driving my 19 year old son Henry to Grantham train station for him to catch an evening train to London. He works there and shares a place with three other guys in the East End.

During the journey, he knows I have been a little down for some months now and says...Dad, why don't you go away for a week or two on your own to the sun, go to some bars and have a change of scenery?

I say...Where am I going to go at my age? I can't be going in Ayia Napa bars on my own!

He says "Dad, you may travelled a lot but surely there must be somewhere in the World you would like to visit? I say...Well yes may be Vancouver, St Petersburg and the island in the South Pacific film, the first film I ever saw.. Bali Hai was its name in the film...but I just don't feel in the mood to go to those places.

I would also like to one day watch a Forfar Athletic game...My favourite Scottish team, by virtue of being the first football shirt I ever had as a child... Second hand off a friend, Kevin Wilson. How did I know it was Forfar Athletic? They were the only side in the whole of the English and Scottish leagues in the late 1960's who played in vertical green and white striped shirts. How did such a child's shirt end up in the City of Lincoln where I grew up...? Absolutely no idea!

We are getting close to the railway station and now my son is pushing me. I know he doesn't want to leave me without feeling that I am OK...And then I remember that an old work friend Paul Newton and his friend Ian are going to the World Cup. I make a joke that I could try to go with them.

My son says "Dad, go for it! It is a chance of a lifetime...You have done so much for us, do something for yourself". It dawns on me that he is right...It is a chance of a lifetime.

I am 55 and securing time off work is not an issue. The next two World Cups are in Russia and Qatar. Realistically, it really is my last chance...At least in this life time…And no finer place to go to see the World Cup than in Brazil!!

TUESDAY 27TH MAY TO FRIDAY 30TH MAY 2014

Paul emails his itinerary saying it is not how he would have planned it but he got the tickets he c/ould around a two week work break. His friend Ian Wood who Paul roomed with at University was 50 this year and this was to be a kind of a celebration....Given that Ian hired a box for his beloved Nottingham Forest against Doncaster Rovers which turned out to be a goalless draw for his actual 50th, it sounds like Ian deserves a good World Cup!

I have a cursory look at flight seat availability and for the most part they seem bookable. It does though feel a bit of a pipe-dream at this late stage.

Paul writes to FIFA regarding a third bed in the various hotel rooms. FIFA eventually respond to say that it will be the hotels' decision and that FIFA will be forwarding the guest details to the hotels on Monday second June.

SATURDAY 31ST MAY 2014

This has nothing to do with the World Cup but it was such a fantastic night that I can't help but mention it. Henry somehow managed to book us two tickets for the Froch v Groves rematch at Wembley. Oh what a night at Wembley Stadium... 80,000 fans packed in!

Other than Joshua securing a first round knock out in spectacular fashion, the rest of the under card were all closely fought contests.

Then the drama of Groves coming out aboard a red London bus and of course nobody then knew that the joke would be that he would go home in a London Ambulance!

What a knock out punch from Froch though and for us living in Nottinghamshire it felt a little extra special. Our man so to speak... My son is now saying... Dad, we have to go to Vegas to see him box out there!

After the fight, rather than queue on Wembley Way, we made the long hike

up to Preston Road tube station where my son caught a tube train back into London and just passed the station, I picked up my car to drive home. On the way back, we rescued countless fans who thought they were walking in to Central London only to be told they were walking further away. Most were from Notts...Poor guys don't get down to Wembley too often these days! And after seeing some of Spurs recent defeats there...Maybe I wish I didn't either!

My son promised to text through a photo of us taken together inside Wembley and it came through as I stopped off at a McDonalds drive through...Or I thought it had but it was a photo of him with Alistair Cook the England cricket captain at Preston Road station! Cook had the same idea as us and they chatted together on the tube back into Central London. Long day for Cook as he had played at Lords in the One Day International decider with Sri Lanka which went down to the final over and Malinga as ever came out on top to defeat us . That was despite a magnificent 100+ knock from Jos Buttler.

Anyway I digress!

MONDAY 2ND JUNE TO WEDNESDAY 4TH JUNE 2014

Paul writes to the hotels who say they have not received the guest lists from FIFA. The Rio hotel also advises it won't be possible to have a third bed in the room.

I write to the hotel and a lady called Vitoria responds to say it will be impossible to book a room. It is completely full. I ask her to bear me in mind if a cancellation is received.

The other main hotel where Paul and Ian are staying in Recife sound a little more hopeful but say they will not be able to advise until Friday 6th June. They also require FIFA approval. I duly send the FIFA letter received by Paul to the hotel which will hopefully suffice.

I scour the internet for hotels in Rio...It is hopeless as the prices run into thousands of pounds for a single room for five nights...Even for hotels many miles away from Copacabana where Paul and Ian are staying.

It was a good idea but at this late stage it seems doomed to failure. I hadn't got my hopes up so it's not a huge let down...Brazil is a long way from the U.K. but right now it feels light years away...

EL GRINGO'S ONCE IN A LIFETIME

THURSDAY STH JUNE 2014

One week before the tournament begins; I have absolutely nothing booked... It's not going to happen is it...

The problem is accommodation in Rio. If I could have just found accommodation there, I would have taken a punt on the rest.

I have again been in contact with the Savoy Othon, Copacabana, Rio de Janeiro where Paul and Ian will be staying...Nothing...Nada...

Then miracle of miracles an email drops into my inbox late Thursday night:

Mr John we can offer you accommodation for the five nights you are looking for in a single room at 600 reals per night plus 15% taxes...I quickly get my calculator out. Wow, it is about £200 a night...That much...But hey the cheapest I have seen since starting my search on Monday...

The song "The girl from Ipanema" comes into my head...And stays there!!

The hotel wants confirmation by 7pm local time which is11pm UK time. It is now 11.45pm....Damn... Not quite the exact expression I used but children might be reading!

I call the charmingly named Vitoria at the hotel who thankfully agrees an extension until 11am next morning which is 3pm Friday afternoon, UK time.

Plenty of time to organise flights...Could the pipe-dream be becoming a possibility!!

The problem is Paul and Ian, who booked a long time ago based around the match tickets they could get, have quite a complicated trip...

They are flying to Lisbon Friday night, 13th June and staying in a hotel for an early flight the next morning direct to Rio.

This route is not possible for me...Hmmm

At this point I should add that I live in Nottinghamshire in England and they live in the south towards London.

The flights and prices coming up aren't too great...Flight times of 48 hours or more with two stops at about £4000 a time...Why do the web sites even bother showing these!

Eventually through good old Skyscanner, I find a 6.25am flight from Birmingham with Air France through Charles de Gaulle (CDG) with a 1 hour 20 minute transfer time. It sounds a little tight but fortunately is within the same terminal 2E for those of you who know Paris. I do as I commuted to Paris for 3 years in the last decade and... I therefore know how often early morning UK flights to Paris are all too often delayed...I can't help feeling a little nervous but it's by far the best option...Booked!

The dream is no longer a dream!

There are probably a few other things I should tell you at this stage...

1) The flight arrives into Rio 5.10pm on Friday 13th June

a) My friends don't arrive in a Rio until 3.30pm Saturday 14 June...A day later

b) My hotel booking is from 14th to19th June...I don't have a bed for the

night I arrive in Rio...
2) My return flight is also from Rio. My friends fly back from Recife...
3) My flight back is overnight with KLM into Amsterdam where there will
be a four hour wait for my connection back to Birmingham
For those of you curious on cost...the return flight cost £1484.
Immediately, I ring Vitoria to try to secure another night at the hotel...She
has left for the day...Fortunately her colleague is able to help and miraculously
I book the night of the 13th and at a reduced rate of 384 reals plus 15% taxes..
Bargain!! Umm not quite the right expression but at least a lot cheaper!!
I now work through Paul's spreadsheet trying through Skyscanner to book
the same internal flights... It is a nightmare! Now I am deep into the middle of
the night or should I say early hours of the morning... Tired, stressed...Can I,
will I be able to get hotels and flights which match Paul and Ian's schedule? Not
to mention match tickets...This is crazy...
I manage to book a flight from Rio to São Paulo in the early hours of the
morning of Thursday 19th June to hopefully go to the England v Uruguay match
which is the second of England's three Group games.
It is a different flight to that of my friends and I don't even know if it is even
to the same airport as them!! To understand my concern...Think of how far apart
Luton, Stansted, Heathrow and Gatwick are...Yet they are all called London
airports!! But I had no choice...The only other flights available arrived too late
for kick off... Not that I even have a match ticket yet!! The more I wade into the
detail of this the crazier it becomes...
I look at the next flight on their itinerary...Oh my...It is on the same day
Thursday 19th at 11.55pm!!! A flight arriving into Recife at 3.20am with a note
against it on the spreadsheet which says ...No hotel room available in Recife for
this night!
I search for the flight...And yes!!! It is available...And you, as objective
readers, in the cold light of day rather than in the middle of the action so to speak...
rightly rationalise...Why wouldn't it be!! Only mad dogs and Englishmen out in
the midnight hours! In my anxiety to reserve a seat with my friends...Booked!
Only the next day do I think to check whether I am flying in and out of the
same São Paulo airports...Which given that I will want to leave my luggage at
the arrival airport is somewhat crucial!! What if it isn't...What will I do...It will
be impossible... It is booked now...
On checking and more through luck than judgement, it is the same airport
and not only that but also the same airport my friends arrive and depart from!
I look at Paul's itinerary again and the next flight to be booked is 5.10am on
Tuesday, 24th June from Recife to Belo Horizonte to watch England's final group
game against Costa Rica...Which of course the way England are shaping up...
could be a non-event.. Quite possible we could lose against Italy and Uruguay
and already be effectively out of the tournament...
But...What the hell...I try to find their flight...No seats available...In fact the
only possible option to arrive in time for the match is a 3.20am departure which

5

with a connection arrives at 9.20am...Whereas my friends are on a 5.10 direct flight which arrives at 6.40am..

Umm...What if there is a delay or a problem with the connection...And in any event, how on earth would I ever find them in Belo Horizonte...? Boy oh boy... The hurdles are rising ever higher as much as my tiredness is overwhelming me...

I decide to have a look at flights leaving the day before and preferably late at night...And lo and behold there is 9.50pm flight which arrives into Belo Horizonte at 6.10am with a 2 hour 40 connection in Sao Luis.

Now at this point, if you are not already, you might be questioning my sanity... I will defend myself! My logic for booking this flight, yes I booked, was three fold:

1) I arrive at a similar time as my friends into Belo Horizonte

2) There is plenty of time not only for the connection but also in case of delays on the second leg of the flight. I should get to the match on time

3) To answer your question about sleep or lack of it...If I had booked the 3.20 flight, I would have left the hotel around midnight for the airport. So...effectively no sleep in a bed. By being on planes for most of the night, I may have a chance of at least the same number of hours of disturbed sleep if not more...

Can you imagine going through this logic at silly o'clock in the morning! Anyway...Booked...Another one crossed off the list!

I decide not to book the Belo Horizonte to Rio flight at this stage. It might not be possible to book a hotel room in Rio and if it isn't, I will stay in Belo Horizonte an extra night and transit in and out of Rio on my return journey home.

It is now 5am Friday morning...I have been working on this for more than five hours nonstop throughout the night. I look outside and notice it is daylight... The birds are singing... Was that the girl from Ipanema haha! I go to bed insanely happy… May be that sentence is one word too long!

FRIDAY 6TH JUNE 2014

I wake around 10am to a text from Paul, which came in at about 7am, saying tickets for some of their games are available on the FIFA web site.

Paul also says as a member of Club Wembley, he will make contact in case an England v Uruguay ticket becomes available.

I run downstairs and open up the web site. Alas all the tickets have gone... The site refreshes ticket availability every five minutes. I have several pages of the site open simultaneously which cuts down the refresh from five minutes to under one minute.

I am looking for a ticket to each of the seven games my friends are going to which are:

Match No. 11 Sunday 15th June Argentina v Bosnia Herzegovina at the Maracana in Rio de Janeiro

Match No. 19 Wednesday 18th June Spain v Chile at the Maracana in Rio de Janeiro

Match No. 23 Thursday 19th June England v Uruguay in São Paulo

Match No. 24 Italy v Costa Rica

Match No. 34 Croatia v Mexico

Match No. 40 England v Costa Rica

My friends then return to Recife to watch USA V Germany. While I return to Rio de Janeiro and will try for a ticket for Match No. 53 Ecuador v France 25th June at the Maracana in Rio de Janeiro.

In not too short a time a ticket becomes available for Italy v Costa Rica in Recife. I go through the booking procedure...In my panic... Suffer the pain of entering the security code and getting it wrong. Will it be snapped up before I enter the correct security code?

I am now officially not just going to Brazil...I am now going to the 2014 World Cup!! Category B £85 for a ticket for Italy v Costa Rica! Any other time, being honest, you just wouldn't...Would you? Here and now though I am jumping for joy...Ecstatic!

Then later a ticket comes up for Croatia v Mexico again in Recife. I book it and it's the lowest category C ...Only £56...Bargain! Actually in the context of the World Cup...It feels as if it is a bargain! As a Spurs fan it will be good to see Modric play again and hopefully Corluka if he is in the squad? Shame Kranjcar is injured but they have a number of talented players as do Mexico and of course Giovanni Dos Santos! I am genuinely excited to be going to this match. Then I check the date again. The match is being played at 5pm, Monday 2third June. It will finish at say 7pm...Didn't I have to book a flight from Recife to Belo Horizonte that night as there weren't any early morning flights???? Oh no... What have I done...In blind panic to get the ticket, booked it and I can't actually go to the match??

Anxiously I check my flight time 9.55pm...Phew...It should just about be doable although I may have to have a taxi on hand and leave a few minutes early. Hmm...What about my luggage? I won't be able to take that to the match. I wonder how far the hotel is from the airport. Can I check in the luggage before the match? I wonder how far the stadium is from the airport...Questions, questions, questions...

I ring the helpful Priscilla at the Beach Hotel, Recife who checks and advises that the airport is 30km from the stadium. It should be ok once away from the football traffic...Isn't there enough stress to contend with already!!

Wow a ticket for England v Costa Rica comes up! Somebody gets in before me. DAMN! This happens a few times...I live in an area with a poor internet connection... Ordinarily it is frustrating but as with everything you get used to it...But now...It's a little more than frustrating!!!

Eventually I manage to secure an England v Costa Rica ticket!!! Yessss... I am going to see an England game in the 2014 World Cup in Brazil...Me excited!!! Let's hope England still have something to play for! It's a category A ticket £110...Would I pay that to watch the match at Wembley? Truthfully I would struggle to justify paying half that! But hey I have a ticket to watch England in the 2014 World Cup Finals in Brazil...Yaay!!

There is though one fly in the ointment so to speak...When booking the tickets, I have to state a Brazilian ticket office I have to go to collect the ticket... Yep Rio obviously as I am there for almost the first week of my trip...I refrain from calling it a holiday...A holiday is a chance to chill out, relax, take it easy, come back refreshed...I actually feel like I will need a holiday after trying to get everything booked and certainly after actually being out there! Being 30 years younger would be great...For so many reasons haha...Well except 30 years ago; watching England abroad was a violent affair. Not like going today hey? Oh wait a minute...Yes this is in Brazil...Violent crime, demonstrations against the World Cup, strikes in Sao Paulo, a lack of inoculations...Nothing too much to be concerned about there then!

Anyway back to the collection of tickets in Rio...The first available appointment is 20th June... I have no choice but to book this appointment. If I don't complete the booking within 15 minutes, I lose it...I book the appointment but the eagle eyed amongst you will recognise that I leave Rio on the morning of the 19th June and won't be returning again until the 25th June... By which date, the matches I wish to attend will have been played...Hmmm...Another worry to add to the ever growing list!

I telephone Priscilla at the Beach Resort, Recife who advises that the hotel still hasn't received the guest details from FIFA. Priscilla is so helpful that somehow I kind of anticipate she will find a way to put a third bed in my friends room...Strange how sometimes you sense such things...And then are proven to be hopelessly wrong!!

It is now 3pm which is 11am in Rio. For the next 45 minutes I am frantically trying to obtain a dialling tone into the Savoy Othon hotel in Rio to speak with Vitoria...It is hopeless...I panic that Vitoria may have released the room and write an email explaining the problem. It would be impossible to find another hotel in Rio and now everything else is booked...

I wait anxiously for a response and thankfully the room is still booked in my name. Vitoria says an updated booking form will be sent to me.

I write back asking for an extra night on the 25th June, to at first be advised there isn't any availability. A second email arrives saying the hotel can offer me a booking for a minimum of two nights of 25th and 26th June at 600 per night plus 15% taxes...

I write back saying I only need one night and as I have already booked six nights for the previous week, could the night of the 25th be added on to that booking as I fly back to the UK on the 26th. The answer came back basically saying the system says no...Now where I have heard a similar expression from a well know comedy sketch... But alas, this is anything but funny!!

I had also asked in my email if the hotel would be able to arrange tickets for the four matches I wish to attend. Vitoria kindly advises that the request will be passed on to the concierge.

I receive the form to fill out...Doing this at home is not the same as when being in an office...

Somehow I manage to download the form on my virus ridden old rickety lap top...Hook up the "some days I will work, some days I won't work" (sounds like London Underground staff...Only joking chaps!) printer to the computer and print the form off.

I complete the form; scan it through the printer to my computer. I then attach it to an email and send it to the hotel in Rio...Having not slept too many hours... This feels a torturous route to just book a hotel room...And very sensitive credit card information is contained in the attachment...I will worry about that later... As a worrier, that means I will worry about a lot...

The hotel write back saying the form has to be completed again and as well they require a copy of my passport photograph as well as both sides of my credit card... A trifle frustrating...Stress, tiredness and frustration are a horrible combination...

Eventually, everything is completed to the satisfaction of the hotel and I have a confirmed reservation...Phew!

Then Priscilla writes to confirm I can have an extra bed in the room of my friends for 100 reals plus of course the obligatory 15% taxes per night!! Wow, now I only have two nights' accommodation to book - one or two nights in Belo Horizonte and, if one, the other night will be in Rio! #fallingintoplace

However, the hours are slipping by and all of the time I am scanning the multi refreshes of the FIFA site searching for match tickets. Nothing doing...

As tickets for the matches I am looking for do not seem to becoming available and in my tired state I suddenly realise if a ticket for England v Italy became available...I would be in the country and could potentially go to England's opening match.. Wow!!

The last time I went to an Italy v England World Cup match was in 1990 in Bari. It was the third/fourth playoff match which Italy won 2-1 in Bobby Robson's last game as England Manager.

So now I have added:

Match No. 8 England v Italy Saturday 14th June to my search.

The frustrating thing about the FIFA site is that you have to look down the list of all 64 matches on each refresh, find the match you are interested in, to then check whether the ticket is available or not.. My oh my... It is painful.

The laptop and home office is now virtually where I live...Anything else happening in the world is almost an irrelevance... I love tennis and had been watching Andy Murray's progress through to the semi-final of the French Open... On this Friday, though, it is semi-final day...Oh he lost...Straight sets...Shame... Back to the more important matters...Has an Ecuador v France ticket become available yet? The reality is that outside of a World Cup...If this match was being played in my back garden...I would struggle to open the curtains to watch it... And that is even with Hugo Lloris in goal!

Now it is, along with the other games I am seeking tickets for, taking over my life!! Crazy...Bonkers...Yes you name it...I am it!!!

Several times a ticket for England v Italy shows as being available. Each time I immediately click on the game which takes me to a page where I confirm yes I only want one ticket (chance would be a fine thing!!) and then a security code has to be entered...Then a new page shows that there aren't any tickets available for the "product" selected. I muse...Never a truer word than "product"... Not a sporting occasion... A "product" and this is how it is described on the Official FIFA web site... As a "product"!!!

Occasionally when I get through, in my haste, I input the wrong security code and have to start all over again. With the dawning realisation that I am competing with many others... Probably including touts and ticketing agencies who are well ahead of me in the race to get the single ticket which has become available #missionimpossible

Then at around 1.30am Saturday morning...Oh no I hear you groan... Surely not... Yep...Mr Persistence, Mr Determined, Mr Stupid Idiot... Make the appropriate selection...Then input your security code...Haha...Insanity taking over here!! Anyway you will never believe it... But I actually get an England v Italy ticket!

Fifteen minutes to confirm or lose it...No problem...Oh wait!! Best go on to Skyscanner to check flight availability...Yes a flight leaves Rio 8.05am and arrives in Manaus 11.30am...The flight back is 10.15pm arriving into Rio 3.10am.

I can do it!! Flight cost £485 return...Umm ...Ok...Down to last five minutes or lose the ticket...Decisions, decisions...Can you feel my tension... What to do? Chance of a life time...As Sven Goran Erikssen would say..."Why not?" Flight booked, ticket booked...Wow!

This gives me renewed confidence to persevere...By 3.20am I am shattered, tiredness takes over and I collapse into bed.

A frustrating but ultimately successfully day!

SATURDAY 7TH JUNE 2014

8am...Straight down to my office and laptop...
Tickets still not showing...

Having been invited along with a number of other friends by Keith Pickering to watch the early morning first New Zealand All Blacks v England rugby test match plus the offer of a bacon rolls... The temptation is too great and I take a much needed break. I catch up with friends and watch a spirited England not quite B side take the mighty All Blacks to the wire...The performance of the Welsh referee upsets England TV pundits, us in the room and many others across the social media network...

One of my friends, Jon Howe says he has a business colleague in São Paulo and will try to get me an England v Uruguay ticket!!

This sets me thinking as to who else I might know...I send a text out across my network. Also as a member of a Worldwide Spurs fans web site called "Come on you Spurs", it occurs to me, not having been to Rio or São Paulo for more than ten years, it would be helpful to ask their general advice on Brazil and in terms of inoculations etc....In my last minute tired and stressful haste...I had to admit to myself that I had not giving this sufficient thought....But now I am and it is bothering me.. The combined flight and match ticket is close to £600...What the hell was I thinking in that mad 15 minutes in the middle of the night...

The responses back from people who are going to Manaus are horrific... Yellow fever jabs amongst others plus malaria tablets etc...Umm I went on to a number of health web sites etc...Oh dear...Even though I am only due to be in Manaus 11 hours... It doesn't sound good...Past experience of Malaria tablets ...Not good...May be a curb on alcohol for a week. As Sven Goran Erikssen would say, as England are knocked out of a World Cup, "it's a pity"...What an understatement!!

I keep scanning the refreshes religiously...Now that my focus is solely on securing match tickets for four games...The realisation that not a single ticket has shown as being available during all of the time I have been looking #unlikelytohappen

I try Stubhub...No World Cup ticket availability...

I try ticket agencies...Ticketbis offers the following

1) Argentina v Bosnia is available for over £678...What??
2) England v Uruguay is £581
3) Spain v Chile £562
4) France v Ecuador £468
5) England v Italy only just over £200...Umm think we know why that is...

I think to myself...No wonder tickets aren't being resold through the FIFA website!!

I need to think of other ways of obtaining tickets...I have various channels to pursue...And set about pursuing them...

After some more hours, I start to give up on the FIFA web site. The good news is that through contacting my network on Twitter, Come on you Spurs web site, text contacts...I learn that quite a few Spurs fans I know are travelling out there.

Colin is actually celebrating his birthday in Rio on the night I arrive...What a great way for me to start my World Cup adventure!!

An email comes into my inbox from one of the travel companies saying that it is not possible to book Recife to Belo Horizonte which included a connecting flight as one ticket. This means that the cost will be an extra £115 and that I will have to collect my suitcase off one flight and check in on the other in the early hours of the morning...Ermm...No thank you... But before I say no thank you, I had better check that there is an alternative and there is...An extra £88 but at least my luggage will be checked through.

I watch the England v Honduras friendly on TV, live from Miami, at night. It is England's last friendly before the serious stuff starts in a week's time. The match is interrupted by an electrical storm!! The Hondurans treat the game as if it is their World Cup Final....Tackles and roughneck tactics are the last thing Roy Hodgson wants...But is getting in bucket loads!!

Even though Honduras are reduced to ten men, England for the most part still look clueless and incapable of breaking them down. The game ends in an uninspiring, drab 0-0 draw...

The prospect of a full days flying on Friday 13th to then wake up early the next morning and effectively fly another eight hours, the equivalent of a London to Moscow day return to Manaus and back is not too appealing...And that is before we factor in the health concerns and having to take malaria tablets for about a week after the trip...Umm...What did I do in the early hours of the morning??

After the England game I return to the FIFA sites in the forlorn hope that a ticket will become available ... And in the unlikely event that a ticket does become available that I will be quick enough to secure it...Yes...Even by now Mr Optimistic here is realising it ain't gonna happen!

Exhausted I fall into bed 1am... An early night!!

SUNDAY 8TH JUNE 2014

My new morning routine...A look on the FIFA web site...As usual nothing happening...

I find myself mulling over the England v Italy conundrum.

The morning is spent spasmodically and almost disinterestedly looking on the FIFA site. For the most part though, I am organising my electronic World Cup files, checking documents and printing off e-tickets and confirmations of my flight and hotel reservations.

With the Manaus return, I calculate that I will be taking 12 flights in 14 days.

I see an invoice for one of my flights has my double digit house number twice making it sound like an American address... A house number such as 6161 rather than say our very British number 61. It is probably ok but make a note to give the travel company a call.

Good that I did... But my word I was held waiting for about half an hour at a cost of 10p a minute...Great profit making enterprise...Reduce staff and keep customers waiting at an extortionate cost.. It transpires that if the flight needs changing, the correct home address needs to be on the invoice #goodjobirang

Nothing is straight forward, I now notice that the e-ticket for my return flight to Manaus hasn't been emailed to me.

I have the booking order page open and click on the "contact us" link. I write and explain due to inoculation issues, by this time I learn that for yellow fever has to be administered two weeks before visiting, would they kindly cancel my booking and refund me the £487.55 ticket cost. They are not under any obligation to do so but... Let's see...

I receive an immediate response which says a response will be forwarded within 24 hours...Which wouldn't give me much time to try to resell the England v Italy ticket on the FIFA web site as the ticket would have to be collected by latest Friday of this week...

In passing time between the FIFA web site ticket refreshes, I decide to clear out my spam folder and open it up to delete the mails. Sitting in my spam folder are two emails from "Go to gate"... I open up the first which says that the payment for my flight has not gone through and that if a payment is not made through some kind of international bank clearing system within 12 hours, my flight will be cancelled. It is a Rio departure ticket and I am panicking as the only flight I could possibly take from Rio is to Sao Paulo for the England v Uruguay game. I look at the time of the email... It is more than 12 hours ago. I go to the second email which indeed confirms the booking is cancelled...Oh no no no...Probably because of extreme tiredness, the feeling of it all falling apart comes over me...

Then I check the booking reference and it is the flight from Rio to Manaus for the England v Italy game...Eureka!! My word!! What a stroke of luck!!

I immediately, well not immediately because in navigating the FIFA web site nothing is immediate or for that matter obvious but as quickly as humanely possible...I put my England v Italy match ticket up for resale...

How strange that the euphoria of booking the ticket is more than matched by the euphoria of the £487.55 flight payment not going through and the match ticket being put up for resale!!

In buoyant mood, I again write to Vitoria at the Copacabana Hotel asking if there is a possibility of a room for one night and as to whether the concierge had managed to organise any of the match tickets for me.

I am also in contact with my network and there are small possibilities of tickets for Argentina v Bosnia and England v Uruguay emerging...Fingers crossed!

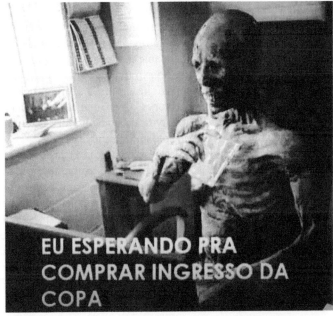

waiting for tickets as depicted on Brazilian on social media!

EL GRINGO'S ONCE IN A LIFETIME

MONDAY 9TH JUNE TO WEDNESDAY 11TH JUNE 2014

Paul emails me a link to a USA EBay web site which is showing lots of tickets as being available for sale...At astronomical prices...

I receive a response from Vitoria at the Copacabana Hotel who advises that a room can indeed be offered for the one night at an even higher price than the £200 per night for my other booking... For one night, the price being offered is 800 reals plus of course 15% taxes ...£240!! This just feels a step too far... actually it feels several steps too far...I politely advise that I cannot pay any more than the price agreed for the other nights and should the price reduce to let me know.

It seems the concierge is still trying to get hold of tickets for me.

I continue to look at the FIFA web site but already know that it will be impossible to obtain tickets for the matches I am interested in through the site.

I am in contact with friends who are flying out ahead of the tournament and look forward to meeting them out there...It's going to be some party! Right now I would be happy to get a ticket for England v Uruguay and just one match at the Maracana out of the three I am seeking... You know the question...Would you take a draw now... Well there is my ticket answer!

I manage to book a single room in the same hotel as Paul and Ian, the Sol Belo Horizonte in... Belo Horizonte of course!

I also manage to book a good fight from Belo Horizonte to Rio de Janeiro on Wednesday 25th June departing at 7.04am and arriving into Rio at 8am in good time for the Ecuador v France game...If I can get a ticket!

I dare to dream that England have beaten Costa Rica in the 1pm kick off the day before and with other friends who we are meeting up with...We can all have a great celebration in Belo Horizonte and I say my goodbyes to Paul and Ian.

I write to FIFA asking for confirmation that my England v Italy ticket has been registered for resale. I am unable to see through my log on. After receiving generic answers to specific questions, I trouble Paul to ask if he can have a look. He has been anyway looking at the site to see if his surplus tickets have been sold for Bosnia v Iran and Greece v Ivory Coast. Good luck with that mate! Paul says he has not seen an England v Italy ticket come up for sale but it could come of course have come up and been sold immediately.

We go through the ticket resale screens and against my reference number it says "refund pending $157.50". Does this mean refund pending a sale or the 30 day delay FIFA build in for repayment purposes? I am further confused by the fact that on the page displaying tickets available, the matches which I have apparently secured a ticket for are colour coded in green... The England v Italy game is still colour coded in green...But surely if my ticket has been sold...I don't have a ticket so it wouldn't be colour coded in green? Does it really need to be this difficult?

Is it really too much to ask for an automated email dropping into my email box saying that the ticket has been made available for resale and a second email to confirm the ticket has been sold?

I also write to FIFA on several occasions asking for confirmation that my three match tickets are confirmed and only receiving generic answers. I receive an email from FIFA at 00.40 hours, Wednesday, 11th June confirming I have a match ticket for Italy v Costa Rica. This sends me into panic mode...What about the other games I think I have tickets for???

I receive an email from FIFA ...Another generic one which has been sent to all members who have applied for tickets but this email provides a Helpline telephone number...Hallelujah...At least I can speak with someone...I call the Swiss number and naturally there is an automated voice but the voice is English and sounds like a Liverpudlian accent...Well it is to do with tickets, it would be wouldn't it! That little joke would only be understood by anyone buying a ticket off a tout for any major UK sporting or music event!

Anyway I patiently work for my way through all the options...There is always an "other "option. Mr Liverpool and me...we are doing really well...Drilling down through the various layers of FIFA, through the labyrinth of corridors to the very nerve centre, the very heart of FIFA...Cracking all the security codes together...My word...What a team we are...But then and without warning, just when you think...That's it we are in...And he might have actually led me to a living human being who I could speak with for simple specific answers...Mr Liverpool does an about turn and says if you want any further answers press 1 or whatever to return to the main menu...Really???

It's a bit like a game of snakes and ladders. I am on number 98 and just need the dice to roll a number two and I am home...But no...The dice rolls a number 1 where there is a big fat juicy snake waiting to slide me all the way back down to number two at the start of the "game" or should I call it a "product" now...

As I write this now, it is 11.30pm on Wednesday, 11 June and I have just sent this email to FIFA:

"Dear Sirs,

I have written a number of times and seem unable to obtain anything but a generic answer when at this late stage I really need specific answers. I have also called but was only able to listen to a voicemail offering similar generic answers.

I fly out to Brazil from the UK in the early hours of Friday 13th June and am asking for clarity on my ticketing situation.

Would you kindly be able to answer the following straightforward questions by close of business Thursday, 12th June with specific answers please:

My user name is xxxxxx:

I have ordered tickets for the following matches:

1) Request number: 701588306: 1 x Match 34 - Croatia v Mexico - Recife / Category 3

2) Request number: 701588211: 1 x Match 40 - Costa Rica v England - Belo Horizonte / Category 1

EL GRINGO'S ONCE IN A LIFETIME

3) Request Number 701588142: 1 x Match 24 - Italy v Costa Rica - Recife / Category 2

4) Request Number: 701589144-1 x Match 08 - England v Italy - Manaus / Category 1

My understanding is that:

a) I have 1 ticket for (1) to (3) above.

b) The ticket for England v Italy has been resold and I will receive a refund of the price less a 10% fee...i.e. I will receive $157.50

c) I will be able to pick the tickets up at Rio de Janeiro airport ticket office on my arrival on arrival at c17.30 hours Friday 13th June.

The booking of flights, hotels, etc has cost me a lot of money and I would really appreciate your response to confirm the above by close of business Thursday, 12th June ahead of my flight to Brazil.

I have tried writing previously and each time received a generic answer. Your response to each of the above specific questions would be greatly appreciated.

Thank you in anticipation,"

I await an answer with about as much expectation as I have in securing any further tickets through the web site. To be fair, it is all a little lastminute.com and I would imagine it isn't one of FIFA's quieter periods...I guess they must be as busy as Santa's elves in the run up to Christmas... Nearly added a cryptic comment then but will leave that one for you, dear readers... Plenty of fertile ground...But may be Sepp Blatter sees himself as a bit of a Father Christmas on board his footballing sleigh spreading the football gospel around the globe and giving hope to the poor...How charitable was I there...Well, I may want tickets for future World Cups, sorry, just heard him say "Inter Galactic Cups" oh my... and that he intends standing again for the FIFA presidency... I had better put a charitable word in for Santa Sepp otherwise I might not be able to apply for tickets at future World Cups in Russia and Qatar... Umm yes precisely... We covered that one at the start of my diary...I have been so absorbed in organising my trip that I only heard second hand that Sepp had apparently accused the British media of racism because it raised the question of corruption around the Qatar World Cup bid. Racism... Russian football fans... 2018 World Cup... interesting combination!

Anyway, back to my own FIFA experience...In business, I have always been taught to delight the customer...I can't say trying to compete with thousands of other fans and probably hundreds of ticketing agencies who are looking to buy and resell the tickets at extortionate prices has been a delightful experience and neither has the lack of simple straightforward communication from FIFA.. All only my opinion and based on my own experience.

Is it really too much to ask to know which tickets I have purchased and whether one has been put up for resale or sold before I fly out to Brazil? Come on FIFA; please let's have some transparency...Now where I have heard that before!

Incidentally, based on the number of tickets at extortionate prices on the

American EBay sites plus usual corporate fiasco at any major sporting event... It won't be a complete surprise if, in spite of the apparently high percentage of ticket sales, there may be, as in South Africa four years ago but perhaps not to the same extent, quite a few empty seats in the stadiums...Hopefully I will be wrong and I write this on Wednesday, 11th June and stand to be corrected...Hopefully by my editor if this diary ever gets that far!

So, as it stands tonight, I have just one night's accommodation to sort in Rio on the 25th June and I believe a ticket for four matches. Now all I have to do is think about buying clothes, toiletries and packing! A thought occurs to me as I write this diary... The time is now 00.25 and I will be flying in exactly 30 hours! But no, that wasn't the thought! The thought was to call my credit card company in the morning and see what transactions have been processed by FIFA...That thought will no doubt keep me awake most of the night...Laughing here but only very nervously!

Some good news does arrive though, FIFA write to advise match day tickets can be collected at certain airports and the two Rio airports are on the list. This is really good news. I will be tired after a full day of flying on Friday but no matter the length of the queues at the airport, it will be great to have the tickets in my pocket on leaving the airport...Assuming I have actually secured tickets of course!

One thing I must write here...If you have managed to wade through the above, you will have drawn your own conclusions as to the state of my sanity or insanity...And yes it is the chance of a lifetime...And I am really looking forward to it... But now having shared the above experiences with me...You might imagine when people hear that I am going to Brazil and say...You are so lucky!"

Yep that's me...It all just fell into my lap!!

THURSDAY 12TH JUNE 2014

So today is the day...The day the 2014 World Cup starts!! The opening ceremony and the mouth-watering clash of Brazil v Croatia to kick off the tournament!

Let's hope Brazil win otherwise suitcases may be slow on arrival into Rio tomorrow...Passport control queues might be even slower!! Come on Brazil...5-0 win please haha

A dreadful night's sleep... Judging by my itinerary...My own World Cup training...Similar to England going to Miami for acclimatisation training! Just too much on my mind to sleep and add the writing of this diary late at night...

The day starts really positively...No, sadly not regarding match tickets... As if! The airline company wrote back overnight to confirm the £488 for the Manaus, England v Italy flight has not been taken... The 24 hour response time elapsed Monday at 3.35pm...Only a 60 hour overrun on their committed 24 hour response! Not too bad then!

I call my credit card company who advise that FIFA have taken cash for all four matches...Great news! I have tickets! Bad news...The England v Italy repayment has not been made yet... But they did say within 30 days. Let's hope FIFA have actually put it up for resale...

One thought I did have overnight...Ring London ticket agencies...A possible chance of a ticket at this late stage...worth a go!

A second thought I had was that I am seeing two of Costa Rica's three Group matches...More than any other team...Now if someone had said that to me at the point of starting this process... Actually yes I still would...I am not going there with any great expectations of England doing well. I am going for the World Cup experience in Brazil... Anything else is a bonus...I say that now but if I have to fly in and out of Sao Paulo and not see the England v Uruguay match as Sven might say "It would be a pity".

And finally a third overnight thought... Now this will sound absolutely ridiculous...But it's amazing how things go through the mind at 2am, 3am, 4am... You get the picture...Virtually no sleep...Well the third silly thought is...Just how much sport I am going to miss...

On the Friday I am travelling to Brazil...Three World Cup matches including Spain v Holland...What a game that promises to be! Sure I will miss many others while travelling too.

The US Open golf which promises to be a humdinger of a tournament.

The final stages of the Stella Artois tennis at Queens and the first week of Wimbledon...In other words three quarters of the four week grass season lol.

The England v Sri Lanka test match at Lords starts today...Paul is taking his wife along to spend some time with him! I wonder how many tests I will miss... Just heard back to back tests so at least two tests matches.

I am a member at Nottinghamshire County Cricket who have a Twenty 20 (T20) match at, what I call, my summer home Trent Bridge tomorrow night... First home match to be missed this season...

There will be a Grand Prix...By the way wasn't last Sunday's Canadian Grand Prix a spectacle...Just a shame Hamilton didn't finish...Long way to go in the season but his team "mate" has won the last two in a row...

Yes... I know, I know...I am going to Brazil for two weeks... And yes I feel incredibly excited and fortunate to be doing so. I was just saying how the brain works in the middle of the night...That's all!!

There are a couple of big children occasions being missed too...Father's Day on Sunday and the most important event of them all... My daughter's 17th Birthday on the 24th June when I am in Belo Horizonte for the England v Costa Rica match. So it all comes at a price and not just the extortionate one to go out there...

As a side note ...I can't believe my daughter will have had a driving lesson by the time I return... Eek!

My son who is responsible for all of this... By encouraging me to go to Brazil...Well he is flying out for his first lads' holiday on Saturday... Six of them are going to Ayia Napa for a week... Oh dear...Don't even want to think about it...

The other random thoughts which went through my mind being that because of the intensity of trying to organise to actually get out to Brazil, I have missed the build-up on the television...Shame really...I keep hearing how good the David Beckham program was... I have recorded it and as well the BBC1 program last night or as is said today Sky Plussed them...It will always be recorded in my head... But realistically when will I have the time to watch them!

What has been quite good though when I have tuned in, has been the TalkSPORT coverage...The shows of Alan Brazil and Adrian Durham being broadcast from Rio is really helping to get me into the mood...Alan Brazil's description of the Moose wandering round Copacabana in a West Ham United shirt, baggy white shirts, white socks and sandals.. Saying he might just as well be in Dagenham and sending him down Muggers Alley in a Rolex!! The Moose interviewing many different nationalities on the beach is really getting me in the mood for the football festival ahead of me... Adrian Durham and Darren Gough's Copacabana beach penalty shoot-out...I can't help but let the child inside me out to play!!

Even the TalkSPORT World Cup song is proving too catchy...But not enough to push out the tune which has been virtually living with me for almost a week now..

"Tall and tan and young and lovely
The girl from Ipanema goes walking
And when she passes, each one she passes
Goes "A-a-a-h"
When she walks she's like a samba
When she walks, she's like a samba
That swings so cool and sways so gentle
That when she passes, each one she passes
Goes "A-a-a-h"
Oh, but I watch her so sadly
How can I tell her I love her
Yes, I would give my heart gladly
But each day as she walks to the sea
She looks straight ahead, not at me
Tall and tan and young and lovely
The girl from Ipanema goes walking
And when she passes, I smile, but she
Doesn't see. She just doesn't see
No, she just doesn't"

Well not quite every word... A lot of humming to cover up my lack of knowledge of the words...Here and now I am determined to learn the words... Love Frank Sinatra, love the song!

The phone has just rung...My 85 year old mother...She loves listening to Radio Lincolnshire...The presenter is talking about people planning holidays... Mum who is a regular caller to the station takes it upon herself to ring in...You will never guess where my son is going tomorrow...I am now waiting for the presenter to call me and speak live on the air...The day started so well...

I keep meaning to call the Health Centre and confirm no jabs are needed... Why am I putting this off...Because I don't want bad news...And now I can't ring just yet...In case the Radio Station call me!

Late afternoon now, the Radio station never called me... But the good news is that I summoned up the courage to learn that no jabs or Malaria tablets are required for the places I am visiting.

Not one but two specific emails drop into my mailbox from FIFA confirming I do have a ticket for each of the three matches I ordered and that my England v Italy ticket has been sold and a refund less a 10% admin fee will be returned within 30 days. Wow... Good news!

I rather cheekily write back to ask if they can help me locate tickets for the four games I am looking still looking for...If you don't ask, you don't get... In this case I more than strongly suspect...If you ask, you don't get!! Worth a try though!

Again sent messages to people already out there and contacts in the UK to try again to obtain tickets for the four matches I am looking for. Message from Rob in Rio saying that prices are off the scale for matches at the Maracana... That doesn't sound too promising...

I again write to poor Vitoria in Rio to ask about the possibility of a room at the "cheap" rate of £200 a night and also as to whether the concierge has managed to obtain match tickets for me.

Trying to print Air France boarding tickets...Proving to be a very slow process... Probably in part due to the slow and inconsistent Internet connection where I live. The Air France site eventually advises that it is redirecting me to the Flybe site...The site keeps failing...Nightmare...Passport details required, job done and boarding tickets finally printed!

So, it is 8.15pm, ITV has the opening ceremony ahead of the Brazil v Croatia match which kicks off at 9pm UK time.

Half time... not the usual drab opening game...Trying to imagine how Marcelo must have felt to score an opening 2014 World Cup ...An own goal against the host nation...

I started watching the game wanting Brazil to win...Sadly the refereeing decisions taint the game...Brazil are very fortunate to be given a penalty at 1-1and at 2-1 for a Croatia goal to be disallowed...Like the rest of the World, I do hope, from now on in...We see quality refereeing performances...but based on previous World Cups I fear not...

I still have my packing to do and have to be up at 3am to head off to the airport!

Another night with very little sleep...Something to get used to!

Alarm set for 3am... You know when you are tired... You take that extra bit of care when setting your alarm for very early the next morning... Especially when ahead of an important, time critical day...You set it... Question... Did I set it correctly? Check... Check again...it says the alarm is set correctly for 3 o'clock... Phew... I can finally switch off and go to sleep. I lay my head on the pillowcase and close my eyes...A sudden thought hits me... Did I set the alarm for 3 o'clock in the morning or 3 o'clock in the afternoon? The light is switched back on... This is me in a state of extreme tiredness at 11.45pm. Yep that's right 3 hours 15 minutes in bed and probably only half of that time asleep before the alarm is due to go off. I have hardly slept since starting to organise my trip just one week ago...But as the Americans would say...I am all set!

EL GRINGO'S ONCE IN A LIFETIME

I confess that my thoughts were not the best before the start of the World Cup. In the situation where Brazil is, I was disappointed to learn that so much money was being invested in this event and little in the evolution of the country. And I was afraid of protests, revolts and the country becoming a big mess.

But everything in life has its good side ...When the crowds of people from many countries began to arrive, I was amazed!

Walking the streets and seeing the various faces and accents, was wonderful. A very good energy!

It was the most amazing moment I could live in my country. I could see a piece of the world, within my country!

It was infectious see people's emotions for their country, and despite the "rivalry" on the field, I believe the World Cup could make people forget their differences and unite their tastes and habits.

I felt at a carnival out of season. A carnival that I wish had lasted more than 31 days.

And yet I had the blessing to make new and good friends, new lodgings outside Brazil (hahaha), opportunities to improve my English and I hope to have made a good impression of what being a true Brazilian is to the people I met.

Brazil has not took the cup, but I loved having participated in every single moment of this "Cup of Cups".

The World Cup was a big party in summary: screams, laughter, disappointments, fun, caipirinhas (of course haha), friends, family, gringos, accents and miss you!

An infinite mixture of feelings between nations!!!

Jessica Souza,
Brazilian with the joy in the smile and soul,
Rio de Janeiro, Brazil

FRIDAY 13TH JUNE 2014

Well, the alarm goes off on time... The thought goes through my mind. Shall I just have another 5 minutes...? Then a second thought... What if I fall back to sleep and miss my flight!! The thought is more than enough to shock me out of bed!!

I set off at 3.30am and the drive to the airport passes without incident arriving just after 4.30am... A few hours later and the M42/M6 road network around Birmingham would be gridlocked! It's actually a pleasure to drive this early summer's morning on what is forecast to be the hottest day of the year.

The airport is as ever very busy at this time of the year and especially on a Friday... There are stag and hen parties everywhere along with holidaymakers and the poor businessmen in their suits trying to cope with the stresses and strains of the day.

Baggage drop done and no longer a person to check your boarding pass...

All machine operated these days... The machine picks up the barcode on the e-ticket in the same manner as self-scanning machines for supermarket purchases. Whatever happened to the personal touch! But then again these days shop assistants are usually serving someone who is either talking on or typing into a mobile phone. May be the phones should just communicate with the self-scanning machines and take the people out of the equation altogether!

Next up security... A machine to check my luggage and another machine to check me. It is amazing how we do all we can to avoid the machine bleeping as we walk through... And yet somehow it still bleeps! It's fascinating to watch people's reactions when the bleep goes off... Some go bright red with embarrassment... others show frustrated body language whilst for a few; anger quickly rises to the surface. Then you have those who get through first time without a bleep... On some... Joy lights up their faces. It's almost as if a year of studying and revising had been endured... But hey look at the result achieved... I passed first time!! Others walk smugly out the other side as if to say... Look at me... Don't know what all the fuss is about... Seasoned traveller here #Iknowwhatlamdoing.

My main aspiration is to avoid having to go through the taking shoes off rig morale... Which fortunately on this occasion I manage to achieve!!

I buy a few essentials at Boots and can't resist the meal deal offer which is actually always very good value. Boots... One of the few of our great British institutions and headquartered in the city where I live...Nottingham... Though if rumours are to be believed... Sadly it may not be British for too much longer...

Browsing through a few books in W H Smith, the optimist in me suddenly thinks... Hey, if this diary is going to sell... I am going to need a publisher... So out comes my iPhone and I take note of a cross section of publishers from books ranging from fiction to sporting books. So Mr Publisher... If I contact you and you agree to publish... This is how I found your name!!

To my relief the flight is called on time... The 1 hour 20 minute transit through Charles de Gaulle airport, Paris is weighing on my mind... And not just whether I can make it but also whether my luggage can too...The first part of the equation I will know immediately... The second part won't be known until the very last bag is delivered onto the conveyor belt in Rio de Janeiro many hours later...

To anyone who knows me well, it won't come as any great surprise to hear that as early as I was in arriving at the airport... The final boarding sign is flashing when I finally reach Gate 9 for my Flybe Flight number BE3001 (AF1869) to Paris, Charles de Gaulle.

The pilot announces that due to air traffic control... My heart jumps into my mouth... The flight will be delayed by 5 minutes... Phew!!

Not sure whether I mentioned but through online check in last night I was able to change my seats for both of this morning's flights.

For the hop over to Paris I managed to secure a front row, extra leg room seat by the window in seat 1a... Years ago this would have been a much coveted business class priced seat... How times change!

I get talking with the guy sitting next to me called Ian Nash who is on his way out to the Le Mans 24 hour race this weekend. Ian works for a company called AP Racing who are specialists in brakes and clutches and will be having a busy working weekend. Ian has been doing Le Mans for many years and regales me with stories of prior events and... The fights to get the French to show England's World Cup matches on television down the years.

I seem to recall that Jimmy Greaves once raced at Le Mans... No idea where that thought came from and Ian cannot recall Jimmy ever doing it. We agree to check through Google and email each other.

Postscript... On my return to the UK... I Googled "Jimmy Greaves rally driver"...

In his first ever rally Jimmy Greaves drove the London Wembley to Mexico City rally...Approximately 16,000 miles (25,750kms) rally with co-driver Tony Fall in a Ford Escort and finished in 6th place out of 96 entrants. It started at Wembley Stadium on 19th April 1970 and finished in Mexico City on 29th May 1970 ahead of the World Cup Finals in Mexico that year.

I forward Ian an email to let him know... I would have been nearly 11 years old when the rally started some 44 years plus years ago so not too bad to pull the rally driver memory from the recesses of my mind... just not the right race!

In writing my diary of events at Birmingham airport, it occurs to me that there wasn't a passport control officer. My passport was matched with my ticket at the Gate by a member of the Flybe staff... Ian confirms my recollection to be correct. When did Her Majesty's Government decide to delegate such a responsibility to airline staff?

I read a little of today's diary and Ian kindly asks me to let him know if it is ever published... May be it was the only way to shut me up. Laughing here... But the truth is although I have never written before I am really truly and thoroughly enjoying the experience.

As we pass over the French coastline I am, looking into the sun, able to take what I modestly

think is a quite stunning photograph for inclusion in my diary. Hope you like it!

We disembark or as our American cousins would say... Deplane at 8.50am which was a flight time of around 1 hour 20 minutes with an hour added for the change in time zone.

The transit within Terminal 2E is very easy with the only issue being that my Boots meal deal drink bought airside in Birmingham had to be drunk or thrown away at security.

This time I am not so fortunate and my rucksack is searched. This is presumably because of the toiletry items also bought airside from Boots in Birmingham. The lady who served me in Boots placed these items in a sealed bag including the receipt... All passed muster at CDG security. The Boots lady was very enthusiastic about my going to the World Cup and made a fuss with her colleagues... She said by my colour, I look as if I have just come back from a sunshine holiday... And it is true, by virtue of my father's Ukrainian heritage, I do tan very easily and through the English almost tropical weather we have recently had, I already have a very dark suntan. No doubt to be washed away by the Rio rain!

In transit there are four very excited English guys singing of going to Brazil. At a distance I am sharing their excitement. They clearly want everybody to know where they are going... And come to think of it so do I!!

My next challenge is to find a socket to charge my iPhone at CDG. This is important to me as I am writing my diary in iPhone notes. The battery is already down to 66%... Although I have an iPhone charger case, it is still a concern as to how quickly the battery runs down.

At this stage I will let you into a little secret... In saying I have never written a novel, I was speaking the truth. However at the moment, I am about 22000 words, circa 50 pages, in to writing my first ever novel. It is a Romcom and not just ironically but also unbelievably, it is a coincidence of epic proportions... The Romcom is set in... South America! And just to be clear, the idea was born a long, long time ago and well before I had any idea of attending the 2014 World Cup and therefore of course of writing a World Cup diary #remarkablecoincidence. So at the grand old age of 55 and never having written a book, I now have two as work in progress. It would though be fair to say that I might not have thought of writing a diary had it not been for finally taking the plunge and starting my Romcom novel last Easter. The inspiration for writing my diary may also have come from the wonderfully written "All Played Out" which gave a fantastic description and fascinating, humorous insight into the passion generated during Italia'90 and England's epic Gazza inspired run through to the Semi Final. If you haven't already read this book, I really encourage you to do so.

I find a socket to charge my battery and continue the writing of my diary. To do so, for those of you who know CDG terminal 2E, I am charging my phone at the internet points at Gate L48. My flight AF444 to Rio de Janeiro departs from Gate L44 at 10.30. I keep looking anxiously along the terminal in my desperation to squeeze every last perentage of charge into my phone. On a number of occasions, the announcer kindly requests outstanding passengers to go to the gate for the São Paulo departure but there is no mention of Rio... And the gate number is different... I check my iPhone charge level which had increased to 91%. I also notice the time on my iPhone shows 9.18... Which in my tired state, I question as to whether it has moved on an hour or not. I am so tired that I cannot actually work it out and look around for a clock... There isn't one...I ask a person sat nearby who shows me his watch... The time is 10.18!! OMG!! The flight is due to take off in 12 minutes.

In blind panic I hurtle across the terminal to gate L44 to be firmly told the flight has closed. I plead; I beg but am told it is not the decision of the staff at the gate. They call the pilot as to whether I can board... The dialling tone seems to ring forever... I am not catching this flight... While the dialling tone continues to ring out... They say the flight was announced and my name called out several times, where was I? I am not catching this flight... It must have been called very silently as I did not hear it... An anxious few moments pass as the gate are by phone in dialogue with the pilot, I curse my French which is much rustier than it was 10 years ago when I worked in Paris. I am not catching this flight...I hear the expression "un peu"...For some strange reason I initially translate this as "afraid" as in about to say afraid the pilot is not prepared to reopen the flight... Although I am not superstitious the thought that it is "Friday the 13th" slips into my mind... I am not catching this flight...Then I remember "un peu" translates to "a little" and try to decipher the context... Then the thought that my suitcase will be on board becomes a comforter I cling on to...It would surely be easier to open the flight and let me on board rather than search in the hold to take off my suitcase?? Finally I am told I can board... Lesson learnt... But waiting to see whether the flight could be reopened was just so so scary...The ramifications were tumbling out of my brain... The hours spent organising this trip...And the only reason I didn't sit at the actual gate was... to charge the iPhone so that I could write my diary for as long as possible during the flight...Oh the irony...

But it just shows how the lack of sleep over the last week is having such an impact on me and impairing my judgement. How I completely lost any track and understanding of the time. With jetlag soon to be thrown into the mix...It is a sobering wake up call... Definitely the correct use of the phrase... Wake up call...I will need to have my wits about me, be aware of my tiredness and judgement going forwards...It will be a fun but also undoubtedly tiring couple of weeks.

As I board the plane, I question where the 1 hour 40 minutes went in transit... And begin to wonder whether I might just have fallen asleep...

Anyway, I board and arrive at my seat 23e to find a French lady sat in my seat who kindly advises me that she has swapped with me and that I am now in seat 42b. Errmmm I think not Madame, Mademoiselle or whatever the equivalent for Ms is in French...I went on line last night and changed to this seat with the extra leg room thank you very much. She had really made herself at home in my seat...So it was a little bit of a drama for her to gather her things together to move 20 rows further back... I didn't feel uncomfortable...It wasn't that she had moved to be sat with family or friends. If this had been the case I would have moved but no...She had just been opportunistic and then had the nerve to tell me that our seats had been swapped... As if it was a matter of fact... Fait accompli!! Again, given that we are still in Paris... The perfect expression...Well except it isn't because she is now shuffling her body and belongings down the aisle to seat 42b...So the perfect expression is...Pas fait accompli!!

The four exuberant English guys are on board and still singing out loud about going to Brazil...This is not only a little childish, rude and unfair towards the other 200 passengers on board the Airbus A330 but also more than a little bit silly...The flight is going to Rio de Janeiro so where they are going is pretty damned obvious...And what's the point of informing the other 200 people around them as guess what...They happen to also be going to Brazil...

They start up a new song... "Gooners, Gooners" which for those of you who may not know... Is a slang word for Arsenal...The next song starts up "We hate Tottenham and we hate Tottenham"...

I may have mentioned earlier, I am not only a season ticket holder at Tottenham but go to all games... Home and away... A veteran of somewhere in the region of 800 games. I live 135 miles away from Tottenham which necessitates a 270 mile round trip to each home game... Including night matches which finish at 10pm with a mile walk to the car before clearing the match traffic to start my journey home. 355th most loyal member worldwide...This little insight probably gives you an indication of my passion for my club and as I call them "my burden" as I have to carry them around for my entire life.

If it isn't already clear, Arsenal and Tottenham are fierce rivals... Their stadiums should by rights be a lot further apart with (Woolwich) Arsenal's being in South London but they moved to within 3 miles of our stadium. I had no intention of bringing local domestic rivalries into my 2014 World Cup diary but...

Of all the planes of all the days to all the destinations...They had to be on my plane!!

As the "We hate Tottenham" song enters its third verse...Yes I think you have got the words by now...I shout out in a loud voice..."And we don't like you very much either". As I am behind them and they have no clue who I am and how many of us there are... But what they undoubtedly do know is that Tottenham's White Hart Lane stadium is not the easiest or pleasantest away game for them to attend...So... Immediately we have silence on board the plane...the French passengers around me probably have no idea what I said... Nevertheless they give me grateful and admiring glances... Probably thinking how could one grey haired old man shut four young men up in the matter of a few words!

For Arsenal fans amongst the readers, I have a lot of friends who support Arsenal and like them... Well as much as a Tottenham fan can like an Arsenal fan... Because as Harry said when meeting Sally, we cannot be friends as the football thing always gets in the way... Or at any rate words to the affect! A lot of lady readers might be thinking... Yes actually football gets even more in the way than the sex! Anyway, decent Arsenal fans would have been embarrassed by these 4 young men and their boorish behaviour...Believe me it was for the best!

It is now 10.54...My iPhone says 9.54...I really don't understand why the phone's software, which can immediately text to tell you the extortionate rates they will charge you should you use your phone in a new country, cannot automatically detect the time zone which the phone has moved into and update the time on the phone immediately.. I recall having this problem earlier in the year when flying out to Riyadh, Saudi Arabia for an interview...There must be a feature within the settings to do this? And as many of you reading this will have iPhones, you are now probably screaming and shouting at this page in the diary as to how to do it!

Sitting on board...We are advised that the flight will be delayed...The plane is still being refuelled...What is it with these airlines? They know the departure time...Why can't they refuel much earlier and depart on time!! Tongue very firmly in cheek here... Think it's called...Giddy relief!!!

10.16 sorry 11.16 the plane finally starts to pull away from the gate.

10.36 on my iPhone is as we have determined 11.36...we take off... An hour and 6 minutes later than scheduled...

And I am probably the only one who is grateful for the delay!

By the way... Whether I will still be happy with the delay on landing will be determined by whether the FIFA ticket office is still open at the airport to collect my match or should I now say "product" tickets!!

The new arrival time is showing as 5.58pm... A flight time of... Wait, in my tired state...This will take some calculating...Rio is 4 hours ahead of UK time which is 1 hour behind French time. That means a 5 hour time difference between Paris and Rio. So if we land at 5.58pm and we took off at what time was it... 10.36 on my iPhone... Which is really 11.36... The flight time must be.... Clunk clunk... 11 hours 22 minutes... Think that is correct??

If you are wondering by this stage why I am not wearing a watch... It is in the jewellers for repair... And has been there getting on for two years now when they completely changed the watch face and wanted £250 for a watch I no longer recognised or liked.. Memo to self... Must resolve this impasse when I return home... So in that time... I have just become used to using my phone as my watch.

However long the flight is... It is going to feel seriously long and get increasingly fractious if Mr Nigeria, sat next to me, persists in elbowing me in the ribs and fidgeting all over the place. He has had one gentle verbal warning... He won't want too many more...Now where was that kind lady who offered to swap seats with me! Just to say I have no clue whether he is from Nigeria and subsequently have heard him speak in French... But Mr Nigeria will be his "pet" name now for the rest of the flight. He is a big boy though...

Isn't it amazing that as soon as drinks and snacks are served and you have the tray out of the armrest...? The bathroom is called for... And the only facilities available are towards the rear of the plane... And yes that is where the drinks trolley is slowly making its way towards...

Thankfully Mr Nigeria has fallen asleep head to head with his buddy... They look so cute together; I couldn't resist a photograph... I know... Naughty aren't I!! Hopefully in his sleep, he doesn't move his head my way... For his sake and mine!

I talk with a Lebanese couple on the other side of the gangway. They are also flying out for the World Cup. They don't have tickets for any games. I ask them which games they will try to see... Argentina v Bosnia and Spain v Chile... I refrained from saying ahh you mean Match Numbers 11 and 19 respectively...

Based on my experience of the last week on the FIFA web site, the prices shown on the agency web sites and from chatting with friends already in Rio through social media... I am thinking unless you have a lot of cash ... Good luck with that...

The food is delivered and I have to say the quality provided by Air France is really very good... The main course of chicken in lemon sauce with bulgur wheat and vegetables is excellent... Very tasty.

Alas and unfortunately, the smell of food has awoken Mr Nigeria from his slumber... After the third elbow in the ribs... Verbal warning number 2 was issued... And now he is fiddling with his TV monitor... This is of course situated on his left hand side... This is of course on my right... Another 8 hours of this... Now he is fiddling in his right pocket, sounds a bit rude! Which necessitates turning to his right with his left elbow in my right ribs...Maybe this is payback... May be he really is a friend of Lady42b... And no I don't mean her bust size... Although now I come to think about it...

Correction to above... Another 8 hours 57 minutes of this

The steward has just decided to do a three point turn of his trolley right by my left hand side...I swear, I have flown hundreds of thousands of miles in economy class, business class, first class and all sorts of planes from private jets to small propellers to huge Airbuses and even Concorde.. But never ever have I seen a steward do a three point turn with a trolley... And it had to be today... And it had to be right by me!!

His trolley is whacking my feet, my ankles, my arms... While on the other side Mr Nigeria at precisely the same moment chooses to put away his food tray... Yes of course on his left hand side and which is again on my right hand side... As he lifts the compartment open. His arm rises in unison and his elbow dislodges my reading glasses...

I have had to stop writing for a few minutes to recompose myself... I have lost it... Utterly and totally lost it... Tears are running down my face...My stomach muscles are hurting... I am having a complete fit of the giggles and genuinely trying to stifle them to avoid embarrassment...

It occurs to me that if I wasn't writing this diary, I would be well and truly hacked off and stressed by now... But sharing with you, whoever you may be and if ever you get to read this... It actually doesn't even matter at this moment... It is just so therapeutic!! The expression "if I didn't laugh I would cry" comes to mind... Except I am doing both at the same time... I am crying with laughter

Wait up... What are we up to now...Oh no he needs his blanket which of course needs to be taken out of its plastic covering...? And guess what that does to his elbows... Now he can't get his blanket resting as he would wish across his body... This guy needs serious space awareness and body control training!!

I swear I have been elbowed more times on this flight already than all other times added together in my entire life...

Landing cards have just been handed out... Family members of Mr Nigeria and partner congregate around us on both sides of the aisle... Mr Nigeria has a name...Ash... I think? Will always be Mr Nigeria in my head! When he responds... I have to confess... A doubt creeps into my mind... Mr Nigeria... Or could it be Miss Nigeria... The curiosity is getting to me... I need to know... I find myself trying to catch a glance on the upper body beneath the blanket... Certainly bumpy... But is that a bit lower and tummy related... I need to be careful... Next I will be accused of being a perverted, lecherous old man... After a vulnerable young lady or... Even worse vulnerable young man under the blanket at 30,000 feet... Imagine a Rio prison; imagine the tabloid headlines...Oh the shame!

A member of the air cabin crew announces over the tannoy that the duty free service is now available. I don't normally look at the brochure to see what is available but...After the iPhone time experience at the airport this morning... And knowing how quickly the battery runs down...An impromptu board meeting is held in my head, strategic options are considered and finally a board resolution passed... I am now the proud honour of a new Hugo Boss duty free watch... Lesson learnt!! The stewardess confirmed the time difference of five hours and I adjusted my new watch to Brazilian time accordingly. Her watch showed 3.09pm. I adjusted mine to 8.09pm

On Air France flights, rather than force feed passengers with the dreaded duty free trolley, if passengers wish to buy any duty free goods, they walk to the back of the plane and buy the goods there. How civilised is that... Perhaps their staff are not bonus driven as some might be on other airlines... Have to say, it feels good to wear a watch again but.., I do question the wisdom in buying a new watch on the way into rather than on the way out of Brazil #streetmuggings. However if I don't buy one, I might end up missing my flight out! Let's say the purchase is a considered risk...

On the way back up to my seat, the first thing I notice is that seat 42b, is the aisle seat on the very back row...Her seat is by the restrooms and the crowd gathering gantry at the back... I see our Lady 42b... Actually that is not entirely true... I see a body with a sheet covering the face and upper body! No doubt protecting herself from the various senses afflicting her!!

As I walk a little further up the plane there is a guy wearing a blue and yellow football scarf... Turns out he is a Bosnia supporter...Rio will be a truly global football party! I sit down on my seat... Hang on a minute... I wonder if he has a spare ticket for Argentina versus Bosnia... One of the games I am trying to get a ticket for... Just going to ask... Will be back in a minute!

Just goes to show... If you don't ask, you don't get! Not that I have got anything yet... But in my broken German I managed to communicate with my new Bosnian friend...His name is Elvis! Yes really!! And Elvis tells me categorically I will be able get a ticket through the Bosnian official agency at the Ibis Hotel between 8am and mid-day on Sunday morning, the day of the match! He will give me the address when he gets his stuff out the overhead locker and come along to meet me there to help on Sunday morning. He asked me which games I have tickets for and as soon as I said Croatia v Mexico... I had to be quick on my tootsies and categorically tell him I was supporting Mexico!!

I just looked at my new watch and the time said 8.56... I think to myself... Is that morning or night? My flight arrives at 5.58pm. How can my watch possibly say 8.56? I then realise that when adjusting the time, I put it forward 5 hours instead of putting it back five hours! I know categorically that Brazil is behind Europe in time zone terms.

After the lack of sleep I have had for well over a week, this is an extreme situation but... To anyone who thinks they can operate machinery, drive a vehicle, and perform a job at the optimum level when tired... Please take from just my experience today... You may well think you can... but the reality is your performance and levels of concentration will to some degree be impaired... 'Elf and Safety lecture over!!

I adjust my watch by ten hours to 11.02 and cross reference to the time on my iPhone of 15.02... four hours difference... So as long as my iPhone hasn't miraculously transitioned to Central European time... We are in good order and Mr Nigeria is asleep under his or her blanket... We are in very good order

I settle down to watch a film called The Grand Budapest Hotel.

The film is enjoyable but I kept dozing off and having to rewind... At one stage I think I just gave in to sleep.

Towards the end of the film, I feel a little peckish and decide to eat my Boots meal deal and... Ouch Mr Nigeria's now got his rucksack on his lap... With both arms rummaging inside and of course... Elbows everywhere... Wonder what he would think if he knew I was here right now sat next to him, writing about him... Making a star of him lol!!

Halfway through my meal deal, whilst eating a packet of crisps, the steward kindly offers me a chocolate ice lolly... In a near 12 hour flight I wonder what odds Paddy Power would have given that in the few minutes I chose to eat my meal deal... The steward would hand me an ice lolly... Now it is a frantic race to finish my sandwiches and cheese and onion crisps before the lollipop melts! At least I have a dessert waiting for me!

I glance at my shiny new watch... It is 2.31... Only 3 hours and 27 minutes to go... The girl from Ipanema seductively rolls into my mind... Tall and lovely... You may have noticed... I do love that tune!!

Uh huh... My iPhone battery is down to 20%... Fortunately the charger case is still in reserve!

New guerrilla warfare tactic is being employed by Mr Nigeria... Not content with just elbowing me in the ribs, he is now at the same time, pushing his left leg out sideways into my right leg. At this point I am thankful that I am not in a window seat by the emergency door!!!

Sorry to record this... But I did say earlier that Mr Nigeria is a big boy... Long hot flight, lot of sweaty clothes on under the blanket... Yes... Think your nose might just be on the scent of what I am writing about... Inevitable I guess... Think a stretch of legs is called for!

To be fair to Mr Nigeria, he is not obnoxious and every time, I put my arm down towards my arm rest and catch his arm... He does withdraw it very quickly. It's just the lack of awareness... And on a 12 hour flight...

I can't leave the plane without knowing where Mr Nigeria is really from! I summon up the courage and ask him where he is from ... Pretty obvious actually... Flying from Paris, speaks French...The Ivory Coast... And yes he is on his way to watch his country in the World Cup Finals... And yes... He will always remain Mr Nigeria to me!

But... I will think of him when I see the Ivory Coast scores... And of course the poor guy sat next to him at the match! Imagine... being sat next to him when he is in a very excitable frame of mind... The carnage if his team score a goal!

So... If you see a guy coming out of an Ivory Coast game with a black eye... I urge you not to jump to the conclusion that violence has kicked off... He was probably just a little unlucky as to who he got sat next to!

Just had a great chat with a couple sat behind me, Sebastian, a Bruges fan and Caroline from Brussels now living in Hackney, East London! Having lived in Brussels and Antwerp in years gone by... We have a lot common ground in terms of places, concerts, and sporting occasions and have a really enjoyable conversation... It also gives me an opportunity to stretch my legs away from Billy the Bruiser...Turns out we were both at Belgium 0-2 Turkey at Euro 2000... they have tickets for a couple of Belgium group games and are justly excited by their team.. How can a country with a population of c10 million produce such a golden generation of players...? As compared to England... Yet sadly for Belgium, they have a likely tough last 16 match v Germany or Portugal... Although, they could easily be good enough to get through against whomever they play. We discuss the possibility of, subject to the airport having TV screens available, seeing the second half of the mouth-watering Spain v Holland clash. Sadly the delayed landing time will probably mean that by the time we queue through passport control and pick up our luggage, fingers crossed! It will be a little too late. With having three Belgians in the side with the possibility of a fourth to join, they are interested in coming to a Spurs game next season. Been to Arsenal and said nice stadium but no atmosphere but thought it was superb during Spurs 3-1 Bruges in the Europa League!! We exchange details and I will invite them to a Tottenham game next season.

A second hot meal is delivered and the battering of my bruised ribs recommences!

4.46pm an hour and 12 minutes to touch down in Brazil!!

Caroline reads an extract of my Romcom and wants to know what happens next between Jeremy and Anabella... Caroline says they have to get it together!

I am feeling a little guilty for neglecting these fictional characters in favour of my 2014 World Cup diary #chanceofalifetime

The fasten seat belt sign comes on. It is just after 5.30 in the evening. The excitement on the plane is palpable. As we circle Rio de Janeiro, people are straining their necks for a first glimpse of this magnificent city, flashbulbs are popping... Ahh bless... Mr Nigeria offers me a piece of chewing gum... So sweet.

Actually the chewing gum is much needed as even with it... The pain in my ears is terrible... The pressure is building... The wheels come down as we commence our final descent. Nightfall had been quite quick and now the nightlights of the city twinkle below us. Come on England... End 48 years of hurt... We can all dream!!

17.53 We have landed!!!! The multinational passengers cheer and clap!! The Arsenal boys let out a tune of "and now you're going to believe us we've landed in Brazil"... Followed by a verse of Inger-land, Inger-land, Inger-land...Oh dear!

Passport control...Rumour starts circulating in the passport control queues that Spain, the defending champions are losing 5 1 to Holland.. Yeah sure...

Japanese on the plane wearing masks to avoid catching germs and also in the passport queue...Takes all sorts to make the world go round...

I am stood with the Bosnian guy who lives in Germany in the queue... He receives a message saying that Spain took a 1-0 lead and then let 5 goals in... It is true... Spain 1-5 Holland is true... sounds like Robben had a fantastic game... My oh my...A shock of epic proportions... It is difficult to absorb a result of this nature without seeing the match unfold...

Chaos in the passport queue but when I eventually reach the front of the queue, a stamp on the passport and exit papers... Unsurprisingly my bag is there waiting for me to be picked up at 6 50pm.

Next stop... Collect 3 match tickets up from the FIFA machine... Ridiculously easy at the airport... No queues!! The electronic process is very quick and smooth. I am now the proud owner of 3 World Cup Group matches... Yaay!!!!!!!!!!!!!

Finally leave the airport 7.50pm... Issue being commission on changing money... Normal exchange rate say 4 reals to £1. To change £10 should receive 40 reals. They wanted to give me 11 reals... There is being ripped off and being ripped off... but to lose 29

reals out of 40 reals on charges is beyond the pale...

Eventually a guy who organises taxis takes pity on me and gives me a rate of 3.7 with no commission. The bus fare to Copacabana is 13.50 reals which is about £3.50.

Showed bus driver the address where I need dropping off. Just hope I don't have a long walk carrying wallet, bags passport, tickets, phone, new watch etc...

Not too many passengers on the bus... Mostly Argentine... Already clear that the locals are like hungry sharks ready to feast on the cash coming in...Once in a lifetime... Now where I have heard that expression before... The opportunity put before them in the shape of genuine football fans coming to enjoy... Yes a once in a lifetime opportunity!!

There are ways and means of keeping the cost down and this local bus service will hopefully show the way it can be done.

The iPhone currently shows a UK time of 00.11h. I have been awake since 3am...

A passenger plays the Girl from Ipanema on his ghetto blaster... All is well in the world!

Beautiful clear evening... A floodlit Christ the Redeemer is clearly visible from above. The air is warm... Around 25 degrees

However if I hadn't been here before, driving through the suburbs at night... It wouldn't feel too appealing... Run down and heavy traffic would be my first impressions...

I realise I am still chewing the gum given to me by Mr Nigeria more than three hours ago!

An hour into the bus journey and not sure but it seems we have travelled from one airport to another!

The idea of joining Colin for a beer on his birthday is starting to look remote...

The bus driver is so helpful. He has no clue where my hotel is but stops twice to ask people... Copacabana beach is now stretching out before me. The place is alive and kicking... Judging by the wild celebrations going on Chile won their opening game tonight.

It really does feel a carnival atmosphere... A football fan festival... So colourful, vibrant, noisy... People from all over the globe mingling together determined to have a great time.

Eventually the driver gestures me to get off the bus and I think from his hand signals... turn down the next right where a block or two back, the road on which my hotel is located runs parallel to Copacabana beach... My hotel number is 995 on Avenue Nossa Senhora... Number 995... Hmm... Let's hope I am at the right end!

A young Brazilian couple kindly walk me to the correct Avenue... I am at number 549... It is quite a long walk with ruck sack, suitcase, valuables etc but it feels very safe. Seems to be a lot of Argentina fans in town and surprisingly quite a lot of Aussies too.

Eventually I arrive at my hotel... The concierge is very helpful and knows a man regarding tickets... Don't you just love concierges who know a man!! Availability and prices will be known tomorrow... I am hoping for a pleasant surprise but am not holding my breath...

Mr Bosnia who goes by the name of Elvis, you couldn't make it up... is my best hope for Argentina v Bosnia and Sebastian of Belgium for the France v Ecuador game...Spain v Chile looks tough and as for England v Uruguay .. I might have to pay quite a bit of money if I want to see this game...

I enter my hotel room number 801... And am pleasantly surprised at how spacious it is...

Having travelled so far... To walk into a room as good as this one... My home for the next six nights... It's a good feeling!

Just had a text conversation with Colin who is in Lapa which is a little too far away at this hour and we agree to arrange to meet up tomorrow.

The journey door to door took 22-1/4 hours... It has for the most part been mostly enjoyable... And that is thanks to you guys for allowing me to share my experiences through keeping this diary. I have now been awake 23 hours and am about to go out and buy some water for the night ahead.

I turn right and walk a few paces along Nossa Senhora to the corner with Xavier da Silveira where there is a little corner bar... I am trying to order a couple of bottles of water and an orange juice ... the language barrier is a real challenge but the guy behind the counter is very patient with me and gives me a number of samples. In my flight induced dehydrated state, all of the samples go down very well!

I go back to my room and send a WhatsApp to Rob at 11.09pm... 3.09am UK time...Rob is encouraging to me come out but he is at the opposite end of Copacabana to me... I am shattered and would need a shave, shower etc... He sends a couple of photographs to encourage me... And as much as I would like to... Big day tomorrow and sleep needed. I say goodnight to Rob with our last text exchange at 11.36pm local time and 3.36am UK time... Time to sleep!!!!

EL GRINGO'S ONCE IN A LIFETIME

This World Cup was about attacking football and changes for the better. From vanishing spray to seeing National anthems of other countries being sung with passion by players and fans alike. In a political world with religious divide, football brings all races creeds and different class systems together to share a common hobby which is the beautiful game!

Russell Young, 42, Grantham, UK

Every two years; for the UEFA Euros and FIFA World Cup tournaments; my two England t-shirts come out from the bottom of my shirt pile. I've had the 'Three Lions' one since '96, the year Ian Broudie, David Baddiel and Frank Skinner won the best football song trophy in perpetuity.

For Brazil, I decided we could dream of a nail-biting third Group match, luck with the opponent in the Round of 16, a glorious win on penalties in the Quarter Finals, Jack Wilshire up to speed by the semis, then... Forty-eight years of hurt has never stopped us dreaming. The 'Three Lions' were lined up for the Italy and Costa Rica games. Unlike our lads, the shirt's still not worn out!

John Hill, Rugby, UK

SATURDAY 14TH JUNE 2014

Wake at 11.40am...Good sleep, much needed!

Catch up on social media and have the vague recollection of hearing pouring rain in the night... Hmmm

Paul text early morning to say he and Ian are on their way to Lisbon airport from their overnight hotel and will meet me at the hotel at 5 15pm.

Peter and Neil send through a great photograph at Lord's today with a jeroboam bottle of Veuve Clicquot......They have no idea of what the score is! Takes me back to my last visit to Lord's in September last year... In a corporate box to watch Notts beat Glamorgan in the CB40 final... Went into London and by midnight was so bad that when talking with a charming American couple I let a full pint of beer slip from my hand and drop to the floor... Now I understand what they mean when using the expression... He can't hold his beer... I literally couldn't! The American guy not appreciating why it had slipped from my grasp... Went straight to the bar and ordered me another pint!

The next day I drove from Wembley to Cardiff to watch Spurs score in the last minute of added time to win 1-0... Paulinho who is a pin-up boy of this World Cup from Brazil, scored the winner... Fair to say Spurs fans haven't seen the best of him yet... But it made the long journey back to Nottingham that day so much sweeter!

Look out of the window and the sun is out but it doesn't look especially warm...

My body is a little achy after basically not doing very much yesterday... You would think it should feel rested after sitting for that length of time...In general

I feel a little lethargic...Shame I lost the morning and missed breakfast...Other than England v Italy I have no idea of which other games are taking place today and at what time. Will need to get down to the fan fest and have a look.

I reflect on the fact that I would have had to be up at 5am to fly to Manaus for the England match and another long day of travelling... Dread to think what I would have felt like on Sunday at being up nearly 24 hours again... The big man in the sky smiled at me in getting me out of that mess!!

I wonder whether Colin or Rob will be up yet... Guessing Colin will be... Rob... Well judging by the intent of his messages...May be up but only by virtue of not having gone to bed yet!!

I receive a good morning message from the UK and send a good afternoon response. They respond in turn to ask if I am drunk as it's still morning there...

I look at my watch... It says 7.51am... I have done it again!!

I had assumed the time on my iPhone was the correct time!!! How tired must I be!!!!!

Yaaaaaay I have got my morning back!! I have got my breakfast back!!!!!!

Both Colin and Rob may well be awake... At different ends of their day!

After a refreshing shower and excellent breakfast I return to reception to see a man about a man.

I meet the man! He has a name! A Brazilian guy called Umberto in the hotel lobby... He offers me tickets for the three Maracana games I am interested in ranging from £465 to £300. Too expensive but we agree to stay in touch and exchange mobile numbers.

After a protracted morning between the hotel reception, Vitoria by phone and email I manage to book a room at the California Othon overlooking Copacabana for £150 including taxes for Wednesday 25th June.

Just the four match tickets to find now...

As I am completing my booking form... Umberto rings my room number with lower prices... I reject them but we are now in negotiation... I am a little more hopeful!!

Colin is in touch. He is staying in Flamengo. When they arrived from the airport they came out of the lift on the 5th floor straight into someone's living room!

A child was watching TV and he wasn't at all perturbed at six middle aged English guys walking into his living room! They were on the wrong floor but... Nevertheless!!

They are drinking at a beach side bar opposite the Budweiser Hotel on Copacabana...Can't miss them...Famous last words!

Walking down Xavier da Silveira I change 300 USD at an exchange rate of 2.20 reals and £100 at a rate of 3.70 reals. All set!!

There is a travel agency and I wonder...Match tickets? I meet a guy called Georges...Yes he can get tickets, the prices are even higher than Umberto's... They come through a Dutch guy called Sam. He tells me where the tickets ultimately come from and I am shocked...Certainly not for publication in this book! We agree to stay in touch.

I make the short walk down Xavier da Silveira towards the beach on the left hand side. On the corner on the right hand side is the Savoy Othon. It is a towering landmark and helpful to remember where to turn off the beach from whilst I find my bearings.

I am now walking along Copacabana's Avenida Atlantique away from Ipanema...The beach is on the other side of the busy dual carriageway. The view along Copacabana is fabulous...The sun is shining, it is winter but my it is hot... An electronic sign...One of many along the beach front which flicks between showing the time and temperature shows 30 degrees! That will do for me...The hotter the better! Memories of 12 years or more ago come flooding back. The girl from Ipanema tune is playing on a loop in my head...I am happy!

In the near distance I can hear a band of some description and singing... Sounds like football fans...It is football fans...As I near, I see yellow and blue shirts... Many with the name Dzeko on the back...They are Bosnia fans and having a huge party at an outside bar. TV crews are filming them... Along come a handful of sky blue and white zebra shirts...They stop outside and start jumping up and down chanting Argentina! Argentina! Argentina!

What an introduction to my World Cup adventure! I take photographs and videos!

It is not aggressive or threatening...Just two sets of fans enjoying themselves and singing together ahead of playing each other at the Maracana tomorrow.

I hang around for 10 to 15 minutes... Just feels right place, right time!

Just passed the bar is the Budweiser Hotel... It has the letters Pestana running down each side of its tower. The pavement in front of the hotel is ring fenced with barriers behind which are stood black suited security guys. Budweiser is heavily promoted on the front of the building.

I cross over the dual carriageway to the promenade beach bars...and after a telephone call or two see a cross of St George flag with a navy blue letter in each of the four segments...T H F C and running along the red central line in the middle the words...Come on England. On the right of the flag beyond the segments, there is a huge navy blue and white Cockerel stood on a football which runs down the length of the flag...The badge of Tottenham Hotspur...I think I may have found them!

The flag is attracting a lot of attention. People from all over the World, walking along Copacabana promenade are stopping to take photographs. Colin bought it from the Spurs shop...And as he says this I recall it being on sale. Of course I didn't pay much attention to it... Why would I...that was late May...I had no idea then that on the 14th June I would be sat here sharing a beer with these guys!! Actually...Come to think of it, I didn't even know these guys were coming until Russell Young told me a few days before I flew out!

The mood is good... Everybody is looking forward to our first game tonight... England v Italy. I learn Uruguay v Costa Rica is the earlier game. So if as expected Uruguay win that one, the expected slow start in the heat of Manaus and a draw for England wouldn't be the worst result.

BBC ask if we would mind being interviewed live on TV for BBC 24 and

EL GRINGO'S ONCE IN A LIFETIME

BBC World News... If you insist! They are having trouble receiving a satellite signal which lines up with a live TV slot...

I get chatting with a couple of English guys on a nearby table... Everton and Newcastle fans. Isn't it funny how football fans describe people...The guys could be serial killers, a heroes, great family men... But no...All condensed into...Everton and Newcastle fans...And I guarantee any Everton and Newcastle fans will now be swelling with pride at reading this! And even if they are serial killers...They will still have some form of affection for them...Well...Because they are Everton and Newcastle fans!

The TV crew are ready... The poor guys lugging the satellite kit and cameras around in this heat... I re-join the group and the reporter asks me a question which I answer and that is that...the guys are aghast...I am immediately nicknamed John Terry... Eventually I ask why... Because I only turned up for the interview... Just like John Terry did for the photographs when Chelsea won the Champions League!

Italian and Costa Rica fans join us...The BBC come back filming us singing and embracing...Just need some Uruguay fans and then we will have the fans of all four teams in the Group together! It is a real party atmosphere here!

Further along towards the fan fest, there is loud singing...Hundreds...No could be thousands of Argentines are gathering.

We finish our drinks and head down towards the fan fest with the intention of stopping off to eat somewhere ahead of watching the Uruguay v Costa Rica game in the fan fest.

As we approach the ever increasing thronged masses of Argentine fans... An open topped car passes...standing on a passenger seat with his torso showing through the open sun roof is the "Pope" dressed in a white gown with both arms out in front of him holding aloft the World Cup! He has an Argentina flag draped across his left shoulder! Everyone is taking photographs... The thousands of Argentines plus all others including ourselves. It is all getting a little frantic. There is a line of Policemen separating the Argentine fans from the road desperately trying to hold them back from disrupting the traffic flow...The arrival of "Papa" has made that task all the more difficult!

Having picked up three or four more England fans on our way...We walk along the central reservation and begin to pass the Argentines. A combination of empty stomachs, sun, beer whatever...But one of our lads thinks it is a good idea to hold up the England flag!!!! Well... You can imagine...England is not exactly the most popular of countries in Argentina...Now the police really have got a struggle on their hands! We sing Inger-land and then someone starts a rendition of "if it wasn't for the Police you would be dead" ... Once we are passed the Argentines a heavy guy and his buddy come running along the road after us...He is from a radio station in Argentina...He asks if we can be interviewed in English of course...His first question and I kid you not!! What about Maradona's hand of God goal!! We say a long time ago... What about Michael Owen...What about David Beckham...! We have a good laugh with him and say our goodbyes! As we keep on walking, more and more groups of Argentines are passing us and singing at us...Just how many of them are here! Copacabana seems to have been taken over by an invasion of Argentina fans!!

We are nearing the Fan fest! What an amazing sight and or site it is to behold. It is visible across the full length of Copacabana which must be four to five kilometres in length.

The fan fest is actually two fan fests. The first is an enormous screen erected on the beach. This is an open fan fest.

Further along, the one which we are now walking alongside. Running partially down the promenade side is a type of enormous white marquee. From the promenade, there is an entry and exit.

Against a purple background in yellow are the words "Juntos num so ritmo" and above in white the words "All in one rhythm" are written across the entrance. It is the official FIFA fan shop.

The fan fest is enclosed by high fencing. Along the promenade, queues have formed to enter the fan fest. At the far end is an enormous screen. It would easily be possible to watch the games from Avenida Atlantique or even the beach on the other side.

We turn down Rua Duvivier... The guys have found a BBQ restaurant which is close to the fan fest and say the food is good quality and reasonably priced.

The BBQ which is called Quick Gelato is rectangular in shape. It has a bar with stools running along both lengths and one width which is street side and the whole frontage is open. The far end of the rectangle is a work area including till and bar-tabs so doesn't have any seats. Running through the middle is the BBQ with chickens, steak and skewered kebabs giving off some heat...No wonder the whole frontage is open! The chef and waiters work inside the rectangle...Drinks and food being delivered, empty glasses and plates being taken away.

It is full but the turnover of people as the name of the restaurant suggests is quite quick and the seven of us are quickly seated in twos and threes. It has a good ambience. Conversation amongst the diners is easy...Strangers become friends very easily. We are talking with Argentines, Iranians and Italians. I have a young spring chicken with chips and a side dish of chopped onions and tomatoes. The food is really very good. The type of BBQ where you quickly dispense with your knife and fork and get down to business with your hands.

On the television Colombia thrash Greece 3-0. Great start by Colombia... Even without their injured talisman Falcao...They still look full of goals...No wonder a lot of people are tipping them to go a long way in this tournament.

Behind us on the side wall is a thoughtful sink to wash hands afterwards... Bill paid and it is on the way to the fan fest for my first visit!!

The queues have reduced and we walk across the beach to the barriered entrance...at the end of the barriers is a huge entrance and a sign "FIFA fan fest Rio de Janeiro bem-vindos". In front of us is an X-ray machine, any bags are also opened and checked and our bodies also just like at an airport.

We are now inside... It is enormous!! At the far end is the huge screen. Down each side are various large tents with interactive games, photo opportunities to be seen virtually holding the World Cup, sponsor outlets, restroom facilities, bars and fans...Thousands of fans stood on the sandy beach. The fences are all covered with sky blue hoardings, the multi coloured official logo and coloured images of the World Cup with the words FIFA World Cup Brazil. All of the colourings are in a mixture of the green and yellow of Brazil plus splashes of a warm purple, white, darker blue and red. The colours give off a feeling of warmth.

Colin leads us towards Bar 5 which is where the England fans have arranged to meet.

As we trudge through the sand passed thousands of people, a fairground ride on our left hand side...Not sure of the name but one of those where about 20 passengers sit in connected seats in a straight line all facing the direction of the crowd...They are airborne and being twisted left and right... Screaming and whooping along the way.

We then walk underneath two cables attached to which is a seat transporting a fan across the width of the fan fest...Must be some view of the fans below!

As we get closer to the screen, the fan fest opens out into a much wider area... An upper open corporate terrace with its own bar is on either side...two other great views!

Bar 5 is on the right side just in front of one of the two corporate areas... No fans are therefore behind us. We queue to buy our drinks tokens and then queue in a separate place for our drinks.

Great chance for Uruguay... Cavani shoots... Wildly wide and high...Had a drink or two but that looked an open goal!

I am having a really good conversation with an Argentine guy while watching the match. Governments may fall out but at the end of the day...We are all people...All football fans.

Holding in the box... Penalty Uruguay...Cavani 1-0!! Even without Suarez, this is looking routine.

Forlan shoots... Deflection...What a save.

Half time 1-0 Uruguay

The excitement is building in the fan fest towards England v Italy. There are a lot of England fans congregating around us...Everyone is singing... Inger-land, Inger-land...Footballs coming home, it's coming home, it's coming...

The second half kicks off...

We are having photographs with fellow England fans. Rica could have scored then...

And again... They are looking threatening all of a sudden...

Cross comes over...Chest's down...Shoots 1-1!! England fans go mad...This wasn't on the cards at all!! Campbell...Somebody shouts out he is the Arsenal guy who scored for Olympiakos against Man Utd last season.

2-1 Rica... England fans go mental!! The Uruguayans are all over the place!! Rica look so fast and pacy... Their counter attacks...Campbell looks sensational.

Paul and Ian are in Rio! I text to say Rico are winning.

We discuss whether we want an equaliser...The guys say no way...I think I would take a draw. If we then draw, to all be on the same points with Italy out of the way would surely be a good thing...

If Suarez was anywhere near match fit surely he would be brought on?

Time running out...Uruguay pushing forward...Rica break...3-1!!!! Oh my!!!

Camera pans onto Suarez on the touch line...He is almost in tears haha!!

I get a text from Paul and Ian to say they are on their way to the fan fest.

Last minute of added time...Ugly tackle...Pereira sent off... Suspended v England...Yesss!!

Game over...Cat amongst the pigeons!! 3-1 in terms of points and goal difference is a commanding position.

Paul and Ian are on their way to the fan fest.

Between games we chat about the ramifications of the result on the group... Even if Rica lose against Italy, they will still be in with a chance of qualifying in their last match v England...Was kind of hoping they would be out by then...Will this change the mind-set for the England v Italy game. Will both teams now go for it as opposed to may be settling for a draw?

Paul and Ian arrive just as Colin and the boys are moving towards the back of the England fans near the corporate section. They will come back later.

Stood next to us is a South African supporting Italy!! I ask why?? Anybody but the Pomes...He supports the underdogs... Then admits he knows little about football...In saying Italy are the underdogs, I had already drawn that conclusion!

We sing the national anthem loud and proud...As do most of the players as instructed by Roy!

1-0 Sterling! Great goal!! We go wild!! Fan park erupts...Sterling must be the coolest guy ever... Just walking back towards the halfway line...I would be going mental! I am going mental! We are all going mental... It was a great goal... Top corner... Wait a minute... The goal isn't given...Why? Not offside...The screen even said England winning 1-0!!! It hit the side netting then somehow ran along the length of the goal as if in the net...

England playing well and looking the more threatening.

I need the bathroom ...Never has bathroom ever felt over exaggerated as in the fan fest... A fence would be...

I have to cross the whole park...And end up at...A fence!

On the way back amongst the Argentinians...Italy score... Everybody goes crazy...Get back to Paul and Ian... Sterling to Rooney crosses ...Sturridge on the half volley... Yessss 1-1 mayhem!!! This time we really have scored! Sturridge looks up to the heavens and raises both arms.

Jagielka somehow heads off the line!!

Half time...Happy...England look threatening going forwards...Come on England!

Queuing for beers and it feels totally against the run of play...Italy score 2-1...Balotelli...Too much space down the left. Welbeck not covering and Baines stood off to let a cross come in...Balotelli unmarked to head home...England poor defensively there. Yet surprisingly I still feel England can win this...Alcohol induced optimism?

Great chance for Rooney... Nooo...shoots wide...Will he ever score a finals goal?

Substitutions start to take place... Brave call but maybe Lambert for Rooney...May be a step too far for Roy who has shown himself to be quite brave.

After 70 minutes... All the talk of preparations being perfect fall apart... England players going down with cramp. Italians seem unaffected... Even Sturridge and Sterling seem to be struggling. Wilshire comes on and promptly plays a cross field ball out for a throw in. Time begins to ebb away...England seem to have run out of legs. Suddenly we are into 5 minutes added time... Pirlo hits the bar...Carelessly we lose possession...And...We lose the match...

I now fully expect the trip to Belo Horizonte to watch England v Costa Rica to be a waste of time...Unless of course you are a Costa Rica fan... Not based on logic as England played well tonight. Just know Suarez will play against

EL GRINGO'S ONCE IN A LIFETIME

England...

Spain lost their opening game 4 years ago and look what happened after... But only a small percentage who lose get through.

After the game an Argentine wants to swap shirts with Ian...I think... Why would you swap a shirt with Messi on the back for a plain England shirt...?

Ian looks rather snug in his new shirt but...He carries it well!!

The drudge through the fan fest after the game is arduous...And would have been even if we had won... Who am I kidding...We would have skipped through it...

We are now sitting in an open air bar by Copacabana beach... The temperature is ...The word perfect is often overused but in this instance it is perfect...!!

The beer is going down well...In fact...Rather too well...We order beef kebabs.

Chicken kebabs arrive... They are awful... Barbecued fat... We have 3 beers each. We wait and we wait to pay... Eventually we give up trying and leave...We walk out without paying for an awful chicken dish and 3 beers each... We did try your honour!

We stop at a restaurant and sit outside... This time we get our beef kebabs and they are lovely and we even pay this time!

On the way back to the hotel we are passing a bar...Live Brazilian music, people spilling out onto the pavement... And yes you are right...We couldn't resist either!

The World Cup in Malta is always a special tournament, as you have top national teams fighting for this prestigious trophy, and being played in Brazil, the mecca of football, made it even more special.

Before the tournament began, the teams quoted in Malta as favourites to win the World Cup were Brazil as hosts, then Germany, Argentina, Holland, Belgium and Italy.

Malta was practically divided into two halves as most fans support teams from England and Italy so you can imagine the hype when these two nations were drawn against each other in the same group!

Italy won and some supporters went out "car-cading" to celebrate until the early hours of Sunday morning!

If you are a football enthusiast, the World Cup always brings that something special, if possible you want to see all the action and all the goals.

This tournament also gives more colour to our little island with roof tops and balconies decorated with so many different flags of various countries participating but that's the beauty of the World Cup and it only comes every four years.

Herbert Azzopardi, Malta.

Parisians are always mouthy... "I do not like this, I do not like that." But during the 2014 FIFA World Cup in Brazil, they were in a good mood, because the team of France played very well.

The whole country was behind them. When the Blues were playing, in the streets of Paris, almost everyone proudly wore the blue shirt, supporters marched like Roosters! Tobacco bars, even those that are often empty were filled with people. Arabs rubbed Jews, blacks embraced whites, and everybody was French. That was the magic of the World Cup football.

Kim Chi Pho, Paris, France

SUNDAY 15TH JUNE 2014

I wake at just after 7.30...Thumping headache...It's a while since I have had a hangover... I vow not to have 14 successive hangovers...

I text Elvis again... No response but his English is about as good as my German...

Luckily my body clock is still on UK time. I dress and jump in a taxi to the Ibis Hotel, Rua Ministro Viveiros de Castro, 134 Copacabana...Only 10 reals.

I hope to meet Elvis the Bosnian and pick up a match ticket for tonight's game

Argentina v Bosnia and back to the hotel for breakfast.

I arrive at the hotel at 8.20... Nobody in the lobby...Hmmm...I ask the receptionist who confirms this to be the only Ibis on Copacabana....He also says there aren't any Bosnians staying at the hotel but there is a Bosnian flag at the Copacabana Mar Hotel across the road ...Hmmm

I text Elvis...No response...I call Elvis the Bosnian...Twice... No answer.... Hmmm.

You know when you meet some people who come across as jack the lads and you just know they will let you down...Well Elvis was exactly the opposite. I had or should I say have a lot of faith in Elvis to deliver...I decide not to write him off just yet and resolve to wait. What else would I do at this time of morning... Sleep? I vaguely recall that concept...

You are not going to believe this...The guests begin to come down for breakfast. Loads and loads of them wearing their colours...The very distinctive red and white check shirts of Croatia...Double hmm...Whilst I am not an expert in Balkan relations...I know enough to know...

So here I am writing my diary in the Ibis Hotel on my iPhone notes waiting for Elvis from Bosnia surrounded by Croatians.

In 1997, flying around the US on a Lear jet on another wild goose chase, doing due diligence on a Group that could never give the required payback... Well...One day we ended up in a place called Tupelo...The sign said population 10,123 or something like that above it...Like the old Western films when the gunslinger rides in to town, kills someone and chalks one off on his way out... Anyway, being a lot younger and a bit of a smart boy...I say to the lady behind the hotel reception...So...What is there to do on a Wednesday night in Tupelo? Deadpan she replies...Well to start with you could visit Elvis Presley's birth place...Certainly put me in my place!!

The thing is...Ordinarily I would be hacked off at being sent on today's wild goose chase but with you guys to keep me company and writing my diary I feel good, even chilled and at one with the World...Wish I had taken up writing years ago!!!

It is now 9am and I text Paul to see what time they will be ready for breakfast and ask him to give me 15 minutes notice.

There never was much doubt as to who I would be supporting tonight.... Argentina! Argentina! My connections with Argentina go back to 1978 when Ardiles and Villa signed for Tottenham... Argentina.... Vamos Argentina!!

I jump in a taxi back to the Savoy Othon which is fortunately only about 15 blocks away and only a £6 return taxi ride...

Never did like his music anyway...

Paul texts back to say they had breakfast at 8am and the plan is to have a walk along Ipanema beach...Sounds good...Tall and tanned and lean and lovely, the girl from re-emerges!

The taxi driver asks me where I am from and when I say England he looks at me apologetically and says sorry... Truth is I am not too downhearted...We played well just a shame that what was once a strength, defence now seems to be a weakness.. Maybe John Terry and Ashley Cole should be playing... Lose in São Paulo and it would take a remarkable sequence of scores to still have a chance of qualifying... And...We just know Suarez will be fit to face England... Don't we?

As I eat breakfast, I look for my room key... It must have come out of my pocket when paying the taxi driver...

Without any form of identification I expect a drama to get a new room key at reception... It was remarkably easy...All I needed to know was my name and room number... Very easy...May be a little disconcertingly so...

Get back to my room... three texts from Elvis come through:

Hallo John ich bin weg. Keine Ticket

Ticket vielleicht bei Stadion Marakana

Ibis Hotel no Ticket

My German isn't great but I get the gist of the first and last texts ... No ticket at the Ibis!

And I guess the middle text suggests trying outside the Maracana tonight...

Open three beautifully worded father days' cards from my wonderful children Henry, Molly and Harvey which melt my heart and just about bring me to tears.

Walking along Copacabana promenade Sunday morning is exhilarating. People cycling, running, walking...Hundreds of Argentinian fans in their distinctive light blue and white shirts...The beach alive with volleyball and an assortment of other ball games.

As I reach the Ipanema end of the beach I take a photograph looking back over the arc of the bay with sugar loaf acting as the backdrop... People out on the water standing on boards paddling with an oar... Never seen that before.

Even the Brazilians suffer the same problems with the weather. It's a little overcast on their rest day.

At the end of the beach there is a large police and military presence outside the Sofitel Hotel... I ask a soldier who advises me that FIFA are staying there. There is likely a man in that hotel I would like to have a word or two with... Maybe you have heard of him... Goes by the name of Sepp amongst many other names he is afforded...

While walking between Copacabana and Ipanema I realise that I have no clue who else is playing today...Being at a tournament is so different...At home, the wall chart would be out, each result being meticulously inked in. The day planned around the games. Whilst at a tournament, snippets of games are picked up here and there...strange!!

Now I am back on Ipanema beach for the first time in what must be about twelveyears... It is of course as beautiful as ever... Where is my girl from Ipanema...Ahh there she comes... Tall and lean and lovely...

Another backdrop of mountains with a large favella nestled in its hills. The bay does not curve in the same way as Copacabana and seemingly less beach games. Ipanema has more apartments overlooking the sandy beach. Being a Sunday morning the road is closed to vehicles.

It is 11.09 and the sun breaks out from behind the clouds.

The last minute.com Timberland sandals I bought are having a baptism of fire and sadly so are my little toes and ankles where the blisters have long since turned red raw...

Text messages seem to be in their own Sunday morning mode ...They are coming through late and in batches. Finding Paul and Ian is going to be tricky.

Text finally comes back to meet at Sol Ipanema where I text to say I was a little while ago!

The Dutch team are staying at Cesar Park and I take a photograph of fans taking a photograph of a player in a car at the Cesar Park Memphis somebody other.

Meet Paul and Ian and we head to the girl from Ipanema bar... We have to stop off on the way. Paul needs the bathroom...No...He really needs it...Rio Revenge! We arrive at the bar...It is 11.45 and ...It isn't open yet! We go to the bar across the road while the girl from Ipanema catches up on her beauty sleep.

Eventually we go into the Ipanema girl bar and take a couple of pictures of photographs of her on the wall. In her heyday ...She certainly was tall and tanned and lean and lovely...And judging by the photographs she has matured well too.

Quite a story...To become famous through just walking down to the beach and someone writing a poem about you that becomes a World famous song and sung by the man himself... Frank Sinatra!!

We walk back through Ipanema and the Sunday morning market...Fantastic paintings on display...I take a few photographs...Moral dilemma...Do the artists mind? Fors and againsts!

We see the media booths looking across Copacabana Bay...Including where the ITV window had been stoned and damaged by protesters after the Brazil v Croatia opening match.

Fantastic models of Maradona and Messi have been erected on the promenade and as you might imagine are drawing lots of interest.

Back to the hotel to change... Sandals dispensed with... My toe is in an absolute mess.

Colin and the boys sleeping off the affects of yesterday on Flamenco beach which is local to them. They are not interested in going to the Maracana today.

EL GRINGO'S ONCE IN A LIFETIME

Social media talk of forged tickets around the stadium...Guy says on Twitter that it is impossible to differentiate between forged and genuine tickets...Hmm

Cheapest price so far £350...How can the prices be so astronomical? Doubt I will be getting in...

Forgot that, Sebastian of Belgium text me last night and could get a Spain versus Chile ticket for $500 and a France v Ecuador for $300 and was continuing to negotiate on my behalf.

I send a text to see if any further progress has made...

Just seen at Half time the Swiss are losing 1-0 to Ecuador.

In reception we book a 5 hour tour for the morning...£67 seems to be good value.

As we do the Swiss equalise... The World Cup is almost a side show!

We order lunch at a corner cafe by Cantagalo underground station...Can I really eat steak every day for two weeks!

Switzerland score a dramatic last minute winner! Wow!! What a difference that goal makes to both teams...With France in the same Group...Could be crucial...

We hear a commotion along the street back towards the beach. There is an army of fans being escorted by police... Naturally we assume Argentine but...We are wrong... Bosnia fans!!

Traffic being held up...Car horns blasting in frustration...

We go to the metro station. As Paul and Ian have match tickets, they are not required to buy metro tickets. I pay 3.50 reals which is less than £1. The walk to the platform is longer than at the revamped Kings Cross to the Victoria line.

The train is full of passionate Argentines...Singing, drinking, dancing, and falling over!

It feels as if other countries fans somehow love their country more than we do...

We come out of the Maracana station onto an elevated walkway. It is rammed with people and a little chaotic. To the left we get our very first glimpse of the stadium... A huge bowl...It looks fantastic!

There is an enormous police and military presence...They are lined across the walkway like a blockade. Only those with tickets can pass. I slip through the ticket check and if I hadn't it would have been a metro straight back to Copacabana.

It is 4.15. The kick off is 7pm. We walk around to the stadium entrance E and F and slip down a side street. At the end of the street more military checking tickets. Paul and Ian go out to look for a ticket but no luck. Lots of people wanting a ticket but not seen a single one being sold.

We walk around the stadium towards the São Cristovao metro station. Amongst the thousands of people, I see an older guy with a satchel and my gut suggests I ask him if he has a spare ticket... Lo and behold he says... Yes! But he says it is a corporate ticket and wants back what he paid...US $1000...About £600. I say no chance and after a discussion he reduces his price by $200. I still say it's too much and offer him $500. He agrees to meet me in 45 minutes at 5.30 if he hasn't sold it by then. I genuinely offer him some sound advice to be careful as there are a lot of fans who would mug him for the ticket.

He walks away and within a matter of minutes returns and says he will accept my offer which equates to 1100 reals. Between Paul, Ian and me we are counting up to 990 reals…A guy comes up and asks him how much he wants... He says $600 and the cash is immediately handed over... Damn...The one opportunity and it has been lost...

We need to find a cash machine!

It is clear he has four tickets and someone wasn't able to turn up at the last minute and he has made a quick buck... Good luck to him but if I had agreed a price with someone and they were trying to rustle up the cash... I hope I would have behaved a little differently...

Continuing our walk to the station, we come across an English tout... A Liverpudlian...What a surprise! He wants £470 for a ticket. The best I can negotiate him down to is £410. I offer my number...He says no point...Clearly expects to get what he is asking...

We go to São Cristavao Station to try to withdraw some money from a cash machine which is two yards the other side of the ticket barrier. Even though Paul and Ian have free underground tickets, they won't let us through and insist that we should walk to another machine. A World Cup volunteer takes us outside and explains how to get there...It seems quite a walk and we again ask for some common sense to be applied. She takes us back inside the station and after some discussion manages to convince the military to let me through to use the machine. The machine is only in Portuguese. The volunteer has to negotiate to come through the turnstile to help me. The machine doesn't accept my card. They won't let Ian through the turnstile to try his card... He kindly passes his credit card to me and whispers his pin code across the turnstile...Yes I know this is ridiculous but wait...It gets worse...Ian's card doesn't work either..

We learn that the machine only accepts Bank of Brazil credit cards! This is a World Cup...Surely there is a clue in the title "World "Cup... May be just may be fans who come from around the world might just want to withdraw cash...

Around the station there is a little more activity and a Hertfordshire tout, Arsenal fan...Yes already a barrier to negotiations...Offers a corporate ticket at $1000 which is c£600... He says with being a corporate ticket... There will be a free drink...I politely ask as to whether that will be for the rest of my life?

There are hundreds of people looking for tickets and only the odd one or two for sale at crazy prices. There is no point in Paul and Ian hanging around any longer... We say our goodbyes and I am doing all I can to get a ticket... The odds seem stacked against me.

It is now after 6pm... Kick off is 7pm...I find a guy who is prepared to sell his ticket for 1000 reals... I negotiate him down to 600 reals... £160... I ask him why he is selling. The gist as I understood it...He points towards a couple of friends... They came together and they can't get tickets and he would prefer to watch the game with them in a bar and make a decent profit. Sounds plausible. He is very nervous as he says selling tickets on the black market is a criminal offence... Which I had previously heard to be the case.

I check the ticket for as long a time as he is prepared to let me and it is on a couple of occasions... The ticket is a little dog eared and clammy... But the feel, texture and look are exactly the same as Paul's.

I look him in the eye and ask him if the ticket is a good ticket and he assures me it is...I ask him if he is a good man...His body language and eye contact is direct and unflinching.

I am not convinced but work through my thought processes...If I walk away and jump on the metro back to Copacabana... I will never know and will always think what if...

A casino manager once said to me that the odds are so stacked against the punter that if you go to a casino... Regard it as a night out like you might for a theatre and or dinner... Determine how much you are prepared to spend and enjoy losing your money as an evening's entertainment...

I begin to regard buying this ticket as a night at the casino and if I actually get into the stadium... In comparison to the prices being quoted... It will feel like hitting the jackpot.

I text Paul to let him know I have a ticket, if not a forgery, to arrange where to meet afterwards if I get in to the stadium.

I show my ticket to pass through the police barricade, walk up to gate D and show my ticket to join the line... It is a long metal barrier queue snaking left then right then left again. Once I reach the front, there is a security entrance similar to that at an airport but no concerns over shoes here! I pass through and no bleep... Passed my exam first time! As an extra check, an officer uses a device across my body and for good measure pats me down before allowing me through.

I go up some steps and approach the turnstile...In my heart of hearts I am still not expecting to enter...

I hand my ticket to the volunteer at the gate who waves me into the turnstile as she places the ticket onto a pad for registration... It doesn't register...The pad shows a light with a red cross ...She tries again and again...Asks a colleague to look and whatever the Portuguese for forgery is said.. I am obviously shocked and horrified...How can this be? Another volunteer takes me down to a type of portacabin office and leaves me to queue. The time is 6.35...Kick off is in 25 minutes...The office has the possibility for five counter assistants. There are seven people in the office but only two counters are open for the sizeable queues.

There is a hint of frustration in the air...Kick off is approaching and people who have paid a lot of money for a ticket are concerned that through no fault of their own they may miss the kick off...The guy behind had his ticket rejected at the gate in the same way mine was but he received his from FIFA through his company...

A small group of Argentines are at the head of the queue I am standing in... One lets out an anguished cry and falls to his knees in tears. It is heartbreaking to see... His ticket is a forgery...I dread to think of the sacrifices he made to buy this ticket, the distance he has travelled...Probably by car...The excitement at actually getting a ticket...And now the heartache...

The people who sell genuine tickets at grossly inflated prices are one breed... The crooks, the bastards who sell forged tickets are altogether another much worse breed...The excitement they create for the buyer and the untold misery they cause...

Eventually I am at the kiosk and I have a small hope that because my ticket is dog eared, the magnetic field may have been disturbed... But alas no...I am told it is a forgery and I leave... I am obviously disappointed but hey two weeks ago I wasn't coming anywhere near Rio... I bought the ticket with my eyes wide open. It was a gamble... Literally... And it didn't pay off. C'est la vie...

I walk back up to São Cristavao station and have a chat with some other English guys who are also looking for a ticket... One is wearing an Everton shirt and I note the irony of a Liverpudlian looking for a ticket...Good guys who decide to hang on a little longer in the hope of getting a ticket. As for me... I am all played out...Laughing at the expression which was the title of the 1990 World Cup diary I read which inspired me to write this diary!

I take the train back to Botofogo. The train is full of weary and dejected fans, mainly Argentine, who were unable to find a ticket at a suitable price. The mood is sombre and in stark contrast to the joyous lively mood of the fans on the way to the stadium.

I chat with a couple from the UK...Warwickshire. The best price they were offered was $1800 for a pair of tickets... We agreed it was just not worth that kind of money. They tell me the metro station at the Maracana only opened a few days ago...And that there is a strong belief Rio could lose the Olympics as it seems they just won't be ready in time. London is apparently being regarded as favourites to host again should that be the case... Not heard this before?

A Brazilian guy shows me the score and the goal on his telephone...Have to say on his phone it looked a weird goal... As if a Bosnian defender back heeled it into his own net!

I change at Botofogo from the Red Line 2 onto the Green Line 1. Line 1 & 2 trains come in on the same platform. There aren't any screens to advise the destination of the next train. Instead each carriage has a red or green light on above the doors to distinguish which line the train is operating on... Reminds me of the Brazilian BBQ restaurants which give you a card...Green coloured on one side and red coloured on the other side. The waiters bring around different BBQ meats and you have your card turned to green to be served that particular dish or red if you don't want that dish. I am looking for a train with a green light for Line 1.

Meet four Argentine fans on the metro from Botofogo to Cantagalo. They are from Cordoba, Ardiles home club. I tell them Argentina winning 1-0.

The Argentine fans ask me to take a photograph of them for my book. We say our goodbyes.

After they get off the train a Croatian man tells me the information I gave to the Argentines was wrong. He said Bosnia were winning 2-0... And had seen it on his phone...I really hoped I hadn't given the Argentine guys the wrong score...

Had the Brazilian shown me a fake goal to go with the fake ticket I received earlier in the night?

The train didn't stop at my station and I end up at General Osorio which is the next stop and is also at the end of the line.

On the platform I check with a Brazilian lady if I am on the right platform. Sure I am but just soo tired...I say how good her English is and that she speaks it with an English accent...She says that's because I am English! We laugh together and the lady explains that she lived in Rio for 7 1/2 years and only returned to the UK in January... No interest in the football but had to come back for ten days and to her horror it clashed with the World Cup! I asked if moving back to the UK had been the right decision and without hesitation the response was a resounding yes...The only downside was missing the weather. The lady didn't miss anything else and when I probed as to why...The answer was that it is so difficult to get things done here. Things that should be easy made unnecessarily difficult...My mind went back to the cash machine farce...I was able to have an understanding of what she meant...

I take the next train back to Cantagalo and go to a bar near the hotel. It is the 44th minute and Argentina are winning 1-0...Wasn't that a strange, pointless conversation with Mr Croatia on the train? In the bar I meet Roy a Man Utd fan and Trond an Ipswich fan both from Oslo. We share a few drinks and stories as we watch the second half. They are also going to Croatia v Mexico in Recife and ask for my number to meet up in Recife and to go to the France v Ecuador game together.

A couple on the next table are from Manchester with their young son and daughter. His son who is I guess is around six years old is a Man Utd fan which is quite problematical...His father is a Man City fan!

I struggle to understand how that can happen...My two sons were in Spurs babygrows. There was never any doubt...And it's a great bonding experience to go to matches together...To always have that in common and never be lost for words.

I learn that France beat Honduras 3-0. With 10 men for quite a chunk of the second half Honduras held England to a 0-0 draw...Hmm not a particularly good comparison against the French performance.

I then realise that the Ecuadorians who we managed a 2-2 draw with a week or so ago lost 2-1 v Switzerland today... Hmm we really can't be that good, can we?

Messi scores a very good goal to make it 2-0... I go to the bathroom and just as happens at White Hart Lane I hear a cheer for a goal... Only this time I am not sure who scored! It was Bosnia to set up an exciting finish!

Both teams are giving the ball away... It's almost like watching a Premier League game!

Argentina hang on to secure victory and I head back to the hotel and post a few photos onto Twitter.

Paul knocks on my door and is shocked by the size of my room... Their room is about a quarter of the size. We could easily have slept 3 in this room... Why didn't the hotel allow it #moneymaking

We meet Ian in the lobby and head back to the local bar we finished off at last night... Already we have our local!!

The atmosphere at the stadium sounded terrific and I am pleased that they had a good night...These guys ordered tickets back in January and spent a lot of time and money on a well planned trip. They deserve a great World Cup.

After a couple of beers, I give in to tiredness and head back to the hotel. I have felt tired since the afternoon and between 3 and 7.45 had been on my feet in the heat without any food or drink... and England players please take note... Not once did I go down with cramp!!

It is now 2.08am and my alarm is set for 8am.

Nigeria is a multi-tribal country where there are more than 250 ethnic groups but there are however only three major tribes. Despite these differences amongst the population, unity sneaks her way into the Largest 'Black Nation in the World' and interestingly the only way this could ever happen is through football. The 2014 Brazil World Cup was another period when, despite the religious crisis coming from a particular sect (I won't mention), Nigeria inevitably came together.

Across the country, pubs, clubs, bars, beaches, viewing centres were filled with Super Eagles fans to watch the games. People would ignore anything to watch the Super Eagles play anytime of the day.

Thankfully, worship hour on Sunday morning was skipped this year unlike the 2002 opening fixture against Argentina when some Pastors who wanted to retain their congregation for the day had to place a television screen beside the pulpit. Pastors blamed our loss to Argentina on the absence of their church members from the Sunday service.

However, 2014 World Cup witnessed a strange occurrence where, according to the BBC News, the religious extremists took about 21 people's lives in the Northern part of the country.

The public screening of football was banned in some of the northern parts of the country but despite the bombing, football lovers were unable to be stopped.

In every other part of the country although fans were more security conscious that wouldn't stop us from enjoying watching our Super Eagles play.

Olasoji Tosin, Ibadan, Nigeria

The World Cup for me is the world's greatest show, even bigger than the Olympics. Even though a Ronaldo inspired Portugal knocked Sweden out in a play-off game, it meant that I and a few million other Swedish football fans spent four weeks sleeping in the day and watching TV at night and we did it without complaining!

Overall the World Cup dominated everything in Sweden for four weeks to the joy for us fans and to the despair for our spouses and children who wanted to go on holiday or just watch the normal TV programs.

Gert Skold, Sweden.

MONDAY 16TH JUNE 2014

Wake up at 6.30am... four hours sleep...The last thing I needed was to wake up this early...

Two days in...Struggling...Soo tired...

I need a holiday!! Have a word with yourself John...You are in Rio de bloody Janeiro... You are on holiday... Have a holiday!! Laughing at myself!

A head-hunter calls and wishes to email a link to some psychometric and competency tests... Hello? I can imagine trying to complete the tests right now... Thank you very much John...Don't call us... We'll call you!! I manage to defer the completion of the tests until I return to the U.K...Thankfully!!

I am, though, soo tired... Have I just said that? My body may well be in Rio de Janeiro but its body clock is still somewhere else... Halfway over the Atlantic Ocean... Get your ass over here pretty damn quick mate... My body needs its clock back in sync!!!

Right starting today I vow to get myself fit... These six nights in Rio are supposed to be an easy few days of rest and relaxation... Yeah right haha!! Ahead of the really tough part of the trip which starts on Thursday morning... Today is Monday already...Hmmm...

In exercise machine terms... You know those machines which show hills and valleys to describe the degree of difficulty... Right now the machine wouldn't be showing any hills whatsoever... I mean six nights in Rio...How could it!!! It can hardly be described as a hardship can it?? I mean... Imagine trying to say to someone sat behind a desk in an office or digging up a road somewhere... No... Not going to work is it?? But from Thursday...Its hills all the way...No not hills... Bloody huge mountains!!! Feeling as tired as this...I wonder whether I will be able to cope...#notasyoungasioncewas.

I have a shower... Don't think I mentioned that there are two shower taps... Rather than having one which can be turned to the optimum temperature... There is one hot tap and one cold tap. I turn the hot tap on and then the cold tap... I cannot get the temperature of the water right... In my jet lagged and tired state... I am now forgetting which way to slow down or increase the flow of each of the two taps... I have a moment of internal hilarity... Competency tests... I cannot even turn a shower on properly!!!

I come out of the shower, get dressed and look at my new sandals... They stare back at me threateningly...They look like implements of torture... Feels like they are saying... Go on...Put us on again today... We dare you...They have made a bit of a mess of my feet and toes, no not a bit...a total mess...Burst blisters on the top of my feet , backs of my ankles and on each of my small toes...The latter being particularly painful and bleeding. With having a 5 hour tour ahead of me, I cannot face another day of pain today. It will have to be my casuals... Not sure what you would call them...Maybe a cross between sneakers and training shoes... Comfortable but they enclose my feet and I will need to wear ankle socks...Not what I would expect or want to wear in Rio...

In England, Water companies such as Thames Water have charts on the walls in the restrooms. These charts explain how hydrated or dehydrated you are through the colour of your urine...Clear water means fully hydrated and very dark water means very dehydrated... Suffice to say I am more than very dehydrated... Obviously not drinking enough beer...Resolve to drink more!!

The next problem is that when cleaning my teeth, my gums bleed...I hardly slept in the stressful week in the lead up to coming to Brazil. This must be a sign of being run down...Just isn't very pleasant...

The next problem ...Dry cracked lips...Probably connected to the dehydration...Not nice either...Add the tiredness and jet lag and I feel a bit of a wreck!! The cocktail of tiredness, bad diet, heavy food, alcohol and no exercise is not a good regime...I again vow to go on a fitness campaign...Starting today... Yeah sure...

I meet Paul and Ian for breakfast. Paul is still not feeling too great...Dodgy tummy...Not good... I hope he can get through the tour ok.

We meet the tour guide in the reception at 8.40am. I pay 810 reals for all three of us by visa which releases some much needed cash until I can find a place to use the bank card.

We get on board through the bus door and are immediately confronted by a second internal door. I am not sure whether this is for air conditioning purposes or to protect passengers from being attacked. When I was in Rio just after the Millennium, there was talk of a whole bus being robbed on the way from the airport...

The first hour of our tour is a tour of hotels to pick up other tourists. The guide says the tour will finish around 5pm... Wait a minute; we booked the 5 hour tour with the intention of watching the second half of Germany v Portugal... On paper, one of the games of the first round of matches! We are told the full day tour and the 5 hour tour have been merged into one tour...It is fortunate that we chose to do the tour today and not on Wednesday when Paul and Ian have tickets for Spain v Chile and I hope to find a ticket...a proper one this time!

The tour guide is very funny and repeating his repertoire in Portuguese, Spanish and English.

We arrive in Gloria Square near the Centre and the tour party breaks up to board smaller minibuses.

As we begin to climb up Corcovado towards the statue of Christ of Redeemer, the guide informs us that Corcovado means the hump of a camel which is the shape of the hill or is it a mountain on which the statue stands towering over the city.

A guy in the front passenger seat takes out his video camera and records the journey of the ascent up to the top. Why?? I am sorry not to be able to give you any more information about him but if anyone invites you to see his video recording of Christ the Redeemer in the coming weeks...Be otherwise engaged doing something more useful like watching the clothes tumble round in a washing machine!

It would be bad enough if the recording was of high quality but we are driving over cobbled stones and being shaking all over... It is that bad I swear if we were airborne, the turbulence would be so traumatic that people would be making the sign of the cross and particularly when the driver is going at such a fast speed round blind bends! The sign of the cross! Quite ironic given where the driver is trying to take us to! We are swaying around so much...Being jerked backwards and forwards that from the outside, people will think we are doing a rendition of that old club classic song... Oops up side of your head... for younger readers... Look it up on YouTube to see what your parents did in their youth #cleanedthedancefloorwiththeirbestclothes.

As we continue our ascent, the natural beauty of the park is all around us... a lush greenness, trees, wild monkeys... It is not difficult to imagine how beautiful it would be to leave the road and enter inside the park.

As we approach the top, there is a guy jogging up the hill... The heat is now like a furnace... The jogger is running up this very steep hill with a rope strapped to his back. Attached to the rope...And I kid you not...is a tyre. The guy is running up this steep hill on a hot day with the temperature being around 25 degrees and is dragging a tyre along on a rope attached to his back...I kid you not #masochist

The thought occurs to me...The way the England players fell down with cramp in Manaus on Saturday...Instead of employing all these fitness coaches and sports scientists...All Roy should do is get Rooney and the boys running up here with a rope attached to their backs every day for a week...Would be a lot cheaper too!

We disembark...Would the Americans say debus? I am not sure! Gosh it is so hot up here. The guide gives us our entrance tickets, the cost of which is within the City Tour price. By coming on this tour, it also means we avoid having to queue to enter. As we approach the turnstile, I know this will probably sound stupid...But all the emotion and nervousness of walking up to the turnstile at the Maracana comes straight back to me. I feel a little anxious... then I am in... Will I be scarred for ever more by the events of last night...by passing through turnstiles...? What about using London Underground with my Oyster card...the next time my credit has been used up and the barrier rejects my card...Will last night come back and whack me around the head?? Is there such a thing as a turnstile phobia!!

We decide to have some exercise...Instead of taking the elevator; we walk up the 223 steps to the statue and are breathing heavily by the end... Altitude... Honest guv!

Sadly it is very misty when we reach the statue and it all but disappears before our eyes... Imagine a statue 38 metres tall (125 feet) being a metre or two away from you... and you can't see it!!

There are a lot of tourists and we are all waiting with our fingers poised over our cameras to take a photograph should the fog lift. It is quite a narrow viewing area which is split level and linked by steps. The fog is keeping people up there longer to try to obtain a decent photograph of what for many will be in a once in a lifetime opportunity. It is getting quite crowded. Ian and I have been previously and have seen the magical views. It is still a disappointment but we feel for Paul as it is his first time in Rio. Paul says he will come back with the family so hopefully he will see the views another time.

The fog does however clear from time to time to show the majesty of the statue. Some photographs are even taken with a clear blue sky. It really is a magnificent construction. The colour is off white and the statue sits on top a great plinth. Christ's arms are outstretched; head slightly bowed looking down on the city and its people below. The right thumb of the statue is under repair following a recent electrical storm but it is so far above us it is only just visible to the naked eye.

The three of us have a photograph together but the fog for the most part envelopes the statue at the point of the photograph being taken. It gives a very celestial almost spiritual feel to the photograph...Or as Paul laughingly said... Jesus photo bombed our picture!

Tourists are having their photograph taken with their arms outstretched on the steps in front of the statue... Their poor photographer having to almost lie on the floor to take the photograph!

We descend the 223 steps and the fog lifts sufficiently to see the Maracana stadium far below us. I try to take a photograph with my phone camera. It feels quite precarious to hold my phone by the wall with quite a drop below. It is not the same as holding a camera which has a strap... Thinking about it... phone companies could consider the option of a strap attachment to the phone...Not just to avoid dropping the phone in such circumstances but also a strap may make it

more difficult for thieves to steal. After all of that, the photograph doesn't come out!! Paul has his camera and promises to email the picture when back in the UK.

The guide tells us the statue is made with reinforced concrete with an outer layer of sandstone and took nine years to build. It opened 12th October 1931 so will be 83 years old later this year. We think but don't ask... Were 7 ½ of those years waiting for the fog to clear! Joking apart... it was some feat to drag the concrete up 710 meters (2329 feet) through the Tijuca National Park in such heat...The guy with the tyre strapped to his back...Easy life!!

We climb back aboard the bus and are returned to Gloria Square where we transfer back on to the larger coach. The driver must be under some sort of time restriction because whilst waiting for the other tourists to return, we drive off from the square and drive round a one way system which brings us back to Gloria Square three times!

Next stop is the Maracana... The guide tells us that the literal translation of Maracana is "small green birds". On the way we reflect on the differing emotions of yesterday's last gasp winner by Switzerland to beat Ecuador 2-1. The elation of the Swiss being in direct contrast to the misery of the Ecuadorians... Can there be anything better or worse than a last minute winner. There just isn't any time for a response and it has such an impact on the next two games for both sides... We get off at the stadium for photographs and bad feelings from last night envelope me. I have bad memories and sincerely hope I have the opportunity to attend one match in the stadium before I return home to replace these with better memories. The statue outside the stadium is of Bellini who captained Brazil to the 1958 and 1962 World Cup successes. We ask the guide why the statue is not of Pele to be told that Bellini is from Rio de Janeiro whereas Pele is from Sao Paulo and played for Santos. There is a statue of Pele in his home city. By the statue, there is a guy juggling the ball with amazing skills... another guy is impersonating Maradona for photograph opportunities and similarly another offers the chance to hold a replica World Cup in the air.

We leave the Maracana and make efforts to try to obtain a ticket for me for Spain v Chile. Paul texts a couple of touts from England who we spoke with last night and I contact Sebastian, the Belgian guy I met on the plane over who texted me Saturday night to say he knew of someone with a spare ticket. Paul also suggests going along to the Botofogo FIFA ticket office in case people collecting tickets have a spare. Good idea...But feels a bit of a bind given we are staying the opposite end of Copacabana.

We arrive at the Sambadrome where the carnival is held each year. It has banks of terracing down either side of the main thoroughfare which leads into a wide square at the end... This is also surrounded by banks of terracing. The terraces hold 90,000 spectators... Wow!

When in carnival, we imagine it looks spectacular but outside of carnival it is a series of empty concrete block terraces. There are a couple of shops and a few people dressed in costume for a photograph opportunity which I take them up on and away we go.

Lunch which is also a part of the deal includes a BBQ...Obviously! But also a buffet comprising meats, fish, salad, vegetables along with desserts and cheeses. This is also included in the City Tour price which is looking more and more like great value. Paul is pleased of the facilities... At least he is holding up ok.

While we are having lunch, the Germany v Portugal game kicks off. An early penalty for Germany! As Englishmen we know the score is 1-0 even before Mueller slots it home... Germans just don't miss penalties!!

As we leave the restaurant we hear the score is 2-0... Wow...Thought this would be a close game...Mr Ronaldo's bottom lip will be puckering!

The Germans always seem to start tournaments well... Just like England ... Not!! A lot has been made of this German squad. After humiliating England four years ago, they reached the semi-final before losing to the great Spanish side... But it will take a lot to win a World Cup in the Americas...Only teams from this continent have won the World Cup in this continent...

I went to the Champions League final at Wembley last year... The skill and energy allied with pace and power of Dortmund v Bayern Munich was incredible to watch...Breathless. It will be interesting though to see how they cope with losing one of their better players Reus through injury. How frustrated must he be to roll an ankle in a meaningless 6 1 win over Armenia and miss the World Cup... In Brazil...A chance in a life time...

Even if as it is now looking likely, Portugal lose this game... It is a tough Group...But with a player of Ronaldo's talent, they should have enough to recover and to beat the USA and Ghana. He carried them to the World Cup virtually on his own in the playoff v Sweden...Scoring a hat trick away to add to his goal in the first leg in his personal shoot off with Ibrahimovic who came up short... Think he "only" managed two goals!!!

Shame one of these two fine players had to miss this World Cup. Ibrahimovic destroyed England with a hat trick in a friendly about 18 months ago... His third goal was a remarkable and breathtaking overhead bicycle kick from outside of the box and if I recall correctly not just out of the box but towards the wing rather than centre #unbelievable.

There are certainly some very talented players missing the World Cup... Not least the World's most expensive player, Gareth Bale...Who is not immune from scoring his own remarkable and breathtaking goals!

I have a personal disaster... Writing my diary on the hoof, I lose the entire contents of this morning's diary... It is gut wrenchingly sickening... I recall as many bullet points as I can remember and with the considerable help of Paul and Ian list quite a lot to write up earlier. A hazard of writing a diary in this way... I resolve to forward my diary to my email address on a more regular basis.

First stop after lunch a 35 year old cathedral São Sebastiao... Designed by Humberto Cozzi of Italy... Cone is 96metres (315 feet) high and it holds 20,000 standing people!

It's enormous! The inside is dramatic... four strips of huge stained glass windows rising up almost the full length of the cathedral.

We get back on board our tour bus...Emotionally the question of a ticket for England v Uruguay is weighing heavily on me... All sorts of thoughts are running through my mind...

Will any tickets be available and if so in Rio or should I wait until the morning of the game when I land in São Paulo?

How much am I prepared to pay for a ticket?

What if the ticket I manage to buy is another forgery...?

After losing the opening game against Italy, the reality is that the England versus Uruguay game is now crucial... Pivotal... For both teams...Uruguay also lost their opening game 3-1 to Costa Rica who now seem to the surprise package of the Group. Whoever loses this game will almost certainly be going out of the World Cup. After just one game of the tournament, it is effectively knock out football from now for both teams. I just have to get a ticket... Life is about experiences... I still remember the Italy versus England experience 24 years ago...

Then there is the question of cash... I can only draw 1000 reals out of my account c£280 each day... I really don't want to experience the same problem as last night when shortage of cash cost me the genuine Argentina v Bosnia ticket.

And of course before the England match, there is the small matter of Spain versus Chile to think about. The old saying... How do you eat an elephant...One mouthful at a time...Feels about the right approach...The old football adage... Take one game at a time!

Couple of English fans are on today's trip...They went to Manaus for two days...Didn't see a single mosquito! Still taking the malaria tablets... One of the guys doesn't have a ticket for the Uruguay game either. They are veterans of previous World Cups and are relaxed about getting a ticket...I am not sure that it will be so easy this time...

The sun is out... Bright clear skies... It is hot...The temperature shows 24 degrees but in the old city, it is stifling...And this is winter!!! The view from Christ the Redeemer would be spectacular this afternoon but also so it will be from Sugar Loaf... We learn it is so named because it is the shape of a loaf and when it has cloud resting on its peak... The cloud looks like Sugar... I wonder how Big Ben got its name...Don't go there John!

The cost of entry is again included in the City Tour price and given the length of the queues, we were given immediate entry. There is however still a queue for the cable car which will take us up 220 metres (722 feet) to the top of Urca Hill. As we board the cable car... The announcer says "mind the gap".... Now where I have heard that before... Good old London Underground!

We walk around the first hill towards the second cable car station...It is incredibly busy with people walking both ways and bustling passed each other along the single narrow footpath as they head in opposite directions.

We are told by the tour guide that Jack Fruit hangs from the trees creating a lovely tree lined walk way and learn that this sweet fruit emanates from

South Asia. In addition to being a fruit, it can also be cooked and eaten with a curry... There you go... We learn something new every day! In fact we learn lots of new information every day...And the majority of stuff we don't retain... Which is why... If you ask me anything about Jack Fruit in a year's time... I will probably say... never heard of it!

The trees though do provide a lovely shade and as we walk along the pathway take in the green smell of the wood.

Hey! Stuart Pearce just walked passed us!! Along the crowded pathway Ian doesn't see Stuart. Before I continue with this part of the story, Stuart Pearce is not only an ex Notts Forest legend and new Club Manager... But no... He is almost a Demi God to Ian who is a huge Notts Forest supporter. Now Ian has felt a little tired and lethargic today... But did this stop him... Oh no!!! He sets off in hot pursuit of Stuart weaving in and out of fellow tourists on this narrow path like a champion slalom skier... And you might think... Ahh but not the same... A skier is under severe pressure. This is where your thinking would be wrong as once Stuart passes through the ticket validation turnstile, these turnstiles are haunting me these days, before Ian reaches him... Then he will be on his downward descent in the cable car and out of Ian's reach.

Some minutes later a euphoric Ian has weaved his way back to us vowing never to wash his right hand again!

We board the second cable car which takes us to the summit of Pao de Acucar some 396 metres (1299 feet) above sea level.

The views from Sugar Loaf are literally breathtaking... The Christ statue stands proudly over Rio with arms outstretched... I would like to say protecting

its inhabitants...But as romantic a notion as it would be to write such words... Well...Let's just say you may begin to question my credibility...

The boats look at rest in the calm waters of the bay; the sun is glistening and dancing on the surface of the blue waters. Huge hills and mountainous rocks provide a stunning almost 360 degree view breaking out into small islands or providing headlands of sandy beaches either side. The runway of the city airport, Santos Dumont, is close by and in the distance, at the international airport; aeroplanes are taking off and landing to and from all parts of the world. Those coming in to maybe fulfil their own World Cup dreams just as I did less than three nights ago... We have packed so much in; it is difficult to believe it is still less than three days ago!!

The England football training camp is below us and in an amazing coincidence the players come out to train during the short 40 minute period we are at the top of Sugar Loaf Mountain.

On our cameras, the players look like ants... Perhaps waiting to be crushed... Hmm perhaps not the correct analogy given our nervousness of playing Uruguay on Thursday... I am using that analogy whilst being sat amongst the clear blue skies sitting atop Sugar Loaf.

The reason being... Uruguay's nickname is... Wait for it and I kid you not... "The sky blue ones" ... Not the best omen... But then again I am not superstitious... And why should I be ... Given the day I had on Friday 13th... Oh the irony!!

A guy stood near to us has an amazingly powerful zoom lens on his camera which can actually zoom in to see the players' faces... Could be quite a frightening experience... And certainly a scary thought in most cases... Sorry lads!

Germany 4-0 Portugal! Mueller hat trick!! Wasn't he also top scorer at the last World Cup? Whatever... What a great start by the Germans!! Not quite as big a result as the Dutch win over Spain but nevertheless, Germany has laid down a marker with this result.

There are certainly some surprising and high scoring games in the first round of group games. Ronaldo will be furious...And Pepe was sent off so will miss the next game and injuries to two other players including the left back... Sounds a catastrophic start for Portugal.

Back down in the cable car to Urca hill and I take a photograph of the first 22 passenger cable car which ran from 1912 all the way through to 1979. Now this cable car worked for all those years without incident... But if you asked people to get in it today... Perception is everything!

I then take a photograph of the 1979 upgrade... Sounds like I went into a cable car showroom and negotiated an upgrade but only on the proviso the old cable car is included in the deal! This second car carried almost three times more passengers...65 to be correct car which ran through from 1979 to 1997. This second car was famously immortalised in the James Bond Moonraker film. Roger Moore in his role as Bond was fighting off Jaws who began to snap the cables with his steel teeth... Yes I know... But the Bond films went a bit on the silly side for a period...

There is a helicopter whirring it's blades at a Heliport on Urca Hill. I recall taking this flight previously...It felt expensive all those years ago and even more so now... 600 Brazilian reals which is about £162 each for a minimum of three passengers for 15/16 minutes from Urca Hill. 600 reals... Now where I have heard that figure before recently? Oh yes the cost of the forged ticket I bought for the Maracana match ticket... Rather perversely, the 15/16 helicopter ride would take in the Maracana... Been there seen it, done it, didn't get in it...sadly...

The Helicopter ride can also be taken from by the lake or a launch pad by Christ the redeemer.

Now back on terra firma... Our energy levels buoyed by the amazing views... Having earlier asked the guide Neto for a list of bars to visit in Lapa we receive a list of bars, clubs and sexy clubs to visit! Not that we ever would... Of course.

Along with many other passengers, we decide to cut short the tour rather than have a tour of Leblon. Ipanema and Copacabana beaches...We know them well having walked along the promenades yesterday. The bus drops us off reasonably close to our hotel.

What a fantastic days tour... All in for £67 including lunch as well as entrance fees... Absolute bargain and Neto the tour guide... What a warm, friendly, funny and knowledgeable man. A sunny smile and the type of positive person you would be happy to have in your life.

Just spent the last hour trying (again!) to find a bank machine which will allow me to release cash on the MasterCard anonymous bank savings card... Started to get more than a little frustrated but even more worried... Then finally

Banco do Brasil has a machine which will accept the card... What a relief!! Then further frustration... It only allowed me to release 1000 reals... With the price of match tickets being quoted here that won't cover one let alone two match tickets...

I am now chilling in my room and posting a few photographs of my day on Twitter...looking at the photographs... Great memories of an amazing day!!

On the television is Iran v Nigeria but it doesn't look too stimulating a game. If I was at home, I would be glued to every game but there is too much going on out here. The three of us watch the closing stages in the hotel lobby...It is the first goalless draw of the 2014 World Cup... Let's hope it is the last one!

Early evening, at nightfall, we take a taxi and head off to Lapa, the bohemian district of Rio de Janeiro.

It is rush hour and as gridlocked as any major city across the world. The noise of car engines ticking over and impatient drivers honking their horns provide the background to our conversation. Looking out of the taxi windows, weary commuters are also making their way home on foot or towards bus stops where queues of people wait for their elusive buses. Away from the beaches and the tourists, the city is alive with the locals carrying on with their daily lives and routines.

The one big difference being that whilst Rio has always proudly shown off its national colours... Right now though, World Cup fever has gripped this fabulous city. The distinctive national flag with its yellow and green colours, blue coloured globe and the words "order and progress" inscribed across it are everywhere.

The shops are awash with green and yellow... Shop windows are adorned with the national flag, posters, shirts and various other trimmings. Flags hang down from apartment blocks. Streets carry bunting and flags.

We will visit three other cites during our two week stay and I would imagine these cities and its people are just as equally proud.

Being amongst the vastness of Rio de Janeiro, it is difficult to comprehend that with its population of c6.3million people, in population terms, the city accounts for only a little over 3% of the country's almost 200 million population!

A World Cup in a country such as the USA, where football or as the Americans would say soccer, is not the national sport, the atmosphere could be somewhat diluted. In the busy daily lives of Americans, including their own jam packed domestic sporting calendar, historically a tournament could virtually pass by without many Americans knowing too much about what is going on. Many at best may only take a passing interest in the drama of the global event place on their own doorstep.

This is not to say that the USA does not have a lot of people interested in football because it does... Whilst it is quite possible that in numbers terms, there could well be more football fans in the USA than say in England, the percentage of the population interested would I imagine, may be wrongly(?) a lot lower than in England. The general census among English football fans is a bit of snobbery against the USA and for that matter Australian football teams...A sort of looking down on them... Which may well bite our collective bum one day!

Here in Brazil, the adopted home of football, no such concerns...There may well be doubts and protests as to whether monies could have been better spent... But right now for the most part this football mad country is taken over by World Cup fever.

Every bar has several televisions showing wall to wall coverage of the World Cup. Every advert even seems to be football related... The young Brazilian striker Neymar is endorsing this product or that product. The weight on the slender young man's shoulders is enormous. Brazil shirts with his name on the back are worn by the masses...

Irrespective of the rights and wrongs of the penalty decision in favour of Brazil versus Croatia during the opening match, the pressure Neymar must have been under as he stepped up to take that penalty... The hopes and dreams of a huge nation which eats sleeps and breathes football... The pressure must have been immense.

It really is impossible to avoid the 2014 World Cup in this football crazy country.

The chatter in the newspapers, the bars and cafés and of all the taxi drivers is football, football, football. I reflect... Despite many of the shortcomings... It is truly a privilege to be at a World Cup hosted by Brazil.

Then, added into the mix of the green and yellow of Brazil, there are thousands of football supporters using Rio as their World Cup base as well as FIFA and many of the teams... The colours of the 32 nations are to be seen across the tourist areas of the City. It is truly a spectacle to behold.

As if to illustrate my point, we pass Botofogo which has a huge sign showing that Russia are using the local club facilities for training purposes.

And ahead of us, through the windscreen, way up in the sky peering over all of this, we have a great floodlit view of the white statue of Christ the Redeemer. Never can the statue, the city have witnessed such a festival, not even in carnival... It is also true to say equally... our eyes like the hundreds of thousands of other tourists, here in this magnificent city, are constantly drawn towards this magnificent and dominate landmark.

The taxi driver drops us at the closed off Rua do Lavradio. We walk down the Rua which has flags of the 32 competing nations hanging across the street. We reach the famous samba club, Rio Scenarium but disappointingly it is closed on one night of the week... a Monday...We have a drink sitting outside a couple of bars. The climate is lovely. It is though quite quiet on this street tonight.

The Ghana versus USA game kicks off... What a start!!! Dempsey scores a cracker for the USA inside the opening minute of the game... Cutting in from the left and shooting into the far corner. What a shaker for Ghana...

We watch the first half in the bars on Rua do Lavradio... Altidore could or should have scored a second for the USA... But by half time, Ghana are unlucky to be behind.

We walk up to a crossroads. There is a bar on each of the four corners! One looks to be quite a large restaurant with high ceilings, large wall paintings and mock standing street lamps which branch out into two hanging lights. We go in to the bar and there is a great atmosphere in there. A lot of USA fans chanting USA! USA! USA! They don't have a huge repertoire of songs but their enthusiasm is infectious.

The second half carries on in much the same way as the first half... Ghana are having the lion's share of the possession, creating and missing chances and the clock is running down. Klinsmann is marshalling his team from the side lines... What the team might not have in terms of skill, they are making up for with team spirit and heart.

After seemingly missing chance after chance after chance... the breakthrough finally comes inside the final 10 minutes...Gyan who left Sunderland for somewhere in the Middle East...Saudi Arabia was it...in a bizarre transfer... plays a great back heel into the path of Ayew who levels with a fine shot for a draw inside the last 10 minutes.. Perfect result for Portugal as well...

The USA fans go understandably quiet... The prospect of Portugal and Germany coming up is a tall order...

Less than 5 minutes to go... Corner to the USA... Brooks is completely unmarked!! He heads the ball down towards goal... It bounces up... And beats the keeper! USA have somehow scored a second!! The bar erupts!! A chant of USA! USA! USA! So loud... The distinctive red, white and blue colours have taken over this bar in downtown Lapa tonight!

That's it! Game over... USA 2-1 Ghana... Not sure how Ghana lost that... But the USA have at least given themselves a chance by beating a good Ghana side!

We pay up and leave the bar.... good food it was too!

The four corner bars are now very busy with people spilling out on to the street. We go into the Provis bar which is quite empty but has a fine samba band playing. We are given a wrist band on entry but don't really understand why. We sit down with our beers and there is a wall which has what looks like sponsors logos on it... I stand in front with a virtual microphone for a photograph as a football manager after the game... Just how much have I had to drink!

UFC is on the TV and having never really seen it before I enjoy watching it. The bar is filling up rapidly... A group of English guys stand by us and we have some good banter... one being a Spurs fan is always helpful!! The bar is now charging people to come in now... Ahh... That is what the wristband is for!

Then two ladies come in... It looks like a mother and daughter. Miraculously there is a table and two chairs available in the middle of the bar. How did that happen? We are chatting with the other English guys... Someone notices the Adam's apple of the "mother"... And Paul coins the phrase... "Anyone up for a father and daughter combo!!"

We leave the bar and walk down the street... The streets are now teeming with people. Music is spilling out from the bars. It is crazy! We head up towards another junction and just before we get there, a little bar with a guitarist playing live music inside. The bar is rectangular in shape...Not that wide with tables and chairs down the side and people standing in the middle listening, dancing and singing along to the guitarist who is playing from the back of the bar.. Beyond the guitarist, there is a room off to the right which houses the bar to buy drinks. It's a great atmosphere in here. We buy our beers and sing along to the music... Often at the very tops of our voices... Losing My Religion, Don't Look Back In Anger and such-like. As the night wears on, it is impossible to buy a drink at the bar...No problem as there is an off licence across the road. Nip in there and bring cans back into the bar. Sadly the other side of Rio is on show... Amongst all the festivities are the homeless sleeping on the streets and prostitutes plying their trade.

We stand outside the bar drinking along with countless others... In the square just ahead of us Argentina and Chile fans are singing and baiting each other with a line of riot police down the middle and tear gas being let off. It is 2.08am and we decide to call it a night in Lapa and take a taxi back to Copacabana.

I don't feel ready to sleep ... Would love to have gone on to a club in Ipanema but the guys have had enough... Fair enough it is around 2.45am!

Paul and Ian go for a last drink...I feel quite tired and decide to head back to the hotel... On the way...An early 20's girl propositions me on the street... 150 reals c£40 for 1-1/2 hours... Umm no thank you!

I decide to take a walk down to the beach. I walk along the beach front... The night air is so warm and lovely...There are various negotiations going on between local girls and tourist football supporters...

There are lots of vehicles parked on Copacabana... Numerous ones being campers... People are sat in fold out chairs, others in the back laid on a sleeping bag...

Some have erected tents...it is fascinating to see the various ways people come and live the Rio World Cup dream...there were over 50,000 Argentines in Rio over the weekend.. Many would have driven the 36 hour, 3000 Kms to be here...imagine those who at the end of the journey arrived at the gates of the Maracana to be turned away with a forged ticket...Little wonder they fell to their knees howling...

I carry on walking and outside the fan fest on the beach there are fans sleeping rough on the beach or in tents on the beach whilst across the avenue, there are others sleeping in 5 star accommodation at probably 12 star prices... Then there are the corporate junkies sitting near the top of this pyramid on their freebies. It must now be getting on for 3.30. The beach side bars are still open for business... Across the road from the fan fest there is a huge crowd on the pavement... I cross over and there is a kind of impromptu street party ...Vendors are selling food and beer... People of all nationalities are sharing stories and bursts of laughter ring out... The party is kind of circled by young Brazilian girls... I would guess teenagers upwards ... They are flirting with the guys... I get talking with a guy who says something along the lines of I can have any girl I like here tonight... But I would have to pay for it...I doubt what he is saying...

I decide to test the theory and talk with a beautiful well groomed and dressed young lady...

She has long dark bushy brown hair, big very dark almost chocolate brown eyes and olive skin which contrasts against her white trouser suit. She doesn't seem to have much on under her jacket which has a number of buttons open but just about keeps her on the good side of, perhaps classy, would be too strong a word but let's say decent. She is about 5'5" in height and she appears shapely but without overtly showing herself.

I ask her if she can speak English and it is immediately obvious that she is very fluent. For good measure she adds in Spanish and her native Portuguese languages as well.

She is very articulate and says she is 22 but shortly after admits to being 29... Which given her maturity and demeanour makes more sense...

When she learns I am English, she enthusiastically mentions of going to St Albans once the World Cup is over... I look at her with incredulity... And say why ever would you to go to a place like that... But it appears to her it is a beautiful place... Obviously a man involved here me thinks...Which she confirms to be a 36 year old Englishman and says they have been together for a year... She adds that she will be going to stay with him for three months and hopes it might become more permanent. She is certainly pretty enough but I do wonder whether this is true...

When I ask who will be paying for the flight... She lets out a friendly laugh and says he is paying for her.

She says at her age she wants to "Stop this, settle down, get married and have children"

So, what the guy said to me a few minutes earlier is sounding to be true...The conversation is relaxed... This feels like an almost unique opportunity to gain an insight into her life, into a different side of Brazil... An old age industry which will be having an out of season World Cup boom...

I ask what she means by "this" and she looks at me as if to say ... Really? And I say but you are a beautiful, intelligent, young woman and then looking round at the other girls asked have you been doing this for ten years...

She let out a laugh and said you think I could do this for ten years!

I then asked why and she replied saying she had completed her diplomas but the money in administration wasn't enough for her. A couple of years ago she took the decision to "to do this".

At this point, I mused out aloud as to where she lives to which she responds in Copacabana...I push it a little and say a favela? To which I get a funny laugh in response and a no I live in an apartment...

I explore further by asking whether 400 reals a day was regarded as good enough to finish her admin role and she says I earn more than that a day... I guess I hadn't thought in those terms and try to find out how many times a day she earns 400 reals. This is not a world I understand but am nevertheless somewhat taken aback when her answer is five times a day!

Doing the maths out loud in front her I am looking at her as I calculate

2000 reals a day at an exchange rate of say 3.7/£1... Around £540... Which then equates to 14000 reals at say £3500 to £4000 a week... She says it may not always be that many times a day... But nevertheless...

She then catches me off guard by asking where I am staying in Rio to which I reply the Savoy Othon...And now she is getting down to business and says as casually as if it were the most natural thing in the World... I can come to your hotel...

After the conversation we have had, I sense the need to let her down gently and suggest an hour and a half wouldn't be long enough for that sort of money... As if I have a masters degree in the price/ time equation in Rio de Janeiro!!

May be it is because of being the early hours of the morning and a little like a taxi driver knowing it's his last fare of the night... Nevertheless she still takes me by surprise...I just want 400 reals... We can extend to two hours, it would be fine... She rightly senses however that it isn't going to happen... I tell her in saying no that it isn't anything to do with her and that she is a very beautiful lady... She thanks me and says she understands... I am not sure what that means but it seems a good way of saying goodbye. I need to find a bathroom and head down a side street to find a bar... I am thirsty and decide for the long walk back to buy a diet coke off the beach side cafe which is finally closing up for the night at around 4am.

Before I set off back, my curiosity gets the better of me... I am intrigued and cross back over to the party to see if the girl from Copacabana is still there. And... She isn't ...May be a guy had been waiting in the wings to snap her up. You know like when the shop only has one of the piece of clothing you want and someone has hold of it...The more they hold onto it... The more you want it... As I leave the party area a roughish young girl grabs me by the arm and says 100 reals... And as I walk back towards my hotel, reflect that in the context of the world she lives in… She is probably under-pricing herself as compared with the 100 reals favela girl...And wonder how much in the high society of London...

I walk back passed those sleeping out on the beach in the rough... I have a spare unused single bed in my room and a spare double sofa bed... And these people who have probably had more arduous journeys than me to be here are sleeping out in the rough...it doesn't feel right... And as I walk back and then think of the US$800 touts are asking of these poor souls for a ticket to see their multimillion filthy rich footballers... The sacrifices we football fans make, all of us including you and me... And then we read the Sunday Times articles on alleged corruption... Rich people wanting to be even richer through having their vote bought...for people on the construction sites dying in building for Qatar... The biggest show being taken away from the footballing heartlands for what appears to be the wrong reasons...gosh the early morning can make one quite melancholy!!

Negotiations continue between the football tourists and the girls on my journey back... And then as I get closer to the hotel... Another new and strange phenomenon to hit the streets... It is between 4.30 and 4.45am and early morning joggers are out running along the Copacabana promenade... At this hour of the day... When many haven't yet gone to bed... Me included!!

Finally I climb wearily into my bed and can't help one last thought of the girl from Copacabana...Where she might be, what she might be doing... Hopefully one day she will land the dream she is looking for...

The World Cup was very happy. I met several people from other countries, and that was really cool. I went twice to the FIFA Fan Festival and enjoyed the party.

Guilherme Azevedo and
Nilda Azevedo

For Belgium this year's World Cup in Brazil was rather special. Our national "Red Devils" participated again for the first time since 2002.

All of a sudden (and with a little help from the media) all the different communities all felt like one nation again - for a while we all felt Belgians again instead of Flemish, Walloon etc.

Flag, scarf, cap and t-shirt manufacturers saw their turnover rise to unseen heights. No street, no pub without a flag. In the village where I live somebody even painted his house in black, yellow and red stripes.

During the matches you could walk the streets and roads endlessly without seeing or hearing a single car. It almost felt like the '70ies when, during the oil crisis, you couldn't drive a car on Sundays.

Our "red devils" in 2014 made us Belgians escape a while from reality. Thanks guys! & "Leve België!" (Long live Belgium)

Lena de Wachter, Belgium

TUESDAY 17TH JUNE 2014

Everyday another part of my body gives up. Today it's my throat and lost voice after our crazy night in Lapa...Losing My Religion; Don't Look Back In Anger etc.

Ian and I finally go down to Copacabana beach to sunbathe. It is has only taken us four days! Paul joins us later...Last night was a heavy one. Ian bought me a strawberry vodka which Paul swapped with me, otherwise, I would have been really struggling today.

EL GRINGO'S ONCE IN A LIFETIME

The sights and sounds of Copacabana beach...The crashing of the huge waves, the whistles of the beach vendors plodding through the heavy sand... Boy they must be fit... May be Roy should get Rooney and the boys to do a little vendor work on the beach for a few days...That would sort their cramp out!

The big bottomed girls in their thongs...May be they really do have injections to beef their asses up...Whatever, their sultry languid walk towards the sea unites the global football fans in mutual admiration!

I go in to the sea and am almost immediately knocked over by the powerful waves. I need to be careful with the trunks and have no idea how the girls in the thong bikini bottoms cope! Looking across the sun kissed bay is a sight to behold. A backdrop of mountains behind the crescent shaped beach. Swimming back in with the waves, the salty taste of the sea...It feels a glad to be alive moment.

Lying on the beach, drying naturally in the hot sun...Is there a nicer feeling in the World??

We get talking with some English lads from Essex who have a sign up looking for four England versus Uruguay tickets. I ask them to make that five! They are a mixture of Spurs, West Ham and Arsenal fans. The Spurs guy, John says they know of a friend's cousin who is selling tickets and calls him. The tickets are US$900 and he takes my number. The recurring theme in my mind is as John described... As much as I am enjoying the sea, the sun, the beach without an England versus Uruguay ticket, it is impossible to fully relax.

We come off the beach to see a TV at a promenade bar showing the Belgium versus Algeria match. Algeria are surprisingly winning 1-0 by virtue of a penalty given away by Jan Vertongen.

We can feel the excitement building for the host nation's match versus Mexico this afternoon. The game is still some two and a half hours away but the anticipation is already in the air. The promenade and roads are a sea of yellow... Like the waves of the ocean rolling in on to the beach, the sea of yellow is heading in one direction...The fan fest at the Leme district end of Copacabana beach.

A camper van drives passed us heading towards the fan fest. It is painted in Brazilian yellow and green. The front passenger door is open and the passenger is stood with his feet on the door frame gripping the top of the frame with one hand. In honour of Ayrton Senna, he is dressed in a red racing driver's suit and wearing a green and yellow motor racing driver's helmet. In his other hand, he is waving a black and white chequered flag. The back door of the van is also open and a guy in a dark blue Brazilian shirt is holding a replica World Cup aloft out of the van. Rising in the air from the driver's

side is a flag pole with a large Brazilian flag waving in the air. It is quite a sight and just shows the effort the fans go to and they are not even actually going to the match!

I call in at the Brazilian travel agency on my way back to the hotel. The Brazilian guy says the corporate ticket prices for Spain versus Chile are ridiculous at 3000 reals which is over £800.

He offers me a ticket for England versus Uruguay. The prices are £450 for a Cat 3 and £850 for a Cat 1 ticket. At least there is a ticket to buy for this match and if I have to pay £450, with England having lost to Italy, this is now such a crucial match...Reluctantly and I can't believe I am saying this, I resign myself to paying this astronomical sum of money. The daft thing is, outside of a World Cup Finals, if this match was being played at Wembley, I wouldn't pay £50 plus travel costs to London for the game. Out here, I have paid to fly in and out of Sao Paulo, have a night without a bed and pay £450 for a ticket #bonkers

The guy tells me the agency is shutting now for the Brazil match as is everywhere else!

A quick change in the hotel room and we are now walking down to the fan fest. The promenade is now a blanket of yellow. Thousands and thousands of yellow shirts, it is an incredible sight.

Whilst walking, a mixture of sounds fill the air...There is a band playing, vuvuzelas being blown, car horns honking...The sense of joy and excitement is palpable.. What else brings a nation together like football?

John texts to say he has picked up his four tickets, is happy that they don't seem to be forgeries and a fifth is available should I want it.

I text and call Colin to let the guys know that tickets are available...The price is a little steep though which they agree with.

EL GRINGO'S ONCE IN A LIFETIME

Paul and Ian have bought some cans of beers and are going to the open fan fest. I go along and sit down to have a beer with them. Whilst sitting there, I feel this is my once in a life time chance of seeing Brazil at a Rio de Janeiro fan fest and decide to go alone to the enclosed fan fest and meet up with them later.

I go through security and walk up towards the front on the left hand side. Passing under the overhead chair lift, I decide on a spot level with the corporate balconies either side of me at the point the fan fest widens towards the large screen at the front.

Health and Safety feels a serious issue in the fan fest and not least because of how loud the music from the band and DJ is...Or perhaps it is an age thing!

The players come out to a huge cheer and the crowd starts to sing. There are also quite a few brave Mexico fans in their dark green colours and they are bravely singing too. It might be better for them to lose!

The Brazilians sing the national anthem. It is sung so loud so passionately it genuinely sends shivers down my spine...

Our section of the crowd is now distracted by beautiful Brazilian girls on the corporate balcony to our left.

I am stood with two Northern Irish lads, George and Robbie, who frustratingly tell me of empty seats at the Argentina v Bosnia game...

They went up to Manaus for four days and said the atmosphere in the fan fest there for the Brazil versus Croatia match was incredible...Much louder than in Rio. When Croatia took the lead, one lone Croatia fan with a flag cheered #braveman!

Bearing in mind my decision not to go there to watch England versus Italy, they hardly saw a mosquito in the Amazonian city of Manaus. I wonder if the week of malaria tablets would have been necessary for the few hours I would have been there. The city had a Uruguayan feel about it with a lot of old buildings and a beautiful main square. Their other abiding memory was the distress of seeing disabled people living on the streets...

They had an amazing experience of taking a boat trip down the Amazon River during which one of their friends was interviewed by Argentine TV!

Brazil score!!! Huge cheer but alas the screen shows the outstretched arm of the linesman's flag...Offside...

Bad tackle by Alves...Should have been booked...After the decisions which went Brazil's way in the opening match...Hmmm?

The smell of marijuana is so strong...I will be high from secondary smoking!

The crowd is now very quiet and tense but there is a constant stream of people barging past us. All of the facilities are at the back...Great planning!! The fan fest also has the feeling of being somewhat overcrowded

A helicopter is circling overhead and adding to the general noise and drama of the occasion.

César the Brazilian keeper pulls off a good save tipping the ball over the bar. A definite corner but incredibly a goal kick is given...Hmmm...

Neymar rises at the far post for a cross...Great downward header into the bottom corner...The crowd are on their toes...A huge cheer building in their lungs...What a save from the Mexican keeper!!

Sporadic chants from within the fan fest Brazil! Brazil! Brazil!

These chants are countered with just as loud a shout for Mexico. I ponder what a fan fest in Buenos Aires might be like were Argentina to host a World Cup again. Just how loud and manic would it be?

I get talking with some guys from Toronto...They are very happy with Defoe who has already scored six or seven goals in the MLS.

Fireworks going off in the background... It needs something to spark this crowd into life! Other than Neymar...The team looks a little laboured.

41st minute still 0-0...Mexico go close...Excited ooohs from the Mexicans matched by anxious aaarghs from the home fans.

Half time 0-0

A Brazilian apologises for brushing passed me. He stops to ask, because I am in a light blue and white striped shirt, as to whether I might be Argentinian... When he learns that I am English he withdraws his apology!

This is my country, my passion, my football match, my team, my beach, my television... He is smiling as he says it and as he continues, brings me and the people around me to tears of laughter!

George, Robbie and I agree that there is more atmosphere at half time with the DJ and fireworks than during the first half. May be for the second half he should be the official cheerleader.

It is absolute chaos at half time. We are being buffeted around, bumped and barged from every direction. Mr Nigeria would love it here...Really in his element! Ffs start the second half!! It is so bad...In the end we give up being frustrated and start laughing at the absurdity of it.

What a relief! The second half kicks off and we are pleased for some peace and quiet. Mr Nigeria and his legion of followers settle down...I think he must have a Twitter or Face Book account with thousands of followers and sent a message out in the first half...Attack John at half time!

Biggest noise of the game so far...The crowd are not happy at Fred being substituted and boos ring out. Within seconds, the boos almost turn to cheers... It's the Mexican keeper again keeping Neymar out. This keeper is amazing...He is virtually keeping Brazil out single-handedly. I ask a Mexican supporter his name...Ochoa and he is now a free agent...Can't see him being so for long after this display!

20 minutes to go and finally the crowd are in the game. They are sensing a goal and I am too,

As nightfall descends over the fan fest, Brazil are piling on the pressure. The fans, aware the clock is running down, are now willing the ball into the net... Vamos Brazil rings out. Come on Brazil! Mexico break into the box, hearts in mouths time...A goal now for Mexico and the unthinkable might just happen...

The Brazilians are starting to trudge out... Was that a cry of we can see you sneaking out from the Mexicans!

Mexico nearly score...As more fans leave, is that the Mexican version of is there a fire drill now being sung?

Mexico almost score again! If there really was a fire drill in the fan fest... Omg it would be a stampede, pandemonium!

Last minute of added time, a Brazil fan's face lights up as she sees her face on TV... I just don't get it...Your team are in desperate need of a goal!

The final whistle...0-0...

There is a sense of disbelief in the fan fest... I say to the fans nearby that a draw versus Cameroon would be enough to qualify. Strikes me though that were Neymar to pick up an injury, this workmanlike team will really struggle. Shame we won't experience a Brazilian victory party in Rio tonight!!

We stand to the side to let the crowd out...Mr Nigeria and his mob will be out there waiting to ambush me!

Oh dear the beer is going down too well...Again...And it's only 6.02pm.... And my last meal was breakfast!

As we walk out the fan fest the Brazilians are indulging in their other passion of dancing and partying. Seems I was wrong and it may be a good night after all!!

The samba drums are still beating on the street. Couples are dancing. Chile fans have congregated outside the fan fest singing and dancing to their songs. It seems to be an amazing lack of tact and diplomacy in front of their hosts!

If Croatia beat Cameroon it sets up a winner takes all Croatia versus Mexico final match and... I have a ticket...Yaay!

As the two fan fest crowds come together, people are literally everywhere. They are on the beach, on the promenade, on the roads. There is a cacophony of noise and colour...Somewhere in the background more samba beat, firecrackers helicopters and yet another group of Chilean fans...Seems they will be outnumbering the Spanish who have surprisingly hardly been seen yet...And just as I write this, I finally see a solitary Spanish flag! May be they are keeping a low profile after the 5-1 drubbing of the World Champions and the prospect of being the first team to be eliminated looming large...

Paul texts to say he is not feeling too well and has to head back to the hotel. This is a tough World Cup campaign In more ways than one!

On a lighter note...I know the view has always been that Brazilian ladies are beautiful but the reality is whilst of course not always true, there really are some, no not right, there are loads of exceptionally beautiful ladies.

The Irish guys feel too old at 31 years of age #ohtobe30yearsyounger!!! Then again...Oh to have the good fortune to still be able to come to such events and places... Maybe a better hash tag is #countyourblessingsjohn!

Walking back towards the hotel amongst the throngs and throngs of people...

Education and health are I am sure enormous issues for these people...But they still have that liberated carefree approach to life which the Europeans including the English seem to have lost along the way. We are so buried in health and safety and political correctness...Do we somehow stop our children and ourselves from living life, enjoying life...So scared of everything we forget how to live and enjoy ourselves...Sure should experts ever read this, they would recoil in horror at such a simplistic view.. But the thought occurred to me and it is my diary... So I share the thought with you!

The climate this evening is again a lovely warm temperature...Another hot sultry evening ahead...It is now 7 05pm. It feels so much later! And with the match starting at 4pm, people started drinking so much earlier...It could be a long night!

Our Savoy Othon hotel is close to the Ipanema end of Copacabana beach. The fan fest is at the other end of the crescent. It is actually some walk...About 30 minutes...The crowds remain almost as dense and loud all the way along the Copacabana promenade. It really is an amazing experience, so much so that I don't want to go back and waste a moment in the hotel room. I want to be outside savouring, absorbing every minute of the Rio 2014 World Cup experience.

The rhythm of a whistle is now accompanying me as I pass the old Help night club which has been replaced by the seemingly much more upmarket Pestana Budweiser Hotel. I never went in the Help nightclub during my previous visits but I once had a beer in the bar next door. I was sat outside and there was a table of big fat disgusting old European men sitting with girls as young as 10 or 11 years old... It turned the pit of my stomach so much so that the memory is still clearly etched in my memory some 12 or 13 years later. I am not naive enough to believe that the problem has been sorted. Dear me, we only have to look close to home at the recent spate of court cases to know we have our own problems... But the transformation from the Help snake pit is a wonderful pleasant and perhaps somewhat remarkable surprise.

In fact, touch wood and I know it will be its best right now...But the whole Copacabana area feels a lot better and safer than it did all those years ago. I hope it feels the same outside of a World Cup.

On arriving back at the hotel, Paul and Ian are waiting for me in the hotel lobby watching the South Korea v Russia game...31 minutes gone and it's scoreless. Some of the fixtures somehow don't hold the same sort of appeal... And yet the stadiums are full for all games!

We talk about the match a little...The performance of the Mexican keeper, the lack of cohesion within Brazil's play and the colour and crowds within the two fan fests.

My voice has just about gone completely now. We go up to our respective rooms for a quick shower and change.

Back in the lobby, we watch the last half an hour of the match. What a howler from the Russian keeper! Straight at him and somehow he let it slip through his hands...1-0 South Korea!!

A Russian substitute comes on and equalises within a couple of minutes of being on the pitch, knocking in a rebound off the keeper. The Russian keeper will be the most relieved man in the stadium!

We head out of the hotel for something to eat. I am conscious that I haven't eaten anything since breakfast...It is now after 9pm.

We end up at a restaurant on the front and have a pizza with a couple (more!) beers.

On the way back, we stop off at our local bar on Rua Xavier da Silveira. After our excesses over the last few days and nights and our various ailments, none of us are up for too a late night! Not that after 1am can be deemed too early a night!

EL GRINGO'S ONCE IN A LIFETIME

To me the World Cup in Brazil almost felt like a last chance saloon. If it wasn't this one, then when would I really go? Russia is a nation currently invading its neighbour and so may be at war in 2018; Qatar is a giant shopping mall in the desert as far as I can tell.

Although I hadn't really planned to be at the Brazil World Cup, I took the chance and don't have a single regret. The Australia versus Netherlands game in Porto Alegre in particular was an absolute treat, partying in the streets all night with the beautiful Gauchas! I don't expect I'll find that in Qatar...

Alex Jordan, Sydney, Australia

Being a Spurs fan in the US for over a decade was always hard to explain to my friends. The World Cup in South Africa opened up the sport in the US a little, but the most recent in Brazil brought everyone out. Friends who couldn't name an English Premier League team became diehard fans practically overnight. I was extremely lucky to win the ticket lottery for every match in Rio. Most of the other Americans there were mostly in for the party and for an excuse to root for the US.

I had never really seen as committed a fan until the match in the Maracana for Spain versus Chile where hundreds of Chilean fans stormed the gates and actually got into the stadium!

In the match before, Argentina versus Bosnia, the chants from the Argentina faithful started at the subway station in Flamingo, lasted 30 minutes on the metro through the journey, and never stopped though the match.

I've been to World Series (baseball) and Stanley Cup (hockey) games and that kind of devotion and excitement is beyond anything I have ever seen before!

Michael Granat, Washington DC, USA

WEDNESDAY 18TH JUNE 2014

My tummy is feeling a little...Uh huh...Bathroom...Oh my... I meet Paul and Ian for breakfast...Which is a bit of a challenge...My stomach feels at best fragile...

Go to a chemist which is an even bigger challenge...They don't speak English...To the amusement of the staff and customers I perform charades... Putting my hand to my mouth to demonstrate eating and then to my tummy with a rapid movement downwards...They seem to understand and I buy some medication.

Back in the hotel room, I open the medication but am not sure what to do so take it down to Reception with the instructions to receive a translation. They explain it needs mixing with water but that I should take it last thing at night to cleanse my stomach first thing in the morning. I say that has already happened and... They start laughing...What is so funny? The chemist has given me medication for constipation...I have diarrhoea... Oh my!! Imagine...

Catastrophe avoided!! The mind boggles at what might have been!

The Reception staff write a note for me to take to the chemist… The chemist staff find it hilarious…I do too but when they won't take the medication back in exchange, my humour subsides somewhat! And then even more so when they say I shouldn't drink alcohol while taking the medication…Hmmm.

After this morning's excitement, we go down to the beach to sunbathe. On the way down, I call in at the travel agent but the prices for Spain versus Chile at the Maracana for today's game are ridiculous…

I have been turning over and over in the mind as to whether to go to the Maracana again without a ticket. There are thousands of Chile fans in town looking for tickets. It feels a similar situation to the Argentina game on Sunday. Am I that bothered about this game…Seeing Messi and Argentina felt like it would be swashbuckling, exciting…The Spanish style of possession football has increasingly bored me.

I walk down to Copacabana beach which really is a lovely place to sunbathe… Some iconic beaches don't always live up to their name…Bondi beach in Sydney being in my opinion an example…But not Copacabana…It is as good as the images which the name conjures within your mind. The waves are so strong but it's a great feeling to stand in front of them, swim through them, swim with them…Just watch your shorts! Paul and Ian leave to get ready to go to the match…Spain versus Chile today…After their disastrous start, it is a must win game for Spain today.

Thousands of Chile fans in Rio…But where are the Spanish? There are a bunch of guys nearby on the beach sunbathing…One of whom has a Spurs towel. I go over for a chat. They are from Norway and a couple of them are indeed Spurs fans. We know Petr who gave up a year to live in Palmers Green, London to follow Spurs and still comes over regularly. Met him in Amsterdam after losing to PSV in the Europa League some years ago now. They are supporting England but no they don't have any tickets let alone spare ones!

Walking from the beach in soft beach footwear to the restaurant to meet Paul and Ian…Road is uneven…I stub two middle toes of my left foot at full pelt against highly raised yellow cats eyes…Incredibly painful…My left foot is now a complete mess…We have lunch at the same restaurant by the metro station as before the Argentina v Bosnia game. We arrive in time for the Australia v Netherlands game on the television. Early on, Robben is one on one and miscontrols the ball. As the camera zooms in on him, rather than show a pained expression he smiles…A hint of complacency perhaps? We are joined by Sam a Spurs fan and his friend Adam who is an Arsenal fan.

They are friends of Paul's and have flown

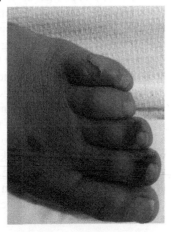

in overnight for the next three games at the Maracana. Robben puts Holland one nil up...Why does such a small country need two names...Is it Holland or the Netherlands? Very quickly after...A long ball is played forward towards Cahill who volleys with a thunderous left foot in off the crossbar for a stunning equaliser!!!

Wow!!!! Surely goal of the tournament so far!! The food is brought over and the portions are twice as big as the other day...

At first we think it must be one between two but as the plates keep arriving... I begin to think of my suspect tummy..! Over lunch I confirm my decision not to travel up to the Maracana... It is unlikely that prices will fall much below £400. I don't really want to pay that for any ticket...But especially a match that I am not that bothered about. England at a push... But even then...A Spurs season ticket for a whole season is only just over £700... Value for money? No I am talking the £400 for a Spain versus Chile ticket...Not the Spurs season ticket...Ok... Fair point!

Earlier I had the chance of a Spain versus Chile ticket for the bargain price of £412...On the basis that the England versus Uruguay ticket is likely to cost even more...I decide to put all my Brazilian reals into one basket!! Penalty to Australia... Surely not...Yessss 2-1...Pigeons and cats spring to mind!! Van Persie quickly equalises in what is turning out to be a not only surprising but very entertaining game. With all the medication...I shouldn't be drinking...four beers later...!!!

As the guys go off to the game and I return to the hotel reception on my own to watch the remainder of the Australia v Holland game. I have a Cinderella moment...A feeling of missing out on the Maracana party...I am on my own... Stop it John!!! Remember where you are! You booked to come out here less than a week before the tournament began...Be thankful for being here! Get yourself down to the Fan fest to watch the match!!

As I enter the hotel reception, what appears to be an error by the keeper gives Holland a third goal and the winner! Another great game...Lot of goals already in this World Cup! I go up to the room to change...Two very badly bruised black coloured toes...Very painful...Could they be broken? As I head off to the fan fest... I may have missed out on a ticket for today's game, I may have two broken toes, I may have a dodgy tummy, I may hardly be able to speak with a sore throat, I may have painful blisters across both feet...But I am happy to be here...What a fantastic experience!

Would just though like to get a ticket for England v Uruguay tomorrow...I don't expect to hear from the touts until after the Spain v Chile game starts...This will be their peak time ...I note the name of the bar we went in a few times for a final drink on the way back to the hotel. It is called "More than nothing" The weather has changed...I am walking down to the fan fest and the skies have gone grey...The clouds are darkening...There is a serious chance of rain...I still need my sunglasses though... Reason...The bars are awash with orange as the Dutch celebrate moving into the knock out phase! Australia are virtually out which given their contribution in the opening two games feels a bit of a Sven's pity... There are a lot of Chile fans in the bars too...Obviously unable to either get or afford tickets...A pity for them too...

Whilst walking towards the fan fest everything seems orange...The colour of the city bikes and holders which are similar to the pay and go bikes in London, the dustbins are orange and even the uniforms of the guys who are always out cleaning the streets and beaches...Who by the way...Given the volume of people on the streets are doing an amazing job...Everywhere is for the most part spotless. As ever television and radio crews from many different nations are out on the promenade interviewing fans...Lugging around the heavy cameras, satellite kit and microphones; waiting for the satellite signal to come through...A text comes through...Hopefully from one of the touts £450 to £550 for an England game... My oh my oh my...

I open up the text, it is from Paul...May be he has found me a Spain v Chile ticket... But...Kick off is in nine minutes...I open up the text...And this is what it says...

"Got you a ticket for Tomorrow England v Uruguay...300 reals. This is not a joke. Have it on me!! Picking up another later. Two Americans not going to SP. YOU ARE A LUCKY BOY"

I can't believe it!!!!!!!!!!! I really can't believe it!!!!!! I am going to watch England!!!!! I am going to finally see a match live...Not just any match...But an England match...A crucial England match!! So so pleased!

I am now down by the fan fest. The Argentines are out in force...Winding up the Chile fans with their singing...This catchy South American football song...#desperatetoknowthewords.

On the beach by the promenade bar, I get talking with a couple of Argentine fans who translate the words of the song for me but before they do, they explain:

When a team beats a team in the World Cup Finals...Until they play again, the winning country is called the father. The last time Argentina played Brazil in the World Cup Finals was in Italia 90 when Argentina rather surprisingly beat Brazil. So...Argentina is the father and Brazil the son.

The words of the song with the catchy words are:

Brazil tell me what you feel,
Having your father in your house,
Even though the years have passed,
It still causes you pain,
We still remember Italy 90, Maradona dribbling and Caniggia scoring,
You have suffered the pain ever since.
You will see Messi and the cup he will give us.
Maradona is better than Pele.

Translated by Nicholas Racedo and Ignacio Lemos from Buenos Aires.

I take their photograph...They give me their email addresses for my book.

What a song!! The words!! The Argentines are singing this time after time in front of the Brazilians!! Fortunately, it is sung in Spanish and not Portuguese!

It's a great song though...The Argentines seem to have a lot of songs...More akin to a club side. I wish England had such songs. Football's coming home was about the last good one and that dates back to 1996...18 years ago!

They tell me the rest of Spanish speaking Latin America copy their songs. The Argentines are supporting Spain against Chile...Local rivalries never die!! It is starting to rain...Chile score...The beach bar erupts... Well not the bar itself of course...Chile fans are going wild!! Chi Chi Chile rings out!! I am having the time of my life!

Chatting with a couple of Aussies from Melbourne and Sydney... It took 40 hours to get here via Sydney, Los Angeles, Miami, São Paulo and finally into Rio!! They leave Rio at 6.30 in the morning and have not been to any of the tourist attractions yet...Not even seen Christ the Redeemer from ground level let alone Sugar Loaf!

Chile score a second...The fans are going crazy!! This is amazing...Spain are falling apart and in danger of falling out of the World Cup in the shortest possible time-frame possible. Chile look a very good side though.

The Aussies prefer to try to have a look inside Copacabana Palace hotel than take their one chance in life to experience the Fan fest on Copacabana...Reason? It might be a bit busy!! Aussies...Strange lot aren't they! Only joking chaps... Love you really...Unless we are playing you at cricket!

I go into the fan fest...Have a chat with some very happy Dutch fans...One guy works for Dutch television and lives in Rio...How good a job has he got! There is a fan in an amazing Ecuador mask. The photograph has to make the book! The fan fest is a sea of Chilean red. There are thousands in the stadium and thousands in the fan fest!! How many in total in Rio!!!

As a Spurs fan I struggle with the colour red...A sort of genetic aversion if you can have such a thing...Even though my birth city is Lincoln...The (not so mighty) Red Imps...Never had a shirt in my life...Never wear red... Never have it in my house...Yes I know...

The second half kicks off. Spain on top in the early stages but just can't score...Raining and getting heavier in the open air fan fest...Chile fans so high some in more ways than one! They are looking down on the rain clouds! Still some nerves amongst them and every save is cheered, every Spain shot that flies wide every tackle... Huge cheers in the fan fest. But without resorting to the obvious...Chile are so hot on the break...Oops I still did resort to the obvious! A third wouldn't be a huge surprise here. I do find watching Spain boring...It's like watching Barcelona when Messi is out injured...Pass pass pass but not going anywhere...No penetration...No plan B...For Juan's sake lads... You are 2-0 down... There are 28 minutes left...You lost the first game... Take some risks...

Bit radical but may be put another striker on...Just as I say that...Torres comes on...Costa goes off...FFS.. Go out...Your era is over...#backtothedrawingboard.

Aranguiz scorer of the second goal goes off...And the fan fest crowd show their appreciation by clapping him off...Hmm should anyone tell them... He can't hear you lads!! Same city but almost an hour away by underground!! Massive oohs as Chile almost score a third...Hit the bar... Olé Olé Olé Olé Olé Chile Chile rings round the fan fest! A huge thunderclap from behind the big screen... All this electrical equipment...No fork lightening...Yet! Slightly nervous...If there was lightening...I don't think many Chile fans will be leaving...Would there be a big enough Mr Brazil with the largest cojones ever to switch everything off... Hmmm...No chance...Would cause a riot!

Naughty tackle from Ramos upsets the crowd who are now frustrated by a penalty appeal being turned down... I imagine if Chile were losing, they would be going crazy. The fans are so much louder and more passionate than the Brazilians yesterday. Would never have expected that. A slide tackle on the left hand side of the box which goes out for a throw in is loudly cheered. This is a fantastic atmosphere. Spain are 11 minutes from going out... Pass pas pass... Finally Cazorla shoots...The keeper comes out to catch a corner... Another huge cheer goes up...Horns are blaring...The mass mood is changing from anxiety to relief and jubilation...It's quite remarkable how you can actually feel the change in the atmosphere. There will be some atmosphere in Rio tonight...One enormous Chilean party...What a save! What a cheer and then an almighty roar goes up when Valdivia comes on...A Chile fan tells me he is coming back from injury and he is their best player!!! A midfielder... Like a fake striker... How did he get in the Maracana!! Fake ticket holders can't!!

EL GRINGO'S ONCE IN A LIFETIME

The last chance...Cazorla free kick...Saved... Into added time Vamos Chile rings out... Who would have thought it when Spain went 1-0 up that they would let 7 in without reply...6 minutes added time...The crowd hoot and whistle... Chaos in the Chile box as Spain finally resort to plan B...Usually England's plan a b c and d...Punts into the box...Two Chile players go to head the same ball...That moment sums up the passion and commitment ...This Spanish team World and Euro champions...Have they lost that hunger? More songs...This place will go wild, crazy in the next seconds...Fans are hugging each other... Almost in disbelief...Chile are on the verge of .. The final whistle goals...Chile have knocked out the Invincible World Champions!!!

Fireworks, firecrackers, singing....The jubilation, the wave of emotion enveloping the fan fest...The disco comes on so loud drowning out the fans... Yesterday it was needed... Today it is an intrusion...Not nothing, not nobody will stop today's party though!

So...Holland and Chile will have a play off to see who qualifies top and second from the group...Both qualified after just two games. Australia and Spain will play off to see who goes home bottom of the table...The disgrace, embarrassment, ridicule and abuse facing Del Bosque and his team is already enormous...It can't get much worse...The end of an era of Spanish domination of world football in such an ignominious fashion...Akin to the collapse of the French capitulation in 2002...The fans don't want to leave the fan fest...And who can blame them!! Large photo gatherings to record this memorable moment in history...Once in a life time!

Where are the Spanish fans? Conspicuous by their absence in Rio this week. What did they know that the world didn't! This morning the country held the World Cup, the Euro, the Champions League winners and runners up and the Europa League...Who could have foreseen this? Yet so few fans seem to be here...The handful of Iranian fans I saw Saturday were almost as many in number as the Spanish! On the way out of the fan fest I have a photograph with Julian of Argentina holding the World Cup. He is a River Plate fan and Lamela is his favourite player...So when he plays on FIFA...Tottenham are his team...Then a photo with a couple of Belgian guys who tell me Belgium improved when Chadli and Dembele were substituted after Vertongen gave away a penalty to go 1 down!! We then have a photograph with Ecuador fans...

Outside the ground...See what I just wrote...Ground! Not ground ...fan fest!! Feels just the same! Out of the fan fest Chile have their own drummer and so many different songs...Apologies as I get closer...It's the Argentines...Obvious!! A strong police presence...The local vendors are walking round with trays of plastic glasses of caipirinha...How they manage to carry them one handed through the throngs of excited fans and collect cash with the other hand I will never know! A Brazilian band has now started up... The cacophony of noise and general happy to be here in this moment of celebration swarms over us all...A jeep just stops in the middle of the road, comes to a sudden halt, a guy with a Chile flag jumps out the driver's seat and climbs on to the roof waving his Chile flag .. All the vehicles behind him including yellow cabs. May be taking people to the airport. They have no choice but to just wait and wait and wait... And wait... Blue and white Police cars...Lights flashing...Its mayhem!

Eventually the Chile fan climbs down, jumps into his driving seat and leaves...Now a red and white minibus replaces him. It is decorated with the faces of the players and stops in exactly the same place...The poor drivers behind him! The minibus has a caricature of who knows who...Could be a Walt Disney character on its roof...Disney parades were never this much fun!! The rhythm of the whistle vendors is everywhere...Adding to the incredible party atmosphere around us on Copacabana...Fans everywhere!!

As if there isn't enough noise... Another band... A ten piece drumming band turns up... If the other music and bands were boxing bouts...They would have been the bantamweights...Now the big boys...The main event has turned up... And boy can these boys bang a drum! As I walk back I realise that the temperature and general climate is back to almost normal...A little breeze but nothing more... How and when did that happen? May be the noise in the ground was too much for it! May be all those drums blew it away or may be just may be Christ the Redeemer put a word in with the big man upstairs...Spontaneous joy and happiness between all his people joined as one...Colour, creed, nation, degree of wealth....Who cares... John Lennon would be very happy to witness this!!

I pass a beach bar... Not difficult as there is one in almost 50 metre intervals and I would almost guarantee that designer and Feng Shui experts were not employed to create at extortionate sums the best possible conditions for people to maximise their enjoyment of life... And I also guarantee that nowhere on earth are people enjoying such a city, house or whatever party... It's all about the people, the mind-set...Where was I...Why did I mention that...Oh yes...With about 20 minutes gone...Croatia are beating Cameroon 1-0. Would like to have seen this game...Spurs old boys... Modric, Corluka and Benoit Assou Ekotto playing.

In the middle of the promenade a couple dressed up in full regalia switch on a ghetto blaster and start a samba dance...Only in Rio! The freedom of feeling alive takes hold of you in Rio like nowhere else on earth. Having been fortunate enough to have visited more than 80 countries and having visited Rio on five separate occasions I feel able to say that with a degree of confidence. If you haven't been yet... Book now and if you still need some convincing... Watch the old Michael Caine film "Blame it on Rio" as that kind of captures the crazy energy and spirit of this fabulous city.

Walk into the hotel room and a text comes in from Paul saying that they are at the beach bar buying drinks for the Americans who sold the ticket to Paul for me for England versus Uruguay...Think I should walk back down there and buy them one too...don't you??? I meet the guys...Two brothers Brad and Michael from Chapel hill, North Carolina and Charlottesville, VA, respectively.

We are having a drink, chatting and watching the Croatia v Cameroon game when finally the rain comes...The Brazilian beach bars are totally unequipped to deal with it and the idea of being protected under the virtual roof quickly evaporates... Shame the rain didn't follow it! We sit in the rain under the virtual covering they drinking beers and me on caipirinha...Croatia are winning 4-0 as the TV set gives up its valiant effort in the face of impossible conditions and comes to a spluttering halt. The conversation is flowing, stories being exchanged, the drinks are flowing and suddenly it's nearly 10pm. We say our goodbyes to our new American friends and head back to the hotel, quickly change and go back down to the front for a pizza and a couple of beers.

We head back to the hotel around midnight...It's been another really great day! Reasonably early night as we have an early start in the morning to São Paulo to see England versus Uruguay!

The bars are full of Chile fans celebrating. Let's hope it's England's turn tomorrow!! On returning to my room...The luggage has to be packed and sorted... The hotel agree to look after my case until I return to Rio on Wednesday 25th June. I will be living out of a rucksack for the next seven days whilst visiting São Paulo, Recife and Belo Horizonte.

To avoid taking stuff to the match tomorrow night, Paul kindly agrees to take some of my stuff in his suitcase which he will check in at São Paulo airport in the morning for our flight to Recife.

I drop the stuff off with Paul first so that they can get off to sleep. Their flight isn't as early as mine but it is still early enough!

Finally I sort my stuff and take my suitcase down to the reception and receive a receipt to handover on collection of my case in a week's time. I ask to settle my hotel bill and am shocked at the size of my telephone bill. I show that a lot of my calls were only for seconds and the receptionist agrees and reduces the phone bill to c30 reals which was about right.

I ask for an early morning call for 4.30 and a taxi to be booked for 4.50am saying that if I am not in the lobby by 4.45 would they come and hammer on my door!! They laugh and say yes!

It is now 1.45am...Time for a couple of hours sleep!

EL GRINGO'S ONCE IN A LIFETIME

Given the Spanish success of the last years, not only in football but also in many other sports, the Spanish people feeling regarding the World Cup was confidence in victory. This feeling, also encouraged by the media, didn't match with the feeling of caution and mistrust that other Spaniards had. Many of us had in mind that the players performance during the season and their fitness status wasn't the most suitable to struggle for a semi-final position. What Vicente Del Bosque did is to reward the effort of his 'old guard" that many success gave him in the past. He didn't afford to renew the Spanish team and the consequence was a shameful defeat.

José Ferrandiz, Madrid, Spain

The football and TV coverage was as I expected. But what really came across was the comments from fans whether on social media, TV or the papers and how football brings so many different people from all walks of life together and the lasting friendships that go on for many years.

Steve Sandall, Bourne, UK.

THURSDAY 19TH JUNE 2014

Hotel reception calls me as planned at 4.30am...2 3/4 hours sleep. It is a good job they remembered to call me as my alarm didn't work....

From many hours of watching the FIFA web site refresh...This date will always be synonymous with Match No 23...England v Uruguay!!!

Paul and Ian are on a later flight than me.

4.50am Chile fans still partying! It is still absolutely lashing it down with rain...Doubt they have even noticed!

Hotel reception organised the taxi as requested and I jump in to be taken to Santos Dumont the domestic airport which is about a 20 minute drive from the hotel. I manage to get in the cab without getting wet...You might think this is not too much of a big deal but I am in a shirt and jeans and...This is going to be a long day as tonight after the England v Uruguay game we are booked on the 11.55pm flight from São Paulo to Recife which is due to land at 3.20am.

My airplane seat will be the closest I get to a bed as we don't have a hotel room tonight in Recife and are going to Italy v Cost Rica tomorrow afternoon...

Remember me saying that the exercise machine starts a steep climb from Thursday!! Good job I had a quiet time with plenty of rest in Rio!!

Health check up in the taxi...

Lip improving

Stomach solved

Blisters...Awful

Toes...Black and painful

Throat...Take a Strepsil... Boy these are strong...Voice still a problem which is going to be much worse after 90 minutes of cheering on England!! In-ger-land, In-ger-land!! Yes I know... In comparison to the catchy and witty songs of Argentina...A bit of a poor effort...But England is England...My country!!

I arrive at the airport and the drop off area is fortunately covered so again I avoid the rain. The fare for the 20 minute journey is 30 reals...About £9.

The Azul check in is easily found but the queue is slow moving. I withdraw from the line.. "line" Good old American expression... My new best friends after they came through with my England v Uruguay ticket yesterday. A very helpful Azul staff member helps me through the electronic check in process which is in Portuguese...I didn't see a change of language option and am not sure there was one...Given that a World Cup is taking place with an Olympic Games to follow... If there isn't one... May be there should be...

I give the Azul staff member my printed booking paper and he taps in the booking code number...Invalidido...My heart sinks...An all too familiar phrase... Argentina versus Bosnia ticket invalidido...The frequent use of this expression when trying to withdraw cash from the 24 hour bank machines...A little tremor of anxiety hits me and as he keys in a different number, I nervously await the outcome with more than a touch of trepidation...The thought that it is "only" 230 miles from Rio to São Paulo provides a small degree of comfort. Finally Mr Azul manages to input the correct reference number; I have a choice of back row or next to back row on the 60 seater plane. My ticket is printed and away I go to the security queues and the thought of taking my shoes off and trying to get my swollen left foot back in my shoe is not an appealing prospect. Thankfully the security process passes smoothly.

The airport is full of bright yellow shirted Colombians which at before 5.30am is a little harsh on the eyes! They are on their way to Brasilia to watch their country play Ivory Coast... Ahh Mr Nigeria...

There are Mexican fans in brightly coloured hats, Japanese in their blue shirts and then the occasional white England shirt...

We look and feel so plain and drab alongside our fellow partygoers... English fans have for the most part grown up in a culture of them firstly looking hard in bovver boots, skinhead air cuts, denims and at one point can you believe wearing scarves around wrists...To then hiding colours at matches and blending in with the crowd...To looking cool in designer clothing such as Burberry caps, Pringle shirts and designer trainers...On to hoodies and non-descript scarves covering faces to avoid CCTV and Police video cameras. In today's world English fans finally feel safe to wear their colours and shirts at matches... But the fun and colour of wearing some of the outlandish costumes we see worn by other nations are not really seen worn by English fans...I mean...Just what would your mates think down the pub...Would never hear the end of it!! And of course it would take a little effort to create a unique outfit and a lot of bravery to stand out...

So a little like our football, we will continue to lag behind the rest of the world...Ironically if we played in our successful 1966 World Cup winning shirt... Just by virtue of the colour...We would look a little more colourful...Hmmm the colour red might be a bit of a challenge for me though!!

EL GRINGO'S ONCE IN A LIFETIME

I walk down to Gate 9 for my 6.32 departure and am now sitting at the gate... Lesson learnt from Paris #nochancesbeingtaken.

There are actually phone charging points by the seats. These are poles with multiple charging points. In the UK, we don't have these of course as the electricity cost to the airport management company would be increased for no value added...Efficiency is the word and everything is done at minimal cost even down to the thickness and comfort or lack of...Of the toilet paper...

Hey, sorry if I am sounding a little negative and appearing to lack a bit of national pride and patriotism this morning...It isn't meant at all in that way... Constructive criticism provided in a positive way can surely only be good... Can't it? Certainly my 14 year old youngest son seems to think so as he will frequently start a sentence with... "Without wishing to cause offence..." And you just know that the next words coming out of his mouth will do just precisely that!!

The 6.32 Flight AD 2401 to Guarulhos is called... I wait until the queue goes down. At the gate my e-ticket is taken off me... I ask for it back but am refused. I then request one final look at my e-ticket to memorise my seat number...All a little confusing...I pass through the gate and walk down a ramp way to a choice of waiting buses.. Hmm which one...I check with passengers on board and am thankfully on the correct bus.

I intended to write more of my diary on the flight but tiredness hit and I woke as we came in to land at 7.55pm... A flight time of 1 hour 23 minutes.

A couple of English guys Austin and David from Luton don't have any match tickets and are not sure where to go in São Paulo. They haven't been able to get tickets to a game yet and fly home tomorrow. I give them the numbers of the touts I have collected...Jason and Matt from the UK and Sam the Dutch guy through the local Rio travel agency.

São Paulo is a massive city with a population of around 25 million which is almost twice the size of London. I know from being here on business a number of times more than ten years ago...The traffic is a complete and utter nightmare and to take care as there are some dangerous parts of the city. Can still recall my first visit in 2000... I arrived on a Sunday morning and asked my appointed driver to show me the sights of this massive sprawling city...All he could offer was a tunnel named after Ayrton Senna, a park and a high rise building which was opened by the Queen. The view was spectacular...Tower block after tower block each seemingly competing with each other for as far as the eye could see... To be the ugliest and biggest in the city. I thought...What a vast monstrosity of a city and if ever there was a case for a city to be torn down and rebuilt...It was this one with all its pile em high cheap and nasty concrete blocks...The more times I came back though, the more I began to enjoy the fine restaurants and shopping centres...Suffice to say though, it wouldn't appear in my top places to visit!

I go along to the information desk with the guys and confirm that Paulista is not only the safest place to go but also the best place to meet fellow fans in places like the Irish and Squat bars. It takes about 40 minutes to get there with one change by Metro 4 reals and one or two reals to get it the metro station by bus or 40 reals directly by bus. We exchange mobile numbers and knowing how I felt yesterday before getting my ticket I wish them well...And just to add I was helping them before I learnt that Austin is a Spurs fan! David supports his local team Luton who after a number of years of trying are back in the football league. I talk of my Lincoln experience in 1989 when Lincoln were promoted back into the Football League...Sadly they need to do it all again #biggerchallengenow

Whilst at the information desk where the young lady who was not only pretty but extremely helpful, Paul texts to say...

"Hope all went smoothly as a few flights cancelled. Ours is on time thankfully. See you soon"

This echoed the message Colin text yesterday... Feel for the guys whose flights have been cancelled...And as well a little perturbed as we have a number of our own internal flights in the week ahead.

Paul's flight is at 8.30 so I should meet up with them just after 10am.

The lady advises me that to meet Paul's Gol flight I must take the shuttle bus to T2 and gives me the details as to where we can leave our bags for the day.

The shuttle bus transfer is very straightforward and while I wait for Paul and Ian I manage to find a socket to recharge my iPhone. Even with the backup of an iPhone charging case, it is still a challenge to avoid running out of battery... Using iPhone notes to write my diary doesn't help in this regard. IPhone must surely be working on ways to provide a longer battery life as it is about the only frustration but constantly aired by all users... On this World Cup trip... Keeping the iPhone charged is an absolute necessity for all fans...

The smell of cinnamon is playing with my senses...Smells can do that to you...And now from not feeling hungry...I am of course desperate for something sweet with cinnamon...I will fight to resist!

As I write, a Brazilian in the blue Man Utd away shirt asks me how long I am going to be as he wants to charge his phone... The old Mad Max film with Mel Gibson on earth post the apocalypse comes into my thoughts...Here though instead of chasing petrol... We are chasing battery charge points!

Quite a few groups of Uruguay fans appear through arrivals. My battery is up to 98% and I can't resist the photo opportunity. They ask me to take one of themselves too...As I hand back their camera, smiling say...Inglaterrra!!

Paul and Ian arrive and we have a croissant and coffee breakfast.

At the bus stop we meet Alex from Sydney, Australia, a marine biologist working in Houston who is on a secondment to Bogota, Colombia for three weeks. Alex is here for two games Australia v Holland in Porte Alegre and today... At yesterday's match they were marched into the centre and ambushed by protesters who fortunately were quickly quashed.

The bus journey is an hour each way and the price is 76 reals return to the stadium about £20.

On the coach, as at the airport, the feel is that England fans will be outnumbered in the stadium.

EL GRINGO'S ONCE IN A LIFETIME

The coach has four seater tables, a television and free Wi-Fi. Paul calls his wife on face time... Technology is amazing... In some contrast, we pass through tower blocks, slums and by a prison...

The slums across the road from the stadium look very poor...

We enter the fan fest which is next to the stadium and meet up with Colin and the boys including Mick from San Diego to buy the second ticket from the Americans.

In the fan fest, we meet up with lads from Nottingham, West Bridgeford and Clifton...All went to Froch v Groves...Swap mobile numbers as going to Vegas if Froch's next fight takes place there. They have a huge England World Cup with which I, like many others, have a photograph.

Aussie Spurs fan joins us... Lot of English in the fest but probably more Uruguay... Also a lot of Colombians here for the early kick off...

Great fun in the fan fest, lots of colourful outfits...Start on the beer early... Two hours before kick off. Few photographs with Spurs flag and mates. Can stay with them in Rio for last 16 if England come second in the group...They will play in the Maracana match on the Saturday. Colombians in the fan fest passionately and emotionally sing anthem hand on heart stuff...One of the Ivory Coast players cries while singing his national anthem. Lot of energy lost there...Fans singing and cheering in fest...Zokora takes a corner well outside the quadrant...Webb and his team missed that one...No surprise there!

So...I have accommodation in Rio to stay in to see England in the Maracana... Please!!!!!

There is only one bar in the whole of the fan fest. It is a nightmare...They are pouring the beers...How slow! Two people serving...Wait now opening boxes of beers. Nobody serving...Security behind the counter asks fans to step back... Why don't you help out and serve mate!

Girl serves half a can... No idea how to pour beer... Can't add up the cost either #shambles

An English lad living out here with an expired visa has his passport and the equivalent of £2000 pick pocketed at the fan fest bar by a local!! He knows who did it and has gone searching through the fan fest... Asked his mates why so much cash on him...Can't leave it where he lives in Port Segura...Not safe... He had asked Rob to get his beer. Rob rightly said no...Can't turn up and expect people you don't know who queued half an hour to do that...Big lad...Wouldn't like to be the guy if he gets hold of him... Seriously...Comes back very stressed... Didn't find him...

Only other story to date of a mugging was prostitutes on Copacabana trying to grab a man in a sensitive area and his natural defensive instinct was to arch backwards. As he did his wallet was stolen out his back pocket...Moral of that story...If a prostitute goes for your whatnots...Let her! Protect your back pocket!

As you can see the Colombia versus Ivory Coast has lost most of our attention! As the second half develops though Colombia are starting to get on top and eventually...Weight of pressure tells...The Colombians go wild 1-0!

Alex tells me a story of an Australian guy at the opening game v Chile match in the VIP section...Needs to sit down on the toilet...Poor quality plastic cuts his ass. He can't pull the chain... No water coming from the tap...Pulls on it...Whole unit comes off the wall!!

I mention this as I am just about to use the facilities in the fan fest and my friends who used them much earlier start laughing.

Well that was an experience... Imagine portaloos at an outdoor concert in the UK...That is just the aperitif in this paragraph... Now let's say it's an Oasis concert...Now let's say Oasis are playing at the same venue for seven successive days...Now let's say facilities management have been on strike for seven days... And we need the "restroom" on the way out of the final...Yes...You have guessed it...The final concert on day seven...You ask about the facilities to wash hands? Seriously?? You think there could possibly be such luxuries!!

2-0 to Colombia!! Mass celebrations... Surely no way back but wait...Gervinho scores a great goal...Arsenal fans must wonder how, why?

The Colombians in the fan fest from thinking the game is over are now anxiously peering at the screen through their hands and fingers. Mr Nigeria will be going crazy!

We leave the fan fest with 15 minutes to go 2-1...The walk to the stadium is ridiculously long... Feels as if we circumnavigate the stadium five times...No toilets... Disorganised...Some barriers overloaded others completely empty.

There are a lot of people holding signs up for tickets in English, Spanish, Portuguese...I feel for them...

I bump into a Spurs fan I know on the way to the stadium. Paul

Revill from Nottingham. What a small world!! He flew in overnight and we talk of the exciting possibility of seeing England in the last 16 in the Maracana... Chickens counting hatch...But hey a win tonight and...This is one hell of a long walk and well over a mile. We all agree the organisation here is poor.

As I approach the ticket machine to validate my ticket, the scars of Argentina versus Bosnia are still with me. Will the light be green for go or red for heartache. I am as confident as I can be...The green light comes up ...I am in the stadium!!

Eventually I am in Block G...Open temporary stand, a long way up...Cat 2 in the corner...I dare to think what Cat 4 tickets would be like. Uruguay other end to us...If it rains...Soaked...If England win...Who cares!! Buy two beers and allowed to take them to my seat! Mick from San Diego joins me.

We are in the steep temporary stand...So high up Mick, who doesn't cope too well with heights, has to leave and try to find somewhere else to sit.

A local Corinthians fan tells me how surprised they were to receive so much money for Paulinho! Most Spurs fans would agree...

Atmosphere mounting...Mixture of excitement, anticipation and yet no real nerves. Suarez playing... No surprise there...Can he really be match fit though?

As the game kicks off, shame to see quite a few empty seats. May be FIFA should allow those outside entry if the seats aren't filled within half an hour of the game starting?

Even game...Ebbing and flowing...Both teams at times having the upper hand...

England fans trying to get an atmosphere going but high up in these temporary stands without a roof...So so difficult...Very cold too!!

Rooney free kick goes close...Uruguay almost capitalise on a defensive mistake.

Cross comes over...Rooney...Surely...Heads against the bar...Should he have scored?

Central midfield very open... No one to receive the ball... Earlier Cahill had to dribble out of defence...Scary but to be fair he did well and released Stirling. Should he really have to be doing that as last man though?

Gerrard in trouble in midfield ...Foul him!! Uruguay cross...Suarez header 1-0...It just had to be...Great goal it was too. The difference between Suarez and Rooney looks stark...And is the difference at half time...Uruguay 1-0 England.

I go down into the lower section...Out of the freezing temporary stands! Nobody stops me...Get talking with an English fan stood next to me...He walked all the way round from the other end without anyone stopping him!!

Second half...Feels a much better atmosphere behind the goal...Feel part of it now. Ball to Rooney's feet just outside six yard box... Surely this time... Nooo... Straight at the keeper.

Hodgson has taken Sterling off...Looked one of the few players who might unlock them...

Felt like a two kilometre round trip to the toilet in the basement...And 28 steps each way! It's a concrete monstrosity.

Just get back... Rooney!!! Yesss!!! 1-1!! Even Wayne couldn't miss an open goal from inside the six yard box. Finally our third highest goal scorer scores a goal in the World Cup Finals. He is a fantastic player in the Premier League and scored important goals in the qualifiers. Let's hope this unleashes the shackles and we see the real Wayne Rooney!!

England on top... Sturridge ffs shoot... Finally!! But a good save from the keeper...Can't help feeling he should have taken the shot earlier.

Brazilians chanting for England!!

Uruguay step up their game...

Comes off the head of Gerrard...Straight into the path of Suarez...Through... Shoots... Buries it...Nooo...2-1...Oh my...We are going out...Two games in and we are going out...The worst nightmare possible...

Brazilian guy starts singing Beatles songs next to me...First "Help, I need somebody, Help not just anybody" and now Yesterday, all my troubles seemed so far away, now it looks as though they're here to stay" What a wag...Not... He can have no clue what it feels like...To come all this way, spend all this money...For such disappointment...When would Brazil ever go out like this...Oh the misery of being an England fan...The torture...

Now I am on the front row...Urging the team to find a last ditch equaliser... Having moved so far down from the top of the temporary stand to pitch side... Might nip on to get the equaliser myself in a minute!

Outside the stadium... "Go home England" being sung into the mobile television cameras.

Ultimately Rooney had three seemingly good chances...one goal...Suarez two reasonable chances…two goals!

Uruguayans celebrate outside the stadium. A poor country with a population of 3.4 million...Against the mega millions of the Premier League and a population of more than 50 million more...Questions should and will hopefully be asked... Again...

If the answer is Premier League teams have reserve sides in the Football League...Heaven help us...

Reality is Uruguay could still go out...Incredible as it sounds...If Italy thrash Costa Rica, England could still qualify... Highly unlikely but we will be there to cheer on the Italians in Recife tomorrow...Straws at clutching...

I came expecting little of England and yet their performances seemed on the whole ok...But defensively, can't let two a game in at this level and expect to win...Having said that if chances had been taken tonight and against Italy, remarkably we would have four points and be top of the group...

Dream on!

Instead England blunder towards 50 years of hurt...

I came expecting us to be knocked out in the group stage and we were.

There was once a time when England being knocked out of the World Cup damaged the tournament... As inventors of the game what do we bring today...? Are we exhilarating? Stylish? Swashbuckling? Innovative? Sadly this World Cup won't miss England a single jot...The bars back in the UK will though...

Graph our World Cup performances and it is just about a straight line down with progress on the vertical axis and years along the horizontal axis. Quarter Finals in 2006; Last 16 2010; Group stage 2014...If this trend continues we won't even qualify in 2018... The Germans found a way of recovering from a drop off in performances in the early part of the new century...Somehow I doubt we will...The all-powerful Premier League rules...

The cold and miserable São Paulo stadium matches the generally perceived view of England fans of the city.

One thing is certain I won't be letting England's demise destroy my World Cup...Once in a life time...Not sure how many times that has been said by so many out here...And it is true...Chance of a life time! Once in a life time!!

I keep being mistaken as a Brazilian...Football wise I wish I was lol

We are back in the fan fest...It's around 6.30pm. It is very cold...England are virtually out of the World Cup. Two and a half hours sleep last night...Our flight is at 11.55pm tonight...Almost five and a half hours away...We land after 3am tomorrow morning without a bed to go to. We haven't eaten since a ham and cheese croissant breakfast at the airport. The evening match ahead of us on the big screen is.... Japan v Greece...If ever there was a classic to look forward to! If England had won...Who would have cared!

Takes me back to watching Spurs being knocked out away in Europe...But a huge difference...After those games all we want is to get home as quickly as possible...But here...Tomorrow is another day... Another city... Another match... Italy versus Costa Rica...As difficult as it is for England to have a remote chance going into the last game... We have to support Italy...Italia! Italia! Italia! Who would have thought it...Cheering on Italy!!

I go across to the Lanchonette snack bar in the fan fest. The menu on the wall is in Portuguese...No other language available...The staff don't speak English... May be the tournament should be renamed the Portuguese speaking World Cup! The only option is to order a hot dog...The sausage is as big as a chipolata... The size being similar to that accompanying your Christmas dinner...Though a lot less meat! The salad camouflage was good enough at the time of purchase! Cheerful tonight aren't I!

Greece have their captain sent off in the first half. We give up on the game just before half time and enter a shopping mall and sit down in the food court.

Would never have thought we would end up in a food court of a shopping mall after an England World Cup match! But we are delighted to be here...It was freezing outside...It is warm in here!

Paul notices it is the first time since our arrival in a place with lots of people, the match isn't being shown... It is 8pm on a Thursday night...The place is heaving!! Lots of Uruguay fans sitting in the food court enjoying a celebratory meal...Must feel good!

Live music starts up in the food court!! Only in Brazil!! Wait 20 minutes for my lasagne!!

Lasagne, diet coke and "One Life" being played by the live singer/ guitarist... Life is good!!

Walking back to sit down to eat my meal...I see a television showing the match...My faith in the Brazilians love of football is restored!!

Then I start to eat the lasagne...It is lukewarm and as I eat towards the middle, it has obviously been cooked from frozen but nowhere enough... It is still cold in the middle...I had to leave it... Hopefully before I did any further damage to my tummy! On taking it back, the chef smiles and gives me the thumbs up...He might just as well have stuck his middle finger up at me.

We walk back and are on the bus by 8.45 for a 9pm departure. The match is live on the television on the bus!

The match finishes 0-0. Mr Nigeria will be delighted. A draw in their final match should just about ensure he is not on the same plane as me! But what will I have to write about on my journey home!

The journey back to the airport only takes twenty minutes...Scheduled to take an hour...Shows the difference outside of rush hour!

At the airport, we say goodbye to Alex. Top guy and we really enjoyed his company. His flight is a little later than ours and from a different terminal.

We sit in a cafe at the airport and I fall asleep at the table! I smile at the irony of the one night of being desperate to go to bed early that I don't have a bed to get into tonight!

We have talked ourselves into believing that we might just qualify...The optimism of a football supporter! Nevertheless it would be good to see Italy win tomorrow to give us something to play for going into the last game.

The 11.55pm Flight 3506 from São Paulo to Recife boards on time from T2 Gate 1b. The screen at the gate shows the flight as going to Teresina. When Paul seeks confirmation that the flight is actually going to Recife, the gate staff smile seems to say...If you expect the flight information on the screen to replicate what is being announced over the loudspeaker...You are obviously not from Brazil!!

I walk down to my seat to find a lady sat in my seat...Déjà vu! This one takes some shifting into the middle seat...Not really sure what the point of discussion is...My boarding ticket clearly shows seat 19d...

I sit down and now she is pointing at the aisle seat 20c where a guy is sitting on his own and I now understand! Why didn't she just say this from the start! I change seats to allow her husband to sit with her.

Another bus arrives from the gate and... Typical!! A group of Uruguay fans sit all around me including in the two seats alongside me. I say to the Brazilian sat across the aisle... "This is all I need" which makes him laugh and he translates to his wife who also sees the funny side.

A good way to end the day and fall asleep on the plane.

This was a one-off opportunity to go and experience the very essence of international tournament football. For me there are two poles to world football. England is the 'North Pole'...The inventor of the game...Wembley and all that. The 'South Pole' is Brazil....Pele, Maracana, 1970, 1982. As English football fans we take the first for granted as we live within this football culture. To go out to Brazil was the once-in-a-lifetime opportunity, taken by all those who went, to experience something akin to a space mission. There was such a great 'festival of football' vibe to the tournament that the actual results themselves... Disastrous from a personal point of view as both my countries, England and Spain, crashed out in the first week (and I was there in person to witness both demises) yet it didn't seem to matter.

Peter Gutierrez, 52, Berkshire, UK

It was our first World Cup and very exciting to be a part of Brazil 2014. Just before kick off we managed to get a ticket for the Uruguay v England for 2750 reals which was much too expensive. The result was a disaster but the occasion was a fantastic experience. The World Cup was amazing and the atmosphere electric!

Austin Melia and David Stockwell from Dunstable, UK

The World Cup meant disappointment for England but a lot of excitement to watch the other games and of course to see the tournament in Brazil...Our second team!

Neil Pereira, 41, London, UK.

FRIDAY 20TH JUNE 2014

We land in Recife at 2.48am and had joked about flying round in a loop to have a longer night's sleep...The joke is on us though as the flight arrives 24 minutes earlier than planned!

I am literally struggling to keep my eyes open to write this.

Never quite understood the logic...As soon as a plane lands the world over, passengers immediately stand up... Some in the aisles, some bent double under the overhead lockers looking most uncomfortable. Why?? What does it accomplish? Wouldn't it be much more comfortable to stay in their seats a few minutes?

I deplane... This American expression will, for some reason, always make me smile! No bus... Straight onto a connecting walkway into the terminal... Feels a big win at this time of the morning!!

A mild panic attack sweeps through me... I think that I have left my ruck sack containing my wallet, all flight and hotel details, etc. on board....It is however in my right hand... I am carrying it... How tired must I be?

By 3.10am Paul and Ian have picked up their bags and we are straight into a taxi to the Beach Club. The whole process of entering a domestic airport for a departure or on landing through to leaving the airport is remarkably quick and easy... So far! Touch wood!

As we exit the terminal, the warmth of a tropical night hits us... A wonderful stark contrast to the cold of São Paulo. The flight time was 2 hours 53 minutes... It feels a little like leaving England on a winter's night and arriving in the tropics.

The taxi ride to the beach resort is only a ten minute, 22 reals journey and we are in the lobby by 3.20am.

We are trying for an early check in which would be an amazing win. Never before have I been happy to fill in a personal details form at a hotel at 3.25 in the morning!!!

This is looking good...Too good to be true...Surely not!!

We are given room keys but... We are not entitled to breakfast in the morning... We are devastated!! Laughing so loudly inwardly here... We have a bed, we are going to have some sleep... We are not going to have to sit in reception until midday before being allocated our room... Wow!! Yaay! You name it... This is fantastic!

On reaching the room, the child bed for me has already been set up. My new home from Friday 3.30am until my flight out at 10pm on Monday night.

There are 29 floors... Wow big place! We are on the 20th floor.

On opening the balcony doors we step out to a wonderful sea view overlooking the promenade. Then straight to sleep!

Slept through to 10am... Around six hours...Wow the longest for some time!

We go to the reception to ask for directions to the stadium and there is a guy with a huge wad of tickets for the Italy versus Costa Rica game. There will no doubt be people outside looking for tickets!

Before yesterday, I hadn't been to a 2014 World Cup match and now two matches in two days... FIFA World Cup games... Just like the number 259 London buses.

To get to the stadium, we need to take a twenty minute taxi ride to the shopping centre, followed by the metro, followed by a bus to the stadium. It is 11am and the hotel receptionist tells us we need to get a wiggle on for the 1pm kick off! There is a group bus service at a cost of 70 reals each return but we choose to make our own way to the stadium.

We step outside and it's raining with sunshine and a coolish breeze. Feels like an English autumnal day. We climb into a taxi to the shopping centre and on arrival ask the driver where the metro station is. He tells us there isn't a metro station at the shopping centre. This is a direct contradiction to what we were told by the hotel reception staff.

Ian lived in São Paulo for three years from 1994 to 1997 and still has a quite remarkable grasp of the language. I have lost count of the number of times where we would have been lost without Ian's language skills.

We arrive at a metro station which is a distance from the shopping centre.

As we step out of the taxi, the heat is back...How the hell did that happen!!!

It was only a short taxi ride!!I am genuinely gobsmacked!!

We get out of the taxi, at Nao Fume station... Haha which is a bit of a shame really as I quite fancy a ciggie...I actually thought that was the name of the station!! Tired or stupid??

With a match ticket, the cost is 7.50 reals return. A lady boy or transvestite or who knows whatever is waiting for us the other side of the barrier... Oo'err!

A wristband is attached for the return journey by the staff.

We board the train at the correct station name...Antonio Falcao on the green line. The locals are very hospitable and when a passenger gets off the tube, a local guy insists I have the seat...Or am I reaching that time of my life!!!! Fortunately he is older than me... May be I just look completely knackered... ✓ we change at Joana Bezerra station on to the red line direction Camaragibe.

I realise I have not had a drink of any description for quite some hours... And as for an alcoholic one... Must be nigh on 20 hours...Sacré bleu!

There are question marks as to whether the line is fully built.

It is now extremely hot on the busy metro train. A Canadian in an Italian shirt, with as it turns out, Italian parents, is enjoying asking us if we are supporting Italy today... And jokes that it is not something we will feel too comfortable with. Paul says a "once in a lifetime" deal...But there might be a second chance if Italy win!

I confirm that "Once in a Lifetime" will be the name of my book... It is the catchphrase of the World Cup!!

We get off at Cosme E Damaio where there are lots of volunteers and barriers funnelling us down to individual buses. It is incredibly well organised and the bus leaves within minutes to the stadium... No doubt to be replaced by another bus for the next batch of passengers. We feel very well looked after.

On the bus, midway to the stadium, an Italian who must have decided to walk and was across the other side of the dual carriageway starts sprinting towards the bus. Amazingly the driver slowed down to let him on. We get off the bus at 12.17pm.

We are walking along a barriered walkway in the countryside to the stadium. Tickets are freely available outside the ground!

There is greenery everywhere... What a difference to São Paulo. The atmosphere is bordering on carnival... Acrobats, samba music and dancers compete with the different music coming from inside the stadium... A little like a fairground when you are walking between rides and can hear the music from both rides...Well except here the whirring blades of the overhead helicopter also compete!

The queue for Block K is a lot longer than elsewhere. Just as I get to the front three early twenties

American guys push in behind me. I tell them the queue is back there which they ignore…These guys are obviously above the rest of us and don't need to join the line #tossers. No way are they getting in ahead of me though #seasonedcampaignerof1970scashonentrycrushes.

My seat is on the fourth tier of a really modern stadium. Inside it is alive with energy and vibrant colours. The fans are singing Olé Rico... I would love to join in with them!!

At kick off there are thousands of empty seats. The game is a sell out on the FIFA website. I am not sure whether this is due to people misjudging the journey time from the City or the ticketing agencies taking a bath…

There is certainly a lot more of the red, blue and white of Rica fans in the stadium than the famous Italian blue whose Italia chant is drowned out with boos and whistles.

Rica fans are cheering every tackle, every attacking thrust...They win a corner down below...The volume goes even higher. It would be such fun to join in with them…Instead I have to will Balotelli's shot to go in... At least he isn't an Arsenal player...Well not yet anyway but if the rumours are to be believed… The North London Fire Service will be on alert #fireworkssetoffinthebathroom.

After 15 minutes or so the match starts to settle down and Italy's retention of the ball starts to take hold... As I say that a careless pass back to the keeper goes out for a corner to whoops of delight from the excited Rican fans.

Another much louder Italia rings out but again it is drowned out.

Being a typical Englishman I am a lover of the underdog... And start to think... What the hell, enjoy supporting Rica...Rooney and co will probably lose in the last game anyway...But I just can't quite bring myself to do it.

The Ricans jeer the Italian passing game. But the Italians have it spot on... The heat is sweltering... Stifling... It's enough to just be sat in the shade in this, let alone play football!!!!

I wonder how England would cope in this heat...Obvious!!

23 minutes gone, there are still people coming into the stadium which is considerably fuller but nowhere near capacity. Good job we got a bit of a wiggle on!

The dreaded Mexican wave... Already done three passes...Thankfully it loses steam... Have the feeling it will return though.

Brazilian yellow dominates in the crowd and they begin to sing their own song...The one which the Argentines so successfully bastardised...The Brazilian words... *"I am a Brazilian guy, with a lot of pride, and a lot of love for my country"*.

Balotelli's through on goal!! Chips the keeper!!! And it drops ... Just wide... Great chance...And somehow if it was against England...You just know it would have dropped in to the net.

Balotelli has another shot...Bounces back off the keeper who grabs it just before an Italian can follow up.

It is one way traffic but wait...An Italian player goes down under a tackle, Rica break and bring a good save from the keeper.

A couple more efforts from Rica. A back header over the bar...They look a good side...Really open game!

Looks a definite penalty to Rica!! Not given...Alex, sat next to me, says the referee must be blind and translates the chant of the Ricans... *"Son of a bitch, Son of a Bitch, Son of a bitch!"*

Before we catch our breath... Cross comes over... Ruiz header back across goal... Did it cross the line? The linesman is sprinting back towards the halfway line...Yessss!! Oh Noooo!! It's a goal!!!! 1-0 to Rica. The crowd, the players, the manager are all going wild!! Goal line technology confirms the goal!!

Half time Italy 0-1 Costa Rica

My oh my!! It will be difficult in this heat, against a pacy counter attacking team, for Italy to get back into this game and score one let alone two without reply.

I swear that whenever I have to support a team I would ordinarily want to lose... When it's a needs must situation and even when they are expected to win... They bloody well find a way to lose.

Let's be honest...If Bryan Ruiz of Fulham was English...He wouldn't get near the England squad. Talking of England, Roy and the boys will be twitching anxiously in their plush, perfect facilities. Roy said the planning has been perfect...The team is predominantly from our top five clubs plus a couple from Manchester United #noexcuses.

Second half underway... Ffs Italy score a bloody early goal...

Rico win the ball back in their own half and burst forward with a number of high tempo passing interchanges to force a corner... Can't but admire this superb attractive and entertaining football #suchfluency.

England are light years away from producing this type of football.

Great Rican save from a long range shot... Italian corner...now Pirlo is lining up a long range free kick...Another excellent save. Straight down the other end and Rica force a save...The pace is frenetic... And in this stifling heat! Great game and the fans are loving it.

As opposed to England last night...Italy always have a man available in the centre circle...Usually Pirlo, come on Andrea work your magic...Please...I can't believe I am saying this!

Few step overs down the left wing has the Ricans cheering loudly...How they are loving this!

What a counter attacking through ball... Buffon comes a long way out of his box and only just gets there to stop an almost certain second.

This is some match!!

27 minutes to go and the Rican fans are giving it the olé as their team knock the ball around... Not against some pub team... But Italy one of the World Cup giants!!!

Rican fans singing out louder and louder...Daring to believe they might qualify for the knock out stages in just 22 minutes time!!

To think when the group was drawn, Rica were regarded as the whipping boys of the supposed big three of Italy, Uruguay and England. They have seen England off and the other two will effectively have a knock out game to see who comes second!!

Italy losing...Mario booked...There's a surprise #toysoutofpram.

Italy break forward but there is a huge gap between the three attacking forwards and the rest of the team...Sheer weight of numbers causes them to lose possession...Looks as if the heat might be telling...The reward for finishing top is to firstly avoid Colombia and then Brazil in the knock out stages #somereward. The final 12 minutes could go a long way to deciding that.

A 40,285 attendance is announced.

6 minutes to go...Rica now looking more likely to score a second than Italy to score one...Let alone the two England need them to score...

The Rica fans are beginning to sniff, to sense victory...Singing and dancing... Italia! Italia! Italia! Rings out one last time before the Brazilians familiar tune takes over.

Corner to Italy 89th minute...Rica player has both arms around an Italian player who just about gets a toe on the ball...So much for FIFA clamping down on holding in the box this tournament.

4 minutes added time...Rica have a thrown in deep in Italian territory down the right wing. Their fans are now singing loudly and dare I say it confidently!! Now they are whistling for the final whistle but... Italy build one last attack... Then, Rica win it back and huge Olé 's ring out.

The referee holds his hands aloft and blows the final whistle...Jubilation on the pitch...Jubilation in the stands...The players get together for a group huddle and dance. Not that it will be many people's thoughts in the stadium...But for at least three of us...The final nail has been hammered into the coffin of England's 2014 World Cup challenge. The fat lady is singing her heart out...England are out...

Back to what is happening inside the stadium...The fans, the players... All are ecstatic! You can see, feel and sense just how much it means for a country the size of Costa Rica to not only beat Italy but to also qualify for the knock out stage.

The whole squad come over to their fans. One player leaps the hoardings and hugs with the fans... The players and fans are united in a way that makes you realise what we in England have lost. Club football is king and it's impossible to paper over the cracks for a tournament every two years. Roy, his predecessors, this crop of players as with their predecessors say the right things. They mean what they say... But somehow, they just don't feel it to the same extent of other nations...That depth of passion. And it's only being out here and seeing the Argentines, the Chileans, Uruguayans and Costa Ricans that it really hits home. Fans are driving 36 hours or more, sleeping on beaches etc...When the match comes, the anticipation, the passion, the colour and the outfits...That fire in the belly. You could see it in the expression of Luis Suarez towards the end of the Rica defeat, just how much it meant. That passion, that fire in the belly all came to the fore.

I meet up with Paul and Ian and immediately we understand why the bus stops are so far from the stadium, to accommodate the large queues after the game! But to be fair we are on the bus very quickly.

Meet three West Stand Upper Spurs season ticket holders on the metro back into town.

They are supporting England but not following them as such. Tomorrow they are flying to Rio to see Belgium versus Russia in the Maracana at the weekend. I still feel the need to experience the Maracana atmosphere once...But will I be able to do so...

The guys are carrying expired credit cards and memberships to spurious clubs plus a few reals in their wallet in case of being mugged #veryclever. Then again they are season ticket holders in the West Upper and you can't afford those prices without being very clever. As Reginald Perrin would say...I didn't get where I am today without carrying around a false wallet for muggers in Brazil!

It is 4.25 and we get off the metro at Recife metro station to catch a bus to the fan fest. There is a truly obnoxious Russian on the bus. He hasn't given us any problems but just the type of drunken yob you would prefer to avoid. 2018 comes to mind...

The Switzerland versus France game kicked off at 4pm. It is impossible to get to the fan fest on time for kick off. Would have been nice if the logistics had been planned a little better so that fans coming out of the stadium could reach the fan fest in time for the next match.

No signs for pedestrians to walk from the bus station to the fan fest. We follow others down a road, across the river and walk in the fan fest to find it isn't yet half time and...

France are three nil up! Missed a penalty too and incredibly with the open goal at his mercy, Cabaye's follow up hit the bar.

We get chatting with Danny now of Oregon, sounds like a character from Lord of the Rings! Danny was born in Bournemouth and is with Dave from Tulsa who is originally from London, born in Chelsea. Both are Spurs fans and there is another from Chicago sat nearby. Danny has brought a small card board cut out of Ledley King, because he feels Ledley deserves to be at the World Cup.

Dave regales me with stories from his childhood. As a young boy he was once sat on a barrier in the Paxton Road end and Steve Perryman shot a ball that smacked him in the face...Splat! Blood everywhere and all the Spurs fans nearby laughing. Typical!!

I know I am a Spurs fan but it's amazing how many we are coming across... Paul and Ian might even agree.

Danny went to the fan fest portaloos and it's not even covered. A plastic strip wraps around your waist to protect your modesty!!! Fortunately I had used the shopping centre facilities next door!

Two guys in fancy dress as Brahma beer cans...Look so funny!

Lovely breeze as we stand overlooking the river with a can of Brahma beer watching the match in a perfect climate as the night falls... Perfect!!

5-0...Wow nearly 6!!

Lloris must wonder why he deserves "virtual" walls... Last season at West Ham, Paulinho and Adebayor brought disgrace upon themselves by turning sideways to avoid the ball hitting them in the chest...Poor luvs...And again today...This time Benzema didn't want to get hurt...A second for Switzerland... Great goal!! 5-2 now...

Get talking to a Brazilian from Brasilia in an Italian shirt...My does he hate France... I say the French are our rivals but nothing to the extent of his feelings... And of course, they have Hugo Lloris! I mention Paulinho and Sandro to him and suddenly a beer is in my hand!!

France score a sixth! Or has the referee blown the final whistle? We haven't a clue! The screen goes off and on comes the local entertainment!!

It's a cracking night...Still not eaten a thing since the half eaten cold lasagne in the São Paulo shopping mall early last night .. Now 6pm...Nevertheless my tummy is taking on pregnancy symptoms!

Enormous inflatable balls are now bouncing around the fan fest! If there was a World Cup in partying...Brazil would win hands down!!

A Brazilian takes a photograph of four Costa Rica fans... Each has a word on their shirt and as drunk as they might or should be...It is important to line up in the right order "Costa-Rica-Pure-Vida". For some reason, my mind goes back to the Charlton Athletic back four of a few years ago...Young-Fish-Costa-Fortune!

Find a football shop and buy my daughter a beautiful sparkling dress in Brazilian colours with the national flag as a centre piece. For some reason, I also buy a Brazilian flag! Actually it must be in my English DNA…When England are knocked out, I like many other English fans support Brazil!

We walk out of the fan fest at 6.25 and stumble upon a cobbled street full of life and atmosphere with a live band playing…Feels like around every street corner there is a party.

We jump in to a taxi and arrive back at our hotel. By the coast, the climate is warm, humid and sultry with just the hint of a breeze…Nigh on perfecto!

As I sit here writing my diary into my iPhone notes in room 2005… Yes on the 20th floor…In this wonderful climate, I can hear the waves rolling in…Nigh on perfecto!

While in the hotel room, on the TV, Ecuador take the lead but Honduras equalise. As we leave the lobby, Valencia heads Ecuador back in front. The 2014 World Cup juggernaut rolls on and at some pace!

We walk along the palm treed promenade and find a steak and seafood restaurant.

There is a Swiss guy sat nervously in front of the TV. If Ecuador hold on to the lead Switzerland only have to beat Honduras to qualify…Assuming of course that Ecuador don't beat France.

At the final whistle, the Swiss guy is happy and gesturing to four Swedish lads on the next table. It transpires that two of the Swedes lost a bet with the Swiss guy and have to do twenty press ups in the restaurant!

EL GRINGO'S ONCE IN A LIFETIME

I go across to congratulate two Costa Rican couples on a nearby table. Two sisters with their husbands and I say that I am a little surprised by the quality of the football being played by their team. They respond by saying…So are we!!! And go on to say, they never imagined that their country would win their opening two games against Uruguay and Italy. Lovely people!

Over dinner Paul and Ian try to convince me that for my book to be a success, I need to be here until the end of the tournament. Their arguments are convincing…Not that I need too much convincing!!

While having a drink after our meal, a Scottish guy notices Ian's shirt and just can't help himself... He comes over to revel in saying how good and funny it is that after two games, England are out…He goes on to say…Can't tell you how much I'm buzzing. There are world class teams here, there are mediocre teams and then there are… I have heard enough... And what does that make Scotland who aren't even here…Again…Oh you can't compare… I ask who can't we compare Scotland with…Countries like Uruguay population 3.2m? Costa Rica?

He comes back with…You boys think you come here expecting to win the World Cup... Really? He then confuses the hell out of us by singing at the top of his voice…A loyalist song!! Excuse me? He walks off and Ian waves him a you're too mouthy goodbye... What a tosser…

The sad thing is that when Scotland, Wales, Northern Ireland, Republic of Ireland play…I along with a lot of English fans want them to do well…I ask Paul and Ian and they say exactly the same…Except of course, when playing England…To be fair most Wales and Northern Ireland fans I know do support England.. What would Sven say…It's a pity!

The Costa Rican daughters are joined by another lady…It must be their mother…

It is their mother! And she has another two other daughters who apparently look just the same…The resemblance is uncanny!!

Then Mr Scotland returns and offers an apology of sorts and a handshake… Wow…But then he goes and spoils it all by saying I hate you… Not quite but as I started writing it… The words of a famous song come to mind…Well with a twist!

It's 10.30 and Paul and Ian decide to have an early night. On warm, sultry nights like this, as tired as I should be, I don't feel like sleeping…What is wrong with me?!!! I decide to stay out and enjoy the World Cup party…Once in a life time!!

Walking along the promenade…It is incredibly quiet…Very few bars…I notice a sign by the beach and walk over to try understand what it says.

Half of the sign is in Portuguese. I have no clue what it says…The other half is in English…Blimey!! Must be an important message… And there in big bold letters

DANGER

Risk of shark attack

And for good measure…Just in case… There is a big picture in colour black of a shark!!

Nearby there is another sign:

CAUTION

In a square a picture of a shark…
Followed by avoid sea bathing:
In the open sea or on areas without the
protection of reefs
At high tide, especially around new
moon and full moon
At dawn and dusk
At river mouths
In deep areas (level above the waist)
In muddy waters (especially in rainy
periods)
If you are alone
If you are bleeding
If wearing jewellery or shiny objects
After drinking alcohol

Bloody hell!! Don't see signs like that at Skegness too often!!

Never knew of a lot of those precautions…Only came to watch a World Cup!!

It is 11.15pm at night and other than a few people out walking or jogging, it is dead…No people, no bars…Nothing whatsoever.

On returning to the hotel I chat with the hotel reception staff who say there are some very good places but you need to go by taxi.

In bed by midnight…There's a first!!

EL GRINGO'S ONCE IN A LIFETIME

Despite all the negative stories in the press, and scaremongering documentaries on TV, the World Cup in Brazil proved to be a success. There was no major trouble, and everybody, including the locals had a great time. Being based in Rio, the weather was great, the drinks were cheap and even England's usual footballing disaster on the pitch couldn't ruin a great trip. Fans of every country had a great time in a carnival atmosphere. It was literally a trip of a lifetime, and one every fan who went, will remember with great affection.

Colin Tatham, Enfield, UK

Being an Australian and living in Switzerland, we only got more engaged in the World Cup because of my eight year old daughter. She told me I had 'ruined her life' because she'd never seen a football game live or on TV and didn't understand what her friends were talking about at school!!!

As she's at the French school, we were then very patriotic followers of 'Les Bleus' and she wore her new cap everywhere. Timing and coverage meant we didn't get to see a single Aussie game. I followed with pride online, but without high expectations for 'my' team. It was actually nice to just enjoy the games without emotional angst!

Office life was quite 'charged' during the period as there are so many nationalities and long-standing tensions. We have just moved outside Zurich, and I discovered how multi-cultural our complex is, with every flag you could imagine on the balconies and lots of cheering and groaning late into the night. Tablets and phones, too, revolutionised supporters' lives - each night you could see commuters huddled together on the train around very small screens watching the games live.

Jenni Dean, Zurich, Switzerland

SATURDAY 21ST JUNE 2014

We wake at 8am, open the curtains to a "to die for view" of the Atlantic Ocean... Problem is after reading the signs on the beach last night...If you do go in the sea above three feet...It may well be a to die for view!!

We have a fabulous breakfast after which Paul and I analyse the World Cup chart in the reception. There are some mouth-watering permutations, although more than a tinge of sadness that England can't now be in the mix.

The one thing we are not really aware of out here is the media and public reaction to England's exit...Greg Dyke has apparently come out and stated that Hodgson will remain as manager through the Euro campaign to 2016.. That is of course if we qualify. Surely coming out with such a statement so quickly is just as much a knee jerk reaction as firing him? This is the trouble with having a nice honourable politically correct manager at the helm...Not so easy to fire him...

The cold hard facts are that Roy was very happy with the squad he selected which was almost injury free and that the planning and preparations had been perfect. Yet this is the worst performance at a finals in my life time...And I am

55 years old... Surely there should at least be a post-World Cup review of some sort before coming to this decision. We do after all have an extra three weeks in which to have such a review!!

Back to what really matters as the 2014 band wagon rolls on! Three more fixtures today: Argentina v Iran; Ghana v Germany followed by Nigeria v Bosnia. We have noticed that the best games seem to be scheduled as the middle game of the day for peak European viewing. The last game usually being the least appealing as most of Europe will be tucked up in bed by then.

We head down to the beach and through Ian's Portuguese language skills... It seems that the beach chairs and umbrellas are free but we must buy our drinks from the guy whose chairs we sit on...We take the chairs.. May be the coke is £20 a time...I mean that which you drink! Fortunately (may be some would say unfortunately!) never been tempted to go down the drugs route...When I was in my late teens growing up in Lincoln... Druggies were regarded as the drop outs in the corner...How times have changed!!

As I doze off on the beach, my phone pings to notify me of a tweet coming through... How can this be? I am about 20 feet from the sea, sat in a beach chair with data roaming firmly switched off...It had better be!! I check and it is...? Phew...So how come? Wow it is the Wi-Fi from the hotel which is across the beach, the promenade, the dual carriageway and the footpath on the far side... Well over 100 yards away!!!

Through WhatsApp my youngest son lets me know that England are 168/1 with Robson 75 and Ballance 61 not out. Good to see the new boys going well but Cook needs an innings sooner rather than later...

It feels so good to be down by the beach...The sun is very hot again today with just enough of a sea breeze to make it feel very comfortable, I absorb the sound of the waves rolling in, creating their froth as they end their journey on the beach. The sand is warm and soft...The sort that it is great to run your feet and toes through as I am doing right now...The smell of the sand and sea is very strong and helps to create that general feeling of relaxation.

The beach is a little unusual in that greenery is growing within 20 feet of the sea and stretches bank towards the promenade creating a break in the eye line of the beach. Palm trees run along the edge of the beach providing a natural barrier from the promenade and traffic...They sway lazily in the sea breeze...

It is a Saturday so the beaches are busy but without being by any means crowded... With over 20 miles of beach to play with... #nowonder

A family of Brazilian adults and children are having a boisterous game of football by the water's edge...Careful chaps...That left back just lurking over three feet out In the water...Norman "bite your legs"

Hunter is a pussy cat compared to this guy!

Multi coloured kites are shooting the breeze whilst the seabirds scavenge the beach for leftovers...As in Rio, the promenades and beaches are spotless.

The vendors are plying their trade and pass by almost as incessantly as the waves roll into shore. Lots of people are taking strolls along the water's edge. The beautiful thonged bikini Brazilian ladies adorn the beach...

Suddenly a genie appears out of my coke bottle...Bejesus...May be there was coke in the coke!! Today Mr John... Is your lucky day...You can have any one wish!!!

Wow...Should I go for Uruguay having fielded an ineligible player and we are awarded a 3-0 Victory? Nah...Would be a waste as Costa Rica will probably anyway be too good for us... Can't believe I am saying that! But sadly it is probably true... As yet another beautiful lady strolls passed...I just can't resist... Can you give me 30 years back please!!

Whoosh I am back on Lincoln High Street just passing Pizzaland on my way towards the Cornhill...Genie come back!! I didn't mean...Too late he has gone...

Just what was in that Coca Cola!!!

Paul decides to go into the water...its 12.30...I turn towards the sea and shout "Hey up lads here comes dinner!"

After a few minutes, Paul returns to say the water is a lot warmer than Rio but that every time the sea thrashes a reef against his leg. There is just that instant when...

While in the sea... He just couldn't get the Jaws music out of his mind!

Ian then lets on he wanted the Jaws music as the bridal walk down the aisle!! He didn't get that but managed to compromise on Mission Impossible as the happy couple walked back down the aisle!

Reminded me of the couple who had as their first wedding song on the dance floor the U2 song... "I still haven't found what I am looking for" which given the happy couple are very happy... Albeit with different partners was the right song to have!

My eldest son Henry rings me from Cyprus... He is just about to board and has had a fantastic time. I am so pleased for him. He has had a really tough year and received some good news whilst on holiday of his first year degree exams... A first plus 2 x 2.1 results #proudfather

I look out to sea and there are bathers out there almost chest high...Is that you Roy?? Don't do it!! And to think previous English managers only had to be concerned about journalistic sharks...

I recall a guide driving me up to the rain forest near Cape Tribulation north of Cairns... We cross a river which has a sign saying "DANGER Estuarine crocodiles inhabit these waters" and a canoe passes by with two guys merrily rowing away... I ask if they would be local guys who know the waters well. The guide replies... "No locals would be rowing in that river!"

We reach a decision... Argentina versus Iran or the beach... What would you do? Yep we are doing the same... The beach it is!!!

Since last night's dinner and the conversation as to whether to stay or return home...I come to a decision that if Colin can put me up in their apartment in Rio...I will try to change my flight and stay for the remainder of the World Cup...I had tried to convince myself that writing with two different perspectives...Being in Brazil for one half of the tournament and being in England for the other half would provide a good contrast... However being in Rio for a Brazil v Argentina final... Yes I know...No comparison... I have to stay!!!

Well I survived the sea!! Those sharks daren't come anywhere near me! Well actually they wouldn't be able to in 18 inches of water!

England have moved on to 300/3...We might pass 400 runs again...That hasn't happened very often in recent times...Can't recall the last time! Sri Lanka's bowling attack or our great batting? Nevertheless...Great for the confidence of the younger players.

Argentina versus Iran is deep into the second half and still scoreless...Paul decides to go back to the hotel to watch the remainder of the game.

I reach up to pull my sunglasses down which are resting on my head. They aren't there??? A moment of anxiety...Did I remove my sunglasses before going into the sea. These aren't just a pair of sunglasses to me...I absolutely love them...I can't recall taking them off and putting them in my rucksack before going into the sea. In fact I am certain I didn't...The anxiety goes up a notch...I go through the small section of my ruck sack...Not there...I go through the larger section of my rucksack.. This is last chance saloon time...Inwardly panic is rising...Not there...I can't remember taking them off...In fact I am sure I didn't...I can't have taken then off before going into the sea which was more than two hours ago... Shit.... I am so upset... I know it probably sounds ridiculous to say but I will never find another pair to buy like these...

I forlornly go down to the sea where I was bathing... Almost two hours since I was laughing off fighting the sharks...They are lost...If the sea hasn't claimed them someone bathing in the sea will have done. There is the odd chunk of seaweed... This is hopeless but still I search...I know it's easily done but I am so cross with myself... I watch a few waves come in from different angles... As I look out to sea...The breeze seems to be blowing the waves marginally right, to my left, as they hit the shore...I walk a little way down thinking the old expression that the sea always gives up it's dead...But then again in my life time I have seen countless footballs float out of the reach of crying children...They will be insured but I have few what I would call treasured possessions.. I mentioned my watch situation whilst flying over from Paris...I don't wear jewellery. It occurs to me...My sunglasses are about my only treasured possession in that regard...I somehow feel good when wearing them... Not least because they cover my wrinkles!!

I continue walking along the beach about 15 feet into the shallow waters... Nothing...Nada...With Paul having already gone back to the hotel and Ian who was looking after my rucksack also wanting to go back I can't look for too much longer. I walk a little further...But this is futile. In the two hours which have since passed, somebody could have picked them up and who knows how far the wind and current could have blown them either along the shore or out to sea... I give up and turn to walk back the some 500 metres to Ian. Something catches my eye beneath the surface. But a wave washes over whatever it is...The seaweed I had seen seems to float that little but higher than whatever this is. I walk a few paces forward... OMG!!!!! There they are beneath the surface...I can't believe it!!!!!! But surely they will be damaged...Hesitantly I pick them up...The mechanics all seem in good order...The lenses are a little misty...But hopefully they will clean? I just can't believe it... And you may think soppy old sod... But I feel quite emotional...Talk about once in a lifetime...This surely has to be a once in a life time find!!! I am so, so happy to have found them!

It is 3.30 and I decide to leave the beach and return to the hotel to see Paul and Ian to organise the rest of the day... Wow! Wow and Wow!!

Me and my sunglasses had a shower! They seem in good order...Fingers crossed...

I look out to sea from the hotel balcony and shadows of the skyscrapers are dancing on the ocean...Fabulous photographs.

I join Paul and Ian in the bar and Germany v Ghana is 15 minutes in and goalless.

Paul lets me know that Messi scored a great curling added time winner for Argentina...Brave Iranian resistance and hearts broken by the brilliance of the little magician...I wonder...Could this be Messi's World Cup?

Half time and its 0-0...Ghana are giving at least as good as they get...And may be a little bit more! If Germany don't win this it will really put the cat amongst the Gerry Francis pigeons! Paul and Ian aren't aware that Gerry keeps pigeons. A conversation thus ensues about all we know about pigeons! Apparently a top pigeon can sell for £200,000!! Bloody hell, that's how much Spurs spent breaking the transfer record for Martin Peters, with Jimmy Greaves going to West Ham as a make-weight in the deal. Yes "the" Jimmy Greaves being the make-weight in the deal. I can still remember the 9 o'clock news headline that day as a small boy... Peters was my favourite player but played for the "wrong" team...So when he signed for us... I must have been the only elated Spurs fan that night and still remember dancing round the room. I went to his home debut a 1-2 home defeat to Coventry... I didn't care... I saw Martin Peters in a Spurs shirt... And he scored!!

As an anecdote further to that story, my mum, as Santa Claus, couldn't get me a Spurs bag one Christmas. So as she knew I liked Martin Peters, she bought me a West Ham bag... Imagine!!'

By the way Gerry, if you are reading this...About time you sorted that barnet of yours out!

Just seen Messi's goal...The bend on that...Why can't England produce a Messi...Genie come back!!

Early into the second half...Normal service is resumed...Cross comes over... Goetze running at full pelt into the box heads the ball down on to his knee and it ricochets into the net 1-0 Germany...As Paul asks...Why don't we get that type of luck..?

We order another round of beers...We are drinking Devassa which has a rather distinctive logo...A side profile of a naked silhouetted lady with her legs tucked underneath her...Her arms arched behind her head.. Very much à lá the entree to a James Bond film...My word!!! Sorry to break off from my ramblings but ...Gyan is through just Neuer to beat...2-1 Ghana...The bar erupts as I suspect does every household across England, Holland, Belgium...Hell...Everywhere... Well apart from of course in Germany!!

Ghana are running riot here...The right ball in from the left and it would surely have been 3!!

Klose comes on...Second highest goalscorer in WC history...Knock on from the corner...In comes Klose...First touch...Goal!! 2-2!! Does that level him with Ronaldo, the original Brazilian version, as the highest WC goalscorer? Need to check...

The trouble with these 4pm kick offs...Is that they kick off at 4pm!! Drinking through to the early hours...It's a pity haha

Its 5.45pm I am feeling tipsy already...Can you tell??

Great game...Ended 2-2...Right at the end, Mueller clashed with a defenders shoulder...Blood everywhere...

It is now 6.40pm., no food again since breakfast...Think it is what is known as a liquid diet...

Taxi down to the fan fest...One of the bars in the fan fest won't serve beers because they aren't cold enough...London pubs take note!

First trouble seen in fan fest...Some old guy having a hissy fit...Escorted off the premises...Too much to drink ...And before you ask...No it wasn't me...We are minding our business getting a couple of brahmas each!

Great start to the Nigeria v Bosnia game... Both teams really going for it... Even Jon Obi Mikel is getting a shot in on goal!! Chelsea fan Paul is shocked... Scored his first goal last season in six years...His last one, Paul reminded Ian was against his team Forest!

Bosnia score...No they don't ...Offside...Oh no...He timed his run perfectly... Wrongly disallowed...

Nigeria 1-0 ... Hmmm... A sense of justice prevails...

A lady dressed in full Argentina colours with the national flag face painted on to each cheek comes over and stands behind us. We are not sure of her intentions. She then comes over to me and asks where I am from. I say England and she says...I saw you come into the fan fest and said to my friend... He is beautiful and my friends said to me to come speak with you!

EL GRINGO'S ONCE IN A LIFETIME

Now it is not every day that this sort of thing happens to me., probably fairer to say not every decade...Actually...It's not that I think of myself as unattractive... My grandma, god bless her soul, used to say I was a lot nearer the front than the back when faces were handed out.. And comparisons with Lineker and Gere are not untoward but...To have a lady come up and say such a thing...Well come on guys...Be honest...How many times in your life? Yes...I was somewhat taken aback and started to look for her Labrador!

We start chatting and her name is Sabina but she goes by a singing name of Tati...I prefer to call her Sabina and in my drunken state ask her if she has seen the film named after her...To then realise that the film was called Sabrina... Not Sabina!! She is with her two friends Vanessa and Ana and her 15 year old nephew called Kevin... I say...Strange name for an Argentine but her sister loves the actor Kevin Costner...So Kevin it is! Sabina is doing all the driving and driven 5000km over the course of three days to watch Italy v Costa Rica and tomorrow will set off to drive 3000km to Porto Alegre for Argentina v Nigeria before returning to Rosario, Argentina...Just the first two legs is a 5000 mile round trip!! The passion of these people...

She said in 2009 she rode her Harley Davidson alone from Rosario to Rio but never got there...The people she met in São Paulo were so warm and friendly that she stayed there. Some journey on a Harley...And alone #bravelady

She is a music teacher and is the lead singer in a bluesy rock band... Having sang in front of 10000 people at a bike fest, I insist she sings... Wow what a voice!! She gives me a business card of her band and says I can see them on

YouTube...And all the time she is saying how beautiful I am...I seriously wonder just how she gets around without her Labrador...

I buy a beer just as the rain comes. Paul and Ian leave to go to a bar and I stay to finish my beer with the girls and some Argentine guys...As ever, as an Inglese they are not keen on me being English... A common theme in my time in Brazil...The Falklands or as they would say the Malvinas is clearly still topical and not least because the Argentine squad held up a banner for a photo shoot just before the tournament.. The damage that has been done and the constant need to do a repair job between ordinary fans...Shame...At the end of the day we are all ordinary fans...In my opinion footballers should not be used as pawns in politics...Only my personal view and I hope FIFA investigate and come down heavily to set a precedent.

Fortunately I have lots of Argentinian Spurs memorabilia on my iPhone photo album dating back as far as 1978 which fascinates them and of course Spurs have an Argentine manager and a rising star in Lamela ex River Plate.

I mention the Romcom I am writing which is initially set in Buenos Aires and the opportunity to speak and mix with this group is priceless...

They share drinks between each other...When I say share...Same cups even... They buy a kebab stick and it is almost an insult not to have a piece...

They stay out in the rain...Who cares about getting wet...Enjoy...No embrace the rain...Be at one...Liberate the senses...Blimey what's in this fan fest beer!!

Kevin who is 15 years old and lives 100km from Rosario asks me why Aaron Lennon is not in the England team...Lennon is my favourite Spurs player...I love Kevin for saying that!

EL GRINGO'S ONCE IN A LIFETIME

They wrap Argentine flags around me for photographs...Oh dear!

The Argentine ladies and their nephew join us in a bar called Burberinho... Very Bohemian in style and Paul says it is where England fans were due to meet should we have played here later in the tournament... Cracking night... There are some Americans on the next table and we have great banter.

We try to pay for the bill...The Argentines won't let us...But in error I leave a 50 real tip...

Sabina may have a spare ticket for Argentina v Nigeria in Porto Alegre... I would love to go to this match...

After they leave, we finish our drinks and head out looking for a Taxi... The streets are rammed, music is thumping out...There is a live band booming DJ style music out...It is as full of life and vibrancy as you can imagine...Very young life... Not for us...Crazy, loud, loco...!

We try to get in the Underground bar...It's one of those bars that is half full but has bouncers who are telling us to queue...Hmmm no I don't think so!!!

We move on to a hotel bar and...I finally have a meal today...its midnight!! A group of 6/7 English guys join us on the next table. They are in their late 50s and are spread across the globe but stay in touch and arranged to meet in Brazil for the World Cup. Sadly one guy only flew in today and England are already out!

After the meal we stop off at another bar and changeover to caipirinhas...By 1am almost 9 hours after we started drinking and a couple of caipirinhas later...

Things start to get a little messy... As I finish this the next morning... The events of last night are a little bit of a blur... #signofagoodnight

When I first moved to the US 14 years ago from England, I couldn't find any football (soccer) on TV. Even my first World Cup whilst in USA in 2002 was hardly covered. Since then MLS has improved every year and even someone called Beckham played here. The World Cup in Brazil was huge by comparison. People at work were talking about it and taking bets, there were big video screens in many cities with huge crowds watching, the USA v Portugal even had more viewers than the NBA finals!

> Alan Martindale, an Englishman living in
> Springfield, Illinois, USA

Because of linguistic and cultural differences, Belgium is a complex country and this is reflected in politics and government structure, but when the "Red Devils" perform well, it creates a sense of unity in the country. All of a sudden, being Flemish or Walloon is less important and the Belgian tricolors appear. The 2014 World Cup did just that, people were proud of being Belgian, flags appeared, rear view mirrors were covered with Belgian colors, shops had all kinds of fan attributes, large screens appeared in village and city centres for people to watch the game. We have high hopes for the upcoming European qualifying campaign!

> Edward Phillips, Belgium

SUNDAY 22ND JUNE 2014

As I wake...The room feels just about stationary...Kind of like being on the waltzer when it gets stuck... And you wait for the guy to give it an almighty push and send your head spinning round and round a la Kylie Minogue...

The weird thing here is though...Whereas in England I have the hangovers from hell... Those with a thumping head...Where it is a struggle to get out of bed unless to make emergency visits to the bathroom to go down on one's knees to pay homage to the pearly white basin... Here as soon as I get up and on with my day...I am fine...#weird

The forecast for today was meant to be rain but looking out of the window, we are delighted to see the sun shining

Ian has gone down to the beach and Paul is going on ahead of me for breakfast...

As he pulls the door handle...It comes off in his hand!! Funnily enough neither of us packed a screwdriver...That was England fans in the 1970s!!

My phone didn't charge overnight...The charger seems to be playing up... Not good...In fact a lot worse than not good...Could be a massive problem... It is incredible how important our phones are on our daily lives...Music, twitter, email, alarm clock, texts, phone calls, internet not to mention Google!! WhatsApp, watch, camera, video, photo album... I am even writing my World Cup diary through iPhone notes...20 years ago we used to have to carry all these things around separately!!

Eventually I manage to start the phone charging process but it feels a little fragile ...On/off... On/off hmmm...

I leave it charging whilst going down for a hearty breakfast...Melon and scrambled eggs...Not together!! The scrambled eggs are excellent here...Just a bit of a challenge to ask for pepper...There is always salt and sugar on the table... But never pepper...And with Ian not being with us...When I ask for pepper... Another salt pot arrives!

We look around the breakfast room...The hotel not only feels a lot busier today but...We can't help noticing that the ladies seem even more beautiful than ever...

I get into a conversation with a Modric shirt wearing Croatian. His English is perfect and amazing isn't it but we were sat nearby each other when Spurs played Dinamo Zagreb at White Hart Lane in a Europa League match!

On returning to the room, my phone has charged up to the giddy heights of 80%. I check my sunglasses... No damage #wellhappy

I look through my emails and see a message from iPhone telling me to back up...I try a number of times but it fails. 155mb of storage left #notsowellhappy

Will have to be selective in what I keep...

I call Colin in Rio who is heading off to the Maracana this morning to try to get tickets for the lunch time kick off...Belgium v Russia. They are flying back to the UK on Sunday 29th but he will have a chat with the Brazilian apartment owner to see whether I can stay from 26th to 29th...Although the owner may have had enough of people living with him by now!

I call Paul from Nottingham and with England being knocked out, they have already put their knock out stage tickets back for resale and decided to go home after the final England game...

With it being a Sunday, the beach is much busier but still nowhere near overcrowded...

We sit in our free chairs...Well...Free as long as we buy the drinks from the guy owning the chairs...A Brazilian family nearby don't buy into this concept and open their own cans of drinks... The vendor comes over to voice his displeasure... One of the group a beautiful but feisty thonged bikini wearing lady takes issue with him...Loud insults are traded..

Then she pours the open can partially on him and the rest on the beach...The passion is quite breathtaking!! They gather up their things and begin to angrily and stompily march off down the beach. Now in their thongs when they just amble down to the sea it is quite a sight but this is quite something else ...Imagine the elephant parade in jungle book...Recall the baby elephants at the back of the herd... The view from behind as they are trying to master their march...Hmmm...

How do I carry on my diary after that exhibition!

Well...

Just when you think there is nothing else to offer...A beach vendor turns up with a plate of freshly caught uncooked fish!!

Followed by a guy pedalling a pair of binoculars...Now I am as hot blooded as the next man... And yes the ladies on the beach are stunningly beautiful but... Imagine being seen laid on the beach peering through a pair of binoculars... Brings a whole new meaning to the term bird watching #pervert!!

How much are they mate? Haha...Only kidding!

Next up is a lady carrying an enormous container hands free on her head...

Difficult enough without the uneven surface of the beach!

Although windier today, the sun is very strong and I can feel myself burning on one or two parts of my body. I have a slight confession to make at this point...

As I was quite tanned before I came out... I didn't bring any sun cream and today is the first time when I have thought...ummm

We again have Wi-Fi on the beach and I decide to take it one step further and stand in the water...Yep...I am standing in the waters of the Atlantic Ocean and have Wi-Fi!! I take a photograph and send a tweet!

Sabina texts to say her brother in law will sell me his Argentina v Nigeria ticket but for US$600... With having to change flights and a hotel in Rio booked I say it's too much.

Along comes a guy with 32 kites...A kite for each country in the World Cup... Showing their national flags and running off one controller. He has taken the trouble to rank the teams in order so flags of countries such as Spain, England, and Australia are towards the bottom!! He even has the teams playing today alongside each other!

I look out along the beach and amongst the bathers is the lady beach vendor fishing...Truly very fresh fish...Will always think of her next time I see a sign saying fresh fish in England...And think...Don't think so!

It is now 1.30 and the winds are blowing in the clouds and a few spots of rain can be felt...Suddenly dangerously large beach umbrellas are flying everywhere... The heavens open...Time to retire to the bar to watch Belgium hopefully beat Russia!

The hotel staff have pulled down a large screen in the corner of the restaurant with a projector producing amazing clarity.

40 minutes gone and it is 0-0.

I meet Paul in the restaurant who has had a couple of disconcerting moments.

Firstly, he has gone up to our room on the 20th floor...Used the room key to activate the elevator...but when he got to our room 2005...The room key wouldn't activate the door lock...Having the door handle come off in his hand earlier...He seems to be having a hotel room door morning! Fortunately the lift is working... Imagine if he had had to walk up and down 20 floors!!

I may have mentioned earlier that the hotel has 29 floors which kind of gives an indication as to the number of guests so...When Paul sits down to watch the match in the restaurant and one of the staff comes over and says... Are you Paul Newton? It is a bit of a shock and he wonders what message he is to be given...

But ...That was it...Just a random... Are you Paul Newton? Now if it was say Hugh Grant and he was a look alike...But he is neither of those... He is just... Paul

Newton... What a strange interlude!

Paul says the game has been quite even but Russia look quite threatening going forwards. Just to confirm his point a cross comes over...Centre Forward... Free header...Centre of the goal...Heads wide... As Paul says...If Russia get knocked out. That will be him heading off to the Gulags!!

Encouragingly for me...There seems to be quite a lot of empty seats in the Maracana...Hopefully this will be the same for France v Ecuador on Wednesday.

As the teams come out for the second half...The cameras focus on a guy in the crowd holding up a placard "Marry me Fellaini" with love hearts around the edges... Judging by the barrage of tweets I read last season...I don't think he will be a Manchester United fan!

Ian joins us and says there a lot of Mexicans arriving for tomorrow's game. Have to say I am quite excited to be seeing this winner takes all game.

Lukaku falls over in the box trying to cheat a penalty...If he had stayed on his feet there was a chance he could have got a shot in or laid off to a colleague #brainless

Seems to be a bit of a challenge to get a beer...We ordered at the end of the first half and are now 20 minutes into the second half...We have had several visits to confirm our order...But no beer!!

Finally in the 23rd minute the beer arrives...38 minutes after ordering...Not that I am counting!

Belgium hit the post and Hazard shoots over...Belgium are finishing the stronger... Hazard dribbles down the wing...Pulls it back...Origi...goal!! We immediately think of the obnoxious drunken Russian skinhead on the bus to the Recife fan fest...

Finishes 1-0...Belgium unconvincing in both games but have qualified for the knock out phase.

I go back to the room to charge my phone...The charger is still very fragile and I have to use Ian's adapter...Mine won't work at all...What happens after Belo Horizonte when I am on my own..??

I am now pondering Argentina v Nigeria...Paul and Ian think I should go to see Messi...

We walk down to the Underground bar...People queuing again...Somehow... We just ignore the doorman and walk in! The bar is full of Americans ahead of their game v Portugal tonight...We sit with three young Brazilians from Recife. Pitchers of beer arrive...I can't get Wi-Fi and one of them kindly tethers his 3G on to my phone. They have a full bottle of vodka between them and offer us a drink...The Brazilians in Recife are really warm and lovely people...So welcoming...Then one, Jose goes and spoils it all by saying that he supports Arsenal because of that Football Fever novel.. Nick Hornby has a lot to answer for!!!

The Algeria v South Korea game is on...1-0, 2-0, 3-0...Wow all in the first half.

We order food...Paul's arrives...Mine doesn't...Not very often I order food and when I do...

3-1...4-1... 4-2...And the goals keep coming! We don't care who wins as long as Russia go out. Capello and the Russian skinhead have polluted our views!

The Brazilian guy take a selfie of the six of us...Yep...Selfies have made it to Recife!

The drinks are going down and the guys are great fun. One of the guys takes my mobile number and puts me in his address book as "John the legend"!

It's now over an hour since I ordered food...I cannot seem to eat in this country!

The pub is full of Americans...A chant of USA goes up...For a bit of fun, the three Brazilians plus the three of us chant Portugal...The end of our special relationship is nigh!!

Then...Somehow, the Americans have managed to adopt the Crystal Palace song...The whoa whoa ohh we follow, we follow the USA, whoa whoa ohh!!

Then when it quietens down we start chanting England!!

The Brazilians say caipirinha is for girls and fathers!!

They also tell us a Brazilian saying... If you don't drink...You go 13 years without sex...Not sure of the connection...It's not as if you need beer goggles for most Brazilian ladies!

After a number of conversations... My food finally arrives!!

We hear it is another Rosberg, Hamilton one two in the grand prix in Austria...These two "team mates" look to be in for one hell of a battle to win the drivers' championship this year!

We might as well be in a bar in downtime Chicago!! We are in a really typical American style sports bar...Neon lights...Too many TVs to count! Mainly tables and chairs with an American style menu burgers ribs etc...Being underground there aren't any windows and with a low ceiling...The singing reverberates loudly around the bar...We have a table service with pitchers of beer. The

American fans, decked out in their American blue, red and white stars and stripes are creating some atmosphere! The US National anthem...They are all up singing at the top of their voices #verypatriotic

A new song...I believe that we will win, I believe that we will win is chanted and booms around the low ceilinged bar. We are in for an authentic American football fan experience!

5 minutes...what a hash 1-0 Portugal...What a disaster...The bar falls silent...

This is developing into some game and the fans are responding! We are enjoying the amazing atmosphere!

The Brazilian guys have two bottles of vodka on the go. One young man Alex is insisting we join in with the vodka...We try explaining it is too early... The night is young...But he is having none of it and we know how this will end #willpeaktooearly

Lots of goalmouth action...Portugal hit the post...Fine US move ends with a pull back and a great clearance off the line.

Jones picks the ball up on the left hand side side of the box, steps inside, and curls the ball hard and low into the right hand corner!! What a goal!!! The bar goes wild!! The Americans are on their feet, now on their chairs!! The singing starts up even more fervently now...Wow these guys are passionate about their team, their country!

One Timmy Howard rings out after a fine save!

The ball is back down towards the Portugal end...Cross from the left... Dempsey leans forward ...With his chest or stomach and the ball crosses the line...Must surely be offside? He wheels away from goal waving his arms...The bar is going mental crazy...This is some experience...The bar is a sea of red white and blue...Shirts, flags, caps you name it!!

Portugal are down and going out of the World Cup...The game moves into 4 minutes of added time...The fans in the bar are delirious...Their team is about to qualify and sit on top of the group.. Above Germany!! The game moves into the last minute of added time...I believe we will win is being sung determinedly...I believe we will ... Cross comes over...Eder...Goal 2-2...The atmosphere in the bar collapses...Stunned silence... Poor guys... It feels like someone has stuck a pin into the atmosphere...Burst it...Just like that...Sport is like this...Incredible highs and lows...It is why we love it so much. Few seconds later and the final whistle blows...Sven would say...What a pity...

I go into the restroom...Alongside the urinals is a huge print of a beautiful woman...She is looking across the urinals... Her expression giving off a look of... Is that all you've got!!!

The talk of the bar is that with Germany playing USA...A draw being good enough for both teams...Klinsmann who of course is German is the Manager of USA...The manager of Germany, Joachim Loew used to be Klinsmann's number two when Jürgen was manager of Germany...This already feels very cosy...Memories of the Austria v Germany carve up of many years ago come flooding back... Either Portugal or Ghana will have to win well in their final match against each other and hope beyond hope that there is a clear cut win in the other game.. The general feeling in this bar and I would imagine in most bars... They might as well pack their bags and head back home...

Ian has gone back to the hotel...Not feeling too well...There is some sort of stomach bug going round which we have all had at some point during the holiday.

We look for our Brazilian friend Alex... He is fast asleep in the corner... Probably a good job...He will be working in a bank at 8am in the morning!!

Our friends recommend we take a taxi to a bar with live music called "UK Club"

The bar bill comes and as Paul predicted it is over 300 reals... Lots of stuff we didn't have...Mini quiches, onion rings, loads of extra beers...We look at the menu, price up what we have had and pay the 150 reals we owe, making it clear that that is all they are getting...They reluctantly accept...The bar is half empty now...As we go outside there is a huge queue.. We tell the guys in the line and the doormen it is half empty...Pretentious...

We walk back to the hotel and Ian is sadly in bed asleep not well at all...We decide to walk to UK club and walk along the sea front before cutting in to walk a few blocks in land. The ladies of the night are on the street corners... A pimp moves away from two of them as he sees us walking towards them. It isn't an uncomfortable walk but probably not one to make alone...We turn a corner into the road on which the UK club is...It is heaving...The queue is probably over a 100 people long.. A guy says he has been waiting over half an hour and is giving up as he has hardly moved forward in the queue.

We jump into a taxi and ask to be taken to another club...The driver takes us to a club near our hotel which is closed!! We get out and go into the bar for a last drink...

A couple of Caipirinhas slip down rather too well...We get chatting with Mexican guys who invite us for a beer ...Giovanni dos Santos rings out...And I tell them the Harry Redknapp quote...If he could pass a bar as well as he could pass a football... They laugh out loud in agreement!

The Mexicans include two brothers working in Saudi Arabia, one in Nuremburg and one living in Mexico... As the beer flows, we are asked whether we are a champignon or a cheeto...We have no clue of what they are talking about!!! It then transpires they are asking if we are circumcised... A mushroom!! Some topic of conversation between new friends!! By the way it wasn't a Spurs related question!! They say one of them is a mushroom and apparently a lady of the night once said she can tell a mushroom by the way a mushroom stands...They apparently have to stand differently as it is a sensitive area! This conversation is getting stranger by the minute!

Paul turns the conversation back to football and says to the guy living in Germany... I guess Mexico will be happy with a draw against Croatia tomorrow... He answers... Fuck that shit...We're going for the win! These guys are hilarious... As with everyone else out here...They say England were unlucky to lose both games but c'est la vie...

Somehow we end up in a taxi going to a club with them...Well except the Mushroom man who is stood a little differently to the rest of us!!

We get out of the taxi in a not too nice neighbourhood...At the Samba club... We are told that we will have to wait 15 minutes to get in and that it is a 40 reals entrance fee...Hmmm

While we are waiting to enter, I go with one of the Mexicans across the road to buy some beers.

There are prostitutes at 200 reals a time...How do I know? Because the Mexican walked straight up to the prettiest one and asked her without any introductions!

Sat outside the shop are two transsexuals...Big guys big breasts! This is way beyond seedy...I buy some beers and quickly get back to the rest of our group... As we wait to go in the club...We are surprised at how lovely some of the girls are who are coming out with their partners... Then a lady comes up to the door, knocks three times and is allowed to enter without queuing...Everything clicks into place...It is literally a knocking shop...The wait is for the girls to come

back... Paul and I jump in a taxi and go back to the hotel #narrowescape
The Mexicans decide to stay on or go somewhere else.
We get back at 2.15am...Another eventful day!

EL GRINGO'S ONCE IN A LIFETIME

Trips like this are the ones that remind you of how beautiful life can be. Not only because of the World Cup, the parties or the breathtaking landscapes, but also because of the people. They say that wherever you go becomes a part of you, well I feel like a part of me never left Brazil. Someday when the time is right I will go back and find these people and have another beer with them!

Gerardo Lopez, Alatorre, proud Mexican

The majority of the people in the Netherlands did not had any expectations. Yes, the Dutch team was undefeated in the pre-qualification but the last European Championship was disastrous and not forgotten. Also the famous "Oranjekoorts", the fever when everything colours Orange in the Netherlands was this time lower than with previous championships.

And the first game against Spain started as expected, till the second half and Holland won with 1-5!

From that moment on the Orange Fever came back. The Dutch team played un-Dutch, very defensive and unattractive, but won game after game to the surprise of everyone. Unknown players became stars, all the players and staff became one team and Louis van Gaal had every game a new surprise for the world.

Guido, Dutchman living in Rijswijk, Belgium

MONDAY 23RD JUNE 2014

Wake with the usual five minute hangover...Can we transfer these to England please...You can take Paulinho as a makeweight in the deal!! Sorry Paulinho...Only joking...But to be fair, five minute hangovers are priceless!

I receive a text from Sabina saying I can have the Argentina v Nigeria ticket for US$500.

On checking flights from Belo Horizonte to Porto Alegre which is the furthest southern based stadium...I look on the internet for flights...It just isn't possible to arrive on time for the lunch time kick off...Pity...

We are going to Olinda today which is where the Portuguese first landed in Brazil. There is an old town and a number of churches there.

I am really looking forward to visiting this historic early 16th Century colony...I think of the Rocks area in Sydney where the criminals were sent from England all those years ago...I am fascinated and in awe of those who travelled the high seas...Not knowing where they were going...Who would they face when or if they got there.

Last night one of the Brazilian guys, Jose gave me a brief summary of the early history...

It seems that after the Portuguese arrived, the Dutch followed...The Dutch invested in the infrastructure and started to collect taxes to cover the cost. The

Portuguese didn't like paying taxes and a war broke out with the Dutch losing and leaving. The Dutch then later went to North America and formed New York!! I recall a New York tour bus guide saying the Dutch, Peter Stuyvesant, bought New York for a single dollar and called it New Amsterdam.

Jose said how different and so much richer the country would have been had the Dutch won the war... Fascinating stuff!

Post note...I Googled Peter Stuyvesant...And he lost a leg in the war in Brazil and returned home to be given an artificial limb and thereafter was called "Silver Leg"...Long John Silver comes to mind! He then sailed across to North America and formed New Amsterdam. Worth a Google and read!

Back to the present day...Good news!! The phone has charged overnight... Can't begin to tell you how relieved I am!!

Paul and I head down for our hearty breakfast while Ian, feeling a lot better this morning, puts us to shame by going to the hotel gym.

The restaurant is jam packed today... Huge Mexican presence with a few Croatian shirts amongst them...The staff are struggling to cope...Juice containers need a refill, out of water melon, out of scrambled eggs...Gradually with well timed runs.. We manage to get all we need. The staff are lovely people and working so hard to keep up with the rush hour!

We take the lift to the 20th floor but the lift doesn't register and seems to have a mind of its own...We have a laugh about the Hollywood Tower of Terror Hotel at Disneyland... Where the lift based on the Twilight Zone takes you up to the highest level before opening up the walls and dropping to the ground floor at top speed...

The lift passes our floor...It continues rising...All the way to the top...We look nervously at each other!! The door opens...We jump out and take a different lift back to our floor!

We eventually get back to the room and with the agreement of the reception, we complete our on line check in and forward it the front desk to print the boarding tickets to Belo Horizonte.

Ian comes back from a 10km run in the gym and is a little red faced, taking a minute to get his breath back #topeffort

I pack to leave the hotel and we get ourselves ready for our trip to Olinda and go down to the reception for me to check out.

The checkout works well and I pay 345 reals for what turned out to be four nights. Ian looks outside and says are you sure you want to go to Olinda John?

It is absolutely pouring down!!

Sadly it is impossible to contemplate...We go into the restaurant to watch Holland v Chile...Not too shabby a second prize! Both teams have already qualified for the knock out phased. They are playing to avoid Brazil in the next round...

This is the first Dutch side not to have a "van" in the side since 2006...Paul is full of these types of statistics!

Ian says a group of Iranians who posted a clip on YouTube celebrating their country's performances in the World Cup so far...Have all been rounded up and arrested for over exuberance... What a crazy world we live on.

Elsewhere a journalist had his mosquito repellent confiscated inside a stadium because... Mosquitoes are not allowed in this stadium! And the Queen of Belgium congratulated Lukaku on his winner v Russia...Only it was Origi who got the winner!!

This sort of trivia always comes out when it's raining...A ha ...First day of Wimbledon...It's raining...Well at least here it is!

Sri Lanka score 457...England 31/0...We calculate that England will need c300 runs to win. Could be an entertaining final day!

It is half time 0-0 but what a run from his own half by Robben just before the break... He must be a frightening prospect for a defender to face in full flight ...Just put it passed the post...Would have been one of the best goals of the World Cup so far.

It is now 1.50 and it is still lashing down with rain...

The Budweiser advert comes on yet again...And for some reason Gary Cahill is the chosen Englishman to appear...It makes us smile every time we see the advert.

The TV doesn't show the highlights or even the score from the other game at half time. Brazilians are clearly not interested in also rans! Paul checks on line and David Villa has put Spain one up against Australia.

We started with such good intentions...Coca Colas and coffees between the three of us... Well that lasted for one round and three chopp (draught) beers are ordered...

Notice my developing Portuguese language skills...Priority words first... Obviously!! Obrigado... Always pays to be polite and say thank you...Two words...At least it's a start!

Finally the Villa goal is shown...Dreadful marking by Australia...

Paul sent some clothes down to the Hotel Laundry on Saturday. The clothes haven't been returned yet...It is now Monday afternoon and he leaves the hotel for Belo Horizonte at 3am tomorrow morning!! Paul now learns that because Brazil are playing this afternoon, the Hotel Laundry is closed for the rest of today and all day tomorrow!

Fer puts Holland a goal up against Chile. Paul says his friend, Bradders who is an Ipswich fan will not be happy! Local rivalries have this impact...Even when the club players are playing internationally!

The crowd at the Holland v Chile are incredibly colourful...A mix of the Dutch bright orange, the red of Chile and the bright yellow of local Brazilians!

Memphis Depay scores a second for Holland... This is the player who was in the car outside the Cesar Hotel on Ipanema beach on our first Sunday in Brazil... As a result I feel some sort of connection #tenuous

England slump to 57 for 5 against Sri Lanka...Plunkett out last ball of the day...We calculate that across their two innings, England have lost 12 wickets in scoring 112 runs... Cook must be under the spotlight...

I go up to the room to charge my iPhone and change into clothes which will need to last me until I check in to the hotel in Belo Horizonte aftr the match tomorrow night...Going to be a long 24 hours...Three flights, two matches, a night in the air or at airports...Whilst in the room I call the reception and hopefully manage to sort out Paul's laundry...

On returning to the guys, Paul says he had also been to the reception and is now assured of receiving his clothes today...I imagine the staff member called in won't be too happy...Not unreasonable to expect laundry to be returned by Monday night...Would have been Wednesday at the earliest...!!

Torres and Mata each score in a game of interest to no one...Actually...Not quite true...Villa has been subbed in his last game for Spain and is crying on the bench...Having being consoled by Casillas. What a terrible decision by Del Bosque...As if he hasn't had a bad enough World Cup already...

So the Dutch top the Group with Chile finishing second. Chile versus Brazil in the knock out phase...Should be some game.

We leave the hotel at 3.08pm ahead of the 5pm kick off and take a taxi to Antonio Falcao metro station. Outside the station I buy some beads in Brazilian yellow and green for my daughter Molly. Inside the station, the same ladyboy or transvestite is there...Good photo opportunity!

We take the metro and after the change of trains at Joana Bezerra, Paul is in desperate need of the bathroom and gets off the train at a station on route. We suggest getting off to wait with him but he won't hear of it and will meet us at the stadium.

EL GRINGO'S ONCE IN A LIFETIME

Colin texts to say I can stay at their apartment in Flamengo from Thursday until Sunday.

Both Ian and I also need the bathroom but not quite as urgently as Paul and vow to get to the stadium #uncomfortable

I text Sabina to ask if it would be possible to hold off from selling the Argentina v Nigeria ticket for 24 hours. If all works out I could see this match in Porto Alegre, fly back to Rio and then hopefully go to Colombia v Italy or Uruguay in the Maracana in Rio on Saturday.

We reach our destination, Cosme E Damaio metro station and are relieved to find restroom facilities at the station...Phew!!

Walking towards the bus, a happy to be alive Brazilian guy insists on a photograph with me. He is a funny man! Strange that expression...It can have different meanings. Just to be clear I don't mean funny as in weird! The English language has such a large vocabulary and yet can still be so confusing!

Just as the bus sets off towards the stadium, Ian thinks he caught a glimpse of Paul coming out of the metro station. Walking towards the stadium, it has the feeling of being a home game for Mexico. The outfits of the Mexicans are amazing...Many in Sombrero hats and wearing the dark green coloured shirts of their team.

At a suitable point we stand to one side of the masses and wait for Paul who joins us within a couple of minutes. We are surprised at how quickly he caught up...Paul says the station master allowed him to use the staff's facilities...Can just see London Underground staff allowing that!!

We say our goodbyes until tomorrow morning in Belo Horizonte.

Walking towards my entrance I overhear English voices and meet Mark Juliette and Jan outside the stadium from Mapperley, Nottingham, and my home city! They tell me that their daughter who was away from them for literally a couple of minutes was robbed at knife point in Jacuma, Natal...It was a truly horrific experience for her...

After the confiscation of the journalist's mosquito repellent, I am worried about my rucksack being searched on entering the stadium...Contact lenses, toiletries etc...Any worries over the search of my rucksack on entering the stadium dissipate...It was thankfully a half hearted effort!

I buy a Coca Cola on the concourse...There isn't a queue...But it takes forever to just serve me...Incredibly slow...The drinks are served in cups specific to each match and detail the stadium, the teams and the date on the outside of the cup. They are collector's items for the fans who can be seen carrying taking them away from each match. I walk in to the stadium to be greeted by a sea of green with quite a lot of yellow too. There is also the odd red and white checked table cloth.

The atmosphere is electric!!

I feel very close to the action...For those who know the stadium...Block 127, Row I Seat 28...Lower tier behind the goal just to the right of the goal between the six and eighteen yard box.

Every Croatian goal kick, free kick, corner... The Mexican fans put both arms out in front of their body and start an off putting noise which gets louder and louder and ends with an enormous roar. At its crescendo, their arms fly in the air. Seeing and hearing fans at English grounds trying to put a keeper off as he launches into a goal kick...Always feels a bit of a pointless exercise...But seeing and hear almost a whole stadium make such a noise...It is a hugely intimidating atmosphere.

There are whistles, horns...It is a cacophony of noise... I have never heard anything like it before in my life #amazing

It is good to see Modric and Corluka again...Dos Santos too! I always enjoyed watching them play for Spurs. After his hair cut, it is not easy to distinguish Modric on the pitch without those long flowing locks. Corluka looks very trim... Seems to have lost quite a lot of weight.

Croatia are trying to take the sting out of the game...Retaining the ball... Trying to quell the noise...Not working...Every single pass is being jeered...Not just by a few...But by every Mexican fan in the stadium #incredible!!!

The black clouds are threatening a downpour but nothing will dampen this crowd...Although being close to the front...I would get soaked...And have a night on the plane in these clothes...A problem for later!

This match needs a strong referee...Would need balls of steel to give a Croatia a penalty!!

Ha...The funny Brazilian guy from outside the stadium is sat, sorry stood four rows directly in front of me urging fans to sing louder...So happy in the moment and having the time of his life!

Mexico hit the bar!! Seconds later a huge roar goes up...Sending shivers down my spine...Tingles, goose bumps the lot!! Brazil have gone one up against Cameroon! This is loco!

The Brazil fans sing their song... A lot of them here considering their team playing...

Never known anything like this...So much noise I can't think straight... So much going on...On the pitch, Mexican fans and now the Brazilian fans #onceinalifetime

Finally I notice to my left Croatia fans are stood trying to make themselves heard... Impossible!!! They are not that far away from me...First time I have heard and therefore noticed them...Sure it's not been for the want of trying...

I feel for Croatia...Two of their three group games...Today and against Brazil in the opening match have been to all intents and purposes away games...Tough on them.

Now there is an authentic Mexican Wave circling the stadium...It is utter and complete bedlam here... Fans wearing sombreros, face masks, loads of colourful outfits...Some spectacle!

The whole stadium is rocking...Me-hi-co! Me-hi-co! Me-hi-co!

Brazil guy with a radio behind me lets out an anguished cry...I put a finger up from each other hand to question 1-1? He nods in frustrated anger...Later I learn he is Alessandro (Alex) Vasconcelos living in Charlotte USA but from Recife and with his parents at the game

Because of Modric and Corluka I want Croatia to win in this winner takes all game but would love Mexico to score just to see the reaction or rather hear the reaction of the fans...The place would go bananas!!

Mexico corner...Melee under the crossbar ends in a scuffle. The fans are right up for that!! Croatia break away...Free kick edge of box... Booking... dangerous position...Crowd jeers even louder if that is possible! The ball dips but not enough and it sails over the bar.

Started to rain... I will get soaked...

Brazil 2-1 Neymar has scored both goals...He could be the pin up of the World Cup! Fans sing their song again. Alex tells me it is sung by all fans at league games too...It is a happy song... Well at least it was until the Argentines

bastardised it!

Half time 0-0...Try restroom with ruck sack impossible and especially with carrying all my valuables... Will have to suffer...

I go back to my seat and Alex asks tells me his nephew Tiago is studying in the UK until September... He is studying in a small place and do I know it...Lincoln?!! Know it? I was born there! Un-bloody-believable. We exchange details.

Alex and his parents suggest I avoid the streets when coming out of the metro at the Aeropuerto station...There is a Passarela...An indoor overhead walkway...I appreciate their helpful advice.

Brazil 3-1...Fred this time...Huge roar again...Song again...They need more songs!

20 minutes to go...Croatia need a goal or they are going out. Still a cacophony of noise... It hasn't relented throughout the entire game.

Mexicans scream for a penalty...Not given...

Mexico corner...I take a photograph as the ball comes over...Marquez rises... Downward header...Pletikosa should do better...But he doesn't...The ball crosses the line!!! 1-0 Mexico!!!!!!!...The roar!!! OMG!!!Pandemonium!!! Drinks flying through the air...The stadium is bouncing!!!

Olé shouts now to every pass

With the goal being scored, I decide now is a good time to use the facilities...I run up the steps...There is a roar of anticipation...I turn round...Mexico breaking...2-0 bonkers!!! Words almost fail

me...Deliriously bonkers...Does that even make sense!!

I go out on to the concourse...Disconsolate, shell shocked Croatian fans are milling around. The clock is running down...The result is clear... Mexico are going through. I just want to sample a little more of this remarkable atmosphere...I go back into the stadium and stand at the back of the lower tier...There is a party mood...All the stress has gone...Mexico corner...Hernandez...3-0!!! Brazil score a fourth!!! Another set of fans go crazy...This is some occasion...It really is!!

Party time...Crazy night ahead in Recife!!

Olé Olé Brazil

Olé Olé Mexico

86th minute Croatia have gone and sadly so have I!!

It is close to 7pm and my fight is 9.55pm...I need to get a wiggle on!!

I run uphill...It is muggy...It is a long way...I have been drinking for the last ten days...I am 55 years old...Hmmm...

I run passed a guy with Van de Vaart on the back of his Spurs shirt and give him the thumbs up.

I am quickly on to the bus and hear that Croatia scored and had a man sent off in the closing minutes! I am on the metro by 7.11 and chatting with Croatian fans. Being English I am able to empathise with how it feels to be knocked out of the World Cup...Once other nations feared England fans...Now they pity us... Is it too much to hope that one day they might envy us! The Croatian fans are disappointed with their team's performance but don't believe the Mexican fans had an influence...May be the pitch...May be just one of those days where the team didn't play at their best...

Croatian fan flying back to Melbourne... Wow!

It is twelve stops to Joana Bezerra metro station where I change from the yellow to the blue line direction Cajueiro Seco for a further six stops to Aeropuerto metro station.

Dave from Boston USA is talking with his friends on the metro and has a twist on a theme... Once in a 24 year lifetime! They take my email address for the book.

Fortunately my iPhone battery seems to be holding up today...Lots of writing and as well photos taken plus a few texts and 4 hours 20 minutes since last charging the battery, it still has 66% left plus the reserve of the battery charger case.

I come out of the Aeropuerto metro station and take the indoor overhead walkway called the Passarela. It takes me straight to the airport...One of the moving walkways isn't working...7 years to prepare...three or four matches will be played here and it isn't not working...Nevertheless by 8.07pm I am inside the airport terminal for my 9.55pm Azul 4254 flight to Sao Luis via Teresina...To then have a 1am to 3am stopover before flying on to Belo Horizonte arriving 6.10am ahead of the England v Costa Rica lunch time kick off. No bed tonight... Hope Roy and the boys read what we fans go through to follow the team...

When I booked everything...The schedule between 7pm tonight and 6am in the morning not only looked quite horrendous but my greatest concern as to whether logistically it would work ok.

My first concern was as to whether there would be enough time from leaving the match to catching the flight. The first leg has been accomplished!!

The second concern was how to manage my luggage in terms of going to the match... Especially as there was so little time to even consider returning to the hotel to collect it after the game. Living out of the rucksack solved that problem!

The third concern is still ahead of me...Will the flight connections through the night work out ok?

The fourth concern of falling asleep between landing at 1.01am in Sao Luis and the 3.10am connection to Belo Horizonte and therefore missing my flight is also still ahead of me.

The fifth concern of protecting my valuables should I doze off whilst waiting for my connection is also very real.

The sixth concern as to whether any of the flights might be cancelled is also still very real...

Six concerns!! Yes I am a worrier and yes it's a driver!!

While waiting for my flight, I reflect on the World Cup and the Brazilian people.

It has been a similar story in Rio de Janeiro, Sao Paulo and Recife and I guess replicated across the other nine host cities...The vast majority of local people getting a glimpse of fans passing through in their colours and outfits like a passing carnival or parade. It is also a once in a life time experience for the locals. They are hanging over bridges, sitting and standing outside their homes to see us...There is an enormous event...A huge party in their district but like Cinderella they don't have an invitation to join the party.

Seeing the ghettos, the Favelas...Many homes are shelters; others have crumbling concrete walls which would be considered as well beyond derelict in the western world...I wonder about sanitation and other utilities...The way millions live...It is easy to understand the concerns as to whether public monies should be allocated to a party which requires paying for afterwards... And yet between the lines of houses, across the makeshift street, the locals have put up green and yellow bunting. They are sharing in the extravaganza as best as they can...

Not to condone but as in most countries, it is understandable as to why some might resort to crime...

Therefore because of the few, the majority sadly can't get too close to us... There is heavy security...It feels as if we need to be protected #shame

I go into a shop and ask if I can charge my phone. Sabina texts to say she will hold the ticket for me.

No restaurant air side. I have a sandwich at the airport and buy a couple of beers for the journey ahead.

The flight to Teresina hasn't been cancelled and is on time! On the flight I chat with a young lady who is with her parents and having been to the game is flying back to her home.

There is a 30 minute wait on the runway whilst passengers disembark and others come on board. Another young lady called Priscilla sits next to me for the flight to São Luis.

I open up a can of beer and halfway through, the waitress takes it off me as alcohol is not allowed to be drunk on the flight...

EL GRINGO'S ONCE IN A LIFETIME

Priscilla looks about 18 but is in fact 30! #staggered. She says that as a student cash is tight. Her family live in her home city of Teresina and takes every opportunity to return home from Sao Luis where she works and studies as a medical student. Overnight flights are cheaper but Priscilla will be at work from 6am until as late as 10pm...Works seven days a week and yet has an infectious personality...Might be coming to London in February or August 2015. I suggest August would be better as February would be incredibly cold for a Brazilian in London! We exchange email addresses and say goodbye on leaving the plane in Sao Luis. It is 1.01am.

I go to the departure gate for my 3am onward flight to Belo Horizonte, charge my phone, update my diary and maybe doze a little, clutching my rucksack with all of my valuables contained therein. The flight isn't cancelled and takes off on time!

I board the plane and eventually close my eyes to signal the end of a very long but enjoyable day.

The World Cup is here again, yippee. Full of excitement, late nights and early mornings; staying up or getting up to watch your team. Bleary eyed, maintaining focus, watching the lads only to be disappointed again. Oh well at least an early exit means we can relax and enjoy the rest of the games. Most memorable game; has to be Australia v Netherlands, open, entertaining, end to end game at a relentless pace that produced the Cahill wonder goal. Not sure my German colleague agrees with me though!

Stuart Patch, an Englishman living in Sydney, Australia

Malaysia is probably one of the most football-mad countries in Asia (if not the world), and I'd struggle to think of another country that has never qualified for the World Cup that would have as much interest in it. There is a lot of interest in football in the country, and whilst some may find it surprising how knowledgeable Malaysian fans are of football in general, I do not. This huge interest is also why there is an influx of Malaysian football club owners (Tony Fernandes at Queens Park Rangers and Vincent Tan at Cardiff - although you could argue if they know enough about the industry to be involved in the first place!). Also, many Malaysian companies sponsor English Premier League matches (many of the pitch side advertising boards have Malaysian brands on them).

During the World Cup, the entire country virtually came to a standstill, and the 13-15 hour time difference certainly didn't deter many from watching the matches. I know of many friends and colleagues who even made their way to Brazil to watch some matches - which is a pretty big investment, traveling almost the entire circumference of the planet when your country isn't involved!

Jia Wei, Kuala Lumpur, Malaysia.

TUESDAY 24TH JUNE 2014

It feels a little strange rolling the calendar forward a day to a new day after an hour or so's sleep on the flight between São Luis and Belo Horizonte...But as much as I would like to have a longer sleep it isn't looking very likely...

Today is my daughter Molly's 17th birthday! I send a text to wish her a happy birthday. I would like to call her but it is mid-morning in the UK and she will be at school. I will call her after school.

It is now 6.49am and I am currently sat in the airside lounge at an uncomfortable angle charging my phone whilst of course using it and waiting for Paul and Ian to land.

The socket is in the wall behind me and the iPhone lead as anyone who has an iPhone will know is very short...So I am contorted in a side on position...Fellow travellers seeing me...unshaven, no sleep, sat at such a funny angle...No doubt rolling their eyes...Gringos!

The day hasn't started too smoothly...

I have been trying to contact Bravofly in the UK to change my flight back to the UK. There isn't any Wi-Fi at the airport to send an email...I try to dial the UK number by dialling the usual international dialling code of 00 44...A message comes up in Portuguese the gist of which is that I have dialled an incorrect number...I try various combinations...Including the zero of the city which would normally be dropped, in desperation ignoring the international dimension altogether but I can't dial back to the UK. On an hour's sleep this is not what I need. I ask a Brazilian couple who listen to the message but are not sure what to do.

They Google and suggest I dial 00 44 41 and then the city code. It doesn't work. They don't know what more to say and I thank them for trying to help me. A few minutes later the lady returns and shows me a page on Google which shows the international dialling code is 00 41 44...it seems I have to dial out of Belo Horizonte which is the reason for the 41 before connecting to the UK exchange number 44...No wonder so many people have been having problems!

I dial Bravofly's number and bravo I get through to an automated message saying that all their operators are busy...Would I kindly hold...Hmm not exactly what you want to hear when dialling from Brazil on a mobile phone... I wait... And I wait...And I wait...Another automated message comes through saying it is not possible to take my call right now... Kindly call back later...Grrrr...

I leave it a few minutes and redial...Same automated message but this time lo and behold I actually reach a person. I explain that I would like to extend my stay in Brazil...The conversation seems to be going well and then he goes and spoils it all by saying he will have to contact the airline to see whether it is possible and what the cost would be. He understands the urgency and will send me an email today...As at this stage I only have confirmed accommodation until Colin returns on Sunday 29th we agree to have multiple dates checked...29th June plus 5th, 6th, 12th and 13th July.

I hope the email arrives in time for my arrival at the hotel when I will hopefully have access to Wi-Fi.

I am in a race against time. It is now 7.23 and I need to go to the Tam desk to understand the possibility of flying to Porto Alegre for the Argentina v Nigeria game which is a 1 pm kick off tomorrow. The logistics suggest the only way would be to have another night of flying but let's see...The race against time is to charge my telephone. It is now up to 94% which gives me approximately 20 minutes to try to sort out flight tickets before the guys arrive.

The Tam sales staff say I can use my Belo Horizonte to Rio flight for the same price to fly from Porto Alegre to Rio and flights are available...Good news!

The problem at the moment...There is only one flight at 6.42 am with Azul... three seats left but at a price of 1138 reals...£308...

Tam doesn't have any availability. Only chance left is Gol...

I queue with the early morning travellers...No chance with Gol...

Since Argentina v Bosnia in the opening days of the tournament...I seemed destined not to see Argentina live...

We arrive at the ground at 9am.

An hour's journey and the bus driver drives passed the ground and drops us 1/2 mile plus away!

Heavy military presence...Ticket check at one end of a 50 yard barriered corridor...And then again at the other end!!

Paul has arranged to meet some friends at a restaurant called Jus Elino. We wait outside for 30 minutes for it to open and pay 30 reals c£10 to enter a bar/restaurant! The price has gone up 5 reals since Argentina played here as they wrecked the place...We are effectively paying an Argentine tax!!

It is so just after 10am and already it is very hot...England fans sitting out with a beer in the heat of the sun...Not sure the England players will enjoy the heat of the sun some three hours later!!!!

We are good boys and all three of us order a Coke Zero...It doesn't last long though and the next round is three beers!! Strangely called Bavarian beer.

The food is excellent...A roast beef risotto with mushroom sauce. Highly recommended when you are next in the area.

The Costa Rican team bus passes by our bar. Oh to be in their position today...

I receive a phone call from Bravofly...Hungary office!! If I change my ticket to Sunday 29th June the adjustment price will be over €1000... That will be a no then! Better news if I change to 6th or 13th July... The adjustment price will be €130... My initial reaction is to stay on until 13th July after the World Cup...I need to sort accommodation though...If I stay it would be easier to take in the Argentina match.

The one hour sleep last night is not helping right now!!!

The England team coach passes and I am able to take a photograph and post it onto twitter almost instantaneously for the World to see...Technology really is amazing...

Paul's friends don't make it in time and suggest meeting in the bar after the game...Another 30 reals entrance fee...Thanks for the offer!

Entry into the stadium seems quicker and easier in Belo Horizonte than São Paulo but it is again a bit of a walk.

Who could have imagined that England would have come into this game on nil points...As also rans...With Costa Rica on six points and having already qualified for the knock out phase...And just needing a point to top the Group.

National anthems played and England fans give a passionate rendition of "God save the Queen" in front of Prince Harry.

Lot of Brazilian yellow in the stadium alongside the white of England with the red, white and blue of Costa Rica settling for third place.

Less than 2 minutes gone Rica almost score!

England's going home is humorously sung by our fans...Can't

help but have a sense of sadness that the game has absolutely no meaning for us. Thousands have saved thousands of pounds to come out here and are at a meaningless match. The renowned English sense of humour comes to the fore!

Sturridge hits a good shot but wide of the post.

Always look on the bright side of life now being sung. It's good not to take ourselves seriously but not sure the foreigners in the ground will quite understand our humour!

A Mexican wave starts...It reaches the England section...England dip out of the Mexican Wave and immediately lose the neutrals with a hail of boos and whistles being aimed at them. The English in general struggle to mix football with Mexican Waves...That goes for me too...The Brazilians start chanting "Eliminated"... England fans respond with who are ya, who are ya...Hmm they are called Brazil five times World Champions! Not the most intelligent of responses!!

Great tip onto the bar by Foster from a Rica free kick... Many fans don't feel Foster deserves a game...Lot of talk in the bar before the game and from people in the stadium...Having turned his back on England for quite a while...The fans feel he should not be picked to play in a World Cup Finals game...

In the heat my tiredness is overwhelming me...Could easily be picked out by the TV crews zzzzing in the corner... The commentator saying something along the lines of...There's an England fan who has had a little too much to drink in the heat! Today nothing could be further from the truth....Well today anyway... And only so far today!

Sturridge goes down in the area at the far end to me...Difficult to know from the opposite end whether it was a penalty or not.

Military police brought in to help the stewards ask the England fans to sit down in the upper tier...They don't seem to be having much success.

England fans now singing...Shall we sing a song for you? Not sure who the song is aimed at...Brazil or Rica?

Sturridge can't quite get on top of the ball and heads over...Shot driven in by Barclay...England looking the better side...Probably go one down in a minute!

England fans start their funniest song yet...It's just like watching Brazil!!

Half time 0-0

An advert for the World Cup comes on the big screen and there is a rapper in a white suit, bald head with and without sunglasses...Looks the image of the Tottenham Hotspur Chairman Daniel Levy!! So that's how you spend the summer Daniel!! No wonder you have to leave all your transfer activity until the 3first August!

It's been said that the most beautiful ladies are in Belo Horizonte...During the interval the camera man zooms in on lady after lady...Drawing applause from the crowd...OK Mr Cameraman everyone in the stadium is convinced!!

Half time passes without any information on the Italy v Uruguay game... Thanks for the communication...Everybody in the world watching on television knows the score...Those that make the effort to come and pay a lot of money even at face value are not informed...Hmmm.

Sturridge misses another chance through a poor first touch...Ffs

Now he mis-controls and shortly after so does Jones...Wilshire elects to take on the whole Rican defence instead of playing the ball out to the right wing... Judgement?

Rica start to time waste aware a draw would be enough to top the group.

Defensive error by Jones and Foster is called on to make a save from a long range shot...

England fans start singing...Let's pretend we scored a goal...Echoes of watching Spurs last season...Sturridge misses again...Banjo and barn door...

Sturridge through again...Takes too long...Tries to make it look as if he is fouled...He wasn't...Corner.

Gerrard and Rooney receive rapturous applause from the neutrals as well as the England fans when they come on for Wilshire and Milner.

We now end the tournament with Gerrard and Lampard in the centre of midfield...Yes the partnership that didn't work in 2002 and has consistently failed ever since...What a depressing way to end a depressing tournament for England.

57283 attendance.

Brazilian guy behind me with 3G tells me...Uruguay take the lead against Italy... My word...Looks like Italy are going out too!!

Into the less 5 minutes and the crowd Olé Rica...Who could ever have imagined a crowd Olé 'ing a string of Costa Rica passes v England in a World Cup Finals match...

Trouble between England and Brazil fans...Drinks and plastic glasses being thrown...Riot police come in...Eliminated rings out from around the stadium...

The riot police are all facing the England fans. The national anthem which was applauded 15 minutes ago is now being drowned out with boos.

It finishes 0-0...An ignominious exit by England...1 point out of 9...2 goals scored; 4 conceded. At least they managed a draw against the Group winners!

The whole squad come over to applaud the fans at the end...And so they should.

The day belongs to Rica who are undefeated in the Group and finish top with 7 points out of 9.

It is an incredibly long walk back to catch the bus into town. Restroom

facilities are at a premium...The bus ride back into town is even longer...We are stood on a crowded bus in the heat, every gear change or braking manoeuvre leaving us clinging on for dear life #cattletrain

We get off the bus and it's a long walk up hill and down dale to the hotel... Very hilly!!

The four star grandly named Best Western Belo Horizonte Sol hotel gives the illusion of being grand... Until I enter the room!! Lights don't work, soap dishes on the bathroom and shower room hang off the wall, the sockets to charge phones are plated over...Luckily I find one they missed. The fan above the shower is so strong it is blowing the glass shower door open...I only told you to blow the bloody doors off comes to mind!!!

I forgot to mention the hotel check in...The hotel registration form which is apparently required by the Police is so detailed...I mean...Could you remember what you had for breakfast 11th January 2012... Well not quite that bad but you get the picture...

I go up to the room and try to sort out the Porto Alegre flight. I can land at 9.07 ahead of the lunch time kick off. The flight will cost c£300. However I cannot get flight to Rio until Thursday so I will need somewhere to stay over on the Wednesday night. The good news is that the airline will transfer my Belo Horizonte to Rio ticket to a Porto Alegre to Rio ticket without any extra cost. If the girls can sort that, I will try to change my Rio reservation from the 25th to 26th with Vitoria...Unlikely but worth a punt...

I text and text again...The network connection seems to be down and there also seems to be an issue for Sabina who had to text from her friend's phone. With being in the South (Alien concept for us to think back to front!), the temperature is also a concern as friends of Paul have fed back as to just how cold it is. I can muster up a pair of jeans but not a sweater or jacket...Paul texts me to say there is a cat 1 ticket available on the FIFA web site which will cause an issue with her brother in law who wants 500USD...

I still haven't changed my flight...At this stage I am still flying back to the UK on the 26th June.

I make the decision that if the ticket is still available and they can put me up for the night I will go down to Porto Alegre to watch Argentina v Nigeria. To avoid risks of getting there and not being able to get in contact by phone...An airport pick up would seem to be a must...Big ask though...

Paul and Ian know where to go for our night out in Belo Horizonte... We set off by foot and it's a long walk to Savassi which is the local happening place... We pass the floodlit Palace of Independence...The streets and roads are very busy in a vibrant way...There is a good feel to Belo Horizonte and also a sense that it is a little wealthier than the other cities we have visited.

On the way I call Molly to wish her happy birthday. Great to hear her voice! She is having a fabulous day!!

Savassi is buzzing...Heaving with people!!! Every corner we turn round... Chocker...The day has been exhausting for all of us...We need to find a bar where we can sit, have a beer and watch both matches on different screens simultaneously! A big ask!! We find ourselves walking a little further out and end up in a small back street bar.

Rumours are circulating of another Suarez biting incident...Surely not again...The rumour seems to have quickly turned into something more concrete...We learn the incident is under investigation by FIFA!!! Oh my...Will this guy never learn...What the hell is wrong with him...If he has bitten a player...This will be at least the third time it has happened...

James scores a cracking last minute fourth goal for Colombia against Japan in the last minute...He looks to be some player...And Colombia look some team...Three straight wins...Scoring 9 goals in the process. Could they be dark horses to win the whole thing? Not only good going forwards but also strong defensively...Only conceded a couple of goals in their three group games...

Mr Nigeria will be very happy!! Bony's equaliser v Greece is taking his team through with 4 points! Bony looked good for Swansea last season and now doing it on the biggest stage of all...Hard to believe Greece won the Euros in 2004... How on earth did that happen!! Strangely Denmark did it too in 1992 having not even qualified...The end of Yugoslavia as a team...

The beer is going down very well!!! Thirsty work today!!

Into added time...Greece attack...Into the area...Penalty given!!! Looks harsh?? Replay...Never a penalty...Samaras standing over the ball...If he scores to make it 2-1...Greece qualify...It looks a shocking decision...I want him to miss...But he doesn't...Poor Mr Nigeria...No time to come back...Final whistle blows...Mr Nigeria's World Cup is over...Somebody is in for a miserable flight to Paris very soon!!! Hope they have their American football playing protection on!!

So...Greece play Costa Rica in the last 16...Wow one of these will be in the Quarter Finals of the World Cup!!! What was I just writing about Greece!! What odds on them winning the World Cup!!

Bars spilling out onto the streets in Savassi!! Its one enormous street party... We can't believe the beauty of the women. Any hot blooded young guys looking at where to go on holiday...Look no further!!!

Just seen that the Italians received a red card...Only my opinion again...But to me it looks a very poor decision...

Now watching the Suarez incident...It looks a clear bite on the shoulder...The guy needs a muzzle...We wonder whether FIFA will fudge it to let him play in the Maracana v Colombia in the Quarter Finals on Saturday...But what if they do and there is another incident??A huge star but...

Not heard back from the Argentine girls. I say it looks like its back to Rio for me in the morning... Paul says... Life's a bitch...What a hardship!

We are drinking in the streets...People have come straight from the game... Great atmosphere... English fans take centre stage with flags of the cross of St George strung up wherever possible. Costa Ricans, Colombians and Brazilians are relegated to the fringes...This is England's last night of the 2014 World Cup and we are determined to enjoy it!!

The beers, the caipirinhas, the vodkas (I may regret the vodka in the morning!) are flowing as are the songs...The full repertoire tonight even the 10, 9, 8, 7... German bombers shot down by the RAF from England song is remembered. The younger English guys are having a great time with the Brazilian girls...That bloody genie...Kissing and exchanging email addresses...it's one huge party...

Food is forgotten...Again...

My voice can't cope with much singing!! I lost it in Lapa a week ago...And it hasn't come back yet...If you were my voice would you!!!

Eventually we leave the square to head back...Walk round the corner and there is a bar full of English fans singing to the music...We can't resist...She loves you, Hey Jude, Wonderwall... Sing a long after sing a long!!! What a night!!!

It is a perfect last evening with Paul and Ian. We sit down for a final quiet beer and reflect on our time together. The end of our joint World Cup experience...I am so grateful to Paul and Ian for allowing me to join their trip and at such short notice; Especially Ian as we hadn't even met before the trip! We say our goodnights and our farewells.

I get to bed at 1.45...Up early in the morning to fly back to Rio de Janeiro... Yaay!!!

EL GRINGO'S ONCE IN A LIFETIME

For me, I always imagined Rio de Janeiro to be some sort of holiday paradise, full of cultural landmarks, scantily clad women on Copacabana beach, and of course football. And it was not too far off my expectations.

Sadly though I felt a little let down by Rio. Our hotel was ten minutes away from Copacabana but felt a million miles away. There was so much poverty, homeless people seemed to be everywhere. I could understand why some people in Brazil felt the need to protest against Brazil holding the World Cup. Sao Paulo seemed to be much worse than Rio. The riches of the World Cup and the money spent in Brazil in holding the tournament as compared with the poverty left a bit of a sour taste in my mouth.

As for the football I had been in the country for less than 24 hours and England had been eliminated. That put a bit of a dampener on our group's trip so we headed to Rio after England's second group game. The final group game against Costa Rica was meaningless for England in terms of the World Cup... So we decided to return to England early rather than go to Belo Horizonte for the final group game. I arrived back to my house in Nottingham and watched us play out a 0-0 draw dreaming of what might have been.

I then re-sold my remaining 'conditional" tickets to FIFA for the semi- final and final. I then had to wait 30 days for a refund which meant FIFA benefited on the interest of about £1450 which I had been required to pay to just secure these conditional tickets. Some might say...Not a bad little earner for FIFA!

Paul Revill, Nottingham, UK

Absolute disappointment......That the class of 2014 will be remembered as the worst England squad to grace the World Cup! The excitement of organising parties, barbecues, altering work, holidays, social and business events to coincide with the England games went out like a damp squib before we had even time to spark up the fire.

Banners, flags red, white and blue outfits were abandoned as we soulfully watched the rest of the world give a dazzling performance as we drank our beer and ate our hotdogs!

Joyce Saul, Birmingham, UK.

It was a day after Italy's first game at the World Cup in Brazil and the expectancy of glory was suddenly high in the country of sun, sea and pasta. Unusually high I thought. Too high...Could it be that the normally so overly pessimistic Italian population when it comes to their national team's chances, were now for once being overly positive? Were they not setting themselves up for a likely fall? I had my fears.

The answer came quickly and brutally in the shape of Costa Rica and Uruguay. And as Chiellini's shoulder slowly healed after the bite marks of a certain Uruguayan striker, Italy found themselves having to start a sporting project for the national team over once again. Both the head coach and president of the FA had left their positions just hours after the World Cup exit. The horizon that had seemed so sunny and promising just weeks ago now suddenly looked gloomy and uncertain…

Claus Wolny, Florence, Italy

WEDNESDAY 25TH JUNE 2014

Alarm call at 4.30am…three hours sleep to go with my one hour the night before.

I still feel a little drunk from last night…Come on John…Wits about you…

Don't leave anything in the hotel room.

Reception organised a taxi for me and it is waiting outside to take me to the airport…It is 4.50am…The driver wants to talk football along the lines of England's demise but I fall asleep to be woken at the airport with a fare of 135 reals…Wtf!!

Check in is automated…The queue is too long for this time of morning and the fragile state I am in…Without even being asked a kindly member of the TAM airline staff completes the check in for my 7.04 flight to Rio de Janeiro. Do I look that bad???

The only non-middle seat is on the back row 24D…I take it and fall asleep…

But isn't it amazing how we wake for a ham and cheese sandwich with an orange juice before falling back to sleep during the hour long flight…Suffice to say I don't wake again until we land.

On the shuttle bus to the terminal, I get talking with a BBC guy who is lugging heavy satellite kit round. He has a friend with two spare tickets for the Colombia versus Uruguay last sixteen game at the Maracana…I would "bite" his hand off for a ticket and he takes my number.

8.15am on the bus from Santos Dumont airport to Copacabana to the Savoy Othon to pick up my luggage and check in at its sister hotel on the seafront.

It feels good to be back into Rio de Janeiro!

I walk into the Savoy Othon to pick up my luggage…Hmm…Breakfast…I didn't have one the morning I left… As Sven would say…Why not? Maybe I did…Maybe I didn't…

It is still early morning, good to relax in the lobby for a while posting stuff on Twitter and catching up with emails before retrieving my suitcase. I really hope I can get a ticket for France versus Ecuador today…As fantastic as the trip has been, as much as I have enjoyed the football I have seen…There would be a sense of disappointment to miss out on a match at the Maracana… The venue of the World Cup Final… The stadium is as iconic to Brazil as Wembley is to England…

I decide to walk to the California Othon on Avenida Atlantique and lug my suitcase a few paces along Nossa Senhora before turning right on to Xavier da Silveira. I stop off at the travel agency...George tells me the price of a ticket for today's game is 1500 reals...Just over £400 for France versus Ecuador...My oh my...

I arrive at the California Othon Hotel and am checked in by 10.30 but the room won't be available until 11.30.

As much as the thought appals me, if I want to see a World Cup match in the Maracana, it seems that I will have to pay the going rate...1500 reals. It feels a once in a life time opportunity and I was fortunate to buy the England ticket at face value...#talkingmyselfintoit

I leave my luggage at the hotel and walk back up to Nossa Senhora to find a bank. I will need sufficient cash in hand to be able to buy a ticket. There are issues with the machines at the first bank but fortunately manage to withdraw up to a limit of 800 reals at the second. Phew that took longer than I expected...On the way back to the hotel, I see a guy in a French shirt and think what the hell...I ask in French if he has a spare ticket for today's game in... And he answers in English....Yes!!!!!!!!!!!!!!!!!

He then says that he wants to recover what he has paid....Here comes the kicker... But no he has paid 125 USD and wants 375 reals... Wow...A decent guy...He says the ticket is at his hotel and would I mind walking back with him... No, not at all!!

He asks me about speaking French and I say I worked in Belgium a couple of times and on Avenue Kleber in Paris...Franck used to work there too and it is highly likely that we were working there at the same time!

Franck has being living in Miami for five years and become more of a US sports fan in that time and especially basketball. I mention being a Spurs fan and that I am looking forward to seeing Hugo Lloris and he admits to not being much of a football fan...With being away from France for so long, he is not so up to date with the players.

Franck is a plastic surgeon and has taken the opportunity to stop off in Rio on his way to carry out work in French Guyana. Unfortunately his Ukrainian girlfriend wasn't able to obtain a visa in time so the spare ticket will actually be sat with him.

We arrive at his hotel and while I wait in the lobby for Franck to bring the ticket down from his room, I hear a group of guys sat speaking with English accents... I think...ummm, it worked once today and ask if they have a spare ticket for the Colombia versus Uruguay match at the Maracana on Saturday... They laugh and say unfortunately not...

I say to one of the guys...You look like Ray Houghton... And he replies... Maybe that is because I am Ray Houghton!! We laugh!!

I say you should have played for my team as your style would have fitted us perfectly...He asks who my team is and I reply...Not sure I should say as when listening to talkSPORT I always feel you don't like Spurs... He is surprised and says not at all... He lives quite close to Tottenham and is a fan... Many of his friends are Spurs supporters...I got that one wrong!

We talk about Suarez and Ray says when he was on air earlier today, he passed a view that his club need to support him...It's not the first time it has happened and it may be that the guy needs help.

We talk about the games we have been to and show photographs of our various games... I tell him the words of the Argentina Italia 90 song which makes him laugh...Ray was blown away by the atmosphere at Brazil's opening game versus Croatia. The noise levels were so loud, he couldn't hear himself think and said that when the fans sang the national anthem at the opening ceremony it made the hairs on the back of his neck stand up. He recorded it on his phone and plays it for me... Wow...How good must it have been to go to a Brazil home game!

We swap twitter addresses... Ray is a great guy...Very chatty, warm and friendly. One of his party is a Luton Town fan we talk about their promotion and the Conference which I have experience of through watching my birth city club...Lincoln City.

Having bought the ticket off Franck, I walk back to my hotel along Atlantique in the direction of Ipanema and am back in the reception by 11.45. Myrelle on reception remembers my name... Good service and says I can have the choice of a room on the fourth or tenth floor. I ask which her preference would be and she says the room on the tenth will have a good view over Copacabana...That does it for me and I take the lift and open the door to room 1003, my home for one night...And after Belo Horizonte last night...Another one night stand!

EL GRINGO'S ONCE IN A LIFETIME

The first thing I do of course is walk straight across to the window...The hotel is in a central location on Copacabana...I look out the window...Wow! Wow! Wow! The view is spectacular!!! Looking out to the left, I can see the whole of the beach, the fan fest and all the way down as it curves towards the rocks at Leme at the end of the beach... In fact I can see beyond the rocks, even beyond Sugar Loaf Mountain to the islands on the horizon.

Stretching out before me is the dual carriageway with the yellow taxis standing out against the darkness of the tarmac, the greenery including the palm trees, the promenade, and the golden sands of the beach contrasting with the nearer green waters and further out the dark blue waters of the Atlantic Ocean.

Looking to my right, a similar view of the curvature of the road and beach, the media centre all the way round to the fort at the end of beach, and the Arpoador Peninsula and rocks and islands beyond. Looking along the skyline of the buildings, the Pestana Budweiser hotel stands out but all are dwarfed by the Rio Othon Hotel at the junction of Xavier da Silveira and Avenida Atlantique.

I try to charge the phone...It is temperamental and getting worse...I am not sure whether it is the adapter into the socket, the UK plug, the cable from the plug to the phone or the connection through the charger case in to the actual phone...All I know is that it is becoming more and more fragile...#notgood

Following emails to and from Bravo, I decide for the price of £113 to extend to July 13th rather than July 6th i.e. until the end of the end of the World Cup.

I make a call to Bravo who say the change of flight has to be made 24 hours before the booked return flight...That means before 7.50p this evening. In the UK it is already after 4pm in the afternoon and as Bravo offices in Budapest and Madrid are dealing with me it is already very close to their closing time for the day...

They assure me, the office dealing with it will call me back immediately. I receive a call within ten minutes...The line is terrible...The call is from Budapest... English is not their first language which makes our dialects anyway difficult to understand...I walk out of the room...No better... I offer to go down to the Ground Floor and they say they will ring back in another ten minutes... They do but it isn't any better...I go outside and they say that they will have to confirm the seat is still available and will call back. I sit in the lobby and watch the Argentina versus Nigeria match...The game I almost went to...Messi smashes the ball in to the net after three minutes! Nigeria hit back within a minute with another good goal...Musa 1-1after 4minutes! Some start to the game!

I would really like to be watching the game in the fan fest but I can't...Time is against me...It is getting quite stressful...

I get talking to a lady in the lobby from Madrid who is living in São Paulo but doing her work remotely from Rio whilst the World Cup is on. She is writing a blog covering all aspects of the World Cup. I tell her of the book I am writing. She asks me if I will cover anything on child prostitution...I say that Copacabana seems to be a lot less seedy than when I was here 12 years or so ago. The Help Club has gone and maybe, only temporarily because it is the World Cup, but it seems a lot safer.

She says child prostitution is still a big issue here just that it is not so visible. She came across an old man with a young girl yesterday with the two of them speaking different languages. She challenged him... He said the girl, who is his daughter, lives in Rio whereas he lives in America and visits every so often. She had serious doubts but didn't feel she could push it any further. There is apparently a telephone number you can call...I say that I haven't noticed it so it can't be that prominent.

After waiting forty minutes, I have still not received a call back from Bravo...I call the Budapest number and there isn't any answer...They must have gone home in Budapest. The lady had said if they go home to call the UK number and reiterated the booking needed to be changed more than 24 hours before the flight time of the existing booking.

I call the UK number and give the reference yet again. The response is that they can't change the booking...It has to be done by the Budapest office. I explain the issue and that the office is closed...No good...I have booked an apartment for two weeks costing 7800 reals...£2100...This is stressful. They will look into it and call me back.

Messi scores a fantastic free kick... This is a great game... and it is so frustrating to not be able to watch it properly...Half time Argentina 2-1 Nigeria.

I go back up to my hotel room and receive a call from a number with a country code 39...Italy now, who say they say will make the booking change...It is a bad line again. I can hear her...I move out of the room again onto the stairs ...Still no good...I ask her to call back again in 5 minutes and jump into the lift down to the lobby. This feels like groundhog day...She still can't hear me...I go outside...Finally but the line is very slow and my sore throat which is affecting my speaking and her Italian English is making this extremely difficult ...She asks for the booking reference number... It is in the hotel room on the tenth floor...I gave it previously but had to leave the room for a better phone signal...She needs the booking reference...Finally common sense prevails... She asks me a series of questions which I answer...We get all the way through detailing the flights, the dates...Confirm the cost of the change is £103..

Credit card number...The payment doesn't go through...She has misheard the number... We go through it all again...Three digit security code, expiry date. Give the date... I can't hear her...I repeat and repeat and repeat and repeat... Line still showing as connected... Repeat again...Getting frantic now...Look at phone connection lost...Nooooooo!! I stare at the phone...She is ringing me back...Finally we get it sorted...I am staying in Brazil until Sunday, 13th July...Only been here twelve days... Have another eighteen days ahead of me... Whoooppeee!!

I go back inside the hotel and Nigeria have made it 2-2! I just get back in to see Rojo put Argentina back in front for a third time off a corner...With his knee!

Both attacks look good but defensively not so good... In the final minutes, cross comes over from Nigeria, Argentine defender mis-kicks but somehow they get away with it...Final Score Argentina 3-2 Nigeria... Argentina have won all three games but will need to strengthen the defence if they are to get beat the bigger boys and challenges ahead...With Bosnia beating Iran, Nigeria qualified for the knock out stages too!

I walk up to the metro station at Cardeal Arcoverde...The name of the metro station sounds like a dodgy auto trader! On the way I get talking with a guy in an Indian cricket shirt with his friend about the Test Series versus England. They are called Major and Jas from Coventry. We take the metro to the Maracana together and have a great chat punctuated by French guys singing La Marseillaise followed by Allez Les Blues!! We exchange mobile numbers and agree to meet up for a beer tonight.

I have some stress going through the various security checks on the way in to the ground... Memories of Argentina versus Bosnia come hurtling back. That night which seems so long ago but is actually only about ten days...So much has happened since then... I hand the ticket to the steward at the gate who places it down for validation...The colour green comes up, the ticket is handed to me and I am in the Maracana...Finally!

I have to queue for forty minutes to buy a drink...Can you imagine...Forty minutes...Almost a half of a football match...It is so badly organised...I buy three drinks to collect the different souvenir cups...Diet Coke, Brahma and the golden Budweiser cup. I show my ticket to the steward who shows me the gangway on the right of the stairs. Taking care not to spill my three drinks, I climb up to my seat, B203 Row Seat JJ18, which having gone through rows A to Z and then through AA to JJ is as you can imagine quite a lot of seats. I get in just before the national anthems are sung. Franck is not in his seat yet. I sit with a couple from Lancashire...Unbelievably, the lady works at Lincoln University, my birth city and lives on Carholme Road in the West End of the City! A couple of guys come along and say I am in one of their seats. It seems this is the wrong block... Hmm...I carefully pick up my three drinks from under my seat and carry them all the way back down to the front of the upper tier. A different steward sends me up the first row to the left of the stairs...Makes sense...I climb back up the stairs to the top. There are some rows beyond the last step of the staircase. The fans sat confirm that the first row is JJ...I ask the guy above the staircase his seat number...He says number 26...I look across and seat 18 is taken...I ask and they say this is not Block 203...The match has started. I walk carefully all the way back down to the front with my three drinks. I ask a steward where my seat is... He doesn't speak English and asks another steward to help me...There are a lot of people who can't find their seats...The people who are sat in the lower seats are getting irritated as those without seats are blocking their view. Eventually after ten minutes a steward comes to help me. By this time, I have drunk one of the beers...It has been a stressful day! The steward takes me back up the staircase that I have just come down from...He speaks in Portuguese to the fans and ascertains that seat 26 is indeed in the wrong block. However without a break in the seating, the numbering changes from a seat number in the 20's of one block to seat number of one the next block! I have to disturb around twenty people to reach my seat. Finally I have a seat in the Maracana! I am sat in the corner of the stadium with a corner flag directly in front of me.

I meet up with Franck who has had his own problems.... He has had his electronic cigarette confiscated at security. He said that he wasn't intending to use it but they weren't interested and obviously it cost him quite a lot of money... He is not a happy man...

Franck is considering flying up to Recife for the USA versus Germany match tomorrow. He doesn't have a ticket and looking at his possible arrival time which would be one hour before kick off, I explain the distance to the stadium. It would be tight enough with a ticket let alone then trying to find a ticket...

Lights representing the colours of the teams are built in to the roof...The red and blue of France and the Yellow and Blue of Ecuador. Never seen that before... Looks good.

France having the better of the play but needed a good save from Lloris just before the interval.

Half Time 0-0

Meet David from Colombia and Sylvia from Ecuador who live in London and are really enjoying the World Cup. Second half France hit bar.

Valencia sent off! Only about five minutes in to the second half...Will be tough for Ecuador from herein...Never really thought of Valencia has a particularly dirty player but was also sent off in the pre-tournament friendly versus England.

73749 attendance.

Switzerland are three nil up... If Ecuador don't win they are out...77 minutes gone, France better side but shooting straight at keeper.

Lloris makes excellent save... Crowd applaud the save.

Franck very keen to capture a goal on video...I am willing a goal for him.

85 minutes...Game is now very stretched.

Ecuador keeper seems to be time wasting...Why? Surely word has got down to him that Ecuador need a goal?

Final Score 0-0

I say goodbye to Franck and again thank him for the ticket. The game may have been goalless but the game was still enjoyable and it has been a fabulous experience to watch a game in the Maracana... The stadium is fabulous and the World Cup Final will be amazing here.

On the way to the metro I get talking with an American guy, Michael from Washington DC...I must have some sort of antennae... He is a Spurs fan and I tell him about the "Come on you Spurs" web site which has a lot of American members. Postscript: I post a message onto the site on my return and Michael, who has joined, responds asking...Are you the guy I met leaving the France versus Ecuador game? Amazing!

I meet up with Major and Jas at their Lancaster Hotel and they take me to a little local bar they tend to start the evening off at. They are quick drinkers and the stories come quick and fast!

I tell them about a couple I met on holiday in Italy some years ago...Brad and Alison. Brad was an Arsenal fanatic and leaving the family holiday to fly off to watch Arsenal in a Champions League playoff match! His wife was at school with David Beckham and as young boy, of 11 or 12 years old, he used to say to Alison and her friend...One day I am going to be famous and play football for England. Over a school dinner one day, Alison and her friend finally said... Well David, if you are going to be famous one day, I guess we should have your autograph. He wrote to Alison love David Beckham and signed it...Alison kept it and still has it today! Brad became a mate of Teddy Sheringham when he started out on his career at Millwall and used to go up to watch him play for Nottingham Forest. A few years later, Brad met Teddy in a bar in Epping Forest and who should come in...David Beckham. Brad says my wife used to be at school with you and when he said Alison, David could remember her...Nice

We move onto another bar and have a laugh with some Aussie guys...One guy left us and took a "girl" back to his hotel...He comes back fifteen minutes later and we all laughing at how quick it had been etc...The hotel wouldn't let him in!! He says...Waste of a taxi fare!

The night starts to get messy...We walk back along Atlantique and I drop the guys off at the Lancaster Hotel...As I walk back towards the hotel, I can see fans sleeping on the beach and in cars along the sea front..

Outside the hotel meet up I meet up with a TV crew from Ecuador. They are being picked up at 6am to film at Christ the Redeemer. They haven't been to bed yet and judging by the amount of beer they still have to work through... They won't be doing anytime soon! They offer me a beer and we stand outside the hotel overlooking Copacabana, drinking and shooting the breeze. We have a cracking night...No idea what we spoke about though! Suddenly, it is 6am and their lift has arrived to take them to their filming work... Alcohol and work not such an issue here! Yes it is 6am!!!

Having woken in Belo Horizonte at 4.30am, I get into bed at 6.15am the next morning...I am sure this sounds repetitive...But after the stresses and strains of the morning...What another fantastic day!

EL GRINGO'S ONCE IN A LIFETIME

As a 15 year old from Argentina, this adventure for me, was one of the more you can appreciate, I had a special time with people from many other countries and I made some great friendships with these people.

My fantastic journey started in the inauguration of the FIFA World Cup in the Sao Paulo fan fest. Then with my aunt and her friend we drove to Fortaleza had the opportunity to see Costa Rica play who were one of the best selections of this World Cup. It was a nice game for the Ticos (Costa Rica) who were victorious beating the great coach of Uruguay Professor Tabares 3-1.

The next day we went to the Fortaleza fan fest to watch Argentina beat Bosnia 2-1. Great friendships were made in Fortaleza!

After the game, we left in the direction of Recife and stopped at Raisin Natal Fan fest where we saw England fans in great force and even after losing to Uruguay for 2-1 in great voice.

As soon as we arrived in Recife, we went straight to the stadium to see Ticos (Costa Rica) beat Italy 1-0 to qualify for the knockout stage. This was a very special moment to share with the team and Ticos fans.

The next day we went to the Recife fan fest to see Argentina win against Iran 1-0. Messi's goal in the 92`30 minute paralyzed the hearts of all Argentina supporters! A huge celebration was made after that great gooool!

We then drove for five days to Porto Alegre to reach the World Cup's most important moment for me. It was to actually be in the stadium to see my country Argentina v Nigeria. It was fantastic and amazing. I was singing and shouting for the whole match. There were good goals in an exciting 3-2 win for my country! Lionel Messi or as he is nicknamed…La Pulga Atomica (the atomic flea) scored two goals… One a great free kick to help my country qualify for the knockout stages!

Brazil 2014 was very special for me. I made great friends and what I most appreciate is that these friendships, regardless of distance and the time which goes by without seeing these friends, is for life!

Kevin Gorr, Rosario, Argentina

THURSDAY 26TH JUNE 2014

Wake at 10am miss breakfast …This is often my only meal of the day! The BBC guy's friend Ciara texts regarding the Colombia v Ecuador match. I call her and manage to negotiate an agreed price of 2000 reals. Her initial asking price was 2600 reals!!

I go to the bank to withdraw cash to be able to pay Ciara and arrange to meet on Copacabana beach.

I check out of the hotel. Great view of Copacabana beach and whilst the room isn't the best, it is worth staying here one night just for the view…Especially from the 10th floor!

I realise my flight back is not on the Monday after the World Cup Final but on the day of the final at 7.50pm… OMG…What a schoolboy error…Extreme tiredness definitely has an effect on my ability to think clearly...With a lot trepidation... I open my World Cup wall chart to look at the time of the World Cup Final...Surely I am not going to miss it... The kick off time is...9pm...Shit, shit, shit...

Wait...Its 9pm UK time!! That means 4pm Brazilian time. Say two hours long...6pm...Flight 7.50pm. An hour to the airport... Even with an online check in...Too tight...And what if there is extra time and penalties...Can easily add another hour...it's true to say I will be Brazil for the World Cup Final ...But where...The airport doesn't feel the right type of environment to watch the World Cup Final...And what if I get a ticket to the final...Yes slim chance I know...But you never know!

I email for a later flight or possibly for the next day or the Tuesday...Not that I have anywhere to sleep on Cup Final night...Sure it will be easy to find somewhere on Cup Final night...Not!!

I am a bit all over the place...

Text to meet Colin, they are on the beach opposite the Budweiser Hotel.

On the way down to meet Colin and the guys, Ciara texts...

Hi John, Ciara here. Tickets sold to a Colombian. Apologies.

What!!!!! We had an agreement...Couple of text message exchanges...Ciara saying we didn't have an agreement...Yeah right...Now says she is on the way to the airport...What happened to her going to the beach...Not worth wasting any more time or texts...The tickets have gone but I promise her a starring role in my diary...I won't include her full phone number but if you know an Irish girl by the name of Ciara who was out in Rio...Please pass on my thanks!!!

I meet up with the guys on the beach with more than 2000 reals in my pocket which was to pay Ciara for the ticket...Doug had his Spurs bag stolen off the beach...400 reals in cash, credit card, phone, wallet, Bobby Robson autobiography...As ever the guys are making fun of the situation and are on the lookout for a Brazilian beach vendor reading a Bobby Robson book!

We leave the beach for a beach side bar to watch USA v Germany...Paul and Ian are at the game in Recife. Both teams need a draw to qualify... The cynic in me questions what the result will be!!

Whilst watching the match, Colin says o2 cut off his phone as the bill went up to £200. He is sorting some problems out at home. He had a chat on line with o2 who sorted the problem. Lo and behold...Two days later the same problem. Another on line chat... Colin says they only have to look at his history...Six weeks ago Las Vegas, now Rio for two weeks and in the last months...Tromso in Norway, Moldova Lisbon etc.!!

Half time 0-0...No surprise there! Although to be fair, it does look a proper game.

Portugal beating Ghana 1-0 at half time.

During half time Colin tells me of their Maracana experience. They went to watch Belgium v Russia. Having paid 300 US dollars each to an agency operating out of the Windsor hotel for four tickets which had the same Brazilian family name printed on each ticket, they were turned away at the entrance to the stadium. They call the agency and are told to pick up a different four tickets nearby. It is all getting a little bit last minute, the clock is ticking down towards kick off...30 minutes no tickets...20 minutes still no tickets...Ten before kick off...Finally!! The tickets arrive and they are corporate!

After the game, they make the most of the corporate hospitality and get absolutely smashed! They are the last in the place... On leaving they see a gap in the fence to take a short cut...And end up straight into a favela. Little kids run up offering to take a photograph of them on their iPhones...Yeah right...Might be drunk but not that bad! Straight back through the gap in the fence to corporate land!!!

10 minutes into the second half...Germany score! Mueller yet again!!! We are all kind of surprised!! Ghana score...1-1 v Portugal...

If Ghana score again it will get very interesting... As the USA score stands... Another goal from Ghana and they will have the same points as USA and the same zero goal difference. Having scored five (if they score!), they will have scored one more than USA. It's suddenly very exciting!! Well done Germany for playing the game in the right way.

One of the guys tells me that Murray got through his second round match at Wimbledon...Normally I would be glued to the tennis...It all feels a little surreal out here!

I show the guys photographs of the view over Copacabana. They say the view wont be quite the same at their apartment in Flamengo

It occurs to us that we asked for a menu about an hour ago...How do these people ever make money!!

Finally we get a menu... All in Portuguese...Ian help!!

I keep it simple and ask for a ham and cheese sandwich. No one speaks any English. Ok...Frites...Hand waving from the waitress...Seems no more food... Another chopp then

Portugal 2-1 up... Barring a three goal movement in 6 minutes... USA going through... Great effort by the USA to get through such a tough group!

Colin asks me the size of my case... Seems it might be better to leave my case at the hotel and just take my rucksack. I am living most of this adventure out of my rucksack...I am finally a backpacker at the grand old age of 55!!

The guys say that when they were in Belo Horizonte, a local guy said that when Argentina played there... It felt like an invasion with thousands upon thousands arriving by car.

Ozil is subbed and an American lady sat behind us says he is so ugly! Her husband calls him Popeye...But without the physique! They know how to go for the jugular!

4 minutes added time...An American on another table asks what date the final is...Got to admire the optimism!

The guys go back onto the beach and I return to the hotel to load up my rucksack. I keep saying my rucksack...It is in fact my son Harvey's rucksack!!The hotel agrees to store my suitcase until Sunday.

The Chelsea guys I gave information to yesterday on what to do in Rio yesterday have had their hire car stolen from the hotel car park overnight! Incredible!!

Walk back to the beach to meet Colin...Advertisement of Suarez with mouth open on the promenade... People posing with their shoulder against his teeth!

The guys have moved on from the beach and I meet up with them at Manuel & Juaquim's restaurant on Rua Siqueira Campos. I finally order my first meal of the day at 5.30pm while watching Russia v Algeria...Good header puts Russia one up in a winner takes all game.

The food arrives... It's steak with what looks like rice pudding!! Ian...Help!!

We take the metro from Siqueira Campos station to Flamengo.

We stop for a beer at a bar to watch the last half an hour...Amazingly it is the same bar I stopped at for a bathroom break at on the way back from the Maracana last night!

Colin and Doug warn me not to lock or close the doors as there have been a couple of incidents of guys being locked in rooms.

Algeria equalise which means if the score stays the same, the Russians will be out... No tears would be shed here...Replay shows a laser is aimed at the keeper from the crowd!!!

Flares in the Algerian end...I think back to Villa away and how the police clamped down that day...

The guys didn't know the Brazilian son Guilherme would be living with them in the apartment!! Seems the mother has moved into his place and he keeps himself to himself in his room designing web sites...And no doubt keeping an eye on the initially six English guys which reduced to four but has now increased to five!!

While we are sat outside the bar having a beer and watching the match, Guilherme's mother walks past us...We are really amongst the local community here. It's a bustling suburb...The guys have felt very safe here and I can understand why...The open air bar is decked out in yellow and green bunting with the canopy having well over a 100 little Brazilian flags.

Mothers with small children are passing to and fro with food, shopping bags or to and from work...Others walking chattering into their mobile phones. Locals ...Men and Women sat outside in the warm climate having a chat and drink watching the match.

2.40 seconds of 4 minutes added time...

Capello out!!

The 5th floor apartment is across the road from the bar and only a couple of minutes away from Flamengo metro station. A perfect location!

We enter the lobby from the street and walk through to the lift which has a slight domestic smell. On coming out of the lift we turn left and knock on the door of the apartment. I enter my new home until Sunday. There is a dining room table and chairs in front of me and over towards the street window a TV sofa and chairs.

On the left side corner is a bedroom with two single beds. I am sharing with Mick from San Diego who is English and still gets over to Spurs games.

Elsewhere Colin, Doug and Rob have beds as well as the Brazilian owner. He is a tall guy with a beard with thick wavy hair and comes across as a warm, friendly, decent guy.

There is a single bathroom which amongst the six of us will be a bit of a challenge...But the place has a feel of university digs...Lads being lads on a football tour.

We take the metro back to Copacabana and have a first drink in the guys local bar Copa Azul. It is on the third block of Rua Duvivier when walking away from the beach on Avenida Atlantique. Copa Azul is only a small bar with tables and chairs outside but with plaques on the wall of the four Rio based football clubs... Flamengo, Fluminese, Vasco da Gama and Botofogo, it has the feeling of being a football bar rather than just a World Cup bar if that makes sense.

Next we go to Mabbs bar which is on the corner of Prado Junior and Atlantique opposite the fan fest. It has Georgian style windows and immediately I am transported back 12 years to when I was in this bar with an American guy. Everything was dude with this guy... He was from San Diego and the most positive happy go lucky type of person I have ever met. He and I walked in Mabbs bar one afternoon...It was empty except for the ten or so ladies sat at the bar...They all without exception swivelled around on their stools and followed our every step. We sat down at a corner table and ordered a beer and their eyes never left us. It was the most unnerving of experiences...As you can tell by the fact that the image hasn't left me all these years later and... That wasn't the end of it... We walked round a street market and another one came up to me in broad daylight in the middle of the afternoon and said "you want fuckie fuckie?"!!!

Fast forward to today and the only difference is that there are a lot more than ten of them and the bar is full of football fans.

The word on the street is that such is the demand, girls are being brought in

from cities across Brazil. The area is heaving with them...And yet it still seems that demand is outstripping supply!

At the bar Mick overhears a French lady tourist innocently try to strike up a conversation with a lady at the bar not realising she is a prostitute!!! "This is my first time in Rio... How about you...How are you finding it?" We laugh... May be...Hectic would have been her answer!

After Mabbs we end up sitting outside an Arabian restaurant and share hummus and kebabs...Really tasty food...Mick has a UK style kebab...We do try to say it might not be the best of ideas...There is a table full of English guys next to us buying the "girls" drinks...One of the girls is a dead ringer for a young Whitney Houston...A Sven pity...

Shortly after midnight we decide to call it a day...Rob, Doug and Colin are intending to be up at 8am to go to Sugar Loaf. We are in a whip of which the cab is 16 reals to my new home in Flamengo.

Doug likens the apartment to Auf Weidersehen Pet...Makes us all laugh...I like being in Flamengo with the guys...Well except the queue for the bathroom!!

It is 1.01am... A chance of some sleep!!!

When Fabio Capello was appointed as manager of Russia, most fans were really excited. Sure there were plenty of naysayers who were extremely against the "Don Fabio", thinking that we need a Russian manager. Still, Russia did well at the qualifiers topping the group ahead of Portugal. At that stage we were extremely positive about our results. Our team played really well, improved in physical and technical conditions. Even the failure against Northern Ireland didn't matter, but it was the first call.

The shadow of incoming problems fell after the finals draw. When Russia drew Belgium, Algeria and South Korea, a lot of people were happy with this group as it was thought as one of the easiest. We then realized that we saw this 12 years ago in Japan and South Korea where we drew Belgium, Tunisia and Japan. And as then, we experienced a huge feeling of déjà vu not more, not less.

First serious doubts appeared when the squad was published. There were almost no questions except for the most important position – striker. One of the brightest strikers of Russian Premier League – Artyom Dzyuba from Spartak Moscow wasn't in the squad. The season before the World Cup he played on loan in Rostov – the middle level team which in the end finished 7th but won the Russian Cup and qualified for the Europa League. This situation started a waterfall of questions, but it didn't mean anything. Nothing changed after the three practice matches in May and June where Russia hardly won against Armenia and Morocco, but played 1-1 with Norway. In all these games our team struggled to convert its chances.

A lot of people were sure with the management of Russian football federation we won't go far. One of the biggest problems is the football culture in Russia as there are a lot of people who really want the national team to fail just to have a laugh on the internet. And this is really disappointing. But still the most popular prediction was the second place because we all knew that it's going to be very difficult to topple Belgium. Algeria and Korea were really underrated by some experts and most of fans.

By our first match vs South Korea, we've been watching top quality football for almost a week and got used to the fact that everything can happen. This made us expect anything from the most stupid loss to the brave victory. The final result was in the middle. At half time we were sure Russia is going to score, but no one could expect Kerzhakov is going to be a one point saviour after the biggest blooper of the first week by Igor Akinfeev. Even after the equalizer from Alexander Kerzhakov fans weren't happy as we expected to get three points in this match.

The second match vs Belgium was the moment when a lot of fans believed in the best result. Russia played way better than before, we had a lot of chances but still failed to convert them. We began to believe we could get three points but again one mistake in the end of the game ruined it all.

The fans and the team understood the game against Algeria was a do or die. Only a victory gave us the opportunity to proceed to the play-offs. The beginning was amazing – ball control, passes, quick goal – we had all the chances to win.

EL GRINGO'S ONCE IN A LIFETIME

We kept creating scoring opportunities but kept missing. The best striker was not in the squad and two out of three goals conceded were personal mistakes by our keeper. The only sweetener was the match between Germany and Algeria. Algeria fought brave and well, and a lot of fans started thinking what the game would be if Russia played vs Germany instead of Algeria. We realized it would have been a disaster and were not that angry or sad, because in the end it was our first World Cup in 12 years. And not the last one.

Alexey Pivovarenko, Moscow, Russia

FRIDAY 27TH JUNE 2014

My body is in shock...6 hours sleep!! Woke at 7am and Mick had left his bed and gone on to the sofa...I was worried that I had kept him awake...Not known to snore... Fortunately it was nothing to do with me...He finds his bed a little uncomfortable. The beds are hard and it does feel like lying on a hard board but I quite like it that way.

iCloud issues having a knock on affect to storage so...First job this morning is to be ruthless with my photo album...Can you believe...1-1/2 hours later!!

The TV coverage is mostly around Luis Suarez...He has been banned for biting an opponent for the third time in his career...The ban is for nine international matches and four months of all Liverpool matches...He is not even allowed to go into the training ground. The talk is of fans wearing Hannibal Lecture masks when Spurs play Liverpool and as to whether he should be made to wear a gum shield or muzzle when playing again!!

Colin, Doug and Rob have gone off to Sugar Loaf. To think.., Twelve days ago when I was up there with Paul and Ian the England team were training below...All our hopes and dreams were still intact. Twelve days on they have packed up and gone home...Some may well be on a beach somewhere by now having their own holiday before pre-season training starts.

There are still quite a lot of England fans in Rio...If we had finished second; it would have been Colombia v England in the Maracana tomorrow...Just how good would that have been. There is a feeling of a sense of disappointment within all of us which we spoke of whilst out last night...The guys flew out Tuesday 10 June and are ready to go home now. Sunday can't come quickly enough for them. I know this feeling from watching Spurs in Europe...If they lose; I just want to catch the next plane home.

The reality is though that by the end of August, we will all be engrossed in the Premier League and the disappointment of England's World Cup campaign will be long forgotten....

Even without England, Spain, Italy, Portugal et al, there are some mouth-watering clashes to look forward to in the knock out phase...Tomorrow alone we have Brazil v Chile followed by Colombia v Uruguay. I really hope Brazil reach the final otherwise Rio and the whole of Brazil will be on a massive downer...

Now that the number of games is thinning out...The final group games were played simultaneously to avoid a repeat of the Germany v Austria fiasco all those years ago...This meant that the evening matches have fallen away... These matches would have been late at night in Europe. This leaves a sense of emptiness on a night...I muse as to how I will feel when the guys go back... How I will fill my time...Today is the first day without football since the World Cup started. Sixteen teams have gone home and by Tuesday night another eight will have joined them to leave just eight teams remaining... After Tuesday the number of football free days will steadily increase...

I just realise that I flew out to Brazil two weeks ago today. It feels another life time...It has been a topic of conversation...Packing so much in gives a feeling of a few days ago being a few weeks ago...I still have more than two weeks ahead of me. It's hard to imagine how distant the memories of the first few heady days will be by the time I fly back to the UK.

Paul and Ian are due to fly home today from Recife which has been in the news due to flooding...It's a shame that their last few days will have been impacted in such a way...It's difficult to imagine when it is expected to be 27 degrees here today...Living in the UK there are relatively small degrees of climatic differences which makes it difficult to comprehend we are in the same country. This country is enormous!

The guys are making me feel very welcome. They are an established group of four but it's all very relaxed.

Amazing what a difference a good night's sleep can do! The idea of 8 hours sleep a night might catch on across the world one day! Invigorating shower... Good start to the day!

Mick says something about keep taking the pills. He had a heart attack eight years ago and flat lined for two whole minutes...

We head off on the metro to get down to the beach opposite the Budweiser Hotel. Mick has to stop off at every beach rest-room on the way...We did warn him about the kebab last night!!

It's fantastic to lie on a sun bed for the first time! Previously it has been a towel or a reclining chair.

With Doug having had his rucksack stolen and hearing of three others also being stolen...We are very careful, almost paranoid, about our bags putting the legs of our sun beds through the rucksack straps and covering them with our towels between our sun beds.

We go for lunch at a beach side cafe and have the rump steak cheeseburger and fries with an orange juice and coca zero...Note...No beer! Mick has to leave us again as it seems he has the bug Paul, Ian and I had early on...Unless of course it was last night's kebab.

It is a very hot day today and the forecast was right...27 degrees....I have a lovely siesta on the sun bed...You know the sort where you close your eyes listening to the waves and the sounds of the beach...Then whoosh you are completely knocked out into a deep sleep...I wake a couple of hours later and

EL GRINGO'S ONCE IN A LIFETIME

Mick's boss Kurt who is here on a corporate joins us... We share a beer and have an enjoyable afternoon in the sun on Copacabana...Life doesn't get much better...It really is a once in a life time experience.

Colombians are now singing at the beach side bar...A bus painted sky blue and white stops by honking its horn...Uruguay or may be Argentina.

Kurt says he doesn't have any interest in football...His passions are golf and baseball...He thought he knew of one player...Messi right? It seems the passion for football is coming through from the younger guys in the States...

One of our group had an incident in the sea... A wave hit him and somehow as he falls over, his shorts are around his ankles and he is covering his embarrassment.

George at the agency is too frightened to speak about tickets as he believes plain clothes police are nearby #clampdown

Talking with guys from Paris...They have been quoted 1200 USD for a ticket to Colombia v Uruguay in the Maracana tomorrow...#crazy

We take the metro and head back to our apartment on Rua Marques de Abrantes in Flamengo

By 6.25pm we are on our way out again. I have borrowed Colin's jeans to go to Rio Scenarium... The belt is not helping...Could be an entertaining night! While Colin is using the whip monies to buy metro tickets, the police with hands on guns are in attendance whilst others unload cash machines.

We take the metro to Cinelandia to go to Lapa for a night out and while walking into Lapa, my daughter, Molly rings to say she has been chosen to play the lead, Dorothy, in the Wizard of Oz at school in her final year before University. I am so pleased for her!!

We end up in the same restaurant as with Paul and Ian...We are drinking very quickly. The beef is as rare as you can imagine...Red raw rare...Tasty though!

The guys take me on a walk through the wild side of Lapa...And boy is it wild...

The walls of the streets are covered in graffiti...Street vendors are selling anything from beer to marijuana...Which by the pungent smells around us is a best seller tonight! People are out on the streets, drinking whilst sat on the pavements and having impromptu street parties. Bob Marley is playing in the background and there is very much a bohemian hippie feel. A guy with lip stick and a bra walks passed us... OMG where am I?

We find the famous mosaic steps.... I am not sure why they are famous and make a mental note to ask at Tourist Information. As we walk up the steps, what an atmosphere...People are sitting on the steps having a chilled out night in the warm night air...Drinks being sold...Caipirinha 75p...It's superb!

We find an open fronted bar...One of the lad's tummy is playing up...Two ladies are banging on the rest room door...He comes out very sheepishly...There is talk of buckets and landlords.. The ladies decide they are not as desperate as they thought were...

Two lads from Wakefield come in. They are staying in a hostel at £40 a night which is mixed with men and women sleeping in the same room. The etiquette is that after a certain time lights are out and stay out for the rest of the night. Those coming back late, use the torch lights on their mobile phones...Well, unless of course you are Argentine...Then at 4am its lights on!!! In the hostel, they are allocated a small locker to keep their passports and cash in. They say there isn't any risk of stuff being stolen from the lockers.

We are having a great night in Lapa...We move on to a street bar and are standing with a beer when police are horseback come through the crowded street!

EL GRINGO'S ONCE IN A LIFETIME

There are street vendors everywhere... It feels as if they are selling everything and anything...

We then walk through the Lapa arches and are amazed by the sheer volume of people on the streets...It is heaving...Feels like thousands of people are on the streets...People are even drinking on a petrol forecourt.

The intention is to go to Rio Scenarium but the queue to get in is more than half a kilometre long...I have never seen a queue this long for a club anywhere... We have a drink at the bar across the road and stop off at a couple of other bars including one with live samba music and some very good dancers amongst the clientele.

We turn right at the four bars crossroad and walk up to the Boemia da Lapa live music bar...The night is getting messy...After quite a lot more beers, we walk down to an open area, we have some banter with the some Aussie fans..

Now it is very messy and there is an incident with a driver who came round the corner far too fast...Time to head back to the apartment...I get to bed at 4.13am

It was a wonderful event, which brought together a wide diversity of people from different places, and at the end everyone was always socializing. This event exceeded all expectations, both Brazilians and foreigners. I just have to say that I just loved it. I met wonderful people, met the culture of some countries and I can say I made friends. All together for the World Cup!!

Victoria Rodrigues Fonseca, 18, Rio de Janeiro, Brazil.

The World Cup to me was both the greatest celebration of football as well as one of the greatest expressions of humanity. The world stopped, gathered, and joined in as one. To be one of the truly lucky ones to be there was a privilege.

Sean Robert Jones, 20, Sydney, Australia.

SATURDAY 28TH JUNE 2014

I wake at 10am...

Five minute hangover can't begin yet because I am still drunk...Honestly!!

Mick is flying back home to San Diego in the early hours of Sunday morning. Sadly he doesn't feel up to coming with us to the fan fest. We hope to see him later but without having his phone with him it might be a challenge. Shame as I really enjoy Mick's company...Hopefully he will make his annual pilgrimage to White Hart Lane in the coming season and we can meet up for a beer.

We walk up to Flamengo metro station to head down to Copacabana. The metro train is absolutely rammed full of Brazilian fans in their bright yellow shirts.

We get off at Cardeal Arcoverde metro station, walk up the staircase and look down on to a jam packed platform full of Brazilian yellow...it is an amazing sight.

On the escalator, there is Brazilian yellow going up to the fan fest and Colombian yellow going down to catch the

metro to the Maracana for their match against Uruguay which is the later kick off.

Coming out of the metro station, we are hit by the atmosphere...

There is yellow everywhere...All walking in the direction of Copacabana beach towards the two fan fests. Horns blasting, whistles blowing, vuvuzelas, car horns...It feels as if the whole population of Rio de Janeiro is heading towards the beach on Copacabana.

This surpasses the excitement and anticipation ahead of the earlier second group game of Brazil versus Mexico match.

We are moving into the business end of the tournament. This is knock out fever...The winners go into the Quarter Final and the losers go out...Go home... Imagine the unthinkable...Brazil going out...This Chile side is very talented... And this though is the crux of it...The Brazil fans don't have any doubt that their country will win. The self-belief and self-confidence of being five times World Champions...These fans are excited at the prospect of seeing their team progress into the Quarter Final...To be two games away from seeing their country, the host nation, play in the World Cup Final in the Maracana, in Rio de Janeiro, in their city!! There doesn't appear to be any doubt in the minds of any of these fans!

The queues for the main fan fest are horrendous. We decide to head for the second open fan fest.

On the way there, the craziness of the afternoon is multiplied...The dual carriageway is closed to traffic and coming towards the fan fest in a mixture of outfits with musicians is a World Cup protest march! Signs are being held up "Fuck FIFA".

Only about 200 in the march but they make their point and at the very least will be seen on local TV stations.

We take some photographs, head into the fan fest and find a spot close to the promenade by the Quiosque Chopor Brahma Beach Side Bar.

Colin is in a Brazilian straw hat. Rob and I join him by paying 25 reals each. Doug is happy in his England shirt and the four of us pose for a rat pack photograph!

Stephen from Argentina who takes our photograph is very knowledgeable on football and Tottenham. He is a River Plate fan and pleased to hear that I have been to see his team at home versus Banfield in a 0-0 draw. I don't say that my Argentinian team is...Boca Juniors!

The crowds go back for as far as the eyes can see on the beach, across the promenades and on the road to the roads beyond. It is impossible to gauge how many tens of thousands of people are on Copacabana...And this is on top of the thousands inside the main fan fest. I have been at concerts of 100,000+ in the UK...The number of people on Copacabana seems to dwarf those sorts of numbers.

The atmosphere sends shivers down the spine. There is a continuous noise of horns and whistles. Everyone in Brazilian yellow and green...Shirts, hats, face paint, bandanas, jewellery, flags and even bikinis!

Chi Chi Chile is sung... We look a little way back and there are a group of

Chile fans not too far away...Talk about attending an away match!!!

The screen switches across to the stadium in Belo Horizonte. The crowd roars! The stadium is bathed in yellow!

The singing of the national anthem...So loud, so passionate and the cheer at the end...Indescribable

The teams come up and unsurprisingly Fernandinho replaces Paulinho.

The English referee Howard Webb and his assistants are in charge of the game. With Doug in his England shirt...Hope Howard doesn't give a penalty to Chile!!

3 minutes...Fernandinho straight through a Chile player...No booking...Hmmm

Corner... Marcelo shoots just passed the post...Huge oooh from the crowd.

5 minutes...Very little play...The opening minutes have been littered with fouls and injuries.

A helicopter is circling above us and the noise of its whirring blades is competing with fireworks, samba drums and TV commentaries from beach bars which are on at full volume!! #onceinalifetime

Every Chile attack causes a wave of anxiety to spread throughout the fan fest. If the scores are level towards the end, there will be mass hysteria in here!

A vendor is selling flags which are hoisted in the air...Blocking the fans view of the screen...He is not a popular man!

Guy trying to push in around us...Just moving him out of the way... A Brazilian girl gives him hell...I love the Latin passion...No holds barred!

Corner to Brazil flicked on...Far post... In comes David Luiz with those flowing locks... To stab the ball home!!!!

1-0 Brazil!!! Bedlam!!

Replay suggests it might have been an own goal? Who cares? Very few around me!!!!

The singing starts up!! Firecrackers...Jubilant fans cheering!!!

Vendors are somehow carrying trays of caipirinhas through the crowd...Others carrying huge drink containers...How do they do it! Worried about cash in my back pocket and holding my iPhone in left hand whilst writing my diary in my right hand.

Neymar has missed a couple of chances but with his long mazy runs is still the most dominant player on the pitch.

Terrible tackle from Vidal on Neymar who lands on his head!! Could have been a really nasty fall...The replays look awful...

Woman carries a baby through the crowd...A baptism of fire!!

32 minutes...Throw in to Brazil on their left by Marcelo to Hulk...Sloppy return intercepted...Passed to Sanchez...Shoots...Goal!!! 1-1!!! Boos around the fan fest except for the Chile fans behind us who are going mad...Brazil fans don't like it...Drinks being thrown.

Neymar heads passed the post...This gets the crowd back up.

38 minutes...Bad miss by Fred...Frustration growing here and I suspect in the

stadium and across the whole country.

Finally a Chile player is booked. Webb has been lenient...Memories of the 2010 World Cup Final when the Dutch butchers were for the most part allowed to get away with it by Webb...Wasn't the easiest game to referee though to be fair!

Great effort from Alves...Tipped over the bar...Whoos sound out from the crowd.

2 minutes added time... Dreadful throw out from César... A scramble stops a goal...

The crowd are living every tense moment.

Half time 1-1...Muted applause...Chile finished the half strongly but it has been some game of football and if it is as hot in Belo Horizonte as it is here... Just wow!

15 minutes of the usual comings and goings...Being bumped and shoved... Oh my, please just restart!

It is 1.50 in the afternoon...The sun is burning on the back of our necks... Dehydrated and fragile from last night...Need to have a strong constitution here! Mad dogs and Englishmen and tens of thousands of Brazilians out in the mid-day sun!

The noise at half time is even louder than during the game if that can be possible!!

We buy a beer...It's all this vendor has...Oh well...Here we go again!

From out of a clear blue sky...Pigeon poo lands on the back of Colin's hand!

Second half...Still frantic...Fernandinho shoots wide.

Chile dangerous on the break...The unthinkable could happen... I really hope not but they do look a good passing side.

The game now feels as if it on a knife edge...

Out of nowhere...Hulk!! Goal!!! Crowd go wild!! Beer through the air... Oh no...Webb has disallowed it...Hand ball...Replay suggests the goal should or maybe could have been given?? No concerns here about showing replays of contentious decisions!! Hulk booked for dissent.

Now Gustavo booked...Howard in danger of losing his homer tag in the most spectacular way possible...

Jo warming up...Crowd cheer! Wasn't he rubbish for Man City?

27 minutes to go...Fred comes off to a round of applause...Jo on.

Great move by Chile. A one two...Cut back...What a save by César!

We are all hot and bothered and as good a game as it is agree this needs finishing in 90 minutes...

Hulk goes down in the area... Elbow in the chest...Not substantial but a penalty could have been given.

Chile looking very threatening on the break...

It is noticeable that the Brazilian fans don't really sing...

Jo misses a sitter...Looked offside but a stinking miss...The fans throw their arms in the air in exasperation.

15 minutes to go...Can feel the tension building...The nervousness...What if???

Neymar header...Keeper saves... Where has Neymar been? Now a goalmouth scramble...

9 minutes to go...Possession statistics come up on the screen and show Brazil having only 46% possession...

Hulk on a run inside the box...shoots...Keeper makes a good save.

6 minutes to go...Brazilian fans have a short burst of singing.

Chile playing the more controlled football.

4 minutes go...Vidal off injured for Pinilla.

The screen shows a Brazilian lady, hands clasped together...It sums up the mood of the nation.

Great back heel sets a Chile player free down the left...To be fair even the Brazil fans show appreciation...Corner...Oh my...Brazil holding on...Scramble in the goal mouth...

I worry for Brazil in extra time...They have put so much in...

Corner Chile...47 minutes... 1 minute added time remaining...The ball flashes right across the box...hearts are literally jumping in to fans mouths!!

Final whistle...1-1...What a pulsating game!

There is a feeling of disbelief around the fan fest. It wasn't meant to be like this...Brazil should be through now and the party about to begin...

Colombians leave to head off to the Maracana for their 5pm kick off with Uruguay...Which could have been England...I could have been leaving too had Ciara not let me down on the ticket. Not complaining...It would be a hell of a dilemma if I did have that ticket...Should I go or should I stay now...Who sang that? Will Brazil still be in the World Cup by the time that game kicks off??? What a thought...

The break until the start of extra time seems a long one...It might help Brazil...

Finally we are underway...Hulk makes a strong run and wins a free kick down the left...He urges the crowd to get behind the team...Seems the same problem as in the fan fest...

Jo booked for high foot on the keeper.

Chile win a free kick...Not sure about that... Does Howard support the Brazilian fuck FIFA campaign...Well he is English after all!

Pinilla booked for a foul on Luiz...Fans cheer loudly...Not sure whether ironic at Webb.

Hulk threatens again...Keeper saves again

Alves now booked... Free kick Chile...Sanchez has the appearance of the ultimate party pooper...But shoots wide...

Half time of extra time 1-1...

Brazil have some excellent and explosive individuals but little cohesion or much to show in midfield...The Brazilian manager Luiz Felipe Scolari will surely be heavily criticised if they go out this early in the competition

Last 15 minutes kicks off...Willian on for Oscar...

One of the beach bar TVs inexplicably switches channels... Sure Brazilian people adore Woody Woodpecker...May be not just right now though #uproar

Game seems to be drifting towards penalties...Fatigue in this heat must be playing a part...

5 minutes to go...Sustained Brazilian pressure but every one of their players wants to take every player on and win it on his own...It's a team game lads...

Webb gives another decision to Chile...The crowd falls silent ...A Brazilian woman shouts out in English in a thick Brazilian accent...Go to hell Webb I fucking hate you... Seems it's not just English club fans he winds up...Is he universally hated?

1 minute to go...The noise level picks up...It is the Chile fans singing! Seems they would have taken the draw at the start of the game?

Chile's Pinilla shoots...The ball smashes against the crossbar... It bounces back well outside the 18 yard box. Oh my!!!!!!!!!!!!!!!!!!!!!!!!! What an effort... There is disbelief all around...From the Brazilian fans that they were inches away from being dumped out of their own World Cup to Chilean fans who can't believe how close their team just came to winning...To neutrals like the four of us...Who can't believe how good an effort that was and deserving of winning any match...And yet I still want Brazil to win!

Brazil break...Should have done better...Chance of a three on one but wasted...

OMG its penalties!! The fans sing their I love my country song...

The tension in the air is unbearable...The Brazilian players look in a bit of a mess on the big screen...

The pressure on these Brazilian penalty takers... Imagine missing and the feeling of letting 200 million people down in their own World Cup.

Well done Neymar!! He is rallying the troops...In a few minutes the mood here in Rio will swing wildly one way or the other...Christ the redeemer... Please!!! Can I ask such a trivial request I hear you say...It doesn't feel very trivial right here right now!

Brazil will take the first penalty...

Luiz...Screams and claps of applause 1-0

César saves... Crowd ecstatic!

Willian misses...Haha sort of...Sorry but club rivalries still pollute a football fans mind and if you don't know what happened last summer...Google will tell you!

Sanchez misses...Crowd up again!

Marcelo scores 2-0

Chile score. It is now 2-1 Brazil after 3 penalties each

Hulk ... Misses... Would you believe it...The pressure is getting to both sets of players.

The fans sing for Julio César around the fan fest...Can he have redemption for taking the blame four years ago against Holland?

2-2...After four penalties...It is now effectively sudden death...

Neymar...Cometh the hour, cometh the man? Steps up...Huge cheers...

EL GRINGO'S ONCE IN A LIFETIME

Scores!!

If Chile miss...Brazil are through...

Steps up...Shoots...Hits the post...Missed!!! Brazil are through...The scenes are amazing!!! Elation, jubilation, relief, mayhem, drinks in the air, the noise...A cacophony of everything!! Sheer unbridled joy!

The most amazing scenes I have seen in my life...This will be some party tonight! This is already some party!!!

Once in a life time!!!!!

The Chile fans gather outside... I go over to them and offer them my condolences... They are very gracious in defeat.

They still chant Chi Chi Chile...

Amongst the noise on the streets, the sirens mingle with the firecrackers, samba drums, vuvuzelas, whistles... Friends meet up in the streets afterwards hugging each other, clapping, bouncing up and down on their tiptoes...Arms aloft, whooping and hooping, screaming at each other...Photos and videos capturing the moment... I dare to imagine what it would be like were Brazil to actually win the Cup...They will have to improve if they are to get anywhere near the final though. Chile played really well and were unlucky... The shot against the bar in the last minute... Phew!!!

The sheer volume of people...Eventually I walk to the BBQ restaurant... Car horns honking everywhere.

We have a BBQ chicken on Rua Duvivier...First food of the day!

We move on to the guys local...Bar Azul...Outside there is an impromptu samba bad playing and a BBQ... Let the party begin!

Over our first drink we estimate there could have been as many as 250,000 people on the whole of Copacabana today.

Empty seats in the Maracana... Can't think why! They will begin to fill up soon!

The party outside Cafe Azul is in full swing...The Samba beat in full rhythm...

The Maracana fills up...It is difficult to focus on the game with the party in full flow!!

What a goal from James Rodriguez!! Chest ...Volley...Outside of the box...Goal...To score a goal like that...Not only in the World Cup Finals but in the Maracana!! Surely the goal of the tournament so far...And it makes him joint top scorer in the finals...

Close your eyes and imagine a bar in Brazil...The atmosphere in this little bar Azul is pure Brazil!! Lots of locals, samba, green and yellow and and...

The barman has a line of tabs open on the bar...How he keeps up with them... We have no idea...Would be easier to pay as you buy... Surely!!

Half time...Doug is setting a sprinters pace tonight! Tonight? Hmmm it's 5.46pm...Tiredness is overcoming me...Needing the bathroom here would be problematical...Enormous queue...Think I had better start to queue as not sure whether it's the type of beer but ...When I need the bathroom I need to go...The queue took 15 minutes! Good job I planned ahead!!

James scores again...Rodriguez is some player!

Colin says that while I was in the bathroom, a guy walked passed dressed as the Pope...Divine intervention was certainly needed today!

A taxi driver felt it necessary to tell the guys when talking to Brazilian ladies on Copa... To understand where a man stands he needs to ask...Are you on the program? Now if we walked into a bar in Nottingham and said to a woman in a pub... Are you on the game?"

The bar is in serious danger of running out of its stock of beers...Would be sacrilege!

Colombian keeper pulls off a good save from a long range shot...The camera keeps focussing on a very miserable looking Uruguay manager...Penny for your thoughts...Suarez...What if??No doubt where he will lay the blame...no Idea what Roy will be thinking...Suarez played two games and Uruguay won both games...They lost the two he didn't play in...Unfortunately; one of the games he played in was versus England...

Loris de Paulla from Rio...A proud Botofogo supporter said the joke in Brazil is... The Pope is Argentine but god is....Brazilian!!!

Another excellent save from the Colombian keeper!

The Brazilian girls in the bar insist on posing for photographs. How could we resist!

Colombia win 2-0...Brazil next in the Quarter Finals...It will be some game and a play off between Neymar and Rodriguez...A mouth-watering prospect!

Oh dear a guy has had too much to drink...The barman man handles him out of the bar...Scuffle...Drinks everywhere...Same the world over!

I get talking with Claudia and Darrick from just north of Washington DC. They have been here three weeks and had a fabulous time...No hassles as the locals think they are local!! We exchange Twitter addresses and Claudia's Twitter address leaves little doubt of her love for football!

Claudia loves Ronaldo...The Portuguese one...I tell her she is in the only person outside of Portugal and Madrid who likes him...We agree to a test and ask a Brazilian who says he is a good footballer and an ok person...I think he has had too many caipirinhas!

Claudia insists on carrying on with the test ...Suddenly she is 8-1 down...I say next time you win at the casino on the first go...Pick up your chips and leave!!

A local lady just told me the apartment I am moving into tomorrow is a transvestite area...OMG!!

We just settled the bar bill....four of us for four hours...Drinking nonstop...The total bill came to 20.75 reals...less than £6... maybe the tabs behind the bar got mixed up!

The Colombians are back from the match en masse...Just when it couldn't get any crazier...May have said that earlier today...But it is true!! Add 50,000 Colombians returning from the Maracana...They say 80% of the stadium was Colombian...And judging by the numbers on Copacabana tonight, they could well be right! The Brazilians and Colombians are shaking hands and hugging each other tonight in anticipation of their Quarter Final clash...May be they won't be so friendly after the game!!

Strange night...We have moved on to another bar and local Brazilian girls who don't appear to be prostitutes are fawning all over of us... We are not interested...Colin has a feeling one might be a ladyboy and there is another concern that they might be after our wallets... One says she is a nurse and says that her friend owns four apartments on Copacabana and is making a fortune on renting them out during the World Cup.

When we won't buy them a drink they get very angry...We leave trying to understand what the scam is...Nick from Oxford, an Evertonion, joins up with us... He has been here three weeks, hasn't booked a return flight and is staying in a hostel... He may move on to do the Inca Trail after the World Cup. I take his number to arrange to meet up with him with another night after the guys return to the UK tomorrow.

Seeing footage on the TV of the main fan fest in Rio tonight... Uruguay and Colombia fans fighting in the fan fest...Not good...Might start to be a common occurrence now that the competition has moved on to the knock out stage #highstakes

We are sat outside Mabbs bar under the canopy with a beer... A young hooker comes up and introduces herself, Nicole from Bahia...In Rio for the World Cup...As we all are...Just for different reasons! "I love money, I likey money very, very much"... She has an infectious character and is making us laugh...

Finally food! We share chips covered in a cheese sauce with bacon bits!

It is now 11.30pm...It has been a long tough day!

Mick's flight home to San Diego is at 2am...We haven't seen him since we left the apartment this morning...We feel a sense of sadness that we didn't say goodbye...

After a few more beers, we jump into a taxi to return to Flamengo...A red traffic light obviously means go to Brazilian taxi drivers!

It is almost 1am ... An early night!!

EL GRINGO'S ONCE IN A LIFETIME

The World Cup was good in Brazil! It was perfect because it is close to us and we can travel there.

The whole of Chile was with the participation of the Chilean football team because they saw strength, effort, enthusiasm and heart. In the field 11 warriors braved the world powers in the sport.

Here people ate, lived and breathed football, some watched on TV, others by radio, or by phone, anyhow! Was a sports festival that lasted just for us, but in the end we were satisfied, although as always expect more.

Alvaro, Santiago, Chile

As a Brazilian guy who is not in love with football, it was just interesting, but a little messy, at least at the Airport in Rio, lots of people sleeping all over the place or better saying, all over the city. As an airline employee, I must say it was great, lots of passengers, often overtime, meaning extra cash, and you know, money always comes in handy, right? Lol.

Aloizio, Rio De Janeiro, Brazil

SUNDAY 29TH JUNE 2014

A couple of times on this trip, I have woken and had no idea where I am...It is very disconcerting, almost frightening... I have had the feeling of waking on a street...I did say the other day about how hard the bed is!! Joking aside though, for a minute or so until I get my bearings, it isn't very pleasant. Other times it has been in the middle of the night in a locked São Paulo football stadium beneath the temporary stands. The match in itself was a nightmare...I don't need to revisit the stadium thank you very much. These wake ups though are disturbing...

I do wonder about the quality of the alcohol...Especially the Caipirinhas from street vendors but I didn't have any of those last night so they can't be blamed...

Bueno...

With Mick having flown back to the States, I had the luxury of a room to myself last night. Today though is the day the lads fly back to the UK. For the next fortnight, it won't just be a room to myself but a whole apartment.

Another new phase or perhaps chapter is a better expression given that I am writing a book!

It has been great with the guys and I will miss them.

Colin has run the whip and it has worked really well... All our expenses for metro tickets, drinks and food came out of the whip which was topped up when needed. There haven't been any discussions as to whose round it is etc...

It will be more of a challenge on my own...The practicalities...Even going down to the beach... If I want to go into the sea...Who looks after my bag and iPhone? When we are out in the day or night be it with Paul and Ian or these guys, we look out for each other...I won't have that safety net anymore...

I hope the apartment is ok...The comment last night about the area being full of ladyboys or transvestites has unnerved me...The hotel staff had said the area would be OK during the World Cup and it is close to the fan fest.. Fingers crossed...Not so bad if with friends but on your own and returning late at night...

Colin and Rob have gone down to the beach early to enjoy a last morning on the beach. Doug comes back from the supermarket and while having breakfast... I do the schoolboy thing of filling out the World Cup wall chart...Paths through to the semi-finals worked out...Could be sensational games...Brazil v Holland or Mexico and Argentina v France or Germany. The dream final for me and perhaps many others ...Brazil v Argentina.

We walk through the Flamengo district on the way to the beach...Not a tourist district at all...Very residential...People out walking their dogs, the local bakery serving up Sunday morning treats. Flamengo has a lovely feel to it. The closer we get to the beach, the better the apartments. It is the same the World over!

Along the edge of the beach is a tree lined park with various sports being played. Looking back inland, there are apartment and office blocks peeking out above the trees along with Hotel Novo Mondo...Standing imperiously above all though to the left is Christ the Redeemer, arms outstretched in his white gown looking down on Flamengo... A quite spectacular view...

The beach itself is very long and straight and looks to be set in a huge cove... Enclosing it on the right is the commanding presence of Sugar Loaf Mountain... Looking straight out to sea there are a number of islands and to the left is the domestic airport.

The flight path of the planes provides fabulous views for the passengers... What an incredible first impression... I can imagine excited passengers taking photographs through the windows...A seat on the right of the plane would be the place to be...The flight path runs along the coastline and as I look from the beach, the flight path in land is right to left. As the planes pass Christ the Redeemer to their right, at the end of the bay, the planes arc to the left out to sea passing Sugar Loaf on their right hand side as they then turn to head back along the coastline to land on the left hand side of the bay..

The planes are a continuous stream and provide quite a spectacle. Only the old city airport of Hong Kong could compete in my affections...As we came in

to land there... You could almost see people ironing their clothes and watching their televisions... Terrifyingly close were the planes to the tower blocks ... And yet at the same time, the most exhilarating of landings...

With it being a Sunday morning, quite a lot of the local residents are on the beach on what is yet another glorious day...It is hot today...Winter!!! Long may it continue!

There is a beach football match taking place...It is very organised with a referee and teams playing in blue and green tops. The level of skill is quite astonishing...Takes me back to the quote of...Who was it...Barry Davies the BBC match commentator? When Brazil are in need of a striker, they can just pluck one off Copacabana beach...looking at these guys playing... Their instant control of a high ball...The precision of their long range passing and dribbling skills... Astonishing.

Further along there is a football volleyball match taking place involving two man teams. Doug and I stand transfixed marvelling at the ability of these guys in bare feet on the beach heading and juggling the ball with both feet to each other before knocking it over the net. The other team somehow scramble to get a leg or head to the ball before it touches the ground...Then keep it up and devise their own strategy to hit a winner back over the net...Which they don't and so the rally continues...What chance have England got of ever winning a World Cup!!

There are more traditional games of volleyball taking place and again the level of skill is at a high level.

Just in case they don't have enough time to harness their skills during the day...Floodlights have been installed for night games. Erected on the beach are flag poles with the yellow, green and blue flag of Brazil there to remind people of just what they are aspiring towards...

On Skegness beach, at the height of summer, the flags would be fluttering wildly in the "bracing" North Sea wind...And if you don't believe me or feel I am being unduly harsh...Look out to sea at the 50+ wind turbines...Here in the depths of winter, the flags droop unmoving, hanging limply against their poles.

The sweet smell of coconut sun cream is pleasant on this hot Sunday morning.

Elsewhere, the beach is alive with the pitter patter of balls on bats. We find Colin and Rob...For those of you who know the beach, we are by building number two half way down to the sea by the guy hiring out the beach chairs... The chairs are the sort which are designed to cause maximise embarrassment... You know the sort... Where you jiggle the arm mechanisms to recline...Nothing is happening...You do it with a little more force... Still no movement...Still sat upright...In frustration, you do it with a lot more force... And suddenly you jerk backwards laid out on the floor... Looking nervously round to see how many people are watching and giggling as you cumbersomely try to raise yourself out of the tangled mess on the sand...

I have a Coke Zero for breakfast...Any sense of normality has gone from my life!!

Just like on Copacabana, the warm soft sand feels good to run my feet and toes through...Unlike Copacabana, we are not besieged with vendors on this more residential beach. The water is perhaps not as clean though. Umbrellas are scattered along the beach and even a bicycle...Riding on a sandy beach...Now that would be a challenge!

Above the usual sounds of a Brazilian beach, we hear the constant rumble of aeroplanes as they come into land and thrust their brakes on as well as the booming sound of planes taking off.

Again though the noise is fine... An added sight and sound to the beach. Whenever I have been to Rio before, I have felt at home and this is the case again now... I can't really describe it... Just a feeling of being relaxed... Of being comfortable...Yes I know what you are thinking... But after a couple of weeks here...The guys are ready to go home... And many people when talking of holidays in general say the same... Not me not here though...

Walking back to the apartment, the community feel is again very apparent... There are open air book stores, a busker strumming his guitar, restaurants filling up for Sunday lunch, guys gathered around street TV bars watching Holland versus Mexico...0-0 at half time...

We are back in the apartment and following a tweet from Paul about the number of empty seats at today's game have a look on the FIFA site... There is a category 1 ticket in Salvador for Belgium versus USA...If it was a little closer I would be interested but there is only so much I can do...

Early minutes of the second half...Dos Santos scores a cracker from outside the box...1-0 Mexico! He is one of those types of players who play better for his country than his club...Well certainly when playing for my club...

It will be a big ask for the Dutch to come back in this game...

The Dutch keeper makes a good save to keep his team in it. The Mexican keeper than makes a point blank incredible reaction save...Tipping the ball onto the post. Goal line technology shows the ball didn't cross the line.

Time is running out for Holland...We are a little concerned at the European teams' performances at this World Cup...Would FIFA try to reduce the number of European teams in future finals?

We take photographs with the apartment owners. The guys buy the mother champagne, chocolates and flowers.

5 minutes to go...Knocked back to Sneijder... Wallop! Into the bottom corner...1-1!!

6 minutes of added time...Robben on a mazy run inside the box...Marquez challenges...There is contact but Robben throws himself into the air... The referee points to the spot...It feels a very harsh penalty. We want Huntelaar to miss...But he doesn't ...The ball is fired into the bottom corner...Leaves a bad taste in the mouth...

Doug gives me his Listerine... May be it will

clear the rot of Robben...Rotten Robben has quite a ring to it! Doug also gives me his sun cream and after sun. I haven't used either on this holiday yet...

It is 3.15 and I have to leave to pick up my suitcase and then head down to my new apartment.

I feel a sense of sadness to be leaving here and saying goodbye to my friends...

Sure those of you who have back packed around the world will know the feeling as you leave one location to move on to another.

I take the metro to Cardeal Arcoverde and turn left on to Ribeiro and after a couple of blocks or so I turn right on to Prado Junior arriving at number 135 in time for my 4pm appointment. The apartment building is on the right hand side as I walk up towards the beach and I find it just one block from the front! So far so good!

I meet the apartment owner in the lobby but security won't allow me into the building because I don't have my passport...It is in my suitcase at the California Othon hotel.

In remembering that a copy of my passport was forwarded to the Savoy Othon when making the booking what seems forever ago, we find a compromise. I am able to open my emails through my iPhone and provide my details on the proviso I can show my passport once I pick up my suitcase...Phew that was difficult.

We take the lift to the seventh floor, come out and turn right and right again. I notice domestic cooking smells in the hallway on our walk down to number 735.

After unlocking the two locks, the door is opened and I am pleasantly surprised by the apartment. It is light, airy and spacious. We walk in across a light and dark wooden floor...The apartment has a good feel and I will be comfortable here for the next two weeks.

The owner's wife is waiting for us in the apartment. Neither speaks English and so they open up a translator application on their laptop. I have to sign a lengthy lease document and reading through, it seems to be a document more suited to a much longer lease term...The terms are quite onerous but being on my own here, I don't foresee any issues arising.

We go through the practicalities of the inventory, how to use the equipment and ensure the Wi-Fi code works on my phone. The owners promise to return with more towels and linen in the week. They are warm and friendly people and suggest if I have any problems to contact them by email rather than by phone.

I unpack the few items in my rucksack and head out on to the street. I walk up to the front and see that Mabbs bar is on the left hand corner which will be an easy landmark to remember.

As I would like to see the Greece versus Costa Rica game in the fan fest, there isn't time to pick up my suitcase so that can wait until after the match.

I am walking along Avenida Atlantique and a lady walks passed with a couple of guys. I only got a quick glimpse in the dark but the lady looked like Jane Sparrow. Jane suffers the same burden as me of watching Spurs home and away and we always see each other in the Coach and Horses pub on the Tottenham High Road before home games.

I turn round and walk back a pace or two...Is it Jane? I shout her name but no answer. I try to catch them up and feel in danger of at best suffering embarrassment and at worst appearing to be a weird stalker! I draw level and as the lady is suntanned and I am still not quite convinced but ask...Is that you Jane? And unbelievably...Yes it is!!

Jane is with her father Clive and her boyfriend Stephen Ford who reminds me that I once sorted a ticket out for him at Wigan away! Wigan pies to Copacabana caipirinhas...Some journey and would actually be a great name for the book.

We go to a beach side bar and order caipirinhas. It is 6.14pm and I realise that I haven't eaten anything at all today...Again...

Ruiz scores 1-0 Rica!! I have to admit having a soft spot for Rica. With such a small population, they are massive underdogs, I have watched them live twice and was thrilled by their football versus Italy and then we met the mother and daughters with their partners in Recife. The ladies were not only identical in looks but such lovely people. Apologies to any Greek readers but...Come on Rica!

Rica red card...Down to 10 men..,

Game just about over...Wow...Rica into the Quarter Finals!

Greece shot comes in...Keeper saves...Rebounds 1-1!!

For the second time today...More last minute heartbreak!! But at least this was a goal without controversy...Greece certainly live on the edge...I recall they scored a last minute dubious penalty to get through to the knock out stages...And here they are doing it again! What resilience from the Greece side!!

Final Score: Greece 1-1 Costa Rica

Extra time and with the extra man Greece must surely be favourites now to go through to the Quarter Finals...The Euros all over again...Slipping in under the radar!

EL GRINGO'S ONCE IN A LIFETIME

I translate the words of the Argentina Italia 90 song for Jane, Clive and Stephen and explain the context of using the word "Father".

Jane then says...So...We are the fathers of Argentina! I hadn't thought of that...But yes it's true!! The last time England played Argentina at the World Cup Finals, England won...Oh what fun to be had with the Argentine's hereon in!

Jane tells me the seats were empty at the Holland game because people had to move back in the shade because of the heat!! Putting aside Robben's antics, that just makes the Dutch comeback in the final minutes all the more remarkable. They must be super fit!

Jane tells me about the problems faced in sorting out accommodation. They booked an apartment on Leblon through bookings.com three weeks before the tournament and paid an £800 deposit. After the deposit had been paid, the owners then insisted on the remaining £3000 being paid in cash! Jane offered PayPal, direct debit but they wouldn't listen. Naturally Jane didn't feel comfortable in carrying around that sum of money in cash. Eventually Jane had no option but to cancel and lose the £800 deposit #ripoff

They strongly recommend a visit to Iguaçu Falls and to stay overnight. It sounds spectacular but I am not sure it will be possible now.

We are drinking quite quickly three beers and a caipirinha already...Food? Hmmm...

I know Jane through a fellow Spurs fan called Phil who I have known for close to 40 years through watching Spurs and I send him a text saying...You will never guess who I am sat having a caipirinha with and of course he responds... Jane!

Extra time comes to an end and the ten men of Costa Rica manage to hold out for a 1-1 draw.

Penalties...

Costa Rica take the first penalty and score. Greece step up...1-1

Both score again 2-2

Rica score...3-2... Greece score 3-3...Good penalties!

Penalties are like tennis to me...Be it during a set or in a tie break... Now we are getting to the business end now where as in tennis a mistake or winner now can be fatal. The tension is mounting...

Rica make it 4-3... Seven penalties, seven goals...Greece step up...Keeper saves!!

The beach bar chants Rica! Rica! Rica!

If Rica score their next penalty, they are in the last eight of the World Cup Finals!!

Yesssss...Goal!! 5-3!!! Costa Rica, the supposed whipping boys of Group D are through to the Quarter Finals of the World Cup to play Holland!!

A population of around three million... Ten men...Wow...So pleased for them! My thoughts are with the family we met in Recife. How happy they must be!! Fabulous for them!!!!

Some effort to score all five penalties...I make a note to check whether they have a German heritage!!

I say my goodbyes to Jane, Clive and Stephen...It was lovely to see them and watch the match together. They are flying up to Brasilia tomorrow to watch France versus Nigeria. Amazing that we met up like we did and so pleased that we did!

I walk up to the California Othon Hotel pick up my suitcase. They can't find my suitcase and ask for my room number. I tell them my room number and they start to look on the computer system. The staff on reception tonight don't appear to speak very good English. I try to explain that I left the case when I checked out last Thursday. This is taking forever... Somehow I pluck out the name of the lady on reception who spoke good English and was on duty when I left my suitcase. They call Myrelle and some minutes later my suitcase is retrieved. Phew that was difficult!

I lug the suitcase across the dual carriageway to pick up a taxi which will be heading in the direction of Prado Junior. We pass Prado Junior which is a one way system in the wrong direction. We take the next left at the Windsor and he signals first left. The driver plays the usual game of making a mistake in the one way system He can't turn into this street as it is one way. He then has to do a u turn and heads back to Avenida Atlantique. We pass Prado Junior again. The meter is climbing and climbing. We are now stuck in traffic heading back towards the California Othon Hotel from where we started the journey.

We have a heated exchange of words with him speaking in Portuguese and me in English. The meter is continuing to climb upwards. In frustration I open the taxi door give him 10 reals and don't wait to hear his protestations...He knows I know his game...Unfortunately I am further away from the hotel than I was five minutes ago and have to lug my suitcase a good four blocks to the apartment building.

On reaching the building, Security won't let me in without seeing my passport. I try to say I will open the case in my apartment and bring it down. This is not acceptable to them... I am now on my hands and knees in the lobby opening my suitcase, hampering the ease with which people can get in and out of the apartment building.

Having lived out of a rucksack for more or less two weeks, finding my way around the suitcase is not easy. To find my passport which would have been put in a safe place last Thursday, I now have to take clothes out and the only place to put them is on the dirty floor. Security already have all of my passport details registered and I have the apartment key in my hand. They won't relent... Eventually, I find it for a quick look by them and it is then handed back to me.

I pull my suitcase towards the two lifts. The security guy calls me and gestures me back towards the entrance of the building to walk down a different passage to the Service lift.

Eventually I reach my apartment and drop my suitcase off, change and am straight out to meet up with Major and Jas! That was an unnecessary stressful hour or so!

We meet up in their local bar for a couple of beers. They tell me it was 33 degrees today!! It felt hot but my word not a bad temperature for the depths of winter!

We talk of Robben's dive and I tell them the old Baddiel and Skinner story about Klinsmann who had a bad reputation for diving. They were watching a Germany match on TV one night. During the game, one of them went up to take a beer from the fridge. On the way, he brushed passed the TV set and Klinsmann fell over!

Major and Jas tell me that in the UK press it was reported that an English fan bit off another England fan's ear lobe at the game v Uruguay...Suarez can't be blamed for creating a copycat incident as this happened before his biting incident. What a crazy story though...Hearing this story makes me realise how totally disconnected I am from what is being said at home...

They take me to Dante's bar and restaurant which is on the corner of Prado Junior and Nossa Senhora. It is literally across the road from my apartment!

We order a white wine and two chopp beers...15 minutes later...A red wine, water and caipirinha arrive...Wtf!!

It is 11.47pm and two guys have just walked passed our restaurant only wearing white Speedo swimming trunks...Only in Rio!!

It is now 11.52pm I have not eaten yet today...In fact I calculate back that my last meal was at around 4pm yesterday...Some 32 hours ago...It is not deliberate...I am a Taurean and love my food...It just seems that I just don't get round to eating out here and....The weird thing is I am not even hungry!

After a few more drinks and I finally have a bite to eat, Jas decides to call it a night. Major is up for going to the Barszin night club in Ipanema on Rua Vinícius de Moraes, 75. We take a 20 real taxi ride and walk up the stairs and into the club. It is quite a trendy place and I am back on my staple caipirinha diet! Major is straight on to the dance floor and immediately in a good rhythm to the beat.

Maybe I am a little tired, maybe I feel a little old, maybe I feel I could be in a trendy nightclub anywhere in the world rather than experiencing a Rio de Janeiro night...For whatever reason, my spirit sinks a little and after about half an hour or so, I finish my drink and take a taxi back to my apartment. Major is quite happy on the dance floor on his own and I am sure won't miss me!

EL GRINGO'S ONCE IN A LIFETIME

The World Cup in the Cayman Islands meant it was in the same time zone so just about every ex-pat of every nationality represented immersed themselves in the folly their own team presented. Businesses shut early pubs were packed and World Cup fever presented opportunity for social gathering without any social conflicts. Ex-pats united for football. Office sweepstakes were won and lost and it was amazing to see myself supporting Germany as I had them in the draw!

World Cup fever certainly gave the island an excuse to party not that it needs one! :)

Chris Bailey, English but living in the Cayman Islands

We had a great time. I have been to the World Cups in 1990, 1994 and 1998 but this was the best. The football atmosphere in Rio was fantastic especially around Copacabana.

The street life in Lapa was an eye opener! The beaches and the warmth of the Brazilians were outstanding.

Robert Hollerhead, Australia

MONDAY 30TH JUNE 2014

Wake at 8.30...Although I must surely have adjusted to the time zone by now, I always have the feeling it will be much later...But it never is!

I am very hot...The room is very hot...The fans may well have to be on 24/7... Good job its winter!!!

I resolve to do a number of chores this morning...

I unpack my suitcase and split the clothes into three piles...Those ok to wear go into the wardrobe, those I won't wear again out here are put into the suitcase and a third pile is created for the launderette.

In packing to come to Brazil, with the amount of internal travelling ahead of me, I decided to travel light. I am however here now for more than four weeks as opposed to the originally intended two weeks. To be honest, I am a little bored with the small selection of clothes to choose from #smallpricetopaythough!

I begin to feel a mild sense of unease as I can't find my two credit cards. The unease starts to build until I am frantically searching and rechecking every possible place. I know that I had left them in my case. It didn't seem sensible to be carrying all three cards and cash across to Flamengo so I balanced it up by taking the cash and one credit card.

I start to think...I had to open my suitcase in the lobby last night when I gave my passport to the Security guy on reception. Were my credit cards inside my passport...? Did they fall out in the lobby? I go down to the lobby...The Security guys don't speak a word of English... I try to make myself understood but they are not very interested in listening...I go back to my room and find the phone numbers to call and cancel the cards. Before doing so, I carry out one last check...When emptying the case this morning; I put all the paraphernalia gathered during my trip into a carrier bag... Worth a look... Nothing... And then I see A4 folded paper and remember!!

Relief...you may wonder why I have chosen to share this with you and I am also asking myself the same question! I think the reason is to show that there are so many variables in play here...Moving between cities, moving accommodation within a city, being split from my luggage for prolonged periods, the effects of travel, tiredness, alcohol etc...So much scope for so much to go wrong...

Now I have my credit card, I call Bravo Fly to try to move my flight back a further day...They write back to say that there isn't any availability on the 14th or indeed the 15th... No surprise there then! The first couple of days after the World Cup Final will have been booked by FIFA, media and journalists etc a long time ago.

I write to ask if there are any later flights on the 13th, the night of the Final or via any alternative routes. If not I will just about see the Final after which I need to hotfoot it to the airport... The flight is at 7.50pm and the match should finish by 6pm, hopefully it will be decided in 90 minutes!

After the launderette and bank, I manage to buy some contact lenses for the reminder of my time in Brazil #surprisinglyeasy.

Domestics finally done... I can finally think about going over to the fan fest to watch the match!

I arrive in the main fan fest in my usual place with thirty minutes of the France v Nigeria match gone and it is still scoreless. It is busy but nowhere near as busy as previously. I had developed a similar feeling on the promenade whilst walking to the fan fest. A lot of people seem to have returned home...Their 2014 World Cup adventure being safely locked in their memory banks forever...Once in a lifetime... All will have different stories... Of their team's performances, of their personal experiences... Some good... Some not so good...

Half time it is 0-0...

I am not in the mood today to start chatting with strangers... Instead I go through my diary...Hmmm...My mood is not so good today...The positive party man needs to return...The weather is not helping... It is overcast and rain is forecast for tomorrow. Although the temperature is 27 degrees, a cooler breeze is definitely noticeable. May be the party man left with the sun!

The opening 15 minutes of the second half belong to Nigeria... France are struggling to keep them at bay... If Nr Nigeria had really been Mr Nigeria instead of Mr Ivory Coast... He would be very happy right now!

The French are putting a few heavy tackles in and a Nigerian player is stretchered off... Lloris is having to make quite a few saves...Giroud off for Griezmann...

The fan fest crowd is well populated by the French but they are very quiet. The neutrals are siding with Nigeria and a few chants with a soft "g" confirm this. An acrobatic clearance by a Nigerian defender brings a further round of applause in the fan fest.

Benzema goes on a mazy run into the box, plays a one two and is through one on one... The keeper half saves but the ball is heading towards the goal... A defender steps in and hooks it clear! Great play though by Benzema!

The Argentines are here again in the fan fest and singing their songs including of course their Italia90 song.

The Griezmann substitution and Benzema run seem to have inspired the French...

Another clearance off the line... A follow up shot thuds against the crossbar...

The pressure is mounting... Keeper flaps at the ball... Pogba rises to head into the net!!! 1-0 France!!

Now a good save from Lloris... Looks like it will be difficult for Nigeria to turn this around but... After the late drama in yesterday's games... Anything is possible!

Allez Les Blues is being sung with increasing confidence as the game goes into the final 5 minutes...The fan fest is much busier now...full!!

The wind is getting up ...It could well rain this afternoon...

5 minutes added time...France score a second... Not strictly true!! Nigeria's Yobo scores it for them!

There is something about the African sides...Even when Nigeria were on top, I still doubted they could go on to win the game and I sense they doubted it too. Maybe this is the thing about African sides?

Final score 2-0 France!

After the shocks in the Group phase... The line-up for the Quarter Finals is still shaping up to be a strong line up... Brazil, Colombia, Holland, France with only Costa Rica the surprise package so far... Add Germany and Argentina plus one of Belgium/USA and we are in for quite a finale.... Not sure what the reaction to the tournament is in the UK but people over here are saying that so far it's been one of the best tournaments for years... Difficult to disagree!!!!

As it is now 3pm... And I haven't eaten or drunk anything today...Yes I know, I know...Going back to the BBQ now before the second game...Promise!!

Meet Patrick from Sweden living in Norway at the BBQ counter. He has been to see a girl in São Paulo for some days and is now in Rio on his own. We exchange numbers.

Patrick says there is a district in São Paulo called Vila Madelena which had two million people on the streets at night... All in party mode! He said it was crazy and so tightly packed that it was a little scary too...Two million...It is hard to comprehend two million people in one district!

Patrick said that in a part of Sao Paulo, the Government give the "would be" homeless huge tenement blocks to live in...It can be quite dangerous to wander into the wrong district! Imagine what it would be like in these blocks...There but for the grace of God...

We get taking with Uruguay fans who say their President has been very critical of FIFA in an outburst today. In their opinion Suarez should have received a one or two match ban!! I asked if they felt he had let their country down and they said the feeling is more of disappointment. They feel football is not a sport of business people and gentleman but for men from the streets...

We go down to the beach and meet Colombians singing and dancing on the beach...

They fancy their chances of beating Brazil!! And maybe they just might! An Argentinian has a very strong joint on the go...It is pungent...Patrick buys us a couple of beers off a beach vendor.

He asked which cities I have been to and when I say Recife... Patrick tells me about a teenage girl from Sao Paulo who had her leg bitten off within the last year by a shark. A brave guy rescued her but it was to no avail and she died either on the way to or at the hospital.

(Postscript...On returning to the UK, I Googled "Recife shark attacks" and learnt Recife is one of the most dangerous places in the World to swim. There have been 59 shark attacks in the last 21 years and not only is the story of the 18 year old girl true but there is also a video...Not for the squeamish or faint hearted...)

We get talking with Martin and Paulo who are part of a group of seven or eight Argentines and in particular... I ask them to sing the Italia 90 song for Patrick which they do. Others join in and now they are singing "*If you don't jump up and down you must be English*"... The other guys aren't aware I am English! This is followed by

Brazil, Brazil,
It is our obsession, to win the World Cup in
Brazil, Brazil

We now have TV cameramen filming us!!

We go into the fan fest and I say to Martin... Tell your friends I am English... But only when I am deep inside the fan

fest!

On reaching my usual place, Patrick and I meet up with Essex lads Jo, Jordan and Harry along with Ross from Nottingham. Ross has been touring South America for six months and met the Essex boys in Buenos Aires. They went to see the Argentina v Trinidad and Tobago warm up match in the week before the World Cup started and have travelled together ever since.

The Germany v Algeria game is already underway...very entertaining... Algeria are giving as good they get versus the might of Germany!

Goal...Algeria... Wow! Oh noo offside... Shame!! This is end to end with both teams creating chances and both keepers making good saves.

Half time 0-0

Patrick has had enough of the fan fest and says his goodbyes.

Ross tells me of a few stories of his trip...

As an entrée, he tells me did a trail to Machu Picchu for four days and for all four days had diarrhoea... ooh errr!

Before a white rapids tour, a half hour health and safety presentation was given to them... The tour was with an "experienced guide" in Grade 2 rapids which is regarded as very safe...Grade 6 being the most dangerous and Grade 1 being gentle. At the first rapids, the boat over turns and they all thrown overboard. Ross was under the boat... Panicking... All survived...But only just and it was a very frightening experience...

In Nicaragua, or Guatemala, Ross can't quite recall but the hostel he was staying at had adopted a monkey. Staying at the hostel was Gary who spoke very loudly with a thick New York accent. Ross described as the type of person who is accident prone and often unaware of what is going on around him! Gary had had some dental treatment and was given a valium supply as a precautionary measure. One night he came running into the bar shouting the monkey has my valium, the monkey has my valium! It seems the monkey broke into his room and took the valium!

They chased the monkey all over the hostel and finally tempted it with a food swap! Fortunately the monkey hadn't been able to open the screw cap container!!

They met an English fan from Middlesbrough in Belo Horizonte. The guy had a huge Afro and he bumped into them again in Rio. However, when he said hello, they didn't recognise him. His head was completely shaven and if he hadn't said hello they wouldn't have recognised him at all...It seems a company sponsored him to have his head shaven...They gave him five tickets and flew him and his four friends to Brasilia for today's France v Nigeria match and also provided a free hotel plus food and drinks!!

In Sao Paulo, the lads booked the cheapest possible hostel for the night before the England v Uruguay game. It felt strange when they arrived at the hostel. It was a long way out of the city and well off the beaten track. Nobody spoke English on the reception desk and nobody seemed to want to register them. There weren't any other football fans or tourists there. It felt like a homeless place. They went out for dinner and came back around 11pm as they were a bit nervous about walking the streets with lowlifes grabbing hold of them. When they arrived back, one of the guys had to sleep around a corner from the others. In the middle of the night, he woke aroused thinking of a dream of his girlfriend. He was in the top bunk and as he awoke, he became aware of a huge shadow by the side of the bunk bed...A presence... He then became aware of a hand rubbing his genitals through his underwear. It was a six feet plus (two metres) bearded guy!!! He screamed out to his mates, who woke thinking he was being robbed, which in some ways he was, and they gave chase... Fortunately for the guy he got away... They left early in the morning and didn't go back for the paid second night. No matter how many showers he had the next day he felt violated...

The second half carries on in the same vein...The fan fest is alive... The Germans are getting on top...Incredible saves and misses.

9 minutes to go... The Algerians seem to be tiring...A German goal feels inevitable...Corner... An Algerian player goes down with cramp...If Algeria are to cause an upset; it feels as if it will have to be in the 90 minutes.

Now a free kick on the edge of the box...Algerians giving their all... Sadly can't see them getting to 90 minutes let alone penalties... And even if they did... We all know...The Germans always win on penalties!

What a waste of a free kick... Howls of derision as a German falls over trying to be innovative...

Schweinsteiger header... Surely... No...!! Keeper saves...again!

Now Neuer is having to rush off his line to clear.

4 minutes added time...

Last minute... What an interception... Algerian keeper catches the corner. Extra time!!

9second minute...Cross...Schurrle 1-0... What a great goal!

Now that the resistance has been broken, could possibly be three or four now...

Ross tells me the countries he has visited in the last six Months...Mexico, Belize, Guatemala, Nicaragua, Costa Rica, El Salvador, Panama, Colombia, Peru, Bolivia, Argentina, Brazil...Some adventure... And many of the countries are those that have featured on news channels with wars and drug gangs during my life time!

Ozil scores to make it 2-0! Puts the result beyond doubt... Brave hearts of Algeria crushed...

My word... I can't believe it. Algeria go straight up the other end and score!! 2-1!! What do I know!!!!

One final push from Algeria...Header comes in... Neuer takes comfortably...

Final score Germany 2-1 Algeria

Very entertaining game with some very entertaining new friends!

We go down to Mabbs... Caipirinhas... Oh dear... The night is young... So are these guys... Their energy is infectious!

The heavens open... To say it's lashing down, torrential, whatever isn't enough... And just when it can't get any wetter... Harry knocks his beer all over Jo...

Ross starts to tell me a story about him and his girlfriend who went home towards the end of their travels...The rest of the lads sing...Ross and is missus; we've heard it all before!

The drinks are flowing...We move on to Mud Bug but lose Jo and Harry on the way.

We pay 20 reals entry fee to go into the Mud Bug bar except we don't... It is another one of those where they give you a card and you pay everything when you leave... Always a little suspicious of paying in this way as the bill is not easy to stay on top of...

We also have to provide passport details...Now where have I heard that before! When we say we don't have our passports with us, they let us enter our personal details on the computer...Which we do... Correct ones of course...

At the bar we get talking with Lawrence a Sky news journalist from Bristol. He says it is 20 years ago today that the footballer Escobar of Colombia was murdered in his homeland after making a mistake at the World Cup. It seems the Colombians want to demonstrate to the World at Brazil 2014 that a new Colombia has been born.

Laurence also tells me of the Alzirao, Tijuca suburb of Rio de Janeiro. It has been holding informal gatherings to watch World Cup matches on a large screen since 1978. This year with the World Cup being in Brazil, FIFA tried to stop it... Eventually and only after enormous pressure, FIFA allowed it to continue but they were not allowed to show any mention of the World Cup or of Brazil 2014.

It is a regular bar and we are having a good night when in walks Rob! Would be difficult to miss Rob...He is 6'11" (2.11 metres) and before you ask...Yes he was a professional basketball player! Finally we meet up!! We have been trying since my very first night in Rio. Rob is staying until the 16th July and insists I change my flight to the same date and stay at his place from the 13th to the 16th so that I can be there for the World Cup Final party. For my book, it sounds the logical thing to do...Robs says his place is about an hour's drive from Copacabana.

There is quite a large group of us now and it's some night... My temporary mood of lunch time went the moment I walked into the BBQ and met Patrick. I love that BBQ!! I feel well set for the rest of the World Cup.

Rob picked a friend up from

airport and on the way back the taxi driver ran a red light while on his mobile phone. It seems that taxi drivers can go through red lights after 10pm...That explains a lot! But not whilst on a mobile phone!! A Police car with sirens and flashing lights is requesting the taxi driver to stop. The taxi driver ignores the request! The Police are making it very clear he must stop and eventually the taxi driver pulls over. They are all ordered out of the taxi at gun point! Rob says... Don't shoot; we are English...And then to his friend...Welcome to Brazil!

Jordan talks about his love of following Millwall home and away...Rob talks of his travels watching Spurs. He has a photo of him in the main square of Kiev when Spurs played out there last season... Behind Rob there are fires and riots...It was the night a hundred people died... What a crazy decision to play that game... It should have been moved weeks before...Spurs helpfully told the 40 fans not to go back to Kiev... As Rob said it might have been a nice gesture to organise a bus to the airport or do something to help them...

The talk moves back to the World Cup and Rob and I agree to take an overnight bus to one of the semi-finals in either Belo Horizonte or São Paulo!

We say our good nights and I get to bed around 3.15am. What a fantastic day and night that turned out to be!

Already one month before the World Cup began, my car got a transparency sheet "Hopp Schwiiz" that meant of course, that I will support the Swiss football team.

Two weeks before the World Cup started, we organised in our company a tote. About hundred teams participated giving their tips. The daily ranking was posted every day on the screen in the warehouse and on the intranet. Therefore many discussions took place every day, especially because the best ranking teams were not the football fans or the ones who really know all about the football.

Women teams were lucky and finally a women team won the tote and got a team prize. We bought banners from all nations who participated at the 2014 World Cup and every day the warehouse was decorated with the banners of the teams who were playing on that day.

In our company, work employees from 22 different countries, so you can imagine how the discussions were and how many emotions and frustrations when a supported team won or lost. It was a very good experience and made a positive contribution to the good working environment.

For myself, the World Cup meant very little sleep, but showed me a colourful world with happy people all around the world.

The people of each nation moved together. The World Cup in the news was top priority and forgotten was, at least for a while, war and suffering in the world. During three weeks the world was a great sportive family.

Edith Zweifel, Switzerland; World Cup Supported Team: Switzerland;
Forecast Winner of the World Cup; Brazil.

Algeria's path was historical for the African level, not only for a country but for all the African continent and all of the Arabian people.

When I talk with the people in France or Brazil they say me what a team! Very seductive!

I think the Algerian Team was the "heart stopper" "le coup de coeur", like we say in French, of the Brazil 2014 World Cup because nobody expects Algeria to perform at that level.

I don't find the words for the heroic Quarter Final game with Germany.

Naoufel Loudjertli, Algerian living in Marseille, France

TUESDAY 1ST JULY 2014

I forgot to turn the volume off on my phone, so you can guess what happened... 7.45am...well at least I managed four and a half hours sleep! Wait for the five minute hangover to wear off! This room is so bloody warm. It could do with transferring some of the heat to the shower... Cold water and hangovers ugh...

The location of the apartment couldn't be better. It is literally one block back from the beach and the fan fest. It feels safe, at least during the World Cup. There are a lot of hookers in the area and a few ladyboys and transvestites, but it doesn't feel threatening...

Although dominated by tourists and football fans... Much more so than Flamengo...You don't have to scratch too far below the surface to see a community going about its daily life...Talking of which... Having pleaded for my laundry to be ready before closing time yesterday, I had better go and collect it!

Events moved very quickly yesterday... Patrick, the Argentines on the beach, the Essex guys and Ross, Laurence the Sky news reporter and Rob... Not sure I mentioned Christi from San Francesco and her gay boy friend... Remind me later... Just in case I forget!

Bit of a shock to find that, having withdrawn 800 reals this morning, the balance remaining is 111 reals which is about £30. Reinforcements needed!!

Looking forward to the fan fest today... Not watched an Argentina game in there yet... Having had the forged ticket experience in their first game I couldn't get back from the Maracana in time...

I text round the guys to see if any will make it in time... Doubtful is my guess given that they also have to travel in.

At around mid-day as I turn onto the promenade, I can already hear the Argentine fans singing. This will be some atmosphere! There is no doubt...The Argentine fans are the most pronounced in this World Cup...This song over and over again is getting a little tiresome though!!

I am laid on the beach catching an hour or so of sun... There are hundreds of Argentines on the beach. Some are as close as 100 metres away. All are in their light blue and white shirts and for the most part with the number 10 Messi on the back. They have huge flags in the same colours, drums and whistles. They are bouncing up and down on the beach singing inevitably the Italia 90 song amongst many others in their repertoire.

It's 12.45... The sun is out... So much for the rain which was forecast!!

For some reason I look incognito today... Sunglasses and Brazil hat... I wonder which is worst to an Argentine... England or Brazil... Not very often England beat Brazil but... Think England would win this one!!

An Englishman in a Brazil hat... Hmmm not sure that was my wisest move of the day!!

I am walking into the fan fest through security... Feels like an Argentina home game and I haven't seen a single away fan yet lol!! I suspect though that I might know who the Brazilians will be supporting!

It must be great to go to a game 100% confident your team is going to win. I can tell that is exactly the mood of the Argentines...Not a shadow of doubt... They are not only here to win today, they are here to win the World Cup. When did we ever have such belief...? May be 1998 and 2002 we had some level of confidence...But nothing like the Argentines. Unlike Ally MacLeod's, tartan army boost in 1978, bless his soul, this is merited... Messi, Higuain, Di Maria... They can even afford to leave Tevez and his diva tantrums at home!

The national anthem is sung loudly and passionately. The fan fest is much fuller than yesterday for the first game... Guess the locals will be at work and can only make the second game otherwise it would be heaving...

Lots of beer being drunk ahead of a 1pm kick off... And in this heat!

Towards the front... It is a little like the mosh pit at a rock concert... The songs being sung by the fans in the stadium are being echoed around the fan fest.

Still a lot of English out here... Crystal Palace, Derby County shirts amongst many others. There are Americans in their red blue and white stripes here for their 5pm kick off, the yellow of Brazil, red of Chile, Mexican green, the Aussie yellow... Finally I see a red Suisse shirt...Brave man!!

The strong smell of Marijuana wafts around the park...so strong I could get high on secondary fumes!!

It's baking hot in the fan fest... 13 minutes gone and still fans are pouring in... Around a dozen or so Swiss just in front of me now in their orangey red shirts

Pele appears on the screen to huge boos of derision from the thousands of Argentine fans in the fan fest.

I get talking with Rowan and Laura from Sydney who stopped off in Santiago and caught the Brazil versus Chile game on TV in a bar. There were hundreds of riot police as when Chile beat Spain there were riots... Yet there was a party atmosphere after they lost on penalties... It seems they riot when they win and party when they lose!

27 minutes... Cut back... Swiss must score... Blocked... What a chance!

Stings the Argentines into life... Cross whipped in... How did someone not get a touch!

Swiss striker through... Just the keeper to beat... Apologies for being unkind but that was a pathetic effort...

Half time 0-0

A computer game of FIFA is being played on the big screen by two ex-players.

Second half and the Swiss are creating the better chances... Hitzfeld has them incredibly well organised.

Based on their games so far in this World Cup and the number of goals conceded by both of these defences, I thought this might be a bit of a goal fest but after 56 minutes it's still goalless.

The smell of herbs is coming from an English guy sharing it with Argentinians... Laura says at least it smells better than cigarette smoke. I have never taken any substances but I can't disagree.

Argentina break down the left... Through... Great save by the keeper at point blank range diving across his goal...

Halfway through the second half... Messi shoots just over the bar. It is becoming a game of Swiss defence v Argentina attack.

Rowan's knowledge of football is amazing... There is an Aussie cricketer called Michael Hussey who was nicknamed Mr Cricket... Rowan is on the verge of being nicknamed Mr Football!!

Laura, a Liverpool fan, asks me to put an Aussie quote in my book... Friends don't let friends support Chelsea or Arsenal. If that was a tweet, I would have to favourite it!

The sun is on the back of our necks. It is incredibly hot and energy sapping in the fan fest. That one coca cola before the game whilst sunbathing on the beach is all I have had food and drink wise today. I make a mental note to buy a few provisions from the local supermarket.

15 minutes to go... Still goalless...

I learn that São Paulo is about 500m above sea level on a plateau which in addition to being further south explains why we were so cold when we went there to watch the England v Uruguay game.

8 minutes to go... Still goalless... The fan fest is full of nervous chatter... Well except for the adopted Swiss from Brazil... Singing Switzerland in Portuguese!

Last 5 minutes... A goal now either way would surely win it...Who would have thought it... I certainly didn't.

Heroic Swiss defending... Somehow getting last ditch tackles and blocks in...

Into added time... Swiss free kick... Could a seismic upset be on the cards here... Free header!!! Over the bar...

Into extra time... It's a tough one... Us Brits tend to root for the underdogs but I want Argentina!!

The Swiss Brazilians in the fan fest are Olé 'ing each Swiss pass...The team is getting stronger by the minute... Laura, who admits to being a lush, is on her sixth beer at 4.10pm in the afternoon. She is now asking me what the difference is between the England team and a tea bag. Yep the tea bag stays in the cup longer... From an Aussie for ffs...

A family from the USA are asking why I am still here... Double ffs!!

Second half of extra time...Penalties looming... Surely one of Messi and co can provide that one moment of magic, of inspiration to win this game.

There is a lot of tension building... The Argentine fans didn't expect this... Just shows what a good coach can do with a squad of players...Is it really the right decision to keep Roy?

Di Maria shoots...Top corner...Keeper somehow gets there to tip it over. Great save! The Argentine fans are in full voice!

Corner to Argentina... The camera in the stadium zooms in on an Argentine lady in the crowd. Her head is bowed; she is clasping her hands tightly and close to her face. This is becoming unbearable for them...

2 minutes or so to go... Messi runs at the heart of the defence one last time... Releases it to Di Maria who...Sweeps the ball into the far corner of the net!!!! 1-0 Argentina!!! The fan fest erupts!!! The distinctive light blue and white flags go up in the air...The Argentina fans having not believed the situation they were in and the possible lottery of penalties now can't believe that they have pulled it out of the bag!

The Swiss keeper comes up ...cross ... Header hits the post comes back hits the attacker... It looks to have gone in...Swiss fans in the fan fest cheer but ... Somehow it rebounds just wide.

Argentina break quickly... Di Maria shoots towards an empty goal from the half way line...The keeper hasn't got back... It's an open goal...Just misses!

This is frantic... End to end stuff... Free kick to the Swiss... Edge of the box... Dead centre... What a chance this is! Could this still go to penalties? Argentina will be on the floor if it does! If Messi was taking this, you would favour him to score. It is taking forever to line up... Steps up and ...Misses and the final whistle blows!

Final score: Argentina 1-0 Switzerland

Huge cheers of relief or celebration... Who cares!!! The screen shows scenes of jubilation in the stadium and also of absolute heartbreak...

The Swiss Brazilians sing in respect of a huge performance by their two hour adopted nation.

Boy, this is some World Cup!!!

Fantastic scenes leaving the fan fest... Brazilian Swiss, Argentines, real Swiss, Mexicans and a whole host of other nations all hugging, singing, posing for photographs... The samba disco starts up in the fan fest... As soon as the music comes on the Brazilian ladies immediately dance to the rhythm of the beat... It is almost as automatic as turning a computer on and the screen appearing in front of you. It is as if they have an inbuilt program to dance and smile along with the music. I could almost imagine the same reaction if Brazil get knocked out... Incredible!!

Jordan texts to say they will meet in the fan fest at the same place as yesterday for the second game.

I head across to the BBQ and am third in the queue. Logistically it must

be a nightmare for the staff... A few minutes earlier and the restaurant would have been empty. Then, whoosh it is full. Everybody wants to be served a drink immediately. As well they all want to order their food, and be served their food... And all at once!

And then there are those of us in the queue who after standing in the heat for over two hours are desperate to get a seat. Desperate for people to leave so that we can sit down and order our drinks, our food!!

Then there is the time pressure. It is 4.11pm and the next match kicks off in 49 minutes! Stress, pressure, deadlines...Sounds just like work...Only joking!

I eventually get a seat next to a guy called Ryan from north of San Francisco... Yet another Liverpool fan. He would like to see the USA win today but in being realistic about their overall chances, would like to see a Brazil v Argentina final with Brazil coming out on top.

Ryan has finished his meal and kindly offers me his mixed rice which is on a side plate. He stays for a chat with me whilst I eat my meal. His friend is flying in tomorrow and his brother on Friday. He accepts my invitation to watch the game together in the fan fest. The Quick Galetos really is a sociable place to eat.

The BBQ chicken is as delicious as ever. We leave the restaurant and head to the fan fest. Wow it is heaving... Incredibly busy...

We walk up to my usual place... It is rammed...The normal half time streaming backwards and forwards of people buffeting us around is continuous throughout the game. There are many more USA than Belgium fans in the fan fest and the chant USA! USA! USA! is heard regularly. On the pitch however, their team is struggling to get out of their own half. There appears to be quite a lot of empty seats in the stadium and yet FIFA site shows the match as a sell-out...Hmmm.

At half time we go from being completely rammed to it being very spacious... Only having restrooms at the back of the fan fest is a disaster... Why couldn't they have them dispersed throughout the fan fest? Everybody has to traipse through the thronged masses to the back. Wading through the sand, barging passed people. With a little more planning, it would have made it much easier for the fans.

Night falls over the fan fest, the lights of the Windsor hotel to our left compete with the floodlights. Above us there is a full moon and a helicopter adds to the noise of the disco. The cameraman hovers on a very pretty girl on someone's shoulders decked out in a USA bikini and flag. As I am writing, Ryan suggests I look up to the screen... And there we are, on the big screen! Me in my gringo Brazilian hat!

Just as the second half starts, a guy taps Ryan on the shoulder. They went to high school together some years ago!!

Howard tips over the bar. The one way traffic continues. Cross comes over... Origi misses the ball from six yards out. I seem to recall Paul or Ian saying that Spurs are interested in him...Hmmm... Another cross... Header onto the bar.... Now a shot over...Great run down the left hand side, pulled back and jabbed just wide... Mirallas comes on for Mertens... One way traffic!

USA chants go up...other than the occasional foray though, Belgium are laying siege on the USA goal.

20 minutes to go... Good save by Howard again.... Wondolowski comes on for the USA... He was studying in Chico at the same time as Ryan.

15 minutes to go and for all Belgium's dominance... Similar to Argentina earlier... The game is in the balance...

Another one on one... Another Howard save...He is having an amazing game.

Great run down the right... Pulled back... Another Howard save... England v Poland all those years ago when Tomaszewski thwarted England time and again comes to mind.

Howard punches clear under pressure... Belgium look a little vulnerable on the occasional counter... Would be a real smash and grab. I said to Ryan at the BBQ, Klinsmann is a winner... For some people, things just seem to happen, I just wonder if tonight is going to one of those nights.

Great last ditch block... Another good tip over by Howard!

5 minutes to go...USA corner but easily dealt with

Kompany starts a counter and gets on the end of a cross. Belgium look a very good side in all departments... If they do get through...The game against Argentina could be a classic.

Into added time...Knock down in the Belgian box... Ryan's mate, Wondolowski, six yards out... Goal at his mercy... Blazes over!!! Klinsmann holds his hands to his face in disbelief... Was that the moment??

Extra time... Ryan's old college friend has had his phone stolen out of his pocket. He thinks it was by an Argentine while buying a beer at half time and has gone off to try to find it. Probably 20000+ in here, I thought I got lucky with my sunglasses in the sea at Recife. This would be on a completely different level!

Second minute of extra time... De Bruyne...Low cross shot into the far corner... breaks the deadlock and probably millions of American hearts. Belgium finally find a way past Tim Howard to take a 1-0 lead.

Vertongen... Chance to make it 2-0 but he is a little slow and the chance is lost.

Great football from Belgium... Mirallas involved again down the right... Howard denies yet again!

Now a move down the left... Lukaku 2-0!! The score line is finally beginning to reflect the balance of play. This is a very impressive performance by Belgium.

Half time of Extra time 2-0 to Belgium

This would take a Herculean effort but... The Belgians will think they are through... An early goal and the momentum could turn but the Americans just haven't shown enough to suggest they have the ability to. If it wasn't for Tim Howard, Belgium would be out of sight.

Green comes on as a substitute for the USA... He is German! First touch... Goal 2-1!!! Wow...This could get interesting! The Americans are back in the game; not just on the pitch but also in the fan fest! The fans are really enjoying this match. The US are going for it! I believe that we will win rings out from the Americans. You know, maybe they just might! For the first time in the game, Belgium look rattled... But they are still dangerous on the counter... Howard saves again! Chadli comes on for Hazard... Really?? It feels like there will be another goal in this game but which way?

Free kick to the USA, a great inventive passing move slices through the Belgium defence... Dempsey one on one...Shoots...Courtois saves! What a game! What a World Cup!!

What a shame England didn't reach the knock out phase! Remember those dizzy days when teams could only beat us on penalties. Oh to suffer that misery again rather than be out after two games...

2 minutes to go... Fans chanting for both teams... Everybody so engaged in this wonderful football match.

Cross comes over... Out for a goal kick...Klinsmann is furious at only 1 minute of added time in extra time being shown on the electronic board.

Game over... Belgium 2-1 USA

The USA will have won a lot of friends with that plucky second half of extra time performance. They showed a great team spirit to come back so strongly from such a desperate position.

Ryan starts talking with a couple of young Brazilians in front of us... He is 24 and I guess they must be around 20... They introduce themselves as Aline and Jessica. Aline has self-taught herself English and her grasp is very impressive.

Jessica seems to be able to understand English but not speak it. Ryan invites them for a drink and we walk along the promenade in the direction of Ipanema as they would prefer to have a drink away from the fans pouring out of the fan fest, nearer to their apartments. During the walk, Aline talks of her career in insurance. She has travelled internationally including to London. She has driven from Strasbourg to Munich on her own! This is a journey I have done, it wasn't an easy one. We are a little taken aback at a lady so young having done all that she has.

Aline has just come back from a holiday in the Cayman Islands. I ask why she is not working today...She was ready for a change and left on Monday of this week without another job to go to...She has applied for a position in Munich!! Remarkably Jessica left her job on Monday too...She was working in healthcare specifically dermatology and wants a career change into media and public relations... She has an all-day interview arranged for tomorrow.

We talk about Brazil's performance so far in the World Cup and the media reaction. It seems the view we have formed about a lack of structure is being echoed across Brazil. Scolari is under pressure to improve performances and quickly otherwise there is a feeling that Colombia might beat Brazil. Scolari is also irritated with the media over suggestions that the match officials are favouring his team.

I ask which club side Aline supports and it is Vasco da Gama who are now struggling in the second Division. I am gobsmacked to hear this as about 12 years ago I saw them play Flamengo in the Cup Final in the Maracana. Aline said she started supporting them in 1994 when her father took her to her first game. At that time, they were on their way to the top and reached the summit in around 1998.

I stop her right there and then...You said 1994 Aline? That can't be right. Its 20 years ago? She said yes that it correct...Ryan and I look at each other in amazement... So your father took you to the game as a baby or toddler...But you can't have made the decision to support Vasco at that age? She starts laughing and says how old do you think I am? Ryan and I agree. 20 may be 21. The response is thank you, thank you; you have made my day... She then says... I am 11 years older than Jessica... Our jaws drop to the floor...Even if Jessica is 18 that would make Aline 29...Impossible to believe and yet with her career it makes sense #confused...

Eventually she tells us she is 34!!!!!!!!! We genuinely can't comprehend it...

We reach the restaurant and Aline asks if we would like to have a bite to eat. We say yes and Aline says her boyfriend Luiz will join us. She then disappoints me by saying her English club is Chelsea... Three of the Brazilian squad play for Chelsea and she has even been to Stamford Bridge to see them beat Man City. I say the next time she visits London, she has to come to White Hart Lane to see two more Brazilians and she agrees! I am a kind of Spurs missionary on this trip convincing Brazilians, Argentines and Americans to support my club...Giving them links to grab onto. Dempsey is a good one for the Americans... But on this trip, there is no doubting the popularity of Liverpool. From Australia, which has a district by the same name and links of Craig Johnston and Harry Kewell, through South America into North America and across into Scandinavia, many fans follow Liverpool. As I write this... I realise Manchester United have hardly been mentioned by the people I have met...Surely coincidental... But I can only write what I have heard people say. Steven Gerrard is by far the most popular player mentioned from the Premier League.

Aline orders a traditional local fish called mandioca/aipim...

We order drinks... Caipirinhas for Ryan and me whilst the girls who are teetotal order soft drinks. Aline's boyfriend Luiz joins us. He is 40 years old and has lived seven years in Toulouse and a year in Auckland...

I ask about how the World Cup is being received in Brazil. Aline says that the opening ceremony was a national embarrassment... Waiting and waiting for it to take off and it just never did... A damp squib...They had such material to work with... The carnival being a prime example but nothing... Nada...

mocking of the opening ceremony as depicted on Brazilian social media

Ahead of the tournament there was a huge concern as to whether the stadiums would be ready and the real possibility of the national shame of not being ready... But in true typical Brazilian style there was a huge frantic dash to just about get there... And amid the panic... There was the sadness at the loss of life of construction workers...

Six months before the World Cup started there were a lot of Brazilian people posting protests on Twitter... Now these same people are posting photographs of themselves inside the stadiums saying look at me...people are retweeting their previous protest tweets which is causing a lot of hilarity...But there is also a serious side to this... Many people don't want Brazil to win the World Cup because it will cause such a wave of euphoria. The World Cup being awarded to Brazil by FIFA and backed by the Brazilian Government will then be seen to be justified in the eyes of the World.

Luiz says the hundreds of millions spent on the stadium in Brasilia is the biggest illustration of waste...The local club only has a support of 500 fans so... Flamengo from Rio will play some home games there to avoid a post-World Cup public relations disaster.

The conversation moves on to crime and safety. For the time being it is safe on the front of Copacabana but just before the World Cup started an American was badly beaten and robbed by six men and as soon as the World Cup circus leaves it will return to as it was before... Dangerous! They advised us to close all our windows in taxis as being stuck in a traffic jam or at traffic lights is when the criminals can strike...

They told a story of an abduction of two ladies... As the car was climbing the hill, the lady in the front bravely grabbed the steering wheel and turned it which caused the driver to brake...She opened the passenger door and started to run down the hill. The kidnappers shouted out to come back or they will kill her friend. Instead she carried on running and screaming. The people living in the neighbourhood came out to help and forced the kidnappers to release the other lady...They lost their phones and handbags but it could have been so much worse.

Ryan then tells us of an horrific incident which happened to him in China... He had been drinking in a night club and while waiting for a taxi he ended up in a conversation with a local who spoke English...The taxi arrived and he jumped In and gave the card of the hotel where he was staying to the driver. The local who he had been speaking with jumped in the taxi just before it moved off and spoke to the driver in the local language. The taxi driver takes them to a warehouse and he is instructed by the other passenger to get out of the taxi at gun point.

He is taken inside the warehouse where there is a gang waiting... He is ordered to empty his pockets and while they are taking his cash he tries to hide his credit card. They spot what he is doing, take his card and demand 10,000 US Dollars for his release. They have a credit card payment machine!!!

During the course of the next three hours Ryan negotiates the price down from 10,000 to 60 US Dollars! He pays by credit card and is released. He is in the middle of an industrial estate, it is the middle of the night, and he has no cash. Bizarrely the kidnappers call a taxi and pay the taxi fare back to his hotel!!

We move the conversation away from crime and Aline says we must find the Rio metro pretty poor and especially when compared with London. I say that although I find London OK, a lot of the locals get very frustrated by it. I ask her to Google the song London Underground which she begins to listen to and bursts into uncontrollable fits of laugher! By the time the song comes to an end, she has tears rolling down her cheeks! I just have to take a photo to capture the moment. We were all laughing so much at her laughing at the words of the song. If you haven't heard it...Google it now!

It is Aline's dream to work in London and after seeing an outstanding letter of recommendation from her London counterparts, I agree to forward her CV to a few contacts.

I warn her of the cost of living, the scraping of ice off cars but she is undeterred. It seems the temperature can be well over 40 degrees in the summer in Rio and the thought of cold weather like she experienced in New York sounds perfect... She saw snow on the ground there but has never actually seen snowfall!! The only issue seems to be the quality of food in the London restaurants that she has been to... That the English eat potatoes with everything!

They suggest we visit Santa Teresa and Bar do Mineiro for a more authentic Brazilian experience than say Copacabana and the usual tourist venues.

Another place to visit is Bar Urca which has fabulous views and excellent sea food. She has a conversation with Luiz and Jessica and then says we could go there tomorrow evening and also bring along Ryan's friend, Gerado, who is arriving tomorrow. It is agreed that we will be picked up from Bar Cervantes on the corner of Barata Ribeiro and Prado Junior at 7.30 tomorrow evening.

After a very enjoyable evening we say our goodbyes and wish Jessica good luck with her interview in the morning.

Ryan and I walk back towards the fan fest and I see a text from Rob asking where I am and to join him as he is with some fellow Spurs fans. I try to reach him but by the time he picks up my message and responds it is 1am and we have already had a few mores beers and caipirinhas...We decide to stay out in the warm open air and have a walk along Copacabana promenade with large caipirinhas from a street vendor in hand. People are still sleeping in campers and cars along the front. Well most are still sat in fold up chairs drinking at the moment... There is a hot dog stall being operated out the back of one vehicle!

It is well after 1.30am... We see a couple of guys coming off the beach after playing football... We get talking...They are called Bhaga and Roo. Bhaga is a sports journalist. He finished work at 9pm, had dinner, and then at 11pm left his house, drove one hour to play in a match which kicked off on the beach at midnight! The match has just finished and he will now drive one hour back to his house and will be up at 6am for work #crazy or #wherethereisawillthereisaway

They are great guys and one is wearing a Corinthians shirt... As usual he says Spurs paid too much money for Paulinho. The Corinthians fans think he is average. Spurs scouting network ...Hmmm. Bhaga is a West Brom fan because they have a player with a similar name to his! I convince him to change to Spurs... But I have to become a Corinthians supporter #smallprice... My missionary work continues!

We walk back to what Colin and the guys called the "walk of shame". There are still loads of guys here drinking, eating and chatting with each other and the hookers. Like me, Ryan has never seen anything like this before in his life...I tell him what we had heard about supply outstripping demand and bringing them in from different parts of Brazil...He can't believe it! A little later one walks up and says hello, we ask where she is from... She says Sao Paulo... Staying in an apartment here and going home after the World Cup!

We get another caipirinha and get chatting with a group of Argentines. The usual... Pochettino, Lamela, Ardiles and Villa... One guy is really enjoying the conversation and says it is a big risk to take this out and show you... It is very valuable and there are lots of people here who would go crazy for it... Furtively he pulls out an old Boca Juniors shirt signed by all the star players... It clearly means so much to him and he risked taking the shirt out of his rucksack to show us..

It is after 3am and we have had enough to drink. Ryan takes a taxi back to his hostel on Ipanema and I walk the less than ten minutes to my apartment. Walking back I reflect on what a fantastic day and night it has been. Great football, great company, great stories and a great insight into Brazilian life from our new friends.

EL GRINGO'S ONCE IN A LIFETIME

From a football perspective, Nigeria's qualification for the FIFA 2014 World Cup came with mixed feelings for the Nigerian people; A feeling of 'thank God we made it" because as "Champions of Africa', we felt we should make it… But due to our past flaws, it made another great achievement for the gaffer; Steven Keshi, who captained us to our first ever World Cup in 1994 and won the Nations Cup both as a Player and a coach for the Super Eagles.

There is no doubting of Keshi's credibility, but a bigger target for him was to take us beyond the last 16 stage for the first time. He also tackled the dilemma of whether to choose fan's favourite Peter Odemwinge. There had been a verbal conflict between them but Peters' stunning performances for Stoke City forced a recall.

Nigeria was grouped with Argentina, and two World Cup first timers: Iran and Bosnia & Herzegovina in Group F. The first match vs Iran was with a very high anticipation for the Nigerian fans who had a strong certainty that the Super Eagles would trash them but it was Iran that pulled off a surprising performance holding the Super Eagle up to a goalless draw.

The second match with Bosnia was with a lesser anticipation… Most fans expected Bosnia to win but Odemwinge repaid the fans' faith with the lone goal. The referee was also kind for disallowing a good looking Bosnian goal for offside

It was the Group F El Classico; a five goal studded showdown that helped the Super Eagles win back the hearts of their fans back (at least for a moment) with a very classy performance. Argentina won 3-2 but the Eagles performance and qualification for the next knock out phase made the fans believe that France could be brushed aside in the last 16 match.

It was a hard fought match between the two countries, but a goal from Paul Pogba and a late own goal from Nigeria's captain Yobo sealed victory for France and sent the Super Eagles packing and headed for home.

This year's World Cup result and performance summed up our pedigree so far in world football…Able to reach the knock out phase again but not yet quite ready to reach the latter stages.

Olasoji Tosin, Ibadan, Nigeria

WEDNESDAY 2ND JULY 2014

I wake up hungry!! There's a first!! The obligatory cold shower…I am trying to get used to it but it is not that easy first thing in the morning…No football day today…A rarity but as the tournament develops, this will become a more common occurrence..

After catching up on social media, I go across the road to Dante's restaurant and bar and order a breakfast of toast, cheese and ham, omelette, coffee, orange juice and melon…What a way to start the day! Why don't I do this every day and all for less than 20 reals…Well it would have been had I not been so thirsty!

I go back to the apartment and a WhatsApp message comes through to say

Andy Murray has been walloped in straight sets...Out at the Quarter Final stage... What a shock! Nadal is out too...Wow! Murray is having a bad year...Doesn't seem to have recovered fully from the back operation he had towards the end of last year which seems to have been compounded by parting with Lendl as his coach...Whatever...It is very disappointing news to receive...

I head down to the beach to make the most of the hot weather and decide to stay local near the fan fest.

Immediately, the cry of caipirinha on the beach booms out...I did say I was thirsty!

At this end of the beach, there aren't any sun beds so it is a chair or the beach. The chair which should come with a set of IKEA instructions.

The beach vendors are as ever in good voice! As are and as ever, the Argentines who are on the beach drinking and singing!

The smell of marijuana is in the air...You don't get this on Skegness beach! Well not out of season anyway!

There are four Brazilian girls laid on their tummies in thonged bikinis nearby. They are laid in line and attracting a lot of attention... Groups of guys walk up for photographs with and of them. It would be fair to say that they are enjoying the attention. I get up to see what the fuss is about... The view from behind makes for a photograph which you might imagine being used in a Rio tourist brochure. I take a photograph...For the book of course!

It is a little frustrating to not be able to go in to the sea...I just dare not leave my apartment key, phone and monies on the beach...

I finally make use of the underground facilities by the edge of the beach. A cost of two reals but they are actually very good and very clean.

I must have dozed off...Is there a finer way of spending an afternoon than snoozing on Copacabana beach in the sun with the sound of the waves behind you. I say behind you because that is the one downside to the beach. The afternoon sun is inland which means that all the chairs are set facing the promenade rather than the sea...The big man upstairs didn't get quite it right there...Or maybe he wants us to be looking upwards in the general direction of his son stood on the top of Corcovado!

Walking back up towards the promenade, there is a Brazil versus Argentina beach football match taking place. It has attracted quite a good crowd...Well over a hundred people are watching.

Argentina win the match and as the players shake hands, a TV crew comes on to the pitch and interviews players from both sides. It seems anything between Brazil and Argentina is very newsworthy at the minute! I try to imagine how many news crews will be in Rio on World Cup Final day should the Final be Brazil versus Argentina!

Back on the promenade, there is a three piece band. A drummer, sax and electric guitarist! Through the quality of their music, they are drawing a big crowd...There is always something happening on the promenade of Copacabana!!

At the top of Prado Junior, I stop off at Mabbs for a drink. Hookers are in the bar area. One comes over and can speak a little English. I want to learn more about her lifestyle so offer her a drink which she accepts. I am open with her and say I am writing a book and would she mind my including her in the book. She says no problem as long as I don't use her name...I say that would be rather difficult as I don't know her name! She laughs and tells me her Christian name...I agreed not to include her name so am honouring that commitment. For the purposes of the diary, I will call her "A"

It is difficult to guess her age so I ask her...She is 29 years old and has a daughter at home who is ten years old. She lives with her mum, two sisters and daughter. It turns out home is the other side of Barra Tijuca and depending on the traffic, it can take her anywhere between an hour and two hours to come to "work" on the local bus. A taxi would be too expensive...

The World Cup means different things to different people. For A, a hooker, it means a much busier life, longer hours and for the most part working seven days a week.

I ask her specifically what that means and she is very candid and matter of fact in her reply.

Outside the World Cup, she works six nights on the streets for anywhere between six and eight hours plus the journey time to and from work.

On average she will entertain two clients during the whole of the six nights and receive 150 to 200 reals for an hour's work. I.e. 300 to 400 reals per week which is somewhere in the region of £80 to £110 per week.

During the World Cup, she works seven nights a week and receives 300 reals for an hour's work and entertains on average two clients per night. This means that she is earning 600 reals, about £160 per night i.e. 4200 reals per week, about £1135 per week!

A is therefore earning more in one night during the World Cup than she would in a normal week!

She says she keeps all the money she earns and doesn't pay anything to any minders which for some reason surprises me; I guess I just assumed there would be minders etc taking a cut of the monies. I gently press on this point but she is adamant that isn't the case.

To illustrate her point, she tells me about a problem she once had when going back to an Italian's hotel room. He was on cocaine and started to slap her face and body. She felt very frightened and on getting out of his room rang the Police who, in her opinion, were not interested in doing anything about it.

She says during the World Cup, there have been a couple of occasions when after entertaining a client, he has refused to pay. She says the price was agreed and then opens the palms of her hands in front of her in frustration and says... How can they do that?

A says doing this work is the only way she can take care of her family and that for the most part she doesn't mind doing the work...And at times enjoys it!

As she speaks, I am surprised to find myself thinking that she is quite grounded and other than the nature of her work, she seems a nice, decent person.

In talking about the Italian guy, I ask her which nationality she likes the best. A replies...Norwegian guys...I can feel the Norwegian guys reading this book swelling...Behave... with pride!!

Naturally I ask why Norwegian guys and not being accustomed to the world she frequents am thinking... I didn't know they were regarded as the hottest and most passionate lovers in the world...Sorry Mr Norway!

Immediately I am made to sound rather foolish as she says...They pay the most money! Not feeling so good now hey Mr Norway... You are overpaying! Laughing here!

She says that most of the girls she knows are ok but there are always a few who can give them a bad name through stealing from people and so on. At this time, a lot of ladies have come in to Rio from all parts of Brazil and are staying together in apartments nearby for the duration.

It all sounds incredibly well organised and I again wonder as to who is organising everything but there is no point in pushing it any further...

Yes there are lady boys and transvestites and these should stand out from the crowd...They are usually the tall, loud ones...

I ask is the biggest frustration the standing and waiting around...And she surprises me by saying it isn't... She said her biggest frustration which happened again to her twice last night was going off in a taxi with a client and then not being allowed into his hotel or apartment block. It seems Security guards can be quite tough at a lot of hotels and even though she has her identity card details with her at all times, they often won't let her in. She not only loses the time in going to and from with the potential client but is also out of pocket as she has to pay for her taxi journey back...

Last night she didn't earn any money and paid two bus fares and two taxi fares.

I look at the time on my phone and am conscious of meeting Ryan and his friend at 7pm ahead of Aline and Jessica picking us up....It has been fascinating listening to her and given me a tremendous insight into her life as a hooker in Rio. I thank her and without any pressure from her side, give her 50 reals for her time.

I walk away thinking she is a decent person.

I get back to the apartment and feel pressed for time...Arrrggghhh...The shower is teeth-chatteringly cold...

I dash up to Prado Junior in the opposite direction from the beach to the junction of Rua Barata Ribeiro where Ryan and his friend Gerardo from Mexico are waiting outside Bar Cervantes. Gerardo introduces himself as Gerry and while we are waiting for the girls, we buy a beer and then a second one from the corner bar.

Ryan and Gerry got to know each other while in the Far East and have been friends ever since.

Aline and Jessica arrive and the three of us climb into the back of the car to head off to Urca. On route, Aline stops off at the foot of Sugar Loaf to show Ryan and Gerry how to get there and we get out to have a look at the lovely small beach nearby.

Aline is delighted to be living on Copacabana and not least because it is much easier to get into the centre of Rio to work from this side of town.

When she lived on the other side of the City in the Todos os Santos district, trying to get into the centre could be a nightmare. Once it took two hours to drive three blocks...Imagine the frustration!

Now the traffic is even worse as the district is not too far from the site of the 2016 Engenhao Olympic Stadium. The elevated Perimetral highway has been removed to rebuild the port area in preparation for the Olympic Games. It seems the locals will have a tough time of it for the next couple of years.

To ease the congestion on the roads and on the metro during the World Cup, a day's holiday is given on every day a game is played in Rio!

Aline used to be a little naughty on her way in to work by going in the wrong lane and pushing in to the correct lane at the last moment. On a couple of occasions, there was a Police car parked at the point where she intended to push in. The Police made her continue in the lane she was in. The problem for her was that the wrong lane led on to the 13km long bridge to Niteroi! This necessitated a 26km round trip and a toll fee of 6 reals. On both occasions, it added two hours to her journey and she arrived into the office at midday! The second time had the added stress of the fuel tank being close to empty. We don't know her well enough to say serves you right! As if any of us would ever push in....!!

We drive on to park by Bar Urca and meet up with Luiz who has come straight from work.

The Bar is in a fabulous location overlooking Guanabara Bay, which will be the setting for the Olympic sailing events in 2016. The views over the bay are absolutely magnificent. Across the bay, Christ the Redeemer sits majestically on top of the camel's camp, Corcovado. There are other smaller mountains and hills across the bay behind apartment, office and hotel buildings. Fishing boats are bobbing gently on the waters. Lights twinkle on the waters. It really is a beautiful setting.

The upper floor of the restaurant which looks out across the bay is full so we buy appetisers and drinks to sit on the wall overlooking the water. As ever the climate is warm and perfect.

As the drinks flow so do the stories!

Gerry says Mexico fans try to something crazy every World Cup...

At France 1998, a Mexican peed on the statue of the Unknown Soldier.

In Japan 2002, a Mexican stopped the bullet train in his drunkenness.

In 2010 a Mexican placed a Mexican Hat on the statue of Nelson Mandela.

In 2014 Gerry was on a boat and a Mexican threw himself off a cruise liner for the sake of "El Tri" which is Mexico's tricolour and for fame... He died...

Gerry from Mexico supports the football clubs, Pachuca and Queretaro and we agree to support each other's clubs... Luiz supports Flamengo and commits to coming to White Hart Lane for a match... A missionary's work is never done!

Talking of Mexico, I recall a donkey at the Aztec Pyramids in Mexico City... There was a bottle of beer on the floor. The donkey would pick it up with his mouth and guzzle down the beer before putting the bottle back on the floor... Thankfully, it is the only time in my life that I have seen a donkey staggering around drunk.

EL GRINGO'S ONCE IN A LIFETIME

Whilst doing CrossFit at the gym, Aline has got to know a guy who works for ESPN. He asked her how easy it is for the locals to get hold of World Cup tickets. Aline says that even though she wakes to log on at 5am each morning, it is impossible...He says he might be able to give her a ticket or two for the France v Germany Quarter Final game at the Maracana on Saturday!

Jessica is stunned.

And possibly...Two semi-final tickets for the semi-final in Belo Horizonte on the following Tuesday... Which might be Brazil against France or Germany!! I jokingly say...Could you ask him to make that three tickets...To my amazement...Aline says yes I will ask him!!!!

Jessica says she will be in Belo Horizonte all of next week because... She got the job!! Which, of course, calls for another round of drinks!!

During the course of the night, Jessica who has had one caipirinha is quite tipsy and suddenly speaking English! Caipirinhas reach the parts other drinks can't reach #confidence

We learn that she moved to Rio from Natal fifteen months ago and shares an apartment with four other girls...One bathroom...We all agree that mornings must be somewhat frantic and stressful!

We head back to Copacabana, six of us in the five seater car. Aline is hungry so on returning we end up having a beer and pizza somewhere. A very obvious transvestite comes in to order pizza....I take a photograph but with those forearms and biceps am pleased he or she did not see me!

As I climb into bed at 2.45am I think of Aline setting her alarm clock for 5am to try to obtain FIFA World Cup tickets and Luiz having work the next morning...

In India, like any other big urban centres Mumbai, Delhi Bangalore go a bit mental during the World Cup. The games are shown in all the bars and most restaurants, at least the early games. The World Cup becomes an important event for non-league watching spectators. It allows people of my parents' generation in their 60's to get involved, because they didn't have access to football growing up, so don't follow clubs. Many girls that can't sustain feigning interest in club football year in year out get into it in a big way...That brings with it more interest from guys who feel the same.

For me though I'm not really bothered by the World Cup or international football in general. I have no real link to football playing nations...I have lived in many of them but never grew attached to a country. For me it's only ever been Tottenham Hotspur.

I was in Greece for a part of the tournament and it was fun watching the Greece games with my Greek friends...I was cheering them on and thought they did very well...During the 2010 World Cup I was in Holland with my Dutch friends and so wanted them to win the final just because the party after would have been wild!

But until India is in the Finals I'm not really that bothered. Though I do take special pleasure in watching England lose …And they don't disappoint!

That can't be said for many Indian people though…Many Indians do follow international teams, some only have international teams and don't have club teams...They wear the shirts of international teams and get riled up if their adopted team loses! I'm not sure how that works really…Doesn't compute with me. For a fair few, England is their adopted team ...

I watch the World Cup because I love the sport, I like good football. I thought the group stage games were fantastic, Ghana versus Germany comes to mind. Some of the second round games, German versus Algeria, Belgium versus USA, and Brazil versus Chile were smashing games... I like to watch new players come into the spotlight... I had seen James Rodriguez play a fair few times and have known his quality for a while now so it was really good watching him transform into a star.

I did have tickets to the Semis and Finals in Brazil but didn't end up going…I had work and in all honesty didn't try that hard to shift it all around... My younger brother went across and spent a month in Brazil, caught all the games in Salvador and then the Semis and Finals. Many other Indian Fans did the same so there is very much a hysteria about it. Although the final few games were not great, they say the experience in Brazil was amazing. It was very well organised and they gave the impression it went by faultlessly.

Rishabh, India

EL GRINGO'S ONCE IN A LIFETIME

THURSDAY 3RD JULY 2014

My day starts frantically...Paul text to say France versus Germany tickets are available on the FIFA web site.

Aline is also looking but Brazilian people access a different site...And only wheelchair access tickets are available in Brazil.

I am trying through the desktop version on my iPhone...It is too difficult...

Paul and my two sons have my log in details, I text to ask if they would mind keeping an eye out for tickets on my behalf.

Cold shower...Not true, today was absolutely bloody freezing...Teeth chatteringly cold...My body is in shock and I just couldn't stay in the shower.

The apartment owner arrives with more towels and bed linen. He looks at the shower and then goes in to the kitchen, looks at the fuse box which is hidden behind the fridge and tells me that was the problem and that it is now sorted He also sorts the air conditioning...Charming guy...All good!

Sorting the logistics of the England v India tickets from an apartment on Copacabana for the five days at Trent Bridge is proving to be a bit of a challenge... Just about there now though...

Remembering that Colin and the guys obtained tickets from an agency; I walk along to the Merlin Hotel on Avenida Princesa Isabel and take the lift up to the seventh floor. I can't see any sign of their office and take the lift up to the top floor...

Nothing...I take the lift back down to the ground floor and ask the Hotel Reception staff who say the agency is not based at the hotel. Maybe they have moved out...It was worth the ten minute walk to check...

Aline picks Ryan, Gerry and I up at the same junction as last night. She has dropped a dumbbell on her left foot during CrossFit this morning and is in agony. We suggest cancelling our visit to Santa Teresa but she won't hear of it.

On route, Aline says forged tickets are selling for 3000 reals...Imagine paying more than £800 for a ticket, arriving at the stadium to be told that the ticket is a forgery #unscrupulousbastards

We stop off at the Botofogo ticket office. There are quite a lot of people milling about outside looking for tickets. There are one of two touts who are trying to sell France versus Germany tickets for 1200 USD, more than £700... What!!!

We are on the ascent to Santa Teresa. The hills are incredibly steep and almost vertical...so much so that you can almost feel the car groaning! The late Amy Wine house stayed at the Santa Teresa hotel for the 360 degree views it offers.

Aline is giving us lots of information about the area and says as heterosexuals, it is best to avoid Ipanema beach station numbers seven and eight plus number nine which is more for younger marijuana smokers!

It is a struggle to find a place to park on the streets and we have to park a little further away... Aline is really struggling to walk...Not good...I suggest she should go to the hospital tonight but she doesn't want to...

We arrive at Parque Das Ruinas which was constructed in 1894. We walk up the steps to the first tier and then up to the top of the building. It isn't pleasant for us to see Aline limping up the steps with a swollen and blackened foot but she is determined to show off her city to us...

The views are 360 degrees and from both tiers they are absolutely spectacular.

The panoramic scenes show off the diverse and unique beauty of the city... Many of the various bays, harbours, the airports, the 13km bridge across to Niteroi, the mountains, the high rise buildings of the city, the nearby favelas, the lush greenery of the habitat all sparkling in the early afternoon sunshine.

Whilst at the top of the building, we talk with Marc, a Bayern Munich fan from Cologne. He believes the best two teams in the tournament to be Germany and Holland and is convinced these two sides will reach the final. He is adamant that Robben has been the best player in the tournament so far and will not listen to my protestations regarding simulation and any other contenders...Then again he is a Bayern Munich fan!

Marc has a whole wad of World Cup cartoon stickers of players. They are not only very well drawn but also very funny such as Zidane head butting! He kindly gives each of us quite a few of the stickers as mementoes of

Sakho
BY MARCO ZIZZI

the World Cup.

We drive to a famous nearby restaurant called Bar do Mineiro which serves authentic traditional Brazilian food. The restaurant is full and people are queuing outside... No idea how Aline could manage to pull off a table for five!

Aline explains that the bar is named after people who come from a state called Minas Gerais who are called "Mineiros". It turns out I have been to the state's capital city...Belo Horizonte where we saw England's last match in the World Cup.

In ordering drinks, the menu shows a caipirinha passion fruit which I can't resist trying...And am so pleased I ordered it #fantasticrefreshingtaste

We have a mixed pastel starter; small square pastries which have different fillings...Beans, meats and cheeses #delicious

Oh noooo...Jessica texts Aline half way through the first day of her new job... The work entails telephoning people to raise funds for a non-profit organisation. She is not really sure the job is for her...

I ask Aline about the tens of miniature trams on the wall ...A person was killed in a tram accident a couple of years since when the lines have been closed for refurbishment. It is planned for the tram lines to be reopened in time for the 2016 Olympic Games.

The main courses arrives..."feijoada" Brazilian...Pork in a sauce with rice, beans, and a white flour mix with green vegetables #verytasty

We all feel very much "in the moment" eating the food drinking caipirinha in this famous old restaurant.

I look at a table just across the way from me and the former Liverpool and England goalkeeper David James has just taken a seat.

We ask if he would mind having a photograph with us and he is very warm and friendly towards us. We go outside for a photograph and while doing so have

a chat with him. He is an absolute gent...Flew in yesterday and is working for ESPN. Olivier Dacourt managed to get him a ticket for France v Germany at the Maracana which he is really looking forward to seeing.

On returning to our seats in the restaurant, Aline looks at her photograph and the older Brazilian she asked to take a photograph chose instead, to take a photograph of her ass and legs...She is fuming but we just about manage to calm her down... As we pass him on the way out, she calls him a jerk and he replies...I love you!

The next step is the Vasco da Gama stadium but the traffic is too heavy and Aline reluctantly gives in and we head back to Copacabana. On the way back she asks if we have sat on the rocks at Arpoador to watch the sunset over Ipanema. We haven't but we will do this evening!

Aline drops us off at the end of Ipanema beach and we go across the rocks and climb up for photographs of the sunset. It is a little misty tonight; woolly cumulus clouds are resting on top of the mountains across the far end of the bay. It is still nevertheless a quite beautiful view across Ipanema as the sun begins its descent behind the commanding almost domineering dark mountain range.

The ocean is splashing up from the rocks....A very strong sea, salty smell. Lights begin to twinkle in the darkening gloom across the bay... There are groups of people and couples sitting together on the rocks looking out across Ipanema. All here for the sun set...Amongst us all is a lone fisherman on the far edge of the rocks. The smell of Marijuana inevitably wafts across the rocks. A vendor is selling beer and caipirinhas. We can't resist a caipirinha!

Gerry swaps his Mexican shirt for a Colombian shirt. He is looking to collect as many national shirts as he can during his time at the World Cup. A guy from Monaco is waving a huge tricolour red white and blue French flag across the rocks.

We are stood on the rocks sipping caipirinhas, the sea a deep green below us, a lone yacht comes in to moor in the bay, guys are still out surfing the waves... The silhouettes of the mountains becoming increasingly pronounced with every passing minute...The red sky gradually darkening, the artificial orange street lights in the hills becoming ever brighter as night falls over Ipanema Bay.

Along with the hotel lights, the beach floodlights are now reflecting back off the beach and sea creating a luminous orange glow. Above us, stars are twinkling and a crescent moon is shining ever more brightly in the darkening skies.

Camera flashes are bouncing back off the rocks around us as we all capture this special sunset.

People from every nationality treasuring these moments...No one is hurrying or stressed...Everyone mellowing in the warm climate... Chilling...nowhere else we would rather be right now just absorbing, drinking in the moment, enjoying each other's companionship...

Night falls and people begin to drift down from the rocks...Walking along Ipanema people are sat at the beachside bars... Drinking coconut juices from their green shells through straws

EL GRINGO'S ONCE IN A LIFETIME

A guy in an Argentine shirt is stood in a waist high tub which is used to keep beers cold...The ice is still in the tub....!!! He climbs out almost as quickly as I climbed out of my shower this morning!

We go to the Girl of Ipanema bar and cross over the road just as Paul, Ian and I did two weeks ago last Sunday...Gosh nearly three weeks ago!

Ryan says Wikipedia has had one of its page changed...Tim Howard is now the US Secretary of Defence!! It was corrected in minutes but by then it had spread all over the USA... After his performance against Belgium, Tim Howard has been elevated to a "god like" status... People want to name a state after him!!

Dempsey and Howard even received a call from President Obama! Ryan shows me a picture doing the rounds across the United States Twitter pages. It shows a picture of a lady about to be bitten by a shark and heroically Tim Howard diving into the ocean to save her!

Gerry says in Mexico, the feeling of the Robben penalty is that it always happens to Mexico... Sounds just like a Spurs fan! The Mexican view is that it was the fault of the referee rather than Robben. The Mexican view is that diving is part and parcel of the game...And that it was the fault of the referee. There are calls in Mexico for greater use of technology for contentious decisions.

A few beers and caipirinhas later, we say our brief farewells. They head back to their hostel on Ipanema for a quick shower and bus over to Copacabana and I go down to Ipanema beach to take a public bus back to my apartment...It is 3 reals and I am at the mercy of a guy on the pavement as to whether the bus heading to Castillo passes Prado Junior. I had asked the driver but his response was ...No Se... I feel like saying why won't you say...But then it is 8.29pm...I am in his country and he is sober and I most definitely am not! Aline had arranged to meet us at metro station Siqueira Campos at 9.30pm which in Portuguese means around 10.15pm...Only teasing Aline!

By way of reassurance...Brazilian buses are just the same as those in the UK...

Every gear change and break either throws you back into your seat or hurtles you five metres forward. Have we really progressed from riding a camel? Traffic jams certainly mean we don't get there any quicker...There is one significant difference to UK buses. There are turnstiles to get on or off the bus. Is this to stop people getting on without paying or deter gangs from mob handedly robbing the passengers? I look out of the-window and there is the Budweiser hotel...We are on Copacabana... Thank you Mr Pavement Man...Yaay!!

On entering the apartment, I receive a WhatsApp message from Aline saying that Luiz wants her to see the doctor tonight...Good news!! She really did struggle to walk around Santa Teresa today...

I go on to Twitter and see a dreadful YouTube clip of a flyover in Belo Horizonte having collapsed onto traffic below killing at least a bus Driver... Tragic... I have no idea as to whether this is a flyover built for the World Cup or not...Accidents happen in major cities all over the World all of the time... It is tragic in its own right...I just hope that it is not anything to do with the result of last minute World Cup "deadline" panic..

Ryan, Gerry and me agree to push back at our meeting time to 10pm and will go straight to Lapa. I text Rob and hopefully he can make it too.

We take the metro... A first time for Ryan and Gerry! This is helpful for Ryan as his brother, Patrick arrives at 9.30am in the morning and it looks like he will have to take the metro later than Gerry and me to the Maracana in our search for tickets #FrancevGermany

I take the guys to the Escadaria Selaron steps which link Lapa with Santa Teresa which is where we were earlier today. Colin and the guys had told me the steps were famous but I hadn't understood why so asked at the Tourist Information Centre. It seems that the steps were created by a painter called Selaron from Chile who changed out old steps in disrepair. He painted the new steps in the colours of the Brazilian flag green, yellow and blue as a gift to the people of Brazil. He had to sell his own paintings to be able to continue his project.

Postscript: On returning to UK and looking on Google... There are more than 2000 tiles from more than 60 countries covering 125 metres! He started the project in 1990 and despite being initially mocked by the locals continued for many years. He was found dead on the steps in January 2013 with burn marks on his body. His steps however have become an iconic landmark of Rio...They have featured in documents and commercials, videos by U2 and Snoop Dog as well as the Rio Olympic bid

At the top of the steps, we have a chat with Tom and Valerie from Raleigh, North Carolina who flew in from Miami via a visit to Machu Picchu in Peru. They didn't know they needed a visa...It is a reciprocal arrangement because the USA requires Brazilians to have a visa to enter the States. There was a mad and stressful panic with the Brazilian embassy in Lima to sort it out...But here they are on the steps in Lapa to tell the story!

While having a beer, Gerry says that in Mexico we call the Mexican immigrants that illegally enter the USA "mojados" which means wet people. This is because there is a river that the Mexicans have to cross to reach the USA; ergo they have to get wet. Since most of the poor people can't get a job in Mexico they see the USA as the land of opportunity...Even though they don't have the documentation they travel through really rough deserts and rivers to get through.

Aline texts to say to meet in 10 minutes...We walk up to the four bar crossroads to meet Luiz, Aline and Jessica who are at Boteco das Garrafas on the corner of Rua do Lavradio and Rua Mem de Sa...The busy "nightlife" street though Lapa. Coincidentally, it is the same restaurant where I went with Paul and Ian and a second time with Colin, Rob, Doug and Mick... The one with the internal bohemian style wall murals and street lamps and well worth calling in at if ever you are in Lapa.

We order drinks and snacks... Aline tells us the good news that her foot is not broken but she is in a race against time to be able to wear heels at a forthcoming wedding...Fortunately us men don't have that problem...Well, except the one we saw in the pizza place last night!

Luiz says Christ the Redeemer will be lit in Brazilian green and yellow tomorrow night...Let's hope Brazil beat Colombia then! When living in Paris, I recall the Eiffel Tower being lit red in honour of a senior Chinese delegation being in town...Great PR with multi million pound contracts at stake. I was in New York when Frank Sinatra died and it was very touching to see the Empire State Building lit blue in honour of "old blue eyes"... A night of sharing memories and stories...

After a few drinks, we walk further along Rua Mem de Sa to my favourite live music bar, Boemia da Lapa but it is a little difficult to stay there as it is very busy and both Aline and Gerry need to be able to sit down...Since the start of the World Cup campaign, our squad has certainly been hit by injuries and illnesses... Talking of which my voice still hasn't returned...

We cross the road and walk down to another bar which is also very crowded. It is getting late so we decide to head back towards Copacabana. On the way to the car, we see a sign which says Hotel Para Solteiros... Luiz and Aline say these types of places rent out beds by the hour for liaisons!

On arriving back on Copacabana, Aline drops us off on Copacabana. Ryan suggests going to the square where the football fans and hookers congregate to show Gerry... It is almost a tourist attraction in its own right...We buy caipirinhas and then walk along Avenida Atlantique to show Gerry all the fans sleeping out on the beaches and in their cars.

It is getting late, Gerry is still struggling to walk and we have an early start in the morning to go up to the Maracana to try to find tickets for the France versus Germany match. We say our good nights. They jump in a taxi back to their hostel on Ipanema and I walk back to my apartment. Every day seems to weave such a rich tapestry...This really is a once in a lifetime opportunity!

EL GRINGO'S ONCE IN A LIFETIME

It was a euphoric experience to be surrounded by the quintessential companions, new and old, knowing everyone is completely committed to that very moment, unable to dream of a more suitable location or atmosphere to be a part of. For me this was a recurring feeling while in Brazil for the World Cup. It will forever be one of my most cherished memories.

Ryan Conway, Chico, California, USA

I can say that I was amazed at the World Cup. It was an incredible event, both structures, such as security, and animation, where it brought together various people, various nations, and the most incredible, with people cheering, joy and happiness with a single purpose. Meet people from other countries, such as John, Gerardo, Ryan and Patrick Conroy, Sabina, have the opportunity to have dinner together, laugh, dance, have fun, and learn more about the culture of each was incredible! No doubt unforgettable, such an event should occur every year, because the longing and hope for the next Cup in Brazil is already in my heart!

Leonardo Silva Santa Rita, 19, Rio de Janeiro, Team Brazil!

FRIDAY 4TH JULY 2014

I wake without any hangover...Not even the normal five minute hangover!
The challenge of the day is to secure tickets for today's Quarter Final France versus Germany at the Maracana...

I am in WhatsApp dialogue with Jason the tout for tickets...He starts with a price of 900 USD but we say no... We say there are four of us and will pay a maximum of 600 USD. He checks with his contacts and eventually says ok...and then it falls through and then the price is 800 USD and eventually he says yes to 600 USD...We are obviously the fall back position if they can't get a better price...

Ryan's brother Patrick won't make it in time so I arrange to meet Ryan and Gerry outside Mabbs on the corner of Prado Junior and Avenida Atlantique to meet Jason at 11.45am...The match starts at 1pm #gettingtight

On the way out of the apartment, I hear an American guy trying to sell a ticket for the game. I say how much and he wants 800 USD... I say oh ok... I am buying for 600 USD...He offers to match it and I say the only way I will take the ticket is for 500 USD...He admits to being a tout and says he needs to make a living...I say no problem and look to walk on...He says ok, ok 500 USD...I am obviously concerned about the ticket being forged...As he had said he is staying around the corner with his wife and son, I insist on walking into his apartment block to ensure security recognise him in his apartment building. I then request his identity papers and take a photograph of them and also take his US telephone number and dial it to make sure it rings...Which it does...He is a little exasperated and says he wouldn't rob me...I say once bitten twice and shy but agree to text him once in the stadium to delete the photograph of his personal details.

I text Jason who seems to be struggling to get the tickets from Ipanema... Code for his contact has a better price...

I meet Ryan and Gerry and we jump on the metro at Cardeal Arcoverde at 12 noon...Kick off is in hour...

Happy Independence Day Ryan!

On route, an Australian couple jump on and overhear us talking about needing two tickets. They say a Brazilian guy was trying to sell tickets in the carriage next door and they decided to leave that carriage and join this one! We get off at the next station and reboard in the carriage that the Aussie's left.

Amazingly, we find the guy and he wants 800 USD... Ryan and Gerry offer 500 USD. The guy is pushing them to agree a price saying he is getting off at the next station...The train pulls in and he says it isn't this station but the next... They agree a price of 600 USD each and exchange the cash for the tickets. It is all very frantic and as soon as the transaction is completed the train pulls in to the station and the guy gets off...

We compare tickets and suddenly we are all nervous as to whether any of the tickets will get us into the game. My ticket is Cat 5 says Winner Match 53 versus Winner Match 54 with a Brazilian name which starts Jessica...I don't look a Jessie in any language! Hmmmm!!!

Ryan and Gerry's tickets say the name of the match...France versus Germany....Hmmmm again... Today is Friday 4th July... France and Germany won their respective last 16 matches on Monday 30th June...The teams contesting this semi-final were only determined three full days ago...Is it really realistic to believe these tickets were printed sometime during say Tuesday sold to a genuine owner and ended up in the hands of a tout by Friday morning...

Then there is the need of the tout to jump off the train as soon as the deal was transacted...I am very nervous as to the validity of Ryan and Gerry's tickets.

I believe my ticket is genuine but... it is in the name of a Brazilian lady....

It makes for a sweaty palmed journey to the Maracana...

Time is also against us... Kick off time is fast approaching...

We disembark at Sao Cristavao and have to go through about six police checks...There is an added dimension...The first check now has a metal fence to pass through..

Once through the checks we sprint in the hot sun up over the flyover down the other side. Continue our run to the stadium... I am too old for this!!

We say our goodbyes as I am in a different section to the guys...Through the metal detector and finally to the gate...Memories of Argentina v Bosnia... The rejection...Come flooding back...Will I won't I get in...Should genuine fans be put through such torture...The steward offers her hand to take my ticket to validate the ticket...I cover the name on the ticket and put it forward for validation...Green for go and boy do I go! I am in!!! Never a moment's doubt haha...My thoughts immediately turn to Ryan and Gerry and I admit to myself that I am worried...

My Cat 5 ticket is at the highest level, I am not just buying drinks for the memento of the cups... I am desperate for drinks and buy three! My seat is behind the goal at the back... Great seat!!

As promised I text the American tout to say I am in the stadium and that I have deleted his details.

I just reach my seat in time for the national anthems...Phew that was some hour! Lots of Brazilian yellow in my section. To my left, the tricolour of red, blue and white of the French fans...The white, black, red and yellow of Germany are mainly congregated at the opposite end of the stadium.

France start well... Couple of last ditch interceptions by the German defence...

13 minutes gone....Free kick to Germany...Mats Humbles rises...Almost centre of the goal, Heads firmly...Scores...1-0 to Germany!! The German fans at the opposite end are off their feet! Where was the French defence? Felt as if it waas a free header...Lloris...No chance... But I would say that wouldn't I...No really though!

Succession of Mexican waves being started by Brazilians.

Germans dominating possession 59/41%...Commanding possession statistics!

1000 gols, 1000 gols, so Pelé, so Pelé, Maradona é cheirador (is a sniffer)

1000 goals, 1000 goals, only Pelé, only Pelé, Maradona is just a sniffer!"

As translated by father and son, Arthur & Miguel Calmon from Leblon who are sat next to me...They only bought their tickets this morning as well!

French supporters won't sit down...Eventually the police come in with batons... French guy helped up the stairs by a steward to an exit... Blood pouring down his face...Ten minutes later, the French are still standing...Withstood the barrage

Great save by Neuer... Allez les blues!

Chant of ticket agencies are all gay comes up from the Brazilians. The term in Brazil is "Cambista"

At the back of the Brazilian end to my right is a group of Colombians who start singing and waving their flags ahead of tonight's match versus Brazil... How brave are they!!!

The Brazilian fans sing something along the lines of "Colombia you can wait... Your time is coming"

The police have had enough and start to escort French fans out...Three pass me... The Brazilian fans are booing them...Defiantly they hold up the tricolour flag and wave it at the Brazilians before being thrown out...

The French fans finally get the message and sit down...

Benzema goes on a run...Cuts in from the left...Beats a couple of players...

Shoots...Neuer saves again! Neuer is emerging as the keeper of the tournament!

The atmosphere is amazing...The game is almost an incidental sideshow...

Half time 1-0

The French are very much still in the game but...The longer it stays 1-0... Chasing the game in this heat may begin to tell...

Miguel the father says James Rodriguez has signed for Real Madrid and Suarez for Barcelona.... The first...Ok ...Suarez...Why!!!

Second half starts...France pressing....Ball comes in...Agonisingly close to a touch past Neuer...

Another cross...Griezmann tries to bring the ball down... If only.

France 5 shots to Germans 2...Professional foul by Khedira to stop a breakaway by France...Booking. Stevie Gerrard...If only versus Uruguay...

Neuer slow to take goal kicks...Brazilian fans don't like it...

Arthur tells me he likes Tottenham because of Aaron Lennon...Never seen anyone run so fast...He is by no means the first Brazilian to say this.

The French are playing some really skilful and imaginative football... The same flamboyancy of their rugby team...The well drilled German machine though is withstanding all at the moment...Schweinsteiger is controlling the tempo...Some player...

An injury and the players take a break in the sweltering conditions...Jordan the Millwall fan texts to say it is too hot and full in the main fan fest.

As the match progresses, the curvature of the stands is creating a bigger and bigger crescent of shade from the sun. The play may well be congested to the side of the French left as they attack towards me...In the shade! Now a German is being escorted out...

74240 attendance

15 minutes to go...France make inroads down the right...Benzema should have left it for his team mate but still gets a shot away...Another break down the right...Neuer in command...He has such a presence. The French final ball is just not quite good enough in this game...But if France do score...The momentum swing could be massive...

A pin ball moment in the German box...The ball ricochets off a German defender passed the post.

Germany break down the left ...They have men over...Free shot on goal... Fine save...Lloris keeps France in the game... Now he comes tearing out of his box to clear.

Goetze for Ozil and Giroud on...One Arsenal player on, one Arsenal player off.

The intensity in the game has slackened in the heat.

4 minutes added time...Brazilians leaving...They have had their feast of hors d'oeuvres...The main course for them is to come...Let's hope they don't choke on it!

Lloris nearly embarrassed dribbling out there...

The final whistle blows...France 0-1 Germany

Germany are in to the semi-final to face Brazil or Colombia...

No great celebrations from the Germans...Winning a Quarter Final is not what they are here for...They are accustomed to that...They are here to end their own 24 years of hurt...To add a fourth star to the three already adorning their famous white shirt.

Arthur and Miguel advise me to catch the metro from the Maracana station rather than Sao Cristavao...I follow their advice and am on the metro back to Copacabana in reasonably quick time.

On the metro, in the same carriage are Tom and Valerie, the couple we met in Lapa last night from North California...What a small world!

On the metro, the Brazilians are in full singing voice...

Argentina go fuck yourself
You have 2 world cups

Pelé has 3 world cups
The Maradona sniffer song again
Messi is worse than Jo!!
Now the national anthem
Song after song all the way back to Cardeal Arcoverde metro station

As we go up the escalator, two Argentines are going down in the opposite direction...They receive a barrage...Not even they dare stay on Copacabana today.

We come out of the metro station on to the streets...Atmosphere amazing... Sense of anticipation...Noise, excitement, colour, all heading in one direction... To the fan fest!

I go back to the apartment to charge the iPhone and send tweets of my day... Feel guilty? Hell no!

I meet Ryan and Gerry along with Patrick, Ryan's brother.

If at all possible it is even busier down on Copacabana than ever before.

Go to the same place as against Chile... Colombians are in front of us...

As the camera pans across the players on the screen, the screams are deafening... The national anthem is sung so loudly...Goosebumps...

A sea of green and yellow...In the stadium, across the screen, across the fan fest... Across the whole of Brazil...Vamos Brazil!!

Paulinho is in for the suspended Gustavo.

3 minutes Fred wins a free kick central outside the box...Neymar ...Tame and wide

6 minutes Corner... Far post...Silva...Off his knee 1-0 Brazil!!!Oh my, the noise is deafening... Even the firecrackers can't compete!!

People bouncing up and down!!!

Colombia free kick...High and wide. Crowd cheer wildly.

Cuadrado ...Oh no...Phew deflected wide!

Good burst into the box by Hulk...Luiz just can't get on the end of the cross... Defender clears

Hulk...Fine save, Oscar...Another save... Fans loving it!!!

Oh no...Colombia break ...three players on one!! A huge gasp from the crowd...What a waste... Silva clears...The game is so open...Now Brazil attack... Is this basketball??

Colombian keeper keeping his team in this...

Group of girls and guys next to us...One asks if I am Flamengo or Vasco... She is Flamengo... I say Vasco...And all the others high five me!! The first girl says Flamengo are the biggest...Her friend says fuck you... The other sticks her tongue out... Rivalries are the same the World over!

Harsh free kick edge of the box to Colombia...Can almost feel and touch the nerves within the fan fest...Day turns towards nightfall... Huge cheers as the ball is cleared...César gathers a cross...

The game still feels so open, so stretched...Neymar shoots wide...Gerry says is it me or does Neymar look like a rooster... All agree he does ...but not too loudly!!

Neymar free kick left edge of box...Closer but not got his range yet...A second goal would ease the anxiety for the majority in the fan fest...They are happy but not happy if you know what I mean...Guv!

Half time 1-0

We are talking with Julia and Leo...Two 19 year old students in biology and engineering from Tijuca. They are the age they look #veryconfusing!

Julia poses for a photo in a Gerrard shirt...Stevie G has never looked so good!

29 minutes to go...Colombia pressing but without doing too much... Nevertheless every time the ball goes anywhere near the box... Huge squeals...We lost Patrick at half time...

We all need the facilities and leave the fan fest...The streets are overloaded...The queues...We

head towards the ocean...Almighty roar... Brazil score!!!! Portaloos queues... Ridiculous...Too crowded...We head towards a street running away from the beach... People spilling out of bars onto not just the pavement but also the roads...

No good...Desperate...Next street...Parked cars...Between them...No choice... Relief...

We get back onto the beach...Penalty awarded to Colombia...James steps up... 2-1...Must be his sixth goal?

Young ladies are squealing behind me....

Neymar down...Carried off on a stretcher...Balance of payments deficit... National disaster? Nowhere near...If Neymar is out of the World Cup...Real national disaster...

5 minutes added time!!! Feels like the referee has decided there will be another half of football...5 minutes will surely seem that long!

The passion!! The samba drums are going on in the background...

Free kick on the right wing to Colombia...Comes to nothing.

The referee blows the final whistle...Brazil are through...

Final Score...Brazil 2-1 Colombia!!!

The fan fest is ecstatic!! Everyone is hugging each other...Taking photographs of today... Of the crowds...Jubilation, relief, happiness all mixed into one.

Brazil are into the World Cup semi-finals!!

Brazil versus Germany on Tuesday...What a mouth-watering prospect!!

The promenade, the roads are just overflowing with people...

On Prado Junior, in the middle of the road is a very tall lady boy in yellow shoes ra-ra skirt and crop top performing her own dance routine...Only in Rio!

In saying that I remember a birthday dinner at a tapas restaurant in Nottingham. There was a group of about twenty of us in the downstairs room with one other table which was shared by transvestites. They left much earlier than us and as we walked through the bar, one of our group, an ex rugby player, Matt remarked "you need some balls to come out dressed like that!" Having all had a drink, we guffawed with laughter...When we got outside, one of our group said to Matt... "You do know as you said that, you were walking past their table in the bar?!!

Everybody wants to party, Patrick re-joins us and three young Brazilians Julia, Leo and Vicki come with us to Mabbs. So much energy in the group... The energy of youth, different nationalities getting together, the buzz of the Copacabana atmosphere and of course the occasion!

Aline texts to say they will come to join us and that the ESPN guys may come too.

We are sat outside under the marquee sharing pizza and drinks, music starts up in the bar...Soon we are inside and the gringos are being taught samba...The steps are easy to learn and having been drinking most of the day, we are now all Samba experts... but alas our efforts are being captured on video...

The staff would like the space for more tables...trying to get us to sit down... But these feet are made for dancing...If only you knew how untrue that is haha...

The staff finally get their way...We sit down in a corner...Luiz, Aline and Jessica join us. Aline is concerned...She says there are a lot of hookers outside and is worried as Rick of ESPN and his friends might be joining us for a drink... They weren't there when we arrived and are not inside but we can move on if she would prefer...She says it is too late now... and we all have another drink.

The ESPN guys come along to say hello but in any event can't stay as they have been invited out for dinner.

It is getting quite late and Julia, Leo and Vikki have quite a way to travel... We say our goodbyes and Aline wants to takes us to a bar on Rua Bolivar... Away from the hookers...We are now sat on stools outside a more upmarket bar with jugs of Sangria... We started drinking around 1pm this afternoon...Beers, caipirinhas and now sangria...

It seems, from what Luiz has heard, the Neymar injury is serious and he is out of the World Cup...There is talk of a broken back...Oh my...Let's hope it is not career threatening or even worse...Luiz goes on to say that Tiago Silva, the Brazil captain and defensive rock, who was booked today, will be suspended for the match against Germany...Hmmm...Can't help feeling...Losing their two best players will make it very difficult against Germany.

Luiz then says that Silva can be replaced by the Bayern Munich centre back Dante...Of course they will have top class replacement! This is Brazil... A football mad country of 200 million...I have to recalibrate my thinking away from England...Nevertheless...It feels as if Neymar has almost carried this team through a number of games...

We getting talk with some Argentinians...One had his rucksack forcefully ripped out of his hands on the beach by three local guys...First time I have heard of a forceful mugging...#unnerving

The tables and stools are quite close and on the next table are two let's say mature local ladies who are sat with a mature German guy. As the night wears on, the guy and one of the ladies becoming increasingly friendly...Now they are all over each other...It is an unedifying sight...No let me rephrase that...It is repulsive! The other lady tries to enter into conversation with me...You look like Richard Gere...Always better than being told Gary Lineker...Sorry if you are reading this Gary! Not saying you are not handsome...But Richard Gere is... Well...Richard Gere!

She is quite drunk...It is a bit of a nightmare...I look across to Aline...And she laughs at the irony...We left a hookers bar where we weren't troubled to come to an upmarket bar...Where... I am being hassled! Ryan kindly agrees to swap places with me...Now she is hassling him!

A group of English fans stop by and I ask where they are from...They say you will never have heard of it...Shrewsbury...I say what Gay Meadow? And am mobbed by the guys! They moved to a new stadium in 2007...Changed the name to Greenhaus Meadow...No surprise there!

We say our good nights and somehow I find my way back to my apartment.

EL GRINGO'S ONCE IN A LIFETIME

France made a good World-cup compared to their recent level and compared to what the French people expected…But in the quarter-final with Germany they were powerless as if they have make their JOB and not more!!

Why the French people don't can dream?? The positive sign for this French team… the new generation Varane, Griezmann, Sakho etc…

Naoufel Loudjertli, Algerian living in Marseille, France

What can I say about the World Cup? It was overall a really good feeling! Even more so after what happened four years ago in South Africa when the French team went on strike and Anelka was dismissed because he insulted the manager, Domenech! It brought disgrace and the competition stopped in the first round for us. So I think everybody was expecting a lot from this World Cup.

For 2014 France didn't qualify automatically, we had to play off against Ukraine to qualify. Having lost the away leg 2-0, everyone was thinking we would not reach Brazil but the return was just amazing!! We won 3 – 0 to qualify 3-2 on aggregate and gain our ticket for Brazil! The French people started to gain trust in the national team

Just before the Finals, the match against Jamaica (8-0) made us, French citizens more confident about the competition. We started to gain trust in the national team! The first round matches were played very nicely by the French team. The 5-2 win against Switzerland was impressive and made us much more confident for the second round. Everybody started to believe that France could do something in this World Cup.

So now, the second round and the match against Nigeria, our first real test. The match was very physical and I recall that the first goal by Paul Pogba came very late in the 79th minute and finally France won 2-0.. During this match we could also see that the entrance of Antoine Griezmann (6second minute) who made a really big difference and that this new player could be decisive for the rest of the competition.

If we do a quick look up at the second round, France, along with Colombia was one of the only team's that made it "easily" to the third round. Just look at the Netherlands' match, Germany or even Argentina, it was really difficult for them to win their second round matches.

Third round: Germany…. We don't feel really confident about this match. Germany is a big team and everybody knows it. The match starts, everybody wants the French team to win but after only 13 minutes Germany scores a goal… Everybody is disappointed but come on there is still 77 minutes to play so let's see. Finally no miracle for France…Germany wins as usual…Comme d'habitude! This match left a bitter taste…We felt we could have taken them.

After the match everybody is at the same time disappointed and happy. Disappointed because obviously we lost and that we were very close to winning this game and maybe go on to the World Cup. Happy because the French Team did a really good World Cup and they just made us dream!

Nikhil Das Gupta, Paris, France

SATURDAY 5TH JULY 2014

M y starts to the day are getting later and later...
My voice box and throat have finally thrown in the towel...

Queues for fan fest enormous... Miss kick off...Meet Tom from Derby now living in London...Arsenal fan...Could get on well but the football thing will always get in the way!

8 minutes...Good build up play by Argentina...Ball played in towards Higuain edge of the box. Almost in one movement he swivels and shoots into the far bottom left hand corner of the net!!! 1-0!!!

The crowd in the fan fest go crazy leaping up and down bare chested waving their flags around.

The Brazilians are singing for Belgium...They are singing their Maradona song...the Argentines are singing their Italia 90 song...May be it's a good thing they speak different languages...And don't seem to know what they are singing to each other. The Argentines have their shirts knotted over their heads to protect themselves against the fierce sun... These 1pm kick offs are tough to watch never mind play in!

The songs between Argentina and Brazil are nonstop. They are all mingled in the fan fest together...In football terms the rivalry is immense and to give you an idea of what is going on around me, I have included the songs I could get translated...

"Argentines have taken over Rio, the place, the woman!"

"If you are not singing you must be Brazilian"

A teenager is carried out the fan fest... Looks like he has fainted in the heat. It is soo hot...

After the shock of conceding an early goal, Belgium starting to get a foothold ...Shot rebounds off the keeper.

In front of me Argentines and Brazilians are winding each other up constantly... Amazed there hasn't been trouble.

Di Maria has to go off injured...Perez on...

A sign on the way to the fan fest said 31 degrees... Must be a lot warmer in the fan fest...

Free kick on the edge of the box... Messi lining it up...There is an anticipation... No wrong word... An expectation... Almost but not quite...

"Neymar is better than Messi"

"I have a lot of smiles because the Brazilians think that Neymar is better than Messi"

I receive a text message from Aline

"It is very sad to see a player in his prime almost immobilised, incapable of play or even walk...But let's stop talking about Fred..." Fred is becoming a national scapegoat!

"Pele likes the children"

"Maradona is a drug addict, Maradona sniffs cocaine"

"Argentina, Argentina it's 30 years since you were world champions."

At this point I am pleased England are not rivals of Brazil...!

"Maradona is better than Pele"

The Brazilians reply... *"I don't understand you"*

Imagine if they both reach the final....

Half time...1-0

The Brazilians in the fan fest form a passage for the fans to pass through... Every Brazilian who passes through is cheered... Every Argentine... Leave that one for you to work out!

"Argentina fans are beach women" is the latest song

Second half... "Belgica" being sung by the Brazilians...

After another "Mil goals" song the Argentines clap sarcastically...

Now the Brazilians sing "Argentina don't sing at their games"... The response is deafening!!

Is there a World Cup quarter cup final on??

Argentina sing "Italia 90" song again...

The Brazilian response is "No entendu, No entendu"

And "You've only got one song"

Higuain nutmegs Kompany through... Shoots...Surely...Over the bar!

Game getting stretched... Belgium having to press forward but not getting any penetration... Argentine keeper largely untroubled... Argentina look more likely to score a second on the break...

30 minutes to go...Fellaini heads over...

Bianca and Carolina from Brazil with Argentine face paint and colours are singing with the Argentines against their own Brazilian fans. They think that South Americans should cheer for their own...hmmm

New song from Argentine..."We must win to shut these shits up"

20 minutes to go...Belgium are in danger of slipping out of the World Cup without really making an impression on this match...

15 minutes to go Chadli for Hazard...Spurs fans the world over will struggle to understand that one!

The sun is so hot...Uncomfortably so in the fan fest...

The second half is drab... Not a lot of action... The heat if anything like here will be having an impact.

Higuain substituted...Huge cheer and applause for his contribution...

9 minutes to go...This looks to be over...

Finally a Belgian shot...Deflects wide...Corner ...Nothing comes of it.

4 minutes to go..."Argentina! Argentina! Argentina!"...The fans are ready to acclaim their heroes!

The Brazilian response..."Cocaina! Cocaina! Cocaina!"

Into the last minute...Belgium will surely be disappointed not to have created more chances

5 minutes added time brings gasps from the crowd...I want this over now...It is so so hot... And this has been one of the poorer games... #uninspiring

Messi through... Just the keeper to beat... The crowd are on their feet... Courtois pulls off a fine save!!

Straight up the other end... Break down the left... Cross... Intercepted... Follow up shot....over the bar!!

The final whistle blows...Beer everywhere...Getting banged about in the excitement, the flags being joyously waved...Cheering...On shoulders, firecrackers!

So Brazil, Germany and Argentina are into the semi-finals... Will Holland win to make two dream semi-finals...? Brazil seem to be massively handicapped with the loss of Neymar...

Having listened to the Argentina "Italia 90" song the entire World Cup... How ironic would it be if the final was to be a repeat of Italia 90...!! Germany v Argentina...Certainly a possibility...But then again so is Brazil v Holland... Would be two fantastic, intriguing semi-finals...!

Walking out the fan fest...A young Belgian is hoisted up on shoulders...They are happy... And maybe just maybe the mentality, the mind-set was a factor...

Belgium seem happy to have reached the Quarter Finals... For the Argentines...It would have been a disaster...They are here to win the cup.., Brazil the same... Germany the same... The Dutch... Having never won it...An interesting one?

I head to the Mud Bug to meet my Brazilian friends. At the bar I meet two Spurs fans from London

who are studying at LSE and Oxford Universities. They along with many others arrived in to Belo Horizonte on a full coach. They were told it was safe to leave everything on the coach while they went to the England v Costa Rica game. When they came back, the coach windows had been smashed. Everything had been stolen...The luggage of 50 people had all been taken!! The Police told them to wait by the kerb...They waited and they waited and...They waited...I recall how hot it was that day...Five hours later...Their entire luggage was returned untouched!!!!!!!!!!!!!!!!!!!! It seems the Police made a visit to the local drug barons...Discussions took place...The outcome of which being the return of the luggage!!!

Aline's American friend Brian is with her, Luiz and Jessica at a table in Mud Bug ... Couple of beers and an hour later... The bill is 40 reals...I say that can't be right... Seems there is a 24 reals, £6.50 entrance fee on a Saturday lunch to have a beer!!

My voice is an ever increasing nightmare... Or lack of voice should I say... For the last two weeks or more, it is so difficult to make myself heard over the noise. It places an even greater strain on my vocal chords... I feel a little flat.

May be we all do...it was hot in the fan fest...I got there to the Mud Bug late to meet Ryan, Gerry and Patrick who are heading off to São Paulo...I have the feeling they will be back by mid-week!

Back to the fan fest for Holland v Costa Rica...It is incredibly busy...Longest queues to date for me. Miss the kick off...Again!

The Argentines are everywhere. In the bars outside, on the beach, in the fan fest queue and the fan fest itself....Think they will be partying until well into the early hours!!

Rob is staying in the Marriott to watch the game. Between us we are hopeless...Met once in three weeks!

I get talking with Vishal and Neil from London in

the fan fest. They say outside of Rio the place to visit is Salvador...But when there...Brazilian lady and Australian landlord as well as all the locals warned them of crime...Huge Colombian influence and drugs is a massive issue. People just shoot people for cash. Guy taking his small daughter for a walk has to pass through a 100m passage to get to a safer area and would take a taxi every time.

Terrible stories of people being held at knife or gunpoint during the World Cup...

A local guy forgot something in his apartment and nipped inside leaving his young daughter in the car...A minute later he was back and the car had been robbed. He was a security guy and his gun had been taken... He found out the perpetrator and within a week not only had the perpetrator been shot dead but also...His whole family...

I am thinking...Thank you for suggesting I go there!!

It is so hot people are actually sitting down in the fan fest watching the match... There's a first... Sitting!! French must have gone home!

Costa Rica keeper versus Holland... Save after save after save...Latest a full length dive to keep out a Robben free kick...

Now a full length dive at the feet of Van Persie... Great goal keeping.

A Japanese fan had a follow Japan ticket plan. He was distraught in Cuiaba at seeing his team lose 4-1 to Colombia in their final group game... He put a tickets for sale notice up in the hostel... Vishal saw it and bought a semi-final ticket in Belo Horizonte and a final ticket for face value!!

Not a football team in Cuiaba ... Stadium built to increase tourism in the area, it is in the far west where rodeo attracts more fans than football. There are wetlands and being rich with wildlife, the hope is to attract tourists...

Carolina is from Brazil, a Carioca from Rio...She wants Argentina to win the World Cup!! She is decked out in Argentine colours including a Messi number 10 shirt...I am incredulous!!! I ask her why??

It seems the mayor of Rio; Eduardo Paes has stated he will shoot himself if it is a Brazil v Argentina World Cup Final... And Argentina win! Carolina hates the mayor so much it is a small price to pay and says many other Carioca feel the same way!! She is a staunch Flamengo supporter and is worried that Argentina will lose as they have adopted a Vasco da Gama song ...The feeling just can't stop... "We are going to win the cup" is the song. Carolina suggests I look up Flamengo songs in English on YouTube!

32 minutes left...Still goalless...The Dutch are dominating... But the longer it goes on....

18 minutes left...Costa Rica seem to be coming out of their shell a little but... Free kick... Sneijder...Shoots...Great shot...Keeper finally beaten ...Hits the post!!

Cross comes over Van Persie coming in less than six yards out... A tap in...1.... Noooo!!! Inexplicably he misses an open goal!!!

16 minute round trip to the portaloos... Everyone is remarkably patient... There are long lines walking through the crowds to get to and from the facilities... The people in each of the two lines... The people being buffeted... All coping

well and respecting each other...So many different nationalities here too...No longer possible to just assume that for example someone wearing an England shirt is English... Ian swapped his England shirt for an Argentine shirt all those days ago... It seems to be the norm to do so... Gerry of Mexico brought many Mexican shirts to swap! Can't ever see me walking around in an Arsenal, Chelsea or Man Utd shirt!!

At the facilities, the steward has his own way of dealing with people peeing on the sand between the portaloos... He goes up to them and holds them from behind and to the delight of the rest of us...Rocks them roughly backwards and forwards...I try not to imagine their clothes from the front!!

In the compounds of the loos... Another couple of guys are using the fence...Suddenly from the side there is a large bang and the fence vibrates ...The guys must wonder what the hell it is... Not content with that the Steward manhandles them away in midstream so to speak... Hoots of delights from those in the queues for the portaloos!!

Into 4 minutes added time, another cross comes in... Feels like half the Dutch and Costa Rica players miss it!!! Wait... Van Persie hasn't... He is beyond the far post... Controls it...This time...Surely... A deflection... A second deflection... Off the player on the line...Loops up onto the cross bar... Bounces... Away from goal...Follow up shot... I have often heard the expression... Charmed life...This is unbelievable!!!!

Game over... Extra time... The Ricans are out on their feet... Just can't see how they can pull this off... But hey...They are a population of less than five million...They are thirty minutes away from the possibility of penalties and a sensational result...Can they somehow pull it off??

Bit of a fall out between an Argentina fan in a Boca Juniors shirt and a Brazilian in a Flamengo shirt ...Seems the Argentine is saying this is supposed to be a party atmosphere not a load of aggressive songs... Interesting...

The Brazilians are now singing...Latin America without Argentina... The more alcohol being consumed... The more aggressive the atmosphere is becoming... Lot of the Argentines seem to have had enough and moved away...

More scrambles in the Rican box... Somehow the ball doesn't cross the line...

3 minutes to half time... Shot... Rica player turns his back on the ball...It hits him on the top of his shoulder... The referee somehow deems it handball... Free kick #harsh

Fortunately Rica block and clear it...Heroic defending, putting in every last ounce of energy for their country add a little luck and...?

Thing with Robben is that everyone knows what he is going to do... Down the right jink inside on his left foot and curl the ball into the far corner...but it seems nobody can stop him!

Half time of extra time... Still 0-0...Fascinating game though!!

Second half of extra time... Suddenly it's all Rica!! Strikers are running at defenders causing panic... Finally...One wriggles clear...one on one... Good save!!

Back down the other end...shot... Yesss... Nooo the Rican bar rattles again!!!

Last minute of extra time... Van Gaal substitutes the keeper... Krul comes on!!

Master stroke or lunacy??? The final whistle blows... The next 10 minutes will tell us!!

The fan fest is back on its feet... I feel out on mine...its tough work standing in here on sand for getting on for five hours a day!!

Rica... Krul guesses the right way but 1-0 Rica

Van Persie... Keeper guesses correctly 1-1

Krul saves 1-1...The substituted keeper is elated on the line.

Robben sends the keeper the wrong way 1-2

Gonzalez 2-2...all three shots to Krul's left... All three times Krul guesses the right way

Sneijder 3-2

Biplanes 3-3 opposite corner but Krul guesses correctly

Kyte 4-3

Krul dives to his left... right way yet again... Saves!!! It's all over!!!

Holland deservedly win but my word Rica have been magnificent in this World Cup...The nation came such a long way... And not just to the Quarter Finals. They have lit up this World Cup. Was the penalty shoot-out their once on a life time opportunity to reach a World Cup semi-final... Quite possibly...

Dutch fans behind me are jubilant... I think of my Dutch nephew Erik Jan who is not too well at the moment...

32 teams set out with their dreams intact on Thursday 12 June... Now on the 5 July... 28 of those dreams have been shattered... Just four intact...

And so the semi-final line up is known...

Brazil v Germany on Tuesday in

EL GRINGO'S ONCE IN A LIFETIME

Belo Horizonte

Argentina v Holland on Wednesday in São Paulo

What a line up!! Bring it on!!!

Outside the fan fest...There are Argentine fans singing songs against Brazil and alongside Brazil fans singing their sings against Argentina...The Argentines have been pretty much used to having a clear run on Copacabana... But today it's the weekend and the dynamics are somewhat different. It's generally in good spirits... If one gets knocked out... You have to wonder whether the mood will change...If Argentina get knocked out it will probably be very short term but if Brazil get knocked out on Tuesday and Argentina win Wednesday...With more Argentines coming for the final...Hmmm.

Couple of caipirinhas at a beach side cafe...No voice or not...Ready to take on the world again!!

Mexicans in fine voice on the front... We are Mexicans, we are the kings, and we do what we want!

All the beach side promenade bars have live music... Oasis in Portuguese!!

Old lady dancing... Must be around 90 years old...Great to see!

Just realised its 10.10pm... Not eaten yet today...

Decide to call in on Rob at Mud Bug to repay him the 200 reals I owe him...

There is a long queue to enter.... Trying to explain that I want to go in and out for two minutes...Remember Basil Fawlty frantically trying to describe the horse Dragonfly to Polly behind his wife's back ... In my case pointing at my eyes, out stretching my arm above my head, saying grand gringo hombre, using my fingers trying to say dos minutes... My fingers walking in, my fingers walking out... Taking reals out my pocket... Pointing to my chest and and and...Eventually... And I am not sure whether it's because he understands me or whether he has been worn down but the rope across the entrance is removed and with a stern look he holds up two fingers and says two minutes and he lets me in!! I imagine the thoughts of the people in the long queue. By the way I did pay an entrance fee a few hours ago... But that counts for nothing in Rio!

I find Rob who immediately wants to buy me a drink...I give the 200 reals and explain what happened with the doorman...Rob goes to see the doorman and says I am with him... No problemo.... I am in...Rob has this affect on people...He may be 6'11" (2.11m) in height but that is small in comparison to his character... The expression larger than life must have been written to describe him...

On entry, customers are required to provide identification papers... If you don't have any you type in your name... It's a little like Jeremy Beadle., tonight I will be....

The bar is rectangular in shape and the actual bar runs down the length of the right hand side...with stools running alongside it...

And so...here I am in my straw Brazil hat, white hair, suntan, sunglasses, shorts, open shirt and beach shoes looking every inch El Gringo!!

As ever with Rob, the vodkas are going down very quickly... I start with a couple of beers... He introduces me to his Rio housemate, John a Chelsea fan, who is already wasted... With Rob he needs a relay team of drinking partners!! John is also in a hat and sunglasses... We have a Blues Brothers photograph together!

Rob introduces me to a lady from Knutsford... And a couple of other guys who are Spurs fans from the States...

You know when you just get that feeling, that vibe about the night ahead... Rob and I are bouncing off each other...Both buzzing... His mate John says I look like Gary Lineker...Tell him I know but prefer the Richard Gere comparison... For a Chelsea fan he seems OK...He shouts out yes I can see that too.

But he seems to decide he wants to call me Wayne Lineker for the night.

Rob tells the girl, he says is from Manchester which she doesn't like... That tonight is her lucky night... She is having the chance of a life time and way above her league... She is laughing...He goes on...In football terms you are Rochdale...

EL GRINGO'S ONCE IN A LIFETIME

It is the draw for the third round of the FA Cup and you have pulled out me... The mighty Tottenham Hotspur...You lucky lucky girl... She is lapping it up... Saying she enjoys a challenge... I add that Rochdale will have to put in one hell of a performance to get a replay... We are all laughing... The girl shows us some photographs of the men and yes the women she has had some fun with... She flicks to a photo of another girl... Rob says she looks like a lady boy.... Her reply...She happens to be my sister!!!!

Rob replies by saying Rochdale take an early 1-0 lead!!

Mud Bag is a disco bar with TV's showing sporting events... Tonight is a huge UFC night with a series of big fights with a Brazilian fighting an American for the World title topping the bill...

All sorts of nationalities are joining us... Many want a photo with Rob... Meeting new people...Rob likes to high five... Now when a 6' 11" (2.11m) guy puts his arm in the air to high five...The petite girls are jumping up with their arms outstretched to try to reach him!!

A tall German guy walks in... Now when you have spent your whole life growing to be the tallest guy... It's a bit of a shock to meet Rob!! We have a photo together... I stand on a stool leg but am still dwarfed... What the hell... I am now stood on the stool!! They chair lift me down... Now we have Miss Ecuador, then Argentines, Brazilians, Italians, Mexicans and and... And the barman is wearing my hat and sunglasses looking cooler than I ever could!!

There is talk of Lapa...But it's around 2.30...John is totally wasted...He is in my sunglasses and hat but swears blind they are his... Rob and I have absolutely no idea where his are... No point in asking John because he thinks he is wearing them!!

We say our goodbyes and I head back to my apartment. En route there is a lady selling hotdogs out of the boot of her car... My stomach is screaming... Stop stop... Feed me!! The hotdogs are delicious... After so long without food... Well they would be!

I get to bed around 2.30... My voice, such as it is, is further strained... I have forgotten what it is like to speak properly... A Spurs friend I know, Louise went out to watch Spurs in Tromso in the Norwegian part of the Arctic Circle...she lost her voice out there and by the end of the season in May... It hadn't come back... A cheery thought to go to bed on at 2.30am!! Another great day though!!

Women sexy and rock roll and...Think there might have been some football in there too!

Five weeks of partying in Rio didn't kill me but first day home, a London taxi driver knocked me over and nearly did...

Great routine of Marriott Copacabana for lunch and crazy nights out in Rio. Lifelong friends made in the Mud Bug Bar!

Routine only broken when travelling to watch England...Not even they could put a dampener on Rio though...

Can we play you every year!

Robert Reed, Luton, England

As a South African living in Paris, I remember being proud of the way my country successfully hosted the World Cup in South Africa four years ago.

I was really looking forward to seeing how the World Cup would be hosted in Brazil but after all the turmoil leading up to the opening ceremony, I was a little nervous for Brazil. Once the tournament started, along with everyone else, I was pleasantly surprised by the organisation of the World Cup, and particularly by the fact that the stadiums all looked full, even for the so called "less popular" nations.

With France making it to the Quarter Finals, I was swept up by the euphoria in Paris, which helped to make my World Cup experience very enjoyable.

Shaun Jackson, South African Manchester United supporter living in Paris, France

SUNDAY 6TH JULY 2014

I wake at 9.20am and relax in the apartment...Catching up with stuff on my phone and writing my diary.

I have the British Grand Prix on the television in the background and become increasingly excited...Yes...Hamilton wins the British Grand Prix!!!

On the way down to the beach I have a fresh fruit drink and a banana to try to soothe my throat...It really is a mess...Will it ever recover!

The promenade is closed off from traffic on one side to allow people to walk, run cycle etc

Walking along the front to sunbathe, I see the green of Wimbledon on a television in a restaurant...Of course, Sunday...Its Men's Finals day and I don't even know who is in the final!! I look in to see Djokovic is beating Federer by 2-1 in sets and is 5-2 in games in the fourth set #matchover

The weather is fantastic...Not at all surprised to see the electronic signs showing 31 degrees!

I take a sun bed by the Budweiser Hotel and almost inevitably start talking with some Argentines on the beach. They have a cool bag containing an alcoholic drink called Fernet with coca cola and ice. They give me a taste and it is lovely... They insist I try it again and say it tastes even better with nuts...and just as I am wondering where I will get a bag of nuts from...Although I am sure a beach vendor could solve that...They produce some nuts and yes it is fabulous. Their English isn't quite good enough to describe what Fernet is and each time I ask, they say not vodka but like vodka!

Postscript: I Googled Fernet and its origins are Italian. It is described as being a spirit called Amaro and is thick in consistency and bitter in taste and its recipe is a closely guarded secret. There is a quote which best sums it up "The easiest way to explain the taste is to imagine Jagermeister without the sugar. You shoot it, immediately getting a strong hit of mouthwash - drying the mouth out, stinging the tongue."

Not much clearer lol!!

They tell me that there was a fight between Brazilians and Argentinians on Friday night on one of the petrol station forecourts situated between the two dual carriageways...As both teams progress through the tournament, the stakes are only going to get higher and higher...

I relax on to my sun bed and continue to write up notes whilst sunbathing. Rob is in touch to say great night and we will have to try to get together again.

One week today it is the World Cup Final...And my departure date...Unless I can change my flight, I will be flying home almost immediately after the final... Last night Rob said he doesn't want to go home...I know the feeling...

I have written to Bravofly again today and await their response.

With it being a Sunday and such hot weather... The beach is packed!

In text dialogue with Aline this morning...The Neymar story is dominating the news...He has fractured his third vertebrae...It seems the injury isn't as serious as it sounds and that he will be able to play again soon...But alas not in this World Cup. Scolari has said he has no idea how he will replace him... There is a tweet doing the rounds in Portuguese showing the bridge collapse in Belo Horizonte alongside one of Neymar laid out in agony on the pitch... The heading is "Brazil's fractured World Cup"... I hope there isn't a third and terminal fracture on Tuesday versus Germany which is coincidentally in...Belo Horizonte...

The Colombian player, Juan Zuniga, who kneed Neymar in the back has been interviewed on TV and is very upset by the outcome...

The Brazilians are still confident and believe they have good cover for Silva in Dante of Bayern Munich.

The sun begins its descent behind the Budweiser Hotel and with it being such a clear day, I decide to have a walk up to Arpoador which is the peninsula between Copacabana and Ipanema to take some photographs of the sunset over Ipanema from the rocks.

Walking along Copacabana, I overhear English guys walking in my direction. Amazingly, they are from the city I live, Nottingham but emigrated to Australia 20 years ago!

Passing under the media gantry, I turn left down a little alley to see the most incredible coloured wall paintings which capture not only the spirit but also the story of the World Cup so far...

There are paintings of David Luiz in his bright yellow Brazil shirt with the number 4 in the middle of his shirt, locks flowing, arms outstretched, eyes and mouth wide open in celebration of scoring...Presumably the stunning free kick versus Colombia, César penalty save versus Chile, paintings of the Maracana, Christ the Redeemer, Sugar Loaf and Copacabana, Casillas with his hand on his forehead and many others...Superb!

I walk through the park on the peninsula on to Ipanema and turn left at the beach front towards the rocks...

Having previously described the mood and the sunset from a few days ago, I won't repeat the detail again but tonight the sunset is truly magnificent...I cannot stop taking photographs of the ever changing colours of the sky...The outline of the rugged hills across Ipanema provide such a spectacular backdrop as the sun sets and turns them in to a dominant and brooding presence across the skyline.

EL GRINGO'S ONCE IN A LIFETIME

Walking back off the rock, I feel very chilled and stop off for a caipirinha at a beach bar. Television pictures show the Colombian team receiving an amazing homecoming from their people. The fans came to Brazil in their thousands, their bright yellow shirts created a colourful atmosphere wherever they went. James Rodriguez came of age on the world stage...His wonder goal against Uruguay in the Maracana will live long in the memory. Colombia brought so much to Brazil 2014.

It is 6.30pm... I have walked along the avenue linking Ipanema beach with Copacabana beach...Night has fallen upon Copacabana. For those of you who know where I am, the crescent beach stretches out before me. At the opposite end of the Bay, lights twinkle atop Sugar Loaf. Intermittently the lights of planes leaving the domestic airport rise into the night sky from the left of and passing by Sugar Loaf Mountain.

Looking along the coast line, the Pestana Budweiser Hotel dominates the skyline with its rooftop disco giving off flashing lights and lasers. In the early evening, people are enjoying a pre-dinner drink at one of the many open air beach side cafés. All the traffic lanes are open again. The beaches are lit up by the many floodlights running the entire length of the beach. I take off my beach shoes and walk along the water's edge. The sand and sea feel good beneath my feet...Why haven't I walked along the water's edge more often! I am breathing in the sea salt air. It is yet another beautiful warm evening...The slightest of sea breezes at the water's edge otherwise the air is completely still...The waves come crashing in...They sound so powerful and yet at the same time seem so relaxing... As a spent force they slowly drift back out to sea and the soft sand partially crumples beneath my footsteps. I am writing as I am walking and occasionally a really big wave will come tumbling in and soak me up to my shorts! It is pure bliss...No place I would rather be...

There are a lot of couples and some singles just sat on the beach watching the white waves rolling in. Quite a lot of fishermen are on the beach and there is a rather odd looking live fish which I take a picture of...It looks odd to me but I think the fishermen, seeing me take a photograph, thought I was the odd one!

As I walk along the beach I ponder as to whether this World Cup adventure has changed me and if so, in what way, and will it have any permanence...I have met people from across the world...Responses to my twitter posts and photographs suggest I am living the dream...And I guess in many ways I am.... But... And here is the thing...It is here for all of us...We just find ways, excuses whatever not to live it... We are mentally blocked...Locked in to the prisons of our routines, what we do...Away from the daily grind, the stresses and strains of the corporate world...Out here it has become apparent to me and to a number of others I have spoken with...Life is about being alive in the moment...Having the mind-set of no place I would rather be...Not on the Santa Claus illusions that Christmas Day will be perfect...Because more often than not it won't be... The presents won't be right, someone will be ill, the dinner will get burnt, and there will be fall outs amongst the kids or the families...No... Forget the future...Life is about the experience of the here and now.

Hmm I come off the beach having walked the length of Copacabana beach to the fan fest...It is now 7.25pm...An interesting hour of thoughts...Perhaps a good job I am back into civilisation before I run off to be a hippy!

Oh and not eaten yet today...Good job I had that banana this morning!

Back into the madhouse of the World Cup...On the promenade a huge Argentine flag is being held up...It shows pictures of Maradona and Messi...In the middle of the two players is a picture of the Pope. The Argentines have chosen to write in Portuguese so that the Brazilians understand the message on the flag which says..."You must respect Maradona and Messi...They are from Argentina"

A Brazilian is wagging his finger at the guys holding the flag....He is saying don't tell me what and who to respect... I will respect nothing...You are in my country...If you don't like it, go home to Argentina...The Argentine guys were apparently trying to be friends but it got lost in translation! The message was meant to convey that they are great players...To be respected...Let's not fall out and fight...It's fair to say the Brazilian guy didn't see it that way! They take the flag down and move off into the crowd.

Across the road amid a host of flashing lights and sirens from police cars and motorcycles a car is escorted into the Copacabana Palace Hotel. Some Argentines say Maradona is in Rio for a TV interview...My feeling is that it will probably be someone from FIFA...All the referees are apparently staying in the hotel. I ask a policeman who confirms it was Sepp Blatter in the car... It has been

said by the locals that from this hotel onwards is the seedy end of Copacabana...
Just saying what the locals say...

The peace and tranquillity of the beach has long since gone!!

It is now 8pm and I stop off at my favourite BBQ on Rua Duvivier which
goes under the grandiose name of "Quick Galetos"!!

A young chicken for less than £5...
it's lovely too! The place is always
full and I manage to get a seat just
before the queue forms!

With everyone sat on stools
in a horseshoe around the BBQ it
makes for a sociable environment.
Tonight I get talking with a couple
of guys working behind the scenes
at the BBC...They have had a pretty
uneventful few weeks out here... Half
hours walk along the beach to start
work around 10am...Known worst walks to work! They say the view of the BBC
pundits is that the England defence let the team down. The pundits were positive
about Sturridge and Sterling and the younger players but felt Rio Ferdinand and
Ashley Cole should have been out here...

They tell me Robben admitted to diving and that the pro view is that without
Neymar, Germany will do a job on Brazil.

They also tell me Djokovic won...But in five sets!!! I am shocked that it went
to five sets... It was 2-1 in sets and 5-2 in games when I saw the score on the TV
this morning...It must have been some comeback by Federer...What a shame that
he couldn't finish it off though #maybehislastchance

I go back to the apartment at around 9.45pm for a shower and to recharge my
phone. I send the photographs taken of Arpoador and the walk along the beach
to Aline and we have a chat about our day.

Luiz is booking hotels for their trip to Belo Horizonte for the Brazil v Germany
match. They will set off tomorrow night and return Wednesday morning having
stopped off at hotels to and from Belo Horizonte. I am delighted for them...To
have tickets to see their country in the World Cup in their country...The only
parallel I can draw is the same in Euro96, coincidentally against Germany too...I
can still remember my excitement so am able to empathise...It will be a fantastic
occasion for them!

Aline asks if I am at my apartment and I say yes but intend to go out again...
She responds with a "wow" and I explain the big man Rob will be texting me.

She sends a strange message... *You should rest...*

Ok...I know I am not young but... did I look that tired when she last saw me!

The next message explains.... *You have a long trip to Belo tomorrow with us!
I got you a ticket!!!!!!!!!*

I am stunned and can only reply with...*What?????????????????*

And then.....*Really??????????*

The answer is ....*Yes*

OMG!!!!!!! Thank you sooooo much......I can't believe it!!!!!!!!!!!!!!!

I was waiting to tell you...You will see Brazil playing!!!

I am lost for words... Brazil in the World Cup semi-final in Brazil!!!!

I am overcome with joy!!!! *Thank you, thank you, thank you so much!!!!*

It will be amazing having you with us... I wish I could tell you in person just to see the look in your face....

I am...We say in English...Gobsmacked!!!

The text exchange continues but as the reader I am sure you get the gist! Not much more I can write about it really....Unbelievable!!! I am having to pinch myself! I ask Aline to send the address of a store to buy a Brazil shirt for the match...

I say to her...Here I was talking about my day, the sun set, the walk along the beach, the BBQ and you managed not to say anything!! Aline said it was on purpose to choose the perfect moment... Aline said she knew from 1pm and was desperate to have contact with me!

Our text exchanges lasted an hour! It is now 10.47pm and I still haven't had a shower yet..!

While chatting to Aline I receive a WhatsApp from Sabina saying if I am free she is meeting some friends on the beach front and I am welcome to join them if I wish.

Cold shower...Who cares!!!!

Eventually I am ready to go out... I text Rob and say contact me by text to say where you are rather than by WhatsApp as I won't have Wi-Fi access...

I walk... no I don't...What the hell am I talking about! I am floating along the promenade...I am so happy...Would it be ok for a white haired 55 year old man to be seen skipping along Copacabana...Who cares!!

There is a small bus along the front covered in a huge patchwork of the national flags...It looks incredible and I take a photograph.

I meet up with Sabina and have a caipirinha to celebrate my news!

I ask Sabina to talk me through her World Cup experience... It is a staggering story!!

The headline is that she personally drove 13000 km, 8125 miles in 22 days!

To put this into some perspective:

London to Rio de Janeiro is only 9259km...There and almost half way back!

London to New York is 5534km...Walk in the park!

London to Los Angeles 8699km...There and half way back!

London to Sydney is 16988km...Didn't drive that far...Lightweight...Haha!

The breakdown of Sabina's journey with her friend Vanesa and her fifteen year old nephew Kevin is quite phenomenal...

Argentina to Cascavel 1300km...Stopped in a hotel then drove:

Cascavel to São Paulo 1200km and stayed two days...Went to FIFA fan fest for Brazil versus Croatia then drove:

Sao Paulo to Fortaleza 3100km in 60 hours...Stopping for only one hour's sleep in 60 hours!!! Sabina didn't have any choice as they had to arrive in time for the Uruguay versus Costa Rica match which they had tickets for.

They stayed two days in Fortaleza before driving:

Fortaleza to Jijoca 300km. They had intended to drive all the way through to Jericoacoara nature reserve but had to leave the car 30kms out because... It was like a desert! They stayed two days by the sea before driving:

Jijoca to Natal 550km. They went to the fan fest to see England versus Uruguay and then drove:

Natal to Recife 300 Km. They had tickets and went to see Italy versus Costa Rica. They also saw Argentina versus Iran in the fan fest before driving:

Recife to Porto Alegre 3900 Km. The driving time was another 60 hours!

They had tickets and went to see Argentina versus Nigeria which was a tremendous finale for them! They then drove:

Porto Alegre to Argentina 1200Km.

A total distance of 13000 Km in 22 days...I am exhausted from just writing it... 59 hours out of 60 driving...And only one person driving #stamina

The total fuel cost was 1440 USD and the total cost including tolls, hotels etc was 6560 USD which they split three ways 2187 USD each..

I asked what problems they faced...Sabina was with a girlfriend and her 15 year old nephew so there was a potential safety aspect but that never felt a concern.

The main problem was obviously tiredness for Sabina who did all the driving...They couldn't have left home any earlier and there was just never enough time in the itinerary to have sufficient sleep.

When in the mountains, the car battery died and they had to wait 3 hours for someone to pass with jump leads! They then had to drive 2200kms on a knife edge as to whether the battery would pack up before they could buy a new one!

They were on the outskirts of Rio de Janeiro in rush hour traffic...The car packed up...Holding up all the traffic...Fortunately it was by an SOS station and other drivers helped push the car onto the hard shoulder.

On the road in the Belo Horizonte region, they were driving in the middle of the night...There were many animals on the road...Horses, chickens etc...Drivers coming in the opposite direction flashing lights on and off...Warning drivers to slow down... Then a horse appeared from nowhere and they had to swerve out of the way...Being in the middle of the night and being very tired...It was a huge shock!

People had warned them about driving at night in Brazil...Criminals etc. but they didn't have any problems whatsoever. Out of the 22 nights...five nights were spent in the car... It was a fantastic once in a life time experience. They started to plan the journey a year ago...And by so doing, were able to obtain good hotel prices.

For the most part, the trip went as planned...And in driving the 13000km, they saw three games live in the stadium and many different regions of Brazil!

I say that I am in awe of the driving she did and very matter of factly she said...A lot of Argentina and Chile fans did the same... It was almost a shrug of the shoulders to say it was nothing!

Having dropped her friend and nephew off at home, with being a music teacher and in school holidays, Sabina took the opportunity to fly to Rio de Janeiro for the final 10 days of the tournament and obviously she hopes to see Argentina win the World Cup in Brazil. The return flight cost her US $1260.

It is a most remarkable story. Sabina hands me a DVD of her band "Belo Rojo Blues". Postscript: On returning home I listened to the CD. Their music is fabulous...Bluesy rock. Do have a look at them on YouTube!

At the same bar are four Algerian French guys, Marseilles fans...Naoufel tells me they are staying in a favela called Rocinha at a cost of 50 reals a night. He says the people are very good and with a big heart but...It isn't so good to see kids of 14 and 15 selling drugs with guns!

Two English Arsenal fans turn up for a drink...One of them, for some reason which he can't recall, is wearing a giraffe fancy dress costume. He knows he got it from an Aussie and he also recalls caipirinhas were involved but that is about as far as his memory can stretch.

He said maybe it is because as he said himself, in this heat, he is sweating like a ...Giraffe obviously! The Arsenal fan says I have never worn a fancy dress outfit in my life... I can't resist the open goal presented and ask him if he has ever worn an Arsenal shirt!!! The comeback was pretty good though...When did you last win a cup!! Good banter at a beachside cafe at... Looks at watch 2.57am...

EL GRINGO'S ONCE IN A LIFETIME

Where does the time go over here!!!

Three Argentines turn up now from Los Angles... Sebastian, Miguel and Ezequiel.

Sabina asked them if they have been in the fan fest which turns out to be a sore point! They went to the fan fest but it was full...They put a trash can against the wall and jumped in to the fan fest by the facilities. They all got in except a friend from Mexico and they could hear the police hitting him with batons outside. Sebastian was concerned and went out of the fan fest to look for him... He even went all the way back to the hotel to try to find him. Sebastian missed the whole game... After the game his friend returns to the hotel drunk singing and had had a great time watching the match on the other open fan fest screen!

The day before their flight to Brazil, Ezequiel went to see his family and said to his younger brother, Facundo...This is a once in a life time chance to see Argentina play in the World Cup in Brazil... You have to come!!Ezequiel came home from work...His brother said... Sold my car...Quit my job... I am coming... And he got a ticket for Argentina v Nigeria...What a game!! He flew back today to...No job and no car but... Memories to treasure for the rest of his life!

Initially Sebastian booked a hotel for him and his mate. They managed to convince the hotel to add Miguel and then Ezequiel wants to join them... Sebastian says bring a rucksack for the 6 days...He has two pairs of underpants, one pair of shorts, two pairs of socks...After sneaking in and out of the hotel for two nights...The hotel staff stop him.. He thinks oh no...There is no way I will get accommodation anywhere in Rio... He decides to tell the truth and the staff say no problem...You should have brought a suitcase!!!

It is 4am; Sebastian needs a pee...He wanders along the edge of the beach... Just as he is about to start... A tramp underneath him screams...Sebastian screams!! They both scream...We are all laughing out so loud!

An American with a beard and bare chest is wandering around threatening everybody...After about an hour of this crap...One of the Arsenal boys gives him a proper left hook...I am not a violent man...But this guy is an absolute pain in the ass...Thankfully it is enough to make him move on.

It is 5.01 and from somewhere a football appears...We go from keepie uppie to football piggy in the middle... I realise I am in danger of overuse but it's true...Ffs it's 5am I am on caipirinha...Early morning joggers are out...We are playing the game where the guy in the middle has to get the ball...And...When the Brazilian who owns the ball realises he is playing with Argentines...He wants 50 reals for his ball... When he doesn't get it...He stomps off with the ball under his arm!!

Florian from Lake Constance is sat with a group of Norwegians and tells us of his of story of travelling the whole country following Germany... There are six of them in a minibus...Had no problems whatsoever until today when they go up Sugar loaf...While at the top their minibus is taken away for being on a yellow line...Surely it's not because Brazil are their next opponents!!!

Julia from Utrecht tells me last Saturday her family had left the day before... It was the day of the Brazil v Chile game...She met a Brazilian guy and spent six or seven hours with him... They are getting on really well, kind of dating, taking photographs etc. Towards the end of the night, she asks him to take a photograph on her phone...She turns round to gather her friends and when she turns back just seconds later, the guy has run off with her phone... The phone is replaceable but it has three months of worldwide travel and memories on the phone which haven't been backed up...#gutwrenching

Julia reports it to the police...A week later she is at the fan fest and behind her is the guy who stole her phone! She goes up to him, holds out her hand and says in a loud voice...give me my fucking phone back...He hands her the phone back!! She looks straight in to the photo album and ...All her photographs have been deleted... She suffers the devastation a second time.

Later Julia goes to use the facilities and the guy follows her...He is saying... It is my phone...Give me my phone back!

EL GRINGO'S ONCE IN A LIFETIME

Julia comes out from using the facilities and he is stood with a security guy. He has told the security guy that Julia has stolen her phone...

The security guy says I heard you stole his phone...We need to sort it out... He has 18 photographs on the phone...Julia knows her code but so does he... Fortunately registering the original theft with the police resolved it... When Julia suggested calling the police...The guy ran off...But all her photographs were lost and can never be recovered... And as well, she missed most of the Holland versus Mexico game.

The sunset I witnessed on Ipanema is countered by the sunrise I see on Copacabana! It comes from nowhere... We are chatting away and have lost track of time...It is stunningly beautiful...Wonderful...I am lost for superlatives... We watch the first tinge of colour come out of a darkened sky behind Sugar Loaf Mountain...The sky is being gradually lit...firstly with dark orange and dark blue which gradually lighten in to all manner of colours... The open fan fest is now visible and as the sun rises, the sky becomes a bright kaleidoscope of colours... Pinks, purples, oranges, blues, yellows... before orange and then bright yellow lights the sky which finally gives way to blue and a new day is dawn... We are on the beach capturing the moment with group photographs...It is a memory which will stay with us forever.

If ever you visit Rio de Janeiro...Even if you decide not to stay up all night...I urge you to wake up early and see the sun rise...Only need to do it once...the images will stay with you forever...I promise!

We look behind us...One guy has missed it... he is laid back in a chair, his head rocked back, mouth open, legs outstretched in front of him and arms outstretched either side resting on the table behind him... A great photograph!

It is 6.45am and the early morning walkers and joggers are out in full force now...The show is over, the night is over...It is time to say our goodbyes...

I return to my apartment and climb into bed at 7.10am. The end of a surreal but extraordinarily special day and night!

EL GRINGO'S ONCE IN A LIFETIME

I am not sure my quote will be useful, as I didn't watch TV for four years now, and even before I never watch sports. I prefer to practice rather than watching.

However, apart from that, I noticed in the street that the linguistically divided Belgium seemed to be united as long as the Belgium team was playing. It was impossible to cross a street without seeing Belgian flags on houses.

When the Belgians lost and went home, everything went back to normal life, in our case, trying to make a new government, the next battle between Flanders and Wallonia. I have to think very hard to remember who finally won the cup. But as long as millions of people were happy and enjoyed it, it is fine for me too.

Not watching TV saves me about 15 hours per week for doing sports myself which is biking!

Johan Braem, Antwerpen, Belgium

I am the eldest of five sisters and as children, our father used to take us to matches in Bogota after Sunday Mass. Growing up, I became a fanatical football supporter and have been to 8 World Cups, 3 Copa Americas, 2 World Under 20's tournaments and the Euro Finals in the Ukraine and Poland.

Brazil2014 was the first World Cup I was able to attend the whole tournament and managed to see 13 matches live including all the games of my beloved Colombia.

For me Brazil was the best tournament ever. The atmosphere and friendship amongst the fans was very special and especially in Rio de Janeiro where every nationality of the teams seemed to be represented and people from many other countries too. It was a magical time of my life.

The experience was not without problems. The lack of English or Spanish language skills in the stadiums and surrounding areas made life very difficult and in phone stores to get a sim card I had to sign a four page contract in the Portuguese language. There was also a lack of hotel rooms which made the prices incredibly expensive. Extra flights could have been laid on but instead seat prices were tripled!

For the country though, ground transportation was excellent and reliable, unfortunately the distance between venues was very large. As an example, in order for me to go to Fortaleza for Colombia vs Brazil I flew from seeing France vs Nigeria in Brasilia to Recife, got there at 1 am and stayed at the airport until 7 am to go to the bus station to take a 14 hours bus ride to Fortaleza.

I met two Japanese guys at the airport during that night and they were going on the same bus with me. We arrived to Fortaleza at 1 am and I learnt that my hotel reservation was declined and I found myself with no place to stay. So my new Japanese friends offered me to stay with them in a Motel (for couples!) that they booked the day before and the cost was $275 US per night. So I spent two nights with them and this was one of the many experiences (adventures) that I had in Brazil.

It was also my best World Cup because Colombia qualified and I felt the team was amazing and the revelation of the tournament. For me they are the World

Champions and I'm sure the only reason we didn't go to the semi or final is because we had to play Brazil. My feelings before the game were positive win or lose, as for me they were already the champions! It was Colombia's first time ever in the Quarter Finals and I am so happy to have been there live to see this happen. The memories of Brazil will stay with me forever!

Maria Teresa Rodriguez, Bogotá, Colombia.

MONDAY 7TH JULY 2014

Ten twenty am...I wake up!! 3 hours sleep is nowhere enough...No hangover... In-cred-ible!!!

7th July... A poignant day...

I am trying to get hold of Bravofly to change my flight...There is a slight possibility of a World Cup Final ticket. It may only be a slim chance but.... imagine!!!

The headline in the Veja newspaper yesterday alongside a picture of Neymar holding his back is..."The whole of Brazil will be the football player for Neymar"

Rob rings...May see him down on the beach later...

I go to an official Brazilian shop as recommended by Aline and buy two Brazil shirts for my sons...It costs an extra 35 reals to have Neymar number 10 on the back of each shirt which is in the region of £10. I will wear one of the shirts to the match tomorrow. I am already starting to feel excited!! It seems to be a Flamengo shop. I ask the young man who is serving me in the distinctive red and black Flamengo shirt if he is a Flamengo fan. He replies yes of course... I move away from the counter and he can't help himself... He discreetly comes up to me and cups my ear to whisper... I am not a Flamengo fan; I am a Fluminese supporter. I do this work just to earn the money! That's the thing...People can lie about almost anything... But not disrespect their football team! There is a young man in the Spurs shop who puts the names and numbers of the fans favourite players on the back of their shirts. He is an Arsenal fan.

Every day in the Spurs shop, he has to wear a Spurs shirt and is mixing with Spurs fans and working with Spurs shirts...Very few people know his secret...I am not sure I could do it but a lot around the UK and the world do!

I pay for the shirts and arrange to collect them on my way back from the beach.

I get down to the beach in my usual place down by the Budweiser Hotel... Between beach stations four and five...The best sun beds ...In my opinion of course!

All the locals are at work and the beach feels almost empty in comparison to yesterday.

Bravo Fly are beginning to bother me...No response to emails and the line although not a discontinued number doesn't seem to be connecting..

Rob comes down to the beach to say hello and confirms I can stay with him until he flies back on Wednesday 16th July.

I have a lovely dozy sleep on the sun bed. This throat infection and coughing is not going away though....It has been with me since going to Lapa with Paul and Ian on our first Monday night in Brazil...

Finally through KLM directly I am able to change my flight back to the UK. The cost of changing my departure date from the 13th to the 17th July would be £900. A day later on the 18th would be £112...So there it is...I am staying until Friday 18th July arriving back into the UK on Saturday 19th July. I will need to find somewhere to stay for the nights of 16th and 17th July...should be a lot cheaper once the World Cup has finished though.

Aline texts to say we will meet at 5.40 to begin our journey to Belo Horizonte... The excitement in me goes up a notch! Brazil v Germany in the World Cup Semi Final in Brazil!!

I leave the beach, collect the Brazil shirts and head back to my apartment. A shower, change of clothes, pack and I am on my way to meet Luiz and Aline

Luiz gets stuck at work...We all know that feeling!! Fortunately the California Othon is close by and I am able to log on to Wi-Fi and catch up with friends through social media.

We meet on the corner of Santa Clara and Nossa Senhora at 7.30. The distance is 465kms but the traffic will be an issue. Luiz estimates it will take an hour just to clear Rio! We are on our way...

Me excited!!

Aline's interview seems to have gone well but it is likely to be August before a decision is made...The timing could work well with a new puppy being picked up on Wednesday!

Aline's phone rings and it is the estate agent as they are looking at buying an apartment in Botofogo. The price sounds too good to be true and they feel there will be an issue of some description ...But they will anyway go to have a look.

Luiz and Aline say five or six very senior people including some close to FIFA and CEOs of connected companies have been arrested. The view is that these people have been selling tickets on the black market for several World Cups.

They say the local people are very proud of the operation by the Brazilian police...Especially as in the run up to the World Cup, the country had been made to feel inadequate...Questions over logistics, stadiums etc and yet now they have been able to do what other countries couldn't and arrested some senior people on suspicion of black market ticketing.

May be Sepp Blatter will be having a chuckle at one of the arrests being a British CEO of a company called Match Services, Raymond Whelan. The first to be arrested was an Algerian. Black market ticketing is a prisonable offence in Brazil.

A number of the arrests have been at the Copacabana Palace hotel which explains the heavy military as well as Police presence there today.

FIFA have issued a statement saying they are collaborating with the authorities. Luiz and Aline say that those arrested have been taken to a maximum security prison in Rio called Bangu. This is a prison where all the drug dealers go. Unofficially they might be able to pay to be in a block of more educated prisoners but the conditions will be somewhat different to the Copacabana Palace....

Now imagine...You are a free man today...You are sitting in the luxury of the Copacabana Palace...You may have done similar things to the allegations being made of those under investigation. What would you do? The World Cup Semi Finals and Final are taking place inside the next week... Do you stay or do you flee the country?

Fair to say if you are to flee...You wouldn't tip the authorities off by checking out of your hotel... A private jet might be needed!!

Aline says a CEO of a major bank received tickets to pass on to clients... The clients he chose were members of his own family!! He was found out and sacked forthwith.

The conversation in the car is going at a quite pace!

People in the media ex-players from Brazil and other countries are saying the Colombian player Zuniga knew what he was doing ... Not to the extent that he wanted to break Neymar's back but enough to put him out of the game. Argentine media are apparently reporting that Zuniga had been threatening Neymar before the incident. On a remarkably positive note...There seems to be a view from some foreign medical specialists that should Brazil get there...Neymar could play in the final!!

The media are also saying that the stretcher used to carry off Neymar was totally inadequate...And is this all FIFA can offer?

I talk about being at Spurs v Bolton when Fabrice Muamba had a heart attack in the middle of the game on the pitch. A season ticket holder couldn't get to the match and gave his ticket to a relative...The relative was a cardiologist and ran onto the pitch to play a major role in saving his life....A truly once in a life time experience for all of us who were there on that frightful night. The reaction of the players such as Jermaine Defoe as events unfolded still sends a shiver down my spine... Bearing in mind Neymar's dreadful injury, it is quite an ironic term to use right now...

Incredibly we have had two other heart attack at Spurs of late in the West Upper and the Paxton upper... It is quite surreal to see arms frantically pumping up and down trying to save someone's life whilst below 22 men continue to kick a bag of wind about...

They tell me a Brazilian man died of a heart attack during the Brazil v Chile match.

We stop for a bite to eat at a well-known restaurant which many of those visiting Petropolis incorporate into their day out. The literal translation is "house of the German" and we enjoy a very tasty hot dog.

Whilst eating our meal, the arrests come up as headline news on the television. Tomorrow's newspapers will make interesting reading....

Aline takes over the driving for the steep climb through the mountains passed Petropolis... Frustratingly, a speed camera flashes...

The road is a good one and a dual carriageway through the mountains but it is littered with speed cameras...

They explain that points are cleared after one year on a driving licence and that 21 points must not be exceeded within that time period. An offence carries 2, 3, 5 or 7 points depending on the severity of the offence. Aline believes she was doing 80 in a 60 which would carry a 7 point penalty and a fine of c150 reals. Last week Luiz overrun a red light which also carries a 7 point penalty...The points are automatically given to the car owner not the driver...Aline is the owner of the car...The driver and owner both have to write in to say that the driver was the driver and will take the points and fine.

The conversation moves back on to football...

A friend of theirs had a spare ticket for the Brazil v Colombia game. He advertised on Facebook to do a swap for another game but nobody came forward. Instead of selling the ticket, he decided to choose someone to give it to! He went out on to the streets and looking at the faces of people he chose a 66 year old popcorn seller whose stall is near the guy's metro station! Although a keen football lover, the popcorn seller had never been inside a football stadium!! Their friend flew him to Fortaleza and took him to the match. The man broke down in tears inside the stadium and asked if their friend would mind taking photographs as his wife would never believe it!!! The friend took some photographs and posted them to his home address. What a heart-warming story!!!! And to hear this on the day of the arrests! I am not sure you could get a greater contrast....

We continue to climb up the mountains...Would be nice if my ears were to pop!

Luiz Googles the place we are staying at... It is 1116 metres above sea level!!

We have travelled about 150kms and paid 24 reals so far in road tolls. The cost each time has been 8 reals.

We have an REM album playing in the car... Losing my religion is such a good song...Takes me back to Lapa!

Santos Dumont 34kms...I ask why the airport is named after a town? Luiz explains that the man Santos Dumont invented the first aeroplane to take off on its own... The Wright Brothers plane was catapulted into flight. The domestic airport in Rio de Janeiro was named after him and as well the name of the town where he was born was changed in his honour.

It is 11.55pm and we have around 100kms to travel tonight. I must have nodded off... It is now 00.55 and I immediately feel guilty...Luiz is driving after a day's work!!

We set off almost 5 1/2 hours ago... And all to watch 90 minutes of football... And life is great...Old Beatles tracks now!! She loves you, Can't buy me love, Yesterday and now Hey Jude and this is what non-football fans just don't get...It's not just about 90 minutes of football it's about the whole day out... The experiences you share, the adventure, the stories, the companionship, the memories being created...

Luiz reminds me of the 2012 Olympics when Paul McCartney went to the Velodrome to watch the cycling and the whole crowd sang hey Jude ... Perfect illustration!!!

We are lost trying to find the hotel...All been there...Long journey... Tired and lost... Then hey presto! There it is!! Well, another sign saying 1km!

We pass through the gated entrance and park up. The time is 1.15am ...Some 6 and 3/4 hours after we set off!!

I realise it is my first alcohol free day since 13th June... Well not strictly true...I was drinking caipirinhas at 5.30 this morning on Copacabana beach!

I get to bed at 1.45 with a 7.30 alarm call booked.

EL GRINGO'S ONCE IN A LIFETIME

Again the World Cup has been vibrant in South East Asia's most populous nation of 250 million people. Never qualified but always behind the big teams, Indonesians have stayed in front of their TV screens vibrating and eating sate ayam (chicken brochettes) and bubur ayam (chicken porridge) until early morning to see the world's superstars playing and battling for world supremacy.

Often supporting "Belanda", the Dutch orange team of their former coloniser it was fireworks screaming in the sky until the semi-final against Argentina.

How long will it take before Indonesia qualifies for the World Cup Finals... Not long as soon as expertise is brought in to harvest the young talents dribbling from morning to dawn in the numerous fields of the 13000 islands' archipelago.

Philippe Bonfils. A Frenchman living in Indonesia

Hundreds of millions of people around the world watched the World Cup soccer tournament including myself and I was very much intrigued not only by the games but by the fans as well. So many fans with such passion and loyalty for their team and who travelled so far away.

As a baby boomer, I grew up with American Football and Baseball in the USA. Organized soccer leagues for kids were introduced in South Texas in the late 70s and early 80s and although my children and grandchildren participated in these activities, I really did not develop an interest or appreciation for the sport until the last four years or so. Now I am looking forward to the next World Cup!

Ralph D Davis, Sugar Land, Texas USA

TUESDAY 8TH JULY 2014

I wake up with the most monumental hangover ever!! Just kidding!!! I awake at 7.15 ahead of my 7.30 alarm call and fall straight back into a deep sleep...

When I wake a second time...Panic...I must have been asleep forever.

It is 7.29 and the telephone rings. Perfecto!! Notice how my Portuguese language skills are developing!!

The mountain air has invigorated me... Great night's sleep!! I am not normally a morning person...But today I have woken in great spirits!

Shower...First hot one since Flamengo...My apartment shower has three temperature settings...Cold, bloody cold and absolutely teeth chatteringly freezing....You never quite know what you are going to get.... Just like Prince Charles talks with his plants, I talk with my shower before I get in each morning... But it is one hell of a cantankerous old son of a bitch. Believe me, harsh words have been spoken. Let's just say our relationship could be better. Not here though at the Senac Hotel Grogoto, Barbacena...We may have only had a one morning stand but I am in love with this shower!!

Then again, today I love everything and everybody!! Some mornings you wake up and the day ahead of you is well just that...The day ahead...Work or whatever...An ordinary day..

But today is anything but ordinary! Today I am going to Brazil v Germany in the World Cup semi-final in Brazil!!! My yellow Brazil shirt with Neymar JR number 10 on the back is laid out before me on the next bed... Boy am I excited!!!

As a child, I remember marvelling at the Brazilians...We used to practice trying to bend the ball round the wall like Rivelino...I have a picture of the 1970 Brazil team on the wall in my gym...44 years later I can still just about name the team...Excuse the spellings.. Felix, Brito. Pensives, Colorado Everaldo, the captain Carlos Alberto, Jairzinho, Gerson, Tostao, Pelé, Rivelino and the substitute Paulo Cézar... Only one substitute in those days!

What a soppy sod I am...I have tears in my eyes...Thinking about me as a child and now here I am... All these years later...Going to see Brazil in a World Cup Semi Final in Brazil...Oh my...Today is no ordinary day... And I am nervous because "we" are playing Germany and I feel comfortable in saying "we", because every time England are knocked out or haven't qualified, I support Brazil.

And we as in being English are playing our old nemesis...Germany...The team who have given us so much misery down the years... 1970...Coming from 2-0 down to beat us 3-2...1990 and 1996 penalty shoot-out losses...2010... Hammering us 4-1...So I am nervous... But no such nerves for Aline who predicts a 2-1 win for Brazil...Luiz thinks 1-0 either way... I just have the "we never beat the Germans" mentality...but this is Brazil...This time it will be different...I am trying to convince myself...But the years of conditioning, of misery and heartache makes it difficult for an Englishman.

Down to breakfast...Not in my bright pristine yellow Brazil shirt...Oh no... No risks of strawberry jam being taken today...Not that I am even having strawberry jam!

Over breakfast Aline says it is very cold here in the mountains and that they had the heater on in the room all night. I say that it is difficult to regulate the use of the word cold as when somebody says it is very cold in England it has a very different meaning to when a Brazilian person says it!!!

I say, an example, is of fans supporting a lower league team called Barnsley in England sing... It's just like watching Brazil...The story makes Luiz and Aline laugh.

This hotel is superb...The rooms are bright, cheerful and spacious. The breakfast is excellent. There is a gym, outdoor pool and the views are spectacular over the mountains and the city of Barbacena. The name keeps making me think of Barcelona! The cost for the room and breakfast including taxes is 138 reals... About £37!!

After breakfast, I go back to my room and the moment arrives to put my Brazil shirt on...I can't deny that pulling the shirt over my head feels a special moment...I am back to being a school boy!!

We set off around 9.15am on our journey to Belo Horizonte. The scenery is magnificent across green hills and valleys. As with last night, the dual carriageway roads are very good. There are a lot of towns in the area and Luiz explains that many years ago it was a gold mining community and the towns developed accordingly with colonial style buildings.

It is 10.35 and we are 65km from Belo Horizonte. This morning, we have traditional Portuguese music on which is typical of the Recife carnival.

The roadworks and lorries pulling out in front of us, cutting us up... It is just the same as in England.

I ask if perfecto is the right word...It isn't...Only Spanish...Ignore my earlier comment!!

We talk about the drink driving laws in Brazil. An offence carries an automatic 12 month ban and a c1000 reals fine. No alcohol whatsoever is permitted.

It is 11.30. We are driving through down town Belo Horizonte, as quickly as possible under flyovers! Third time lucky, we find a car park in the Holiday Inn at 11.44.

So...The game is a little over five hours away...We know Dante of Bayern Munich will replace the suspended Tiago Silva ... But the question remains as to who will replace the irreplaceable Neymar..

We walk out of the hotel and immediately Aline bumps into Gabriel an old school friend!

We walk around the corner and there are bus ticket sellers competing with each other to sell tickets to the stadium...It is chaotic and I almost feel guilty for choosing to buy from one seller as opposed to the other twenty...

The car park location is perfect though...We will be able to get off the bus and be in the car within a matter of minutes to set off on our return journey.

We walk around the next corner and Luiz bumps into his oldest friends... Brazil...Such a small place haha.

Over a frango oops sorry Portuguese, showing off now, chicken lunch, Luiz tells me about the team coming back from the USA with the World Cup in 1994. They flew home to Brasilia in the morning with the intention of meeting the president before a tour of the city and then to fly on to do other city tours.

By mid-afternoon they hadn't left the airport! Everybody was wondering what was happening. The players came back with all kinds of electrical goods believing as World Cup winners they would get through Customs, after all they are World Cup winners! Customs was having none of it...The usual rules were upheld. It is rumoured that the "CBF", the Confederation of Brazilian Football, paid the bill.

The newspaper headline for today's match reads..."The day to overcome"

Inside the headline is ..."Shark behind the bars" and "Whelan...Ticket mafia!"

We head for the bus queues...Judging by the people in Savassi, Germany will have a strong presence in the stadium.

We board the bus at 1.40pm. Even though I am sitting down the bus lurches me backwards and forwards...I remember the return journey into the city after the England v Costa Rica game...Hmmm...

The couple of beers in the sun have made me feel drowsy...I am trying, but sleep is impossible on this bus!! The bus arrives at the stadium and drops us off at 2.18.

Global TV is having a competition to create new songs for Brazilian fans. Better late than never!!

The fans are making an effort and on the walk to the stadium are singing

If you are German,
You only have three world cups,
One less than Zagelo

Not many countries in the world can taunt the Germans! Three world cups... If only!!

The champions are back,
The champions are back,

Hmm...Not very innovative...Can't see that one getting too far in the competition!

We are given Neymar card board masks on route to the stadium. He might not be playing but he is certainly not forgotten and with all these masks will be very visible today!

After going through the various Police and Military ticket checks, we take photographs outside before entering the stadium. There is a guy wearing a green Incredible Hulk mask and gloves who poses for me.

We buy drinks with the semi-final details inscribed on the cups to keep as a souvenir of the game.

EL GRINGO'S ONCE IN A LIFETIME

The seats are fantastic! Near the front, on the first tier between the 18 yard line and half way line.

A huge cheer goes up...The big screen shows the Brazilian team coach arriving into the stadium! The anticipation...The excitement is ever increasing!

We meet up with the ESPN guys from America. Rick Abbott who kindly offered the tickets to Aline through getting to know each other at the gym where Aline does CrossFit, Rubem Prado with his wife and son and Chris Fowler.

Chris Fowler flew in this morning from commentating on the men's final at Wimbledon on Sunday with McEnroe. Chris commentates to the US audience on all the major tennis tournaments. I am a huge tennis fan and used to regularly go to tournaments around Europe in the Tim Henman and Greg Rusedski era. It is fascinating to hear Chris talking of the players and the Andy Murray coaching situation etc.

It is some week for Chris:

The Wimbledon men's final in London on Sunday followed by...

First World Cup semi-final Brazil v Germany in Belo Horizonte on Tuesday followed by...

Second World Cup semi-final Argentina v Holland in Sao Paulo on Wednesday followed by...

A few days in Rio de Janeiro followed by...

The World Cup Final in the Maracana on the following Sunday

Chris admits to there being more than a few envious followers on Twitter!!

As the stadium begins to fill up the white and light blue seats begin to turn yellow.

Having seen Brazil matches on television down the years and not least during this World Cup, being amongst the Brazilian yellow in their own stadium, it is genuinely a moment to truly savour, to cherish and treasure forever.

The teams are announced and Bernard is in for Neymar which when announced gets the loudest of cheers. Bernard and Fred are local boys from Belo Horizonte.

We put our Neymar masks on and pose for photographs... The photos really do look funny.

Kick off is approaching and away to my left in the corner is the official away section for Germany. The section is bathed in white shirts and the distinctive black, red and yellow flags. They are singing their hearts out and making some noise.

It takes me back to the Euro 96 semi-final at Wembley...England v Germany. The German fans were away to our right and having just beaten us on penalties, their players went over to celebrate with their fans. The images and disappointment will stay with me forever.

If any team is capable of playing a host nation and beating them...Germany have proven themselves to be that team...The ultimate party poopers...Nerves of steel... As shown over many years in their ice cool approach to penalties.

The national anthems are sung and I think back to what Ray Houghton said and copy him by recording the Brazilian on my phone. When meeting Ray, never in a million years did I, could I, imagine ever seeing a Brazil match live at this World Cup.

The singing of the national anthem really does make the hairs stand up on the back of my neck!

The game kicks off!!

Brazil start well but seem to be playing long diagonal balls...Missing midfield out completely.

Germany look far more a team...more organised more compact...Adopting a passing game. A terrible error by Marcelo, down the left wing but he gets back to correct at the expense of a corner. Cross comes over ...Mueller...Completely unmarked 0-1...

The German fans to my left go wild...What a start by their team. It looks as if Brazil are trying to come to terms with the loss of Silva in organising their defence on the hoof on the pitch so to speak...How can a player be left unmarked at a corner in a World Cup Semi Final?

Germany are looking a class above Brazil...What has Scolari been doing with this squad?

Every time Marcelo goes forward...Either he or Hulk loses the ball and the Germans are breaking down the space provided...

Now it's two...This could be any score... Klose! Breaks Ronaldo's highest ever goal scoring record!

A third from Kroos follows within a couple of minutes...The Germans are literally walking through the Brazilian defence...Emotionally they are all over the place. If this was a boxing match it would be stopped...

Bloody hell it's 4 after 25 minutes!!! Kroos again! Germany are not even having to work particularly hard here...

29 minutes ...5-0...Khedira gets in on the act...Every time the Germans attack, they look like scoring...

There is a sense of disbelief in the stadium...The German fans are going crazy!! Why wouldn't they be...Less than 30 minutes gone and the score is Brazil 0-5 Germany!!! Unbelievable!!

The rest of the stadium is sat in stunned silence. Some people are crying, others have their heads in their hands...It is difficult to comprehend....The stadium is in shock. I am sure the country is in shock. The whole world will be in shock...

There is a sense of embarrassment, of shame in the stadium...

Silva is a huge miss but nevertheless ..,

The fans singing to the president... "Go fuck yourself' There is an election this year...Surely not a hope in hell...

The worst is that it doesn't even feel as if Germany have had to work particularly hard for this...They are playing a good passing game...Keeping it simple...Passing and moving...

I feel English again...Germany the ultimate party poopers... But my how you have to admire and respect them.

Half time Brazil 0-5 Germany

Luiz says each player is playing with 100 extra kilos on each leg...Emotionally after the second goal they were all over the place...The Germans with ruthless efficiency and simple passing to unmarked players exposed the lack of Scolari's team structure...Brutally...

Second half...Brazil will have to go for it but ... What could happen. Hulk and Fernandinho replaced by Paulinho and Ramires.

In all my years of watching Brazil, they have never been a long ball team.

Until now, until their own World Cup...What terrible timing...

Brazil start the second half really well...Couple of good saves by Neuer.... The crowd are staying with the team.

Fine tip over by César...Brazil are huffing and puffing...

The crowd are now getting restless... Fred booed... Now Oscar...For me, this doesn't feel to be a problem of individuals though...This feels more to do with organisation, structure and team work. Brazil have lacked this throughout...And without their talisman and captain...Their two best players...A football crazy country of 200m... How can this be?

César is on his own...No defence against two German strikers... Somehow he comes out and slides to clear the ball.

Incidents in the seats breaking out around the stadium causing the fans to stand up to all over the place to see what is happening...Guess it's over exuberance from German fans sat around the stadium...Who can blame them!!!

Passing move down the left...Schurrle scores 0-6!! The Brazilian fans start clapping the goal....

Fred is substituted... The camera pans on to him sat on the bench, he is loudly booed... Scapegoat comes to mind. He hasn't had a good World Cup and like a number of players including Paulinho is nowhere near the level of form shown just a year ago in the Confederations Cup, but he is hardly responsible for the six goals flying in at the other end.

Incredibly, the Brazilian fans are now Olé 'ing German passes against their own team.

German fans head out to get a drink...The Brazilian fans applaud them...This could still get closer to 10 if Germany want it...I take no credit for saying this after 5 minutes.. It was obvious.

58141 attendance.

What a goal from Schurrle!! 0-7 The Brazilian fans are on their feet clapping... It is worthy of being applauded...Smashing in to the net off the woodwork!

Now the Brazilians are attacking...The fans are booing. Marcelo shoots tamely wide... The crowd boo his effort. It must be agony for the players out on the pitch...It is like seeing a wounded animal dying before your eyes...It would better to blow the final whistle and be done with it..

Brazilian fans are Oléing each German pass. There can be no greater insult to the Brazilian players and management.

The German fans are a long way from home...They have paid a lot of money to be here...They are having an absolute ball. Almost from kick off, the game has been a relaxing walk in the park. They have sung nonstop throughout...

EL GRINGO'S ONCE IN A LIFETIME

Imagine for one minute being a German fan...7-0 up against a team unbeaten in apparently 55 home games...The most successful team in World Cup history... At home ... And the score is 0-7... If this was a tele printer (seven) and even that wouldn't do the score justice... A few exclamations would surely be required!! This must be one of, may be the most, sensational scores in the history of the game.

Through ...8??? No... A bad miss...Oscar scores 1-7...It won't be considered as much of a consolation...

Game over...The Brazilian fans sing their proud song...The announcer rubs salt in the wounds by announcing the score. The Germans fans are asked to stay inside the ground.

The Brazilian players form a huddle in the middle of the pitch with Scolari joining them. They break out of their huddle and clap the fans in all four corners. All four corners boo.

The German players walk over to applaud their fans. The Brazilian fans are applauding the German team!! Great sportsmanship!

Sven Goran Erikssen would say in his understated way.... It's a pity...

German fans are now told to wait inside the stadium for 30 minutes. This is the first time I have heard such a message...

The stadium is emptying but away to my left the German fans are having one hell of a party and I think of my friend from Copacabana beach Florian, and Dirk and Silke Brakemeir sat at home watching the game on television in Hannover.

The general feeling is that it would have been more upsetting had Brazil lost by a last minute goal...

The latest joke is that the players decided to support Neymar...As he wasn't able, to play.., neither were they...By the time we get into Belo Horizonte there are dozens of jokes doing the rounds.

On the bus back I get talking with a Norwegian guy, Christian, who is a Spurs fan. He has had a fabulous World Cup travelling around the country and thinks the people are wonderful. The spirit of camaraderie between fans... Win, lose or draw has stood out for him. When in Porto Alegre an American guy insisted he take two tickets even though he and is mate already had tickets...Sell them and make a few bucks was the response! He didn't want to sell them on the black market...Instead he wanted a Brazilian father and child who otherwise wouldn't be able to afford a game to have the tickets.

He got talking with a local guy who said he had a daughter. He makes a call and within what seemed minutes the mother was dropping the daughter off. He gave them the tickets and received a photograph from them in the stadium. Christian said no amount of cash could compensate for the buzz it gave him to see their joy.

The journey back into town is a long one...The match finished just before... Well it didn't because Germany scored a seventh...But you know what I mean!! Gallows humour! We took some photographs after the game...Nevertheless it is 9.18pm when we start our journey back towards Rio de Janeiro

On the way back Luiz says one of the biggest selling cars in Brazil is called the Volkswagen Gol... But not even they could make five Gols in less than 20 minutes!

We stop off for a refreshment break... I feel quite cold and have a hot chocolate... A hot chocolate in Brazil!!

A few post-match titbits of information filter through... The Brazilian TV commentator who is quite an emotional person couldn't cope with the unfolding disaster and couldn't speak live on air....

Ronaldo was commentating on the game and Klose broke his record as the highest World Cup Finals goalscorer...

We get back into the car at 11.55pm with a 100kms to drive to our hotel. The services staff say it is about an hour's drive.

By 00.48 Aline is wiped out so Luiz takes over the driving.

We arrive at the hotel at 1.19am.

It is 2.20am and I finally go to sleep. Alarm call set for 8am...

It was always going to be a never forgotten day...But not in this way...Like everyone else, I could never have imagined this...Once in a life time...

EL GRINGO'S ONCE IN A LIFETIME

Ruined my illusion that merely being Brazilian meant you were a naturally gifted footballer. Players cheating in front of an audience of millions ....And without shame! Skill overrides passion. England really are poor!

Danny Best, Birmingham, UK

I woke up with the excitement for the first game of the World Cup, but then realised I had a massive barricade in front of me; SCHOOL...But every conversation at school was about the World Cup, and even the lessons were based around it, which was a horrible surprise for the non-football fans!

There was so much excitement building for the first match Brazil vs Croatia and it definitely didn't disappoint, in just the first match there was an own goal, a controversial penalty and a vibrant Neymar, which led everyone into believing this would be one of the great World Cups.

I remember coming out of the cinema one night after Spain vs Netherlands, we had all predicted an easy 3-0 win for Spain only to hear from our friend Charlie Aspden that the Netherlands had won 5-1. We all said to him "haha good one, now tell us the real score' and so found out he was not joking!

The World Cup was amazing in the first couple days until I saw that England were playing Italy in their first match, the nerves grew every minute towards kick off. I had lots of mates over for the match, and I was definitely prepared with loads of balloons and drinks (soft!) and with that the match had started.

All of us sat there, all eyes on the TV, tension growing every minute until Raheem Sterling struck at goal into the top corner! Everyone started kicking balloons around the room going mental! We had gone 1-0 up in our first match, except the question on all of our lips was 'why isn't he celebrating? He's just scored a top corner screamer in the World Cup'. We then realised it had hit the side netting and all felt so silly. We ended up going 1-0 down but then two minutes later "DANIEL STURRIDGE LEVELS IT FOR ENGLAND!" But then who else could it of been...Mario Balotelli scored the winner for Italy. Later on in the match I fell asleep with all my mates at my house.

The stand out match for me was Germany 7-1 Brazil. Five goals in such a short space of time, they could've had ten. Although I wouldn't have predicted 7-1, you could slowly but surely see Brazil were progressing by one goal or a dodgy decision every match, and Germany were an army who might open Brazil up.

This was undoubtedly a great World Cup and there hasn't been one like it while I've been alive. The great thing about the World Cup is that it brings football fans all over the world together and every four years no matter how good or bad your team is you always have renewed hope you might well win the World Cup.

Harvey Ellis, Nottingham, UK

WEDNESDAY 9TH JULY 2014

The alarm clock wakes me at 6.45...Now you might well ask why I set the alarm clock for 6.45 when we are meeting for breakfast at 8.30am. I didn't ....but the person who stayed in the room the night before kindly did... How thoughtful!!! It isn't too difficult to fall back to sleep...

The hotel reception staff give me an alarm call as requested at 8am and I am ready to start my day.

My phone hasn't charged...The cable seems to have a faulty connection and it has been a perennial problem during the trip.

The first challenge is the shower....

There is a television programme in England called "The Cube". Each contestant walks into a very larger glass cube. A series of mental and physical challenges are set inside the cube...One might be for example standing on a rotating platform and trying to throw a ball into a basket in the opposite corner of the cube while standing on the rotating platform.

This shower would make for an interesting challenge on The Cube... It is not a wide cubicle...The depth from the door to the back is probably a little deeper than the width. This makes stretching to the back wall to turn the separate hot and cold water taps on a little bit of an over reach. There is a sign in Portuguese and English in big red letters saying "Be careful...Very hot water".

The shower head is not adjustable...The water jet is aimed straight at you...

There isn't enough room to climb in the cubicle and avoid the jet...Over to you!!!

Over breakfast I ask the name of the city we slept in. It is called Juiz de Fora which is about 150kms from Rio.

Aline and I are still suffering with a tickly cough and cold...

Aline translates the newspaper headlines and key points:

Scolari: my responsibility...

When the team arrive back in Rio after games there is usually a huge crowd waiting for them...Last night only six people turned up....It would have been quite ironic if a seventh had...One for each of goal...

The statistics show that Brazil didn't have a single shot on target in the first half!

Luiz says a person bet £20 on a 7-1 German victory and won £46000... Wait a minute, let's analyse this... Brazil are at home. I heard a statistic that Brazil were unbeaten in 55 home matches...The last time they lost by a six goal margin was in 1920. I think whatever possesses someone to wake up one morning and think you know what I am going to bet £20 on a score of Brazil 1-7 Germany...Even now writing it...Having actually been there to witness it...It still feels unbelievable...

Pato's sister says her brother should have been picked. There will also be questions as to why Kaka etc. weren't picked. I would imagine there will be many such stories coming out in due course...

For what it's worth, I agree with Scolari that is his responsibility. He has also said the team collapsed emotionally and Luiz feels the same way...The pressure and shock of the second goal going in was too much for the players.

The German papers lead with:

Bild: No words

Berlin courier: Buy this newspaper for your grand children

Berlin Grosste: Sorry

Zeitung: Phenomenal ... Which is a double entendre relating to Ronaldo

Schweinsteiger issues an apology to the people of Brazil saying he is sorry and that Brazil have played a major part in making this World Cup such a major success...

I think clever move ahead of the final and to protect the German fans from retribution...There has been talk of the Rio fan fest being a dangerous place to be last night..

Luiz is due to start work at 10am but his boss is very understanding about coming in later.

10.04... We set off from the university city of Juiz de Fora. Luiz and Aline say it is regarded as a good city to live in...Very vibrant with the energy university students always bring to a city.

Seeing the sign for Rio de Janeiro prompts me to ask the question as to why the city is called "The river of January". Luiz explains that when the Portuguese arrived for the first time it was in January and might even have been on the first of January. They arrived at Guanabara Bay and thought it was a river... Hence the name Rio de Janeiro!!! In English it reads beautifully...

As we are talking it occurs to me...I have been fortunate enough to have travelled to most of the major cities in the world and if I had to choose a favourite... Maybe it would be Rio de Janeiro... Aline says I should come to live here for a while...How tempting!!!

The drive back in daylight offers some stunning views across the mountain range.

Seeing the road signs...It takes me back to 12 or more years ago when I visited Petropolis which is on this route...The views down over Rio and the sea are breathtaking.

Aline says even though we lost, it has been a great couple of days and Luiz and I have to agree....Very tiring but a fantastic adventure. We have had a lot of fun, laughs, some wonderful stories and a once in a lifetime match and result. As Aline says...A match ticket to keep forever... Memories to treasure forever!

Looking forward to this afternoon, there is the second semi-final. The fan fest will be interesting for Argentina v Holland.

Argentina have won the World Cup twice and lost at least one final.

Interestingly they have won and lost a final against the waiting finalists Germany.

Holland have never won the World Cup... They have lost in finals against today's opponents in Buenos Aires in 1978 and to the waiting finalists Germany in 1974 in Germany. They then lost to Spain in the last final four years ago... And what a horrible nasty final that was...I am not a big fan of Howard Webb but as referee that night, he had an almost no win impossible task... If he had started booking and sending players off so early in the game, he would have been accused of destroying the biggest football show on earth...As it was he took a lenient position early on and was accused of not coming down hard enough... The real fault lay at the door of the Dutch...

In this World Cup, the Dutch have for the most part been fabulous...Starting with that jaw dropping 5-1 win over Spain. I had just landed in Brazil and couldn't believe it.

Then there was the fight back from being 2-1 down versus Australia in what was a very entertaining game.

In their final group game, they gave a professional performance to beat Chile 2-0.

In the last 16, came the controversial last minute penalty winner versus Mexico which sadly marred and deflected from what was a great comeback in very hot conditions.

In the Quarter Finals, they battered Costa Rica but couldn't get the elusive goal which led to winning through the penalties lottery...Van Gaal pulled off the master stroke of changing keepers with a minute of extra time remaining.. And Krul repaid him by pulling off the winning save.

Reflecting on their progress, the Dutch have so far had a wonderful World Cup.

Argentina meanwhile have not yet reached their full potential...Messi got them off to a great start in beating Bosnia 2-1 but there were a lot of nerves after Bosnia pulled one back.

They then beat Iran 1-0 with a great added time winner by Messi...Iran could and may be should have been in front by then though...

In their final pulsating group game, they beat Nigeria 3-2 with two more very good goals from Messi. Defensively though they looked very frail and could easily have conceded a late equaliser...

Into the knock out phase, a very late extra time Di Maria winner broke Swiss hearts when penalties seemed inevitable.

In the Quarter Final an early Higuain goal knocked out Belgium who just didn't seem to turn up on the day.

It seems Di Maria will not be fit for the semi-final...Will Aguero make it? Could be vital!! Reflecting on Argentina's journey, without playing particularly well, they have made it to the semi-finals through their big players scoring big goals. Can these big players out score the Dutch...Not sure...Should be a close and great game

At the end of the Group phase... It seemed inevitable that South American teams would dominate. Only six European teams made it into the last 16...

Now it wouldn't be a huge surprise, if as four years ago, we have an all European Final. The big difference here though is that a European team has never lifted the World Cup in the Americas...Could this be another if not once certainly a first in our life time experience??

Aline drops Luiz off at work and then me off at the junction of Ribeiro and Prado Junior. I settle up the fuel and thank them for getting me the match ticket and taking me with them. It has been a truly amazing and memorable experience.

I go into the apartment and drop my bag off and head straight down to the beach near to the fan fest.

Today Copacabana belongs to Argentina. I meet some Argentina fans from Santa Fe... I am in my Brazil shirt and hat...They think I am Brazilian...I say no Inglese...I am not sure there could be a worse combination to an Argentinian... An Englishman in a Brazil shirt!!

I get chatting with them...They are great guys...Very knowledgeable of English football and like Crouch and Defoe!! Santiago is a 25 year old coming over to Europe to stay for some months in France. He wants to come over to London and meet me to watch Tottenham. They share their beer and vodka. Sebastian is dressed in a blue and white punk style wig!

Santiago says Tevez isn't in the squad because Messi doesn't like him... Can that really be so?

The atmosphere on the beach is building...There is a real sense of anticipation... Their biggest rivals are out...They are heading to the Maracana to win the World Cup in Brazil!!! Other than beating Brazil in the final...It wouldn't get any better for these guys. They say if Argentina win today... Everyone they know will be jumping into their cars to drive over the border to Rio.

On the way in to the fan fest a steward tells them they can't bring in an empty polystyrene drinks holder...People are allowed to bring all kinds of bags in but poor Santiago has to run back towards his apartment to drop it off...

The fans have been drinking since this morning. They are bouncing up and down in the queue...They expect to win...As in previous games there isn't any doubt...I have my doubts though and wouldn't be surprised if we don't have a blockbuster of a third/fourth playoff in Brasilia...Brazil v Argentina. It would surely be the most fiercely contested third/fourth playoff in World Cup history.

I meet some guys from South Africa...They have travelled around the country watching the World Cup...They say not just the stadiums in South Africa were top notch but also the stadium environs. $10 billion was spent in 2010 and according to them $12 billion has been spent in 2014...They say there is lots of unfinished works. Where has the money gone is the question they keep asking.

The fan fest is packed...Huge support for Argentina. I head to my usual position. Argentines all around me...There are thousands of them in the fan fest! The atmosphere is electric.

The opening 10 minutes have been very cagey...Almost as if the events of last night have scared or may be scarred both sides...The fear of being out before the semi-final has started...The game is beginning to settle down now...Free kick on the edge of the box...Messi...Round the wall .. But a comfortable save...

20 minutes gone and Argentina have had the lion's share of the last 10 minutes.

Lavessi is making inroads down the right...Corner from the left...Diving header over the bar...Dutch keeper nearly lost the ball...Smart dribble to beat Higuain but surely Van Gaal would prefer not to see it....

I am concerned about my phone, there have been so many thefts, and am grasping it tightly. Even on the rare moments I am not writing the diary and it is in my pocket I am holding onto it. Mascherano loudly cheered as he comes back on after a clash of heads.

30 minutes gone...Holland in danger of doing a Belgium... Not turned up yet...

Of course as I write this, they whip two quick crosses in...Keeper under pressure and elects to punch both crosses clear.

Half time 0-0 Not a great game...Fair to say it needs a goal.

Night has fallen over the

fan fest... I get talking with Carlos Maria Araujo from Buenos Aires. The nerves, the tension of what might be...Carlos says if we get to the World Cup Final, I have to be in the stadium...Help me! We exchange numbers. Usual buffeting takes place during the interval!

The second half is underway and the Dutch have come out with a little more intent... Free kick from Sneijder...Sails high over the bar...

Dutch keeper comes off his line...Ricochets off Messi... The ball heads goal wards... An empty net...Passed the post...

It is pouring with rain in São Paulo where the match is being played... I feel for the fans in the upper temporary stands...20 minutes to go... A moment of magic from Messi or Robben... Or if fit...Aguero off the bench...What an option to have!

With the clock ticking down the tension of one goal being enough is rising in the fan fest...

Messi manhandled ...Ref waves play on... Cross...What a goal!! Argentina fans going crazy....Not given...Off side or is it the same as Sterling's virtual side netting "goal" verses Italy?

Offside...Replay shows it to be very close...To be fair the Argentina fans accept it and move on...

Argentina bring on Perez for Palacio and Aguero for Higuain.

5 minutes to go...Both teams passing the ball along their back four and seem to be settling for extra time...

3 minutes added time...Holland pressing...Robben through down the left side!

Shoots...What a block by Mascherano!!!!!!! It seemed a certain goal! Where did Mascherano come from to get a block in...? Surely kept Argentina in the World Cup with that tackle...Fantastic effort!

Full time 0-0

A gang of young Brazilian kids are wondering around...Everyone is moving them on... Everyone knowing what they are up to...Everyone protecting their pockets and bags...

5 minutes of extra time gone...Van Persie replaced by Huntelaar... The game feels like a stalemate...Penalties seem to be beckoning...Sure commentators around the world will have been saying for a while words like...One moment of magic or inspiration or possibly one error... Let's hope it is not decided by a Robben dive...

Argentina's final substitution...Maxi Rodriguez for Lavessi.

Huntelaar blatant foul...Rightly booked...Free kick...An Argentine fan in the fan fest turns his back...He can't look...

Now Argentina are pressing down the right...An inviting cross...Messi coming in... Can't get there...

Half time of extra time 0-0

The Argentine fans are singing their Italia 90 song. They still believe.

The Dutch keeper likes a dribble...Now done Aguero like he did Higuain earlier in the game...

Zabaleta catches one in the face from Kuyt...Comes back on mouth bloodied...

9 minutes to go....The tension is unbearable...Sophia from Buenos Aires in front of me is rocking from side to side...Hands clasped over her face...Half in prayer, half in fear.. Her hands are clasped behind her head now...

There is nothing happ... Wait... Palacio through... Ball bounces up... Header... Easy save...

Four minutes to go but should be some added time for the Zabaleta injury.

Messi beats his man...Gets to the by line...Crosses to the far post... Rodriguez unmarked! Shoots tamely into the keeper's hands.

1 minute left Dutch probing... Cross... Shot deflected... Keeper wrong footed...

But safe...

Dutch looking threatening...1 minute added time...Last attack. ..Ball runs into the keepers arms...

Full time of extra time 0-0...Penalties...I am not sure the fans can cope with this...

I seem to recall the Dutch generally have a poor penalty record?

The Dutch haven't changed their keeper this time...

Vlaar steps up...Keeper saves! Sergio Romero second choice keeper for Monaco but right now the toast of Argentina!

Messi... Goal!!!

Robben scores!!

Garay scores!!

Sneijder...Saved...Romero again!

Aguero scores

Kuyt scores

Maxi Rodriguez scores ...Oh my....Beer everywhere... The place has gone crazy...Correction the Argentines have gone crazy! Pandemonium!!

Argentina are in the World Cup Final!

Almost the whole fan fest is up cheering... The firecrackers overhead don't stand a chance... Carlos and his friends are ecstatic and involve me in their celebrations. It is a wonderful moment of brotherhood and

camaraderie between fellow fans and nations. People are hugging, kissing, crying...Grown men overcome with emotion... Bloody hell even I have tears... The passion of the moment is too much...The singing starts...The Italia 90 song... I may be wrong, they may not win it but throughout the whole World Cup, it has felt like their destiny...Their fans have made it their destiny. They have brought so much to this World Cup...

Outside the fan fest is a lady carrying her baby. I have to talk with her... Her baby is two months old and is called Camila!! The mother Vanessa didn't go in the fan fest but her husband Osca did. They are from Salta in the north of Argentina...Out on the streets to celebrate... Grandmother is there too!! No self-respecting Argentinian would miss this party!!! We have some photographs together. Osca loves my picture of the Boca pennant but not the photograph of Ardiles who played for River Plate... He is Boca Juniors...Full stop!!

A guy comes out of the fan fest in an Argentina shirt on crutches!! I am in awe...

If any of you readers have been in the fan fest on the beach... You will know why!! It is exhausting...Energy sapping and tough enough as a fit, well fit before this World Cup haha, and able bodied person... Never mind being on crutches!! I have to take a photograph of him.... Out comes another on crutches...I give up! There are no lengths these people won't go to...Many sleeping in cars, others on the beach...Incredible!!

I bump into Sebastian...We embrace like old friends...He can't find his friends...His friends have his money...He has 1 real! He had drunk a bottle of vodka before the game... He won't take 5 reals off me for the metro to get back to his apartment in Botofogo. Eventually he does but insists on giving me the 1 real he has... These guys were sharing their drinks with me before the game and now it is a struggle to reciprocate and help him out with four reals...Just over £1!!

So...We started out with 32 teams on Thursday, 12th June and now some 27 days later on 9th July we are effectively reduced to just two teams!!

The third/fourth place game will be:

Saturday 12th July in Brasilia: Brazil versus Holland

I would imagine it is a game both teams for differing reasons could do without...

The main event though...The 2014 World Cup Final at the Maracana, Rio de Janeiro on Sunday 13th July will be:

Germany versus Argentina!!!

Three times winners Germany versus two times winners Argentina.

Two finals against each other with the honours even!

It is 28 years since Argentina were last crowned World Champions in 1986 versus Germany! The score 3-2.

It is 24 years since Germany were last crowned World Champions in 1990 v Argentina! 1-0.

South America v Europe! Will Germany become the first team outside of the Americas to win the World Cup...In the Americas!!

How ironic that the Italia 90 song sung all through the tournament by Argentina has ended up with the same teams contesting the final as in 1990!!

I so hope I can get a ticket...But then again, I am sure there is an army assembling across the border plus all of those already here...Who will all be hoping for exactly the same!!

The atmosphere is amazing on the promenade! The Argentina fans are singing and celebrating...It will go on long in to the night!

EL GRINGO'S ONCE IN A LIFETIME

I go back to my apartment, not least to charge my iPhone. Rob texts to say he is in the Mud Bug but I am not sure...Not eaten since breakfast and am quite hungry!

I go to the Amir Lebanese restaurant on Rua Ronad de Carvalho which I went to with Colin and the boys. It is on what we call the "walk of shame" as the hookers pass up and down with their clients! The food is fabulous and filling...I have a kebab with rice and accompaniments...Delicious!

After my meal, I go for a walk along the front of Copacabana... It is still crazy on the promenade and beach! Colombians are on the beach, Mexicans are out and still smarting about how they went out. Argentinians are erecting tents and some are sleeping on the beach!

Whilst walking, I buy a couple of caipirinhas from street vendors. After the long couple of days and all night out, exhaustion overwhelms me. It is now well after midnight and after the tiring journey, I return to my apartment for hopefully a good night's sleep.

This World Cup was a farce. The worst technically I have ever seen...
> Philippe Bonfils, a Frenchman living in Indonesia.

For us Dutch, the World Cup was an unexpected journey of delight and especially redemption. After our gut-wrenching loss to Spain in the last World Cup Final, the soul searching afterwards in light of our style of play over there and the horror show at the European Championships two years later, absolutely no-one was expecting our team to do quite so well.

With key players missing through injury, and a squad mostly made up of players plying their trade in our own Dutch League (not the strongest in the world by any means), expectations couldn't be lower. No manic "Oranje"-fever this time around; most fans expected an exit at the group stage, with Spain and Chile the favourites in our group.

For Van Gaal's men to first thrash Spain, then win the group with a perfect score, knock out Mexico after an unbelievable comeback and then win a penalty shoot-out for the first time ever (Krul's magic moment) was an unending source of delight. Game by game, the mood in the country became more upbeat and positive.

The semi-final shoot-out loss against Argentina was a disappointment, certainly, but it didn't create any bitterness. The positive mood lingered on and was capped off by a great win against Brazil in the third place match. We had stayed unbeaten throughout the tournament, created a lot of positive talking points and genuinely done ourselves proud. Even though we didn't win, we could certainly return home with our heads held high. And that is a good enough feeling for any genuine fan...
> Mark Koppers, 's-Hertogenbosch, the Netherlands.

THURSDAY 10TH JULY 2014

It is 9.20...I wake up in my own bed for a change. What an earth am I thinking... My own bed?? I have forgotten what my own bed feels like!! When you return after a holiday... Isn't it always such a great feeling to climb into your own bed? Especially back in the day when cheap Costa holidays had a bed which doubled up as a trampoline...I am sure I could feel the springs through the mattresses in those days!!

So today it's Thursday...The names of the days don't matter anymore...There are only two types of days in Brazil for me...Football days and non-football days...

Today is a non-football day...In fact of my nine remaining days...Only two are now in my preferred category...Nine days is that all? Yet if I was on a two week holiday, I would be five days in and thinking early doors. What a strange expression, I think Ron Atkinson started it? Anyway it would feel early doors... But now it feels as if I am on the last lap #spoilt

Looking out of my apartment window, it looks a little overcast...Hmmm...A day's sunbathing would have been perfect. The Belo Horizonte adventure was really a trip of a life time. It was, though, as I am sure Luiz and Aline will agree, also very tiring... And I didn't even do any of the driving!! So today a chill on the beach in the sun would have been ideal but alas...I know by the feedback on Twitter...You will all feel very sorry for me..... Not!

I meet up with my old friend...The shower... I get cold water today...Not bloody cold or even worse... Today is it just plain cold...Maybe absence does make the heart grow fonder. May be the cantankerous old so and so missed me after all.

Suited and booted I will not be deterred by the weather...I am English and if we didn't do anything because of the weather ... Well we would never do anything.

Foreign readers may say...Well you don't anyway... At least not in the World Cups... I go down to the Tourist Information centre on Copacabana. Those sleeping in their cars and campers have adopted their usual positions... Fold up chairs on the pavement around their vehicles with mate in hand... Mate the drink, not mate the mate...Isn't language confusing!

When I was here in the early noughties I went to Barra da Tijuca but to the shopping mall rather than the beach...The locals say the beach is lovely and as it has a lovely sounding name, I decide to join the locals on the bus service and look out for number 308 or 523. Names can have this impact on you...My mum didn't want to see the film "Four Weddings and a Funeral"...The title didn't appeal...

There are three bus lines and each line seems to have a million and one different bus numbers which pass by the bus stop at a bewildering rate! Except of course numbers 308 or 523!!

Wait there is a 308...It is in the middle lane...This guy has no intention of stopping!! In a last ditch effort I forlornly stick out my hand and amazingly out of the corner of his eye, the bus driver must have caught sight of my loud stripy shirt. The bus somehow changes lanes and shudders to a halt all in one movement! I board the bus at 11.05am and pay the princely sum of 3 reals, about 80 pence.

Talking of stripy shirts...I love the "Stripy Nigels" nickname Millwall fans have given Crystal Palace fans!

On route it starts to rain...A Sven moment...

The bus driver tells me I have arrived at Barra da Tijuca. I get off the bus by a lake with beautiful houses around it. Barra Tijuca already has an upmarket feel.

On the drizzly but not cold walk down to the beach, I stop off for a coffee at a bar. The television screen is showing the Rio carnival parade grounds. They have been opened up for Argentina fans to park their cars, pitch up tents or sleep in their cars! There is only so much space on Copacabana either on the beach or car park spaces to sleep in!

The first 140 cars are there already. This morning though Copacabana was as full as ever. The authorities are expecting another 17000 fans to arrive. Somehow

I think that number might be somewhat understated...Add another nought on the end and we might be getting close!

The report switches to a Brazilian reporter saying to a German. We can forgive you... But only if you can score eight goals against Argentina!!

Walking down the avenue towards the beach, the feeling is more of being in California than Brazil... A tree lined boulevard with brightly coloured shops and overhead cable lines crossing the street. It has a chic upmarket feel with the local community stylishly dressed in their latest outfits.

I arrive at the beach and for those of you who have been here...Looking out to the Atlantic Ocean, I am at the far left hand side of the beach. Behind me, the large rocky terrain towering above Barra da Tijuca is shrouded in cloud. I stop at the Tourist Information kiosk on the promenade to be advised that this is the longest beach in the Rio area. It is 14kms of beautiful sandy beaches... And unlike the long beach at Recife, it is possible to swim in the sea.

They also highlight the shopping area as the place to go...Been there, done that and sorry ladies but shopping is not really something near the top of my agenda. The main bus terminus is also there and it is about an hour's walk... Perfecto! Yes I know we have established perfecto to be Spanish rather than Portuguese...But I am in a foreign country and do like to use the word! Do I sound in a particularly good mood today...I feel good!!

Down to the water's edge, rain in the air, shoes off...It feels wonderful. So liberating! The beach is a lovely light sandy colour...Very fine and soft underfoot.

EL GRINGO'S ONCE IN A LIFETIME

The sea is more a green with a hint of blue. As at Copacabana and Ipanema, the waves are big enough to attract surfers and even in the rain!

Barra Tijuca really has a classy feel to it. An easy place to fall in love with... I begin my walk along the water's edge...My feet are sinking so deep into the sand... It is a lovely sensation and looking back down the beach my lone foot prints are very noticeable.

After walking for 15 minutes or so, the rain starts to get a little heavier and I make for a beach side bar. There is something quite appealing in a warm climate, to sitting under a canopy, with the rain pouring down and eating a ham and cheese toastie with a cup of hot coffee. I am really enjoying my day out at the seaside!

The television is inevitably covering the World Cup...It shows the Argentine players jumping up and down on the pitch after the penalty shoot-out...Incredibly they are singing the Italia 90 song which disses the Brazilians!!

The coverage then shows the differing emotions of the Dutch watching the misery unfold in their own bars before switching across to Avenida 9 Julio, Buenos Aires...The streets rammed with celebrating Argentine supporters. We have all been through the elation and misery...What a contrast!!

I set off walking again...The Radisson hotel with its twin towers looks spectacular. It is raining again...As I walk past a sea front bar... A guy is passing me arms outstretched above his head carrying a concrete block. After a while he takes it down and starts using it as a biceps lifting exercise as he continues to walk and then as a chest press. A couple of Brazilian guys in the bar look at me and point to their head...Loco....It's hard not to laugh out loud and agree!

This time the heavens really open... I have to take refuge in yet another bar! This is in danger of becoming a Barra da Tijuca pub crawl...Caipirinha? Yes Please!

Even sitting under a canopy which is attached to the side of the bar, it is not enough. The rain is torrential and sweeping in. The bar tenders struggle manfully to put side canopies up...The rain is pelting down on the canopy above the bar... It is giving off the sound of a waterfall. The water rolling out of the drains is a waterfall! The guys have done a great job but there is still a feeling of being under siege... Another caipirinha might be in order!

I get talking to four English lads 18 and 19 years old ...Will, Dan, Ali and Greg from Cheltenham who are on a gap year. They have been travelling since landing in New York on the 14th May and have visited Peru, Bolivia and Argentina before arriving into Brazil.

For the most part their travels have been incident free until Will fell asleep on the bus on his way back to Barra Tijuca after going to the fan fest for the Brazil v Colombia game..

He fell asleep on the bus, only waking up on arriving at the bus terminal. He takes another bus, gets distracted in a conversation with people on the bus and misses his stop. He gets off at the start of Leblon and a guy pulls a gun on him... Instinctively he emptied his pockets and the guy took the 30 or so reals he had and walked off. Fortunately, the guy didn't check for any other belongings and therefore did not find the, as they call it, "fanny bag" under his shirt and shorts which contained his and friend's iPhones plus his credit card etc. He didn't have any cash though and had to walk back to their accommodation. It was a four hour walk, barefoot in the rain! He had had a bit to drink and quickly sobered up when walking through tunnels with oncoming buses literally passing within inches of him... A night he will never forget...

It does remind me of a story though. Murph, an Irish Spurs fan from Lincoln, had been drinking heavily at the Spurs v Aston Villa Charity Shield some years ago. He caught the train from Kings Cross in London to go to a party with some fellow Spurs fans in Grantham. He fell asleep and woke up at the last stop... In Leeds... He bought some more beer and caught the next train back south to Grantham....Fell asleep...And woke up back at Kings Cross, London! He then caught the next train north and fell asleep again but thankfully only missed Grantham by one station and woke up as the train pulled in to Newark. He took a taxi to the party in Grantham and arrived in the early hours of the morning... Just as the party was ending!!!

In the fan fest Ali felt something in his pocket... He reached down and found a hand inside the pocket of his shorts which was at thigh height. The guy held his hands in the air in apology and they walked off. They only realised afterwards that rather cleverly, the guy in pulling his hand out of the pocket and putting his hands in the air also pulled out Dan's credit card, which Ali was looking after. He must have dropped it on the floor when he put his hands in the air and calmly waited until they walked away before picking the credit card up...

It is now 4.09 and the rain is showing no signs of slowing down. The guys say the weather forecast doesn't look too good through to Monday...

I ask the barman which bus to take back to Copacabana and he says the approaching number 535 bus to Leme goes via Copacabana. I make a dash for it and offer the driver a 10 reals note. I am not sure what he is saying but one thing is clear, he isn't interested in taking my money. It's pouring...A local overhears the exchange and it seems I need the Brazilian equivalent of an Oyster card... Hmmm, it's lashing it down. Where the hell am I going to buy one of those? The bus stop doesn't even have a shelter let alone a machine to buy an Oyster card...

The local tells me the driver is offering to let me get on the bus free of charge. As there is a turnstile at the front, the driver is trying to gesture for me to get on board through the door at the back of the bus! Wow, how very kind of him!

Relieved, I run to the back and jump on board and sit on the backseat.

My mind goes back to the driver who for the sake of 20 pence forced a young female student off a late night bus in Nottingham. She had pleaded with fellow passengers who wouldn't help out and the bus driver refused her offer to draw money out of a cash machine. She called her parents to come to collect her. By the time her mother arrived, she had been raped by a drunken drug crazed thug... Although he was arrested and was sent to prison, it is an incident that with a little humanity should never have happened...

EL GRINGO'S ONCE IN A LIFETIME

The traffic is very heavy. It is now 5.11pm and the bus has so far made it to Ipanema. A ticket inspector gets on...

I am now in a prison cell...Fortunately they have given me my iPhone back...I am trying to explain what happened but through broken English they say the driver denies all knowledge...

Did you believe that!!! Sorry only joking...Caipirinha in the afternoon...If the weather stays like this, it may need to become a habit over the next few days!

Finally at 5.52pm I get off the bus at Duvivier and walk the remaining blocks to my apartment. I walk into my apartment at 6pm...It has taken almost two hours to return the few miles from Barra Da Tijuca...I have needed the bathroom for more than three hours...Relief!!

It is actually nice to chill in the apartment...Catch up with emails, Twitter and WhatsApp... Jessica has spent the day with Aline who brought the puppy Nikki home today. They send me photographs of her...She us adorable...So so cute!!

I fall asleep and suddenly it's 9pm... And it is still raining!'

I text a few touts to understand the prices for the World Cup Final tickets. I have heard ridiculous prices of 5000 US Dollars but struggle to believe the prices can be anywhere near as much as that.

I get ready and head towards my local sociable BBQ on Duvivier dreading that, as it is approaching 10pm, it will be closed... But it's open!!

I order the beef kebab and get talking with three guys living in Australia of whom, two are English. One who is a pilot in Alice Springs says he is from my home city of Lincoln! He was actually born in Lincolnshire in Boston but nevertheless I am surprised by how often Lincoln has come up in conversation

on this trip. As a Liverpool fan he is delighted to see the back of Suarez...I am not following the news or listening to the sports call in shows in the UK and wonder whether that is how the Liverpool fans feel...My gut instinct is that they will be devastated to lose him...

The other English guy is from Brighton and is wearing a Spurs jacket...He says it's great living in Melbourne but really misses going to White Hart Lane and watches every game on TV and even the silly o'clock ones in the middle of the night.

The Aussie also lives in Melbourne and is wearing an Arsenal top. To be fair he is quite a happy chappie and is delighted that his team has just spent £35m on Sanchez.

They tell me the story of a Brazilian guy who was captured on the television sobbing his heart out at the Brazil v Germany game. He was holding a plastic World Cup and was recorded giving his World Cup to a German. It has become a Facebook sensation. They sat down at the BBQ tonight and... The guy was sat next to them!

I eat too much too late at night.

Coming out of the restaurant...It is still raining!! I feel very tired and decide to go back to the apartment.

By the time I get sorted it is half past midnight...But still an early night for me!

EL GRINGO'S ONCE IN A LIFETIME

The World Cup for me…Encapsulated in a few single weeks the current state of English football; hope and ultimate disappointment. A golden generation of youngsters: Sterling, Sturridge, Shaw, all who promised so much but delivered so little.

My memories of the group games consisted of an Ayia Napa backdrop, hot in nature, but unusual in atmosphere. Although the games themselves are a complete blur, the feeling of disappointment still drained through - particularly after the Uruguay game.

As a football fan and a football lover, it was amazing to see the passion shown by fans all around the globe particularly in Brazil.

In this book, hopefully my father has shared his life changing experience through the eyes of a fan, instead of through a television screen.

Henry Ellis, Nottingham, UK

While some of the group stage kick off times made for very late viewing or necessitated recording in Budapest, the lack of the usual early raft of draws set the scene for one of the more enjoyable World Cups in recent times… Highlighted by Germany's demolition of the host nation. The performances of less fancied sides like Costa Rica was also a breath of fresh air, and in contrast to the poor performances of individual English Premier League stars such as Lukaku, Hazard and Oscar.

Grahame Howells, an Englishman living in Budapest, Hungary.

FRIDAY 11TH JULY 2014

After a restless night's sleep I wake at 9.18am. Last night's BBQ was too late… It isn't planned this way but I seem to be going all day without any food and then eat late at night…#stupido. I actually have stomach ache this morning. It is a feeling of my stomach being stretched from eating too much #doublestupido. A Norwegian guy, Christian Nielsen, I used to work with in Brussels would say… Eating late at night…Are you training to be a Sumo wrestler? I certainly feel big enough this morning…

You are not going to believe this…It is still raining!!! I brought some books with me to read…the latest works of Boyd, Child, Billingham and Grisham… It has been so busy that I haven't even thought about reading…But today might just be the day! Tourist Information first though and there is a large FIFA 2014 World Cup shop by the fan fest which I keep meaning to go in and have a look at.

I catch up with the cricket…England's travails continue… Having taken 4 wickets for 2 runs…The last pair somehow managed an 111 run final partnership… And then… Captain Cook failed again scoring just 5 runs….The tennis, the cricket…All the things that are usually so important to me somehow seem less significant out here…

I have a WhatsApp conversation with Jason the tout who says tickets for the final are 6000 USD... I say no chance...I am not in that bracket...He asks me how much I am willing to pay... Hmmm seems like the tickets will go to the highest bidders...I say let's keep in touch between now and the final and he agrees to let me pass his number on to a couple of Argentine guys.

I forgot to mention that last night before I went out I met with the shower. I had warm water!!! It seems the shower is just not a morning person!!!

It has finally stopped raining!

I decide the best way to clear this feeling of bloatedness is a long walk and decide to walk the length of Copacabana and Ipanema return...That should do it!!

Walking along Copacabana, an Argentine guy has a sign up...Tickets for sale for the Brazil v Holland third/fourth playoff. He wants 300 USD for one ticket but is willing to take 250 per ticket if two or three are bought. He has five in total which he bought through FIFA at 225 USD each.

I ask why he is looking to make a profit and he says he isn't. The Argentine Government charge a tax of 35% for the use of credit cards outside of Argentina! He therefore paid 302.75 USD per ticket. I take his number and text Aline to gauge her interest.

I call in to see George at the travel agency. He tells me the ticket prices are 4500 USD but thinks they may reduce tomorrow and takes my number...

Aline texts back to say flight costs would be high and it's a 1200km drive to Brasilia...It also seems Rick won't have any extra tickets for the final...

I walk onto Ipanema and there is Rio Ferdinand, Tim Vickery, Alan Shearer and Chris Waddle along with Mark Chapman, sat at a table on the promenade

picking their best 11 of the World Cup for BBC television. I can't quiet hear it all but think Neuer was the chosen keeper, Lahm also made the 11. They were talking about Neymar, not sure he got in but think Rodriguez did.

Afterwards I have a good conversation with Chris Waddle who is joined by Rio Ferdinand and we have a photograph together.

I notice Mark Lawrenson in the background. With Alan Hansen retiring after the World Cup Final, the boys are doing some kind of rendition of Billy Joel's song Piano man. Mark is waiting for the camera crew to be free to record his lines.

Mark tells me the sad news that Ray Houghton had some kind of panic attack and that rather than commentate on the final he has flown home. Having had such a lovely chat with him...I am pleased to hear that it is precautionary rather than serious. It seems Trevor Stevens will stand in for Ray.

We get talking about the final and like me Mark wants Argentina to win. Mark says not least because they have not acted like big time Charlies and stayed in medium to lower level accommodation. The irony should Messi score the winner in the Maracana!! I translate the words of the Italia 90 song which makes him laugh.

We really have a good chat covering a wide range of topics from the book I am writing, to his team Preston playing Liverpool in a preseason friendly next Saturday... Yes I was surprised that his team isn't Liverpool too! We also talk about the difference Harry Redknapp might have made as compared with Roy's safety first approach. Mark feels the importance of man management at this level cannot be understated as illustrated by Costa Rica and how Van Gaal is managing the diverse characters in the Dutch dressing room.

Good to hear that Mark is impressed by the innovative approach of the Spurs new manager Pochettino.

Mark is sorry to tell me... He thinks Sanchez will prove to be a great signing for Arsenal.

With the £75m move of Suarez to Barcelona having been confirmed, Mark is worried about Liverpool's chances of top four next season...

Mark is as engaging in person as he comes across on television and radio. It was a real pleasure to chat with him.

I continue my walk along Ipanema. The sky is overcast but at least it hasn't rained since first thing this morning. It is 2.08pm and the temperature is 25 degrees.

Aline's news on the World Cup Final tickets is not unexpected and I am very grateful to have had the opportunity to go to the Brazil v Germany Semi Final. It is an occasion I will never forget!

The American tout calls me to offer a ticket for the final... 6000 USD... The World has gone crazy!! He asks me what I am willing to pay...I say I am not in that type of bracket but let's stay in touch between now and the final...

It is now 2.33pm...I feel light headed...I realise I have not had anything to eat or drink today... What the hell is going on with me!!!???

At 2.37 the sun peaks out through a cloud laden sky!!!

The coca cola zero went down very quickly at the promenade beach bar... More refreshments may be needed...

The atmosphere in Rio is changing...The joyous hordes of genuine football fans are being replaced by the corporates...Flying in to watch the final...Some as I know from my own previous corporate experiences will be on a jolly with very little interest in football let alone an allegiance to either country contesting the final. C'est la vie...

The saving grace are the Argentines...They are flying and driving to Rio in their hordes...Proper passionate football fans... The vast majority of them will be without tickets and also with little to no chance of getting a ticket.

They just want to be here in Rio for the party...To be where their team win the World Cup...

I imagine what it would be like if they weren't here...If it was a Holland v Germany final...Rio would be a lot less colourful and a lot less busy...

Argentina reaching the final has at least retained an element of the earlier World Cup party atmosphere.

It is now 3.01 and I have passed through Ipanema and walked to the end of Leblon beach. I turn round to commence my walk back.

Walking back along Ipanema I meet a couple of guys from New Zealand... They managed to get tickets for the World Cup Final through a relation who works for the IOC..I wonder whether I should have pursued my sporting contacts...Not really in my nature to do so though...

There are two beach football volleyball matches taking place alongside each other in front of a sizeable crowd. There is a girl in each team and the level of skills being shown is just phenomenal. Just to win a single point seems to take forever... And this is in no way an exaggeration. The rallies are minutes rather than seconds and when a point is won it really comes as a bit of a surprise!!

EL GRINGO'S ONCE IN A LIFETIME

It is 3.59pm and I reach the end of Ipanema to cut through the park to Copacabana.

The wall artist is in the middle of painting Klose with an arm aloft which must be the moment he became the all-time leading goal scorer in the history of the finals. When talking with Mark Lawrenson...The record being taken from a true great... The real Ronaldo... Sven would say.....It's a pity!

Nothing ventured nothing gained...Walking along Copacabana there is a man in a suit with a FIFA accreditation round his neck...World Cup Final ticket...I ventured...Nothing gained!!

It is 4.22...10 minutes ago I captured a photograph of Sugar Loaf with a cloud covering its peak and now...It is clear! Patches of blue cloud are emerging... The sun is shining... Hurrah!!

I speak with an Argentine tout on Copacabana. He has tickets for the final but is selling for 6000 USD...I have spoken with an Argentine, an Englishman and an American...They are all quoting a standard price...A cartel on black market tickets??

The Brazilians and Argentines are singing at or should I say taunting each other with their songs on Copacabana.

Finally at 5pm I sit down to a meal in a street off Avenida Atlantique just passed the Pestana Hotel. For 23 reals I have a banquet of chicken, egg, ham, toast, salad and chips...There is a commotion around the restaurant...I find out the reason and have a photograph with the Boca winger Clementos who played for Argentina in the last World Cup.

The Argentina fans are in full voice along Copacabana with a new song:
"The hands of Messi comes to make us champions"
Obviously trained by Maradona then....!!!

Walking along Copacabana, there are tens of Police motorbikes heading towards the Copacabana Palace...More arrests??

Further along on the beach outside of the fan fest there is another group of 300 or more Argentines singing. Some are on top of the beach football crossbars. Flags are waving...It is already crazy...What will it be like by Sunday...!!!

There are a few Germans scattered around and keeping a low profile but I am sure they will start arriving during the course of the weekend...No matter how many arrive...They will be heavily outnumbered in Rio de Janeiro..

There are still a surprising number of Colombians and Mexicans here too!

The moon is shining brightly through a partial break in the dark clouds above the fan fest... It looks fantastic!!

Ahead of the third/fourth playoff match...Both managers are saying the right things...Van Gaal has said that he considers the result against Argentina as a draw and wants to return to Holland unbeaten...Although it seems both he and his players are apparently calling this meaningless and want the game scrapped.. Scolari is saying the new dream is to finish third...Hmmm...

Aline mentioned that in his last domestic managerial position, Scolari took Palmeiras down to the second division...No surprise there!

Ray Whelan has appeared on the television...Something about being a fugitive...In view of the importance of the subject... I break a golden rule and visit the BBC Web Site which according to an article on the site says...

It seems his company have been working alongside FIFA for 30 years and make a profit of £52m per World Cup by selling tickets from $700 to $100000 per ticket as part of a hospitality package.

This makes me wonder if this is what is driving black market prices to levels well outside the scope of ordinary fans...Similar to Wimbledon debenture holders having to pay high prices to secure their seats... If they sell individual days they want their money back plus perhaps a profit of some kind? This is only a personal thought rather than any inside knowledge.

Whelan has left the Copacabana Palace hotel with his lawyer...The Brazilian Police are saying he is a "fugitive from justice" who is wanted for questioning in respect of ticket touting.

This must account for the Police activity I saw. His company Match Services are saying he is free to travel within Brazil and is with his lawyer...

The company is allegedly earning $90m per World Cup.

The Brazilian Police carried out "Operation Jules Rimet" which led to 12 people being arrested and facing charges of "criminal organisation, ticket touting, bribery, money laundering and tax evasion".

There is a tapped telephone conversation in which Whelan talks of $25000 of cash sales...His Company say these sales include hospitality packages...

Jaime Byrom, Executive Chairman of Match Hospitality, has said that the Police responsible for the investigation "are not experts in FIFA World Cup ticketing or hospitality" and deny any wrongdoing by Mr Whelan.

As I write this, my apartment is not too far from the Copacabana Palace Hotel and the sound of Police sirens continue to echo around the area...

On the television, it says 2600 military and police are on duty this weekend. 15 national presidents will attend the World Cup Final including Putin of Russia...

Anti-terrorism measures will be being taken... Managing the Argentines, the Presidents and Raymond Whelan must be a logistical nightmare for the Brazilian authorities....!!

I have a very cold shower...It seems the shower is not a Friday night shower either... May have to leave her for another shower soon...!

It is raining again....I walk down Rua Bolivar to ZOT bar to meet up with Luiz and Aline. We have a very enjoyable evening and some of the Brazilian conspiracy stories are very funny such as...

There are apparently pictures of Neymar arriving at the hospital but it has been proven not to be him as the tattoos on the wrists are not there. This is probably because they used a diversion tactic but the conspiracy theory is...The Brazilian team were bought to lose the match versus Germany. Neymar was the only one who could not be bought which is why he did not play!

Statistics of the Brazil versus Germany match show that Fred ran 7km ...One more than Neuer!! He will not be picked for the last match versus Holland... I wouldn't like to be Fred...A foreign transfer might be in order!

We talk about who the next manager will be and it seems there isn't an obvious choice...There is a lot of talk of a foreign manager taking over...Names such as Pep Guardiola and Jose Mourinho are being mentioned. I doubt they would give up club football at this stage but also think...It was bad enough England trying a foreign manager but Brazil....Surely not!!

It is incredible that Scolari went from relegating a team to be chosen to manage Brazil in their own World Cup....

The press are talking about the issue being much greater than the responsibility of the coach. It seems that Brazil are not producing the players of yesteryear.

There are concerns over the coaching of children, the players moving to Europe and losing their natural flair. There is a concern of the structure of football in Brazil. Hmmm... As an Englishman I have heard these types of stories many times...Well except not enough of our players gain experience in foreign leagues...

Scolari as depicted on Brazilian social media

There is no doubt that the Brazilian footballing soul has been scarred by the events of Tuesday night... On a personal note, I really hope they, as the 2014 Budweiser advert says, "Rise as one" from this... For me football needs a flamboyant Brazilian side...

Romario wrote an open letter to the Brazilian newspaper "Extra" yesterday talking of corruption inside the CBF and naming individuals!

There is also talk as to why, when Brazil apparently had the opportunity to choose where to play in this World Cup, they chose to play in smaller venues... Luiz says Brazil never seem to play friendlies in the Maracana... The view being that it seems to be for political reasons. It is strange as like Wembley is synonymous with England, I liken the Maracana to Brazil...But this perception seems to be a wrong one.

It has been reported that before the Brazil v Colombia game, in the middle of the night, the Brazil fans were letting off firecrackers outside the Colombian hotel...

Similarly 1000 Argentine fans sang outside the Dutch hotel in the middle of the night on Ipanema.

Those old tricks are still allowed to continue!!

A funny story has emerged about an Argentine hooligan who is banned from attending matches. For the Argentina v Switzerland game he painted himself in the colours of Switzerland. When Di Maria scored a late winner, people thought it strange that a Swiss fan was going wild with the Argentina fans inside the stadium!!

Luiz and Aline invite me for a birthday lunch with one of their friends tomorrow at 1pm. They have a Spurs supporting friend who will be there who they would like me to meet.

On the walk back to my apartment I stop off for a caipirinha at a beach bar. I do like a caipirinha! This time next week I will be on an aeroplane flying back to the UK... A fitness campaign is awaiting me!!

I get talking with a Colombian lady with a young Japanese man. Maria Teresa lives in California and has been to 13 games! She travels to each World Cup and even flew out to the Ukraine and Poland for the Euros #footballcrazy!

EL GRINGO'S ONCE IN A LIFETIME

We learn that we are staying on the same road, Prado Junior and the three of us begin to walk back. I pick up a hot dog from the lady operating from the boot of her car. They really are delicious and we decide to have another caipirinha from the street stall. Boy is it strong!! A lady of the night approaches Maria Theresa and says you are beautiful...Would you like to come with me!!

We finish our drink and it begins to rain...Again! We walk back and say our good nights. I enter my apartment at 3.30am

Denmark failed to qualify for the World Cup which meant that the World Cup was 100 % entertainment. I didn't really care who won the games, I just wanted to be entertained. And that was the general feeling in Denmark.

While it was relaxing not to worry about results, it didn't quite feel like a proper World Cup. I missed the patriotic feeling you get when your national anthem comes on before a big game and I missed the unity with my fellow Danes.

Martin Lorentsen, Copenhagen, Denmark

In Thailand, the World Cup in Brazil is not only a tournament that we all love to watch but it also helps in boosting our morale and in bringing the joy back to us in this most difficult time for our country.

Itt Apichartbutr, Bangkok, Thailand

I love the atmosphere in Toronto during the World Cup because it is such a multicultural city - there is a district that supports every different country in the World Cup from Greek Town to Little Italy to Little Portugal. If you go to those areas, they are decked out in the country colours. Everywhere you go there are cars with different country flags and there is always someone celebrating a win. It is quite a joyous atmosphere which contrasts with the UK which can be quite cynical especially once England inevitably gets knocked out.

Kirsty Vlemmicks, English lady living in Toronto, Canada

SATURDAY 12TH JULY 2014

I wake at 10am...Today is a football day!! Yaaaaaay!!
Still no contact from Rob...I begin to wonder if he has had his phone stolen...

I am due to stay with him from tomorrow night...I have been trying to contact Rob since Thursday.

There is a worry emerging over the horizon...What if I am not able to make contact with Rob? I am checking out of the apartment tomorrow...Sunday... World Cup Final day...Hmmm... I need to make contingency plans as I don't want to be struggling for accommodation tomorrow....

I write to the owner of this apartment and as well to the Hotel Savoy Othon. The Othon immediately respond to say there isn't any room availability.

I trawl through the internet for apartments and hotels for the period Sunday 13th to Friday 18th July. A mild form of anxiety sets in...With Sunday 13th being World Cup Final night....Everywhere is full.

I contact the people I stayed with in Flamengo...Phew they will take me in for 200 reals a night...A fall back option and for the rest of the week if I would like to stay... Relief!

Luiz and Aline also very kindly offer to put me up on Sunday night. I look on the Booking.com web site for accommodation for Monday 15th to Friday 18th July...Hey pesto...There is lots of availability and unless I am misunderstanding... The price for four nights is lower than what I was paying for one night during the World Cup! And in what looks to be fabulous four star accommodation! May be I should stay longer ...Haha!!

Another cold shower...I have had enough and say...I am leaving you tomorrow and even if I don't have another shower to go to...That's it...We had a trial separation when I went to Belo Horizonte...No change...I will never use you again... Well after tomorrow anyway!!

I set off on my walk to meet Luiz and Aline at 1pm at the junction of Avenida Nossa Senhora de Copacabana and Rua Santa Clara...I have options!

The fan fest is already in full swing with live music booming out. The screen is so high and large it can be seen from the road outside of the fan fest. As it is a Saturday and Brazil are playing, the dual carriageway closest to the beach is closed off to vehicles. As usual joggers, cyclists, walkers etc are enjoying the extra space...I am sure they will be delighted once the World Cup is over... Their route is constantly blocked by fans. I know from running myself that the constant disruption will be infuriating them...

It is very busy today...Intermingled a much larger police presence than normal...Today has to be a high security alert with thousands of Argentines in town and probably still thousands of Brazilians coming to the Copacabana Fan Fest. Today could possibly be the biggest red alert day of the entire World Cup...

As I walk along Copacabana, the sky is overcast but it is warm and the temperature is showing a comfortable 25 degrees...Hark at me! A comfortable 25 degrees! What we would give for that type of temperature on a daily basis in the UK...Here lest we forget it is winter!!

As ever on big match days, there is the constant sound of horns, vuvuzelas and whistles competing with the boom boom coming from the fan fest.

Walking along Copacabana, there is a whole assortment of vehicles coming in from Argentina...Flags waving, car horns honking...The atmosphere ahead of the final is already building...On route I learn that it is a tradition for Argentines to get together the day before a game and they have chosen beach number six on Copacabana to congregate today at 2.30....2-1/2 hours before Brazil kick off and not that far from the two fan fests...Hmmm...

I am happy to be going to a Brazilian birthday party!! As I wait for Luiz and Aline looking down the street towards the beach, patches of blue sky can be seen! Hopefully the sun will return for my final week in Rio!!

They pick me up at 1.30, Luiz did say when we first met that Aline has many strengths but perhaps time keeping is an improvement area...For those who know me...Yep, for me too...

We pass São Joao Baptista cemetery which is set between Sugar Loaf and Christ the Redeemer who is looking down upon the graves. This is the most expensive cemetery in Rio and it is a little like trying to get a hotel on World Cup Final night. It is impossible to find a space. In fact it seems impossible to find a permanent resting place anywhere in Rio! Families can rent a grave for three years and then are required to go back to collect the bones!!

Burials rather than cremation are still by far the most common but with the resting place issues, cremation is beginning to be a little more popular.

We pass through Rebouças Tunnel which divides the city and leave the South Zone into the more populous North Zone towards the party in Tijuca.

The North also includes the Maracana which is now on our right. Overhead are two police or military helicopters circling the stadium... No doubt concerned over terrorist activity and desperate Argentine fans trying to get into the stadium... They are passionate enough to be digging a tunnel in to the stadium as I write!

The party is at Meu Cantao, Rua Dona Zulmirra, Maracana, Tijuca. We have our own, out of the way, alcove to give the feeling of having a room of our own.

It is Jo's birthday and there is a party of 14 of us.

The Spurs fan, Vander, nicknamed "W" is introduced to me across the table and promptly knocks his beer all over the table including over his phone!

We sit down and I am offered a beer called Therezopplis. I cannot recall seeing this Brazilian brand. Luiz tells me coincidentally, Therezopplis is the name of the place where the Brazilian squad are staying during the World Cup. It is quite a strong beer...I wonder if the players indulged before the Germany game...

The conversation quickly moves onto the football and our trip to Belo Horizonte. They watched the game in a bar and started laughing after the fifth goal went in! Having seen my own side suffer in the past... I get that!

Their friends are laughing at how Aline got tickets. They say instead of spending hours in front of the FIFA website they should have put gym clothes on and gone down to the local fitness centre!

The friends got to know each other through work but mainly through a common friend who was not able to join the party today. They formed a group called the "Boteco hunters" and met in a different bar every Friday night. They developed their own brand, T shirts and Facebook page. It sounds highly organised!

Today they say I am the group's "adopted gringo"!!

They all want Germany to win the World Cup. There could be no bigger humiliation for them than seeing their President handing over the World Cup trophy to Messi in the Maracana, their stadium in their country in their World Cup.

We have a mixed appetiser starting with a tray of sausages which is followed by battered prawns. The main course is the traditional "feijoada" Brazilian meal we enjoyed at Santa Teresa. It consists of separate dishes of beef, pork in a sauce, rice, beans, "farofa" which is a type of white flour mix and "couve" green vegetables.

Afterwards a huge birthday cake arrives...It is the height of a Kit Kat stick!! How do I know? Because the outside of the cake is surrounded by Kit Kat sticks!! The centre is covered in M&Ms and the inside is typical Brazilian style cake. As is the tradition the world over, we all sing happy birthday!

In Brazil, it is a tradition on your birthday to make a wish and to then make the first cut of the cake from the bottom of the cake upwards to make the wish grow. The first slice of cake is then handed to your first love. Jo cuts the cake and hands the first piece to her husband Luiz. The first time Aline gave the first slice to a boyfriend rather than her father...He didn't speak with her for a week...I am a father with my own daughter...I understand!

As their "adopted gringo" I am given the second slice of cake and it tastes fantastic!

By the time of eating the cake I feel full and sleepy...It is 4.06 in the afternoon...My body clock is not used to receiving food this early in the day!

We order a coffee...A caffeine shot ...Perfecto or in Portuguese...Perfeito... That surprised you!!!

As a bit of fun one of the guys, Glaucio tied the birthday ribbon round his head as a bandana and made a gay pose for the camera...I point out it is the colour of Argentina and everyone starts chanting Argentina! Argentina! Everyone is laughing...He can't get the ribbon off quickly enough!!!

All in, the price is 36.50 reals each...Just under £10 a head. It would probably be triple that price on Copacabana!

I feel fortunate to have been invited to the birthday party with such a close knit group of friends. They are all lovely people and made me feel so welcome. A very special occasion...A three course meal...I just feel sooo stuffed lol!!!

On the way back we pass the carnival arena. It is packed with Argentine cars!! They have even been given their own fan fest big screen and a place to eat for a few reals.

They drop me at Prado Junior and I arrive back at the apartment just as the Brazil versus Holland match kicks off at 5pm.

An email from the landlord says I can stay until Friday for an extra 500 reals... Hopefully job done!! The landlord wants to meet at 5.30 umm clearly not a football lover and no concept as to why I am here!! I suggest 7 to 7.30pm after the game. I text Aline who agreed that although the area after the World Cup is a little more of a concern, it is the best option. Aline feels cold showers are not acceptable and I should try to negotiate a reduced price of 400 reals.

I get down the open air fan fest with 33 minutes gone. The Dutch are winning 2-0...Oh my...I feel so sorry for the Brazilian people. This is turning into a never ending nightmare...

No wonder the majority of the fan fest is sat down. I am surprised they aren't flat out completely...

Free kick comes in...Luiz has a defender with two arms wrapped completely around him...When is this type of infringement going to be punished...?

Van Persie brings a diving save out of César.

I learn that Robben was brought down for a penalty from which Van Persie scored after just 3 minutes and Blind got a second after 17 minutes...

Cross comes over...Two Brazilians at the far post...Even Luiz can't stretch far enough to get a touch for a tap in...

Ramires running through...Dutch defender goes to kick the ball...Misses and kicks Ramires full on...Ouch! Free kick hits the wall...

Half time Brazil 0 2 Holland

I see the goals on the big screen during the interval...

Robben didn't dive... It was a genuine penalty. Pulled back from behind... Only saw it the once but was it a last man and sending off offence? Van Persie smashed the penalty into the net and went on a celebration run...Relief? Is he under pressure from the Dutch media perhaps?

Blind's goal was again the result of poor defending...Set up nicely by Luiz... How did Chelsea manage to sell him for €50 million?

First 5 minutes of the second half and the Brazilian players seem to have come out with some of Scolari's fire in their bellies.

A Brazilian lady behind me implores her team to just score a goal. It shows just how far expectations have fallen in just a week.

The screen starts to blur... Almost as if in sympathy...As if it can't bear to bring any more misery to these wonderful Brazilian fans...

A tackle from Tiago Silva on Robben brings gasps from the crowd. The replay shows the tackle across Robben's ankle to look quite bad. It also shows Silva almost does the splits which with Robben tumbling over his back would have been incredibly nasty.

Ramires moves the ball to his right...Shoots...Screws it wide.

58/42 possession in favour of Brazil... Statistics often don't tell the full story...

Outside on the street, the Argentines aren't helping...They have now mustered a full band together and are singing the "rub your noses in it" Italia 90 song continuously.

Sadly after four weeks of hearing it over and over, its originality and clever wording is beginning to wear off...

What seemed like a dive brings another free kick on the edge of the box... Another Luiz free kick comes to nothing...The ghosts of Rivelino, Roberto Carlos Zico, Branco et al are haunting me let alone their own countrymen...

There is a fabulous full moon in the darkened skies to the right of the fan fest screen. Helicopters are as ever buzzing around overhead.

Oscar goes down in the box. The referee blows his whistle...The crowd cheer... But instead of pointing to the penalty spot, the referee pulls a yellow card out and books Oscar for simulation. Replays suggest the referee got it right...

Hulk shoots high and wide...Seems to have been a recurring theme during this World Cup.

A promising move down the left...Hulk running with the ball...Options...But loses possession...how much did Villa Boas want to pay for him...£30m+? I seem to think Zenit St Petersburg may have paid £40m....

11 minutes to go...Spirited second half performance so far from Brazil but the Dutch keeper is not being forced to make saves...Just the odd cross to collect...

High ball into the box...Well controlled on the chest by Robben...Defender shoulders into his back...Penalty!! Not given...Sympathetic decision?? As last man it would have been a sending off... Quite ironic that when Robben is genuinely fouled in the box, a penalty isn't given!

5 minutes of added time.. Dutch move down the right wing...Wijnaldum sweeps the ball first time into the net at the near post...Academic but could César have done better? Maybe...Maybe not...Spurs had a brilliant Brazilian keeper who seemed to be prone to lapses in concentration...Once recall Spurs fans on the underground at Seven Sisters after a game singing about him. Brazilians on the train sitting nearby asked me to translate...the words were "Huerelho Gomes, you are the love of my life, Huerelho Gomes I will let you make love to my wife" or words to that affect. The Brazilians were in pieces crying with laughter. Tears literally streaming down their faces. In the end, I had to ask...Don't you have fan songs in Brazil? Yes, yes of course but my mum is the sister of Huerelho Gomes!!! Through fits of laughter, they showed me photographs of sister and brother together!

Van Gaal brings his third choice keeper on...Nice touch...

The Argentine band is back in full swing... This is blatant rub your noses in it Brazil...

The referee blows the final whistle...

Brazil 0-3 Holland

Holland finish the World Cup in third place. They went through the whole tournament undefeated except for a penalty shoot-out.

The open wound of Brazilian football is gaping. Within the space of four days...Two games at home...An aggregate score of 1-10...60 years plus of self-confidence, almost invincibility has been shattered into tiny pieces. It feels as if it will never ever fully recover to the previous levels...It will take a mammoth Herculean effort to even bring it back on to an even keel.

I climb up to get a view outside of the fan fest. There is a mob of a thousand or so Argentines singing and dancing. The Brazilians are congregating waving German flags and singing their own "Mil gols" song.

This must be about as good as it gets for Argentina. They are in the World Cup Final in Brazil who have lost their last two games 1-7 and 0-3. They are right outside the Brazilian fan fest effectively taking over Copacabana...Although vastly outnumbered they are the dominant voice...

The only way it can get better for them is for Argentina to win tomorrow night!

I admire the Brazilians restraint... There would be a riot in many other countries.

As we look upon the Argentine spectacle I talk with a German guy from Berlin. He says they can have as many of them singing as loud and as long as they want... We will still beat them tomorrow night. It wasn't said nastily or even arrogantly. I guess when you have just beaten Brazil 7-1 away, it is somewhat of a confidence builder!! No wonder it was said with such assured confidence. He had me believing him and I frightened myself by almost wanting to believe him... Germany...Oh my!!!

I walk back to the apartment and open up an email from the landlord saying he can't meet this evening and that the price is 500 reals per night... 2500 for five nights! I check the four star hotel including breakfast is 920 reals for four nights ...And...It is!!

I copy and paste the hotel rate into an email and offer him 800 reals total plus a requirement for hot water and await his response.

I send a WhatsApp to Aline who thinks I am joking about the price of 2500 reals. At least I know I can stay with Luiz and Aline tomorrow night which takes a lot of the pressure off as there is a lot of availability from Monday onwards.

Aline tells me that it is reported that there will be 26,000 security people at the Maracana for the Final tomorrow.

On the way down to the Budweiser Hotel, an Argentine in full view of everyone is urinating into a plant pot at the entrance of the Copacabana Hotel. It is not a pleasant sight. Further along, people are laid out on the path outside of their cars and in the cars. I doubt the authorities would allow it in Europe.

Copacabana is absolutely heaving tonight. Possibly the busiest I have seen it! There are a lot of drunken Argentines, Brazilians and a few more Germans but not really in great numbers... May be keeping a low profile or on another beach such as Ipanema.

It is 10.30pm. While I am waiting for Luiz and Aline outside the Budweiser Hotel, a lady, I would guess in her late thirties/early forties approaches me and says you didn't acknowledge me walking along Atlantique. Taken aback I apologise and say I hadn't noticed...She speaks with an East European accent and I learn she is half Polish and half Brazilian. This is interesting...I wonder whether she is on the program! She asks if I would like to go for a drink and I say that I am waiting for friends. She then says may be another night and hands me a card which reads:

ESCORT
Hot company, speak English. Create pleasing moments, toys, massage, etc....
Phone +55 (21) followed by not one but two numbers!
Claudia

Never a dull moment in Rio!!

I meet up with Aline and Luiz and life returns to normal! They walk me to three hotels and the Atlantico is the most appealing. It is a four star and the cheapest... It is almost around the corner from where I started this adventure at the Savoy Othon at the Ipanema end of the beach.

As we walk towards a bar, a car flashes passed with Argentines standing on their car seats and the upper half of their torsos being visible through the open roof top of a car waving the blue and white Argentine flags. Crazy!!

We sit down at a beach front restaurant and Jessica joins us for a shared pizza and a couple of drinks. Luiz, Aline and Jessica are such beautiful people. I feel very fortunate to have met them. They are already filling my days with social events for the coming week!

Aline says that Scolari said in his TV interview after the game that he will not resign. He thinks the team played quite well today and is building for 2018... Really?

Fred apparently interviewed well...The reporter said it can't have been easy for you with all the high balls being played up to you. He said he accepted his responsibility for not performing well in this World Cup. He thought he played well in the Confederations Cup which Brazil won last year...It just didn't happen this year.

In the canopied restaurant and the adjoining restaurants, Argentines start chanting the Italia 90 song. Now they are jumping up and down .These are not teenagers but grown men. Their band strikes up outside...It goes on and on and on...Now I can imagine how people felt trying to go out for a drink in their own country when England fans used to be out on the town across Europe!

On another subject, Luiz shows me a photograph taken by a member of the general public. It shows Whelan and his lawyer using the local bus service to leave the Copacabana Palace hotel! This is highly embarrassing for the Brazilian authorities. I wonder whether the lawyer will suffer a backlash should Whelan flee the country.

We say our good nights and I walk back towards the hotel. It is 2.10am and both sides of the promenade are still incredibly busy...The beach looks to be full of fans. I turn onto Prado Junior...Incredibly a tent has been erected between cars in the street.... The occasional smell of urine on the streets has been a regular feature of the World Cup. The volume of people in the fan fests, on the promenades, at street parties and sleeping in cars or rough...The public facilities just can't cope with the demand...Tonight it is at its worst...The local businesses will miss the World Cup trade but the locals must surely be keen to have their city back!

I climb into bed but there is little chance of sleep...It is the eve of the World Cup Final...Horns are being honked and there is a total disregard for anyone who may be trying to sleep. If your country was in the World Cup Final wouldn't you be doing the same!

We came a lot farther than we had anticipated. Even though we did not lose any of the qualification matches the expectation was that Holland would be on the first plane out of Rio!

From a bunch of individuals, some of whom had never played for the national team before, Louis Van Gaal managed to create a real team. And the team spirit of winning and being proud to play for your country was embedded and certainly visible on and off the pitch. At the end, finishing in third place felt as a real achievement and put Dutch football on the global map again.

With different football than the introduction of 'totaal voetbal' in the 70's under Johan Cruyff, Van Gaal introduced a system where the players could play several systems depending on the opponent and the players were willing to fight for every ball and to help each other.

Leo, Dutchman living in the Rijswijk area of Belgium

To be honest the Dutch fans didn't have any confidence that our new team would get through the group phase. But when we took revenge on the ruling World Champions Spain (by 5-1!), the winds changed for the better. Although we did not get into the final our third place, by winning from Brazil (3-0), was considered to be a great success.

Ed van der Tak, Rotterdam, Holland

SUNDAY 13TH JULY 2014

I wake at 8.35am having had a couple of hours sleep. The last time I looked at my watch it was 6.31 and at that time I hadn't any sleep whatsoever..

The Argentines sleeping on the streets made sure those of us in beds didn't get much sleep either...Blasting car horns throughout the night, shouting, singing... The streets are teeming with Police and Military who just let them do as they please...If Argentina win tonight I guess it will be even worse...And if they lose... Who knows what will happen!!

The sun is shining...Hooray!!!

I check my email...The landlord of the apartment has not responded yet... Hmmm... What to do...?

I guess the sensible thing to do is to have a shower and start packing under the assumption that I will be moving out today.

It would be worth one last effort to try to obtain a cup final ticket but the only way that would be possible is by paying through my Visa card. This would suggest walking down to see George, the travel agent guy who has Dutch contacts. It is a good half an hour's walk from here...

On a couple of hours sleep, today feels a little bit of a logistical nightmare...

I decide to put off my start to the day by looking at the England v India test match cricket score.

The last time I looked, England were 9 down in their first innings trailing by more than a 100 runs.

I open the BBC web page and it suggests England have a first innings lead...I am very tired and reread it...Yes India made 457 and England made 496...I don't understand...How can that by...I scrawl down the page...Root 156 not out... Anderson out for...81? I pinch myself and reread and yes there it is...

Anderson c Dhawan b B Kumar 81...

Last wicket partnership 198 runs!!!! Wow, wow, just wow!!!

I thought India's last wicket partnership of 111 runs was staggering...I am literally lost for words...Anderson 81 runs!!!! I then think what a shame he didn't make a century...

My mind goes back to Trent Bridge last year when in the First Ashes Test, the young Australian spinner making his debut batting at number 11 scored 98 runs.

England's lower order also responded and England clinched a nerve jangling last day win.

Sadly with India on 217/6 at lunch...It looks as if this match will end in a draw. Nevertheless what an innings from Jimmy Anderson...Not forgetting Joe Root who is developing into a fine young England batsman.

Sport has the capacity to completely shock you...In a good way as well as a bad way... Just like the Brazil 1-7 Germany score...

I wonder how the World Cup Final will play out today.

I can still hear car horns honking incessantly outside...To be honest it is becoming a bit of a nightmare...To the point where if Germany win...I won't shed any tears...Never ever would I have imagined saying that!

It is now 9.33am...Time to go see the shower....Not knowing whether it will be our last time together or not!!

The shower bless it ... As consistent as ever...Cold!!!

I am having an email exchange with the landlord who wants to come at noon...I want him to come as early as possible. After a couple of email exchanges we agree 11.30.

I don't know whether he has accepted my price or not...I therefore have no option but to pack... I may be unpacking again shortly but I have no option.

The landlord, Mauro arrives on time which given that all lanes on Avenida Atlantique are closed today and the knock on effect to all other roads is quite an achievement!

He sets up his lap top with English to Portuguese translator and Portuguese to English translator.

Mauro starts the laptop conversation by saying he is confused. I think me too!

He has travelled in from his home near the Maracana to check me out but thought I wished to stay until Friday. He can offer me an 11.8% discount to give a price of 500 reals per night which would be 2500 reals for the five nights through to Friday 18th July.

I respond by saying that I can stay with friends this evening and then for the following four nights I can book a room in a four star hotel on Copacabana including breakfast for a total cost of 960 reals for the four nights through to Friday 18th July. I say I am prepared to pay 800 reals for the five nights inclusive but that I would need hot water as I haven't had any in all if the time I have stayed in the apartment.

Mauro responds by saying that he thought I wanted the room and I said I thought his offer had been 500 reals for the five nights which seemed about right as compared with the hotel price. I apologise for the misunderstanding and understand that the price might not be acceptable.

He replies by saying that he could offer a price of say 450 reals per night for one or two nights if it would help me. It is the family apartment and they have a baby to bring home. Money is not everything and he fully understands my position and there will be no bad feelings if I decide to leave.

I say he is a good man and thank him for his explanation and that I will leave.

Mauro writes to say I would always be welcome to stay in the future and to remain in contact.

I thank him, sign the release documents. We shake hands and say our goodbyes.

Out on the streets, it is manic...Massive traffic jams...The obvious but challenging task is to walk with my bags to a main road in which the one way traffic system is heading in the right direction towards Luiz and Aline's apartment.

Upon doing so and in 14 reals time, I am outside their apartment block. After Security check the gringo can be allowed in, I go up to their apartment on the third floor.

On entering the apartment, Nikki the pup immediately runs away from the gringo speaking in a foreign tongue.

We check various web sites on line before I book the Atlantico Hotel, bed and breakfast for the four nights 15th to 18th July. The cost is 960 reals through Bookings.com...I have found this web site to be very good.

We print off my reservation. Luiz and Aline decide to go to his father's on Ipanema and watch the game on television.

It is 3.10pm and I am walking along Copacabana towards the fan fest. The Brazilians are wearing black, red and yellow in support of Germany. One of the local sides Flamengo play in black and red...There are a lot of their shirts on display today.

On arriving at the first open fan fest, amongst the mayhem, colour and noise of the football fans, there is a "Jesus loves you rally"!

Walking a little further along, there is a Hari Krishna rally...They are all out in force today!

I walk up to the main fan fest...It is full...it has probably been full for hours with passionate Argentina fans.

There are Argentina fans everywhere...Absolutely thousands of them...Tens of thousands of them!

Amongst them is a famous Brazilian TV presenter trying to give a news report on the promenade.

Finally I manage to work my way on to the beach of the open fan fest...It is the most packed it has ever been...Just how many Argentines are here!!

The players are shown coming down the tunnel...The crowd erupt...If Argentina score...

The national anthems... Ticker tape is thrown in the fan fest. Argentina fans sing their anthem so loudly, so passionately...A really emotional rendition...These people have driven a long way...Slept in cars, campers, on the beach, in tents, at the Sambadrome...They have sung their song of destiny...Many times over!! The manager, Alejandro Sabella appears on the screen and is loudly applauded.

Now a stunning shot from above Christ the Redeemer looking down on to the Maracana comes up on to the screen.

The 2014 World Cup Final Argentina v Germany kicks off!!

Suddenly a quietness descends upon the fan fest...The moment they have waited for...Dreamed of...The World Cup Final...Argentina in the World Cup Final in Brazil... Can they take that final step and become champions of the World...In Brazil...

A German free kick is charged down by the wall...Suddenly Argentina break...

Excitement in the fan fest...Higuain shoots across the face of the goal... Neuer not troubled...

Fernet and coke is the order of the day around me...A very traditional drink for Argentines.

The early exchanges in the first 7 minutes are surprisingly open.

8 minutes...Messi weaves his magic down the right...Gets to the by line... Pulls the ball back... Cleared...

Another intricate Argentine passing move down the right...Pulled back... Avoids attackers and defenders...Now a corner to Argentina...Cleared...

Yet another attack down the right...Neuer gathers... Are these attacks down the right, the German left tactical or coincidental?

Free kick to Germany...Argentina fan next to me says the Germans are eggs... Fragile as eggs!

20 minutes gone...Kroos heads back towards his goal...No idea who to...But it is a perfect through ball to Higuain...Dead centre of the goal...One on one... Surely 1-0... Shanked wide of Neuer's right post...The miss is as bad as Kroos error...

Chances like that in a World Cup Final are as rare as well... It is a dreadful effort...Should have at least made Neuer make a save. It could well be a crucial moment. If it is, at least Higuain can escape back to Napoli... Just imagine if it had been Fred for Brazil!!

An aerial shot over the Rio fan fest comes up on the screen...We look amazing haha

Schweinsteiger booked for a professional foul...

Another break down the right...Where the hell is the German left back... Cross...Higuain... Goallllll

Beer absolutely drenches us...The crowd are going wild!! I am frantically trying to put my Brahma beer down to take a photograph. Holding a can in my left hand and writing in iPhone notes with my right hand is not easy...But I have had a month of practice!

I look up again to the screen...Higuain has been given offside...The replay shows the decision to be correct...Soaked for nothing!

Kramer goes off injured...Schurrle comes on... Not a bad substitute to bring on... The scorer of their last two goals in the Semi Final!!

Lavessi brought down again...Now another foul on the right wing... Another booking...This time Howedes.

Messi running in from the left...Chooses the wrong option...

Romario diving save from a German left wing thrust and Schurrle shot.

38 minutes gone...Argentina seem to be on top...But the score is still 0-0

39 minutes...Down the right again...Messi wriggles through...Pokes it passed the keeper...German and Argentine players race to the ball...Cleared.

43 minutes...Now a German attack, played in by Ozil...Clear sight of goal...Romario saves from Kroos.

2 minutes added time...Corner to Germany...Howedes header...Hits the post!! Follow up...Surely...Offside...Wow that was close!

Half time 0-0 but a surprisingly open game.

I meet Grace and Kate from New Zealand...They travelled to Buenos Aires and Peru separately before meeting up in Brazil for the final two weeks of the World Cup... Paid 220 USD for a hostel on Copacabana...Had a fantastic time in Brazil. Grace had her phone stolen in São Paulo...But blames herself for it... Sounds as if the Brazilian guys took advantage of them having had a drink...

Lot of kissing being shown on the big screen at the fan fest... Two ladies come up on the big screen...They look at each other...Not sure what to do...An Argentine solves the problem and snogs one of them!

Pelé comes up on the screen from inside the Maracana...The word "Puto" echoes around the fan fest... Somehow I don't think it is a term of endearment...

Second half starts....Cross from right inside the box... Begging to be put in... Higuain offside...

Now Messi through on the left... Just Neuer to beat...Time to pick his spot...

Inexplicably he puts it passed the far post...

This is all within two minutes of the restart. Ball played up in the air to Messi left hand side of the box... He heads it across goal to his strike partner Higuain...He misses his kick...

Amazing shot of the sun setting... Lighting up Christ the Redeemer #stunning

11minutes into the second half and

the game continues in the same vein as the first half...

Two flares are lit near me...Light blue and white...Not pleasant...

Long ball down the right...Higuain chases just inside the box...Neuer comes rushing out... Goes over the top of Higuain to punch the ball clear and on his follow through crashes into Higuain...Referee gives a free kick to Neuer... Not sure what Higuain did to cause a free kick to be given against him?

A penalty could have been given and Neuer sent off for dangerous play?

Romario makes a save...

Argentina can't afford to keep missing these chances...Such profligacy in front of goal... Germany are quite capable of snatching the lead... Mascherano booked for a foul on Klose

26 minutes to go...I need the bathroom...

Aguero booked...Late challenge on Schweinsteiger...

I learn from an Argentine that Puto means gay...Another Argentine overhears and says not gay...Very gay...Not sure discrimination laws have reached Argentina yet!

The second half has been much more even...

In the last five minutes or more...The Germans seem to be getting a much stronger foothold in the game. Physically, they appear to be looking in better shape...The longer the match continues...And if it were to go to penalties of course...

It is 5.33...16 minutes to go...Messi cutting in from the right...Trying to get a shot away...Good defending forces him across goal...Somehow he creates a smidgen of space to unleash a shot...But wide...

Night is falling...Marijuana being smoked not too far away...Palacio for Higuain...

A kite is for some reason flying over the fan fest...By the elevated big screen, someone has somehow placed an Argentine flag up there!

The floor is littered with beer cans...The guys and girls around me are urging me with body language to squat and kick sand over it...I point to my grey hair... Too old or may be too reserved...

Into the last 10 minutes...A goal now would surely settled it...

Kroos shoots just wide...

Another spectacular shot from the sky of Christ the Redeemer overlooking the floodlit Maracana...

The Brazilian guy squats...I give him the thumbs up... The Argentines on the other side of him don't like it...Oh the irony...But then again would you want someone peeing on your bed!

EL GRINGO'S ONCE IN A LIFETIME

5 minutes to go...Gago for Perez.

Becoming more a war of attrition now...Goetze for Klose... Is that the end of his goal scoring feats?

An Argentine hands an empty coca cola bottle to his mate...We know what will happen there...

5 minutes added time...Germany almost create a last minute chance...Goetze shot saved by Romario.

Schurrle brings another save from Romario...Germany definitely finishing the stronger...Romario the busier keeper...

Full time 0-0

Amazing how it has ended goalless!

If I hadn't changed my flight... Departure time 7.50pm...I would have had to have left sometime between 5 and 5.30pm #gooddecision

A caipirinha salesman slaloms through the packed crowd with a tray of drinks on one hand...An amazing feat but sadly for him not quite the same rewards as for the skills of the footballers on the big screen. Aline

told me the guys selling drinks on the beach are making over 10,000 reals a month during the World Cup!

Within the first minute of extra time, Germany create a real opening down the left...Romario saves.

2 minutes in...Argentina break down the left...Pull back surely...Instead a cross to an empty box...

The other Brazilian younger guy pees into a beer can...I am stood next to him in shorts and worry about splash backs...I needn't have...Precision personified.

The Argentines are still singing...But as you might imagine, they are fully engrossed in the game...A goal either way now feels as if it would be decisive...

6 minutes...Ball into the box...Palacio chests it down...Just an onrushing Neuer to beat...Palacio lobs over Neuer towards the empty net...It bounces wide...

Mascherano...Foul on Schweinsteiger...Could easily have been a second yellow...Common sense prevails...

Half time of extra time 0-0

How is it still goalless?

The Argentine fans are singing their songs

Second half underway...Schweinsteiger goes down under a heavy challenge.

Schweinsteiger goes up for a header...Aguero leads with an arm... Schweinsteiger goes down...Puto is screamed...I say to Argentines that would have been a red card in England...They totally disagree...Schweinsteiger goes off with a bloody face...

8 minutes into the second half...Run down the left...Cleverly lofted ball into the box by Schurrle...Chested down by Goetze and almost in one movement he volleys the ball passed the oncoming keeper....What a goal!!! Fit to win a World Cup...Which may just be the case!!!

A scuffle breaks out behind me...

Messi header flies over the bar...Is that Argentina's last chance...

2 minutes to go...The Italia 90 song is sung defiantly by the Argentina fans... But there is a sense of total disbelief...This is not meant to happen...

2 minutes added time... Free kick...Cometh the hour, cometh the man? Up steps Messi...Too far out....Surely? But if anyone can Messi can! Germany trying to make sure it's the last kick...Schweinsteiger is down injured...I wonder if he would be down injured if Germany were a goal down!

Talking with Argentina fans...Argentina have had a number of clear cut chances but put everyone wide...Can anyone recall Neuer actually making a save?

Over the bar...The Argentine fans start clapping their team...They know the game is up...All played out... The title of the Italia'90 book...The same teams, the same score...The irony...

The referee blows the final whistle to bring the curtain down on the 2014 World Cup!!!

Germany 1-0 Argentina

The 2014 World Champions are Germany!!!

The Argentines are leaving in their droves...A Brazilian walks passed the group near me chanting the Brazil "Mil goals" song...He would be lynched in

EL GRINGO'S ONCE IN A LIFETIME

England...

Incredibly the fan fest screen switches to the disco and we won't see the celebrations or the World Cup being lifted...The screen now goes completely blank...Goodnight Vienna...Or should I say goodnight Rio de Janeiro!

Omg!!!! It's kicked off big time...Argentines and Brazilians...Right in front of me...Ring side seat...Except there isn't a ring...Fists are being thrown...Chairs are being used as weapons...One guy takes a huge whack across his chest and doesn't flinch an inch...This is violent...Very nasty...People are running for cover...From nowhere in wade the riot police...Batons flying indiscriminately. Time to get out of here...

The promenade is crowded...Brazilians are singing jubilantly...Argentina losing the World Cup Final in their country...The avoidance of total humiliation for them for years to come!

A group of Brazilians gather on the corner of Rua Rodolfo Dantas and Avenida Atlantique...They are singing and celebrating in the faces of the Argentines... An Argentine walks up saying 7-1 and showing seven fingers... Other Argentines are saying similar things but it is generally good natured. I am taking a few photographs...Suddenly the Police come wading in to the Argentines...I am nearby and have to run to avoid receiving an indiscriminate baton across any part of my head or body... Just as I avoid that charge... Another Police charge comes from a completely different angle and now another...This is bloody dangerous...I am trying to get away from this but have no clue which way

is safe...Possibly to stand with the Brazilians as the Police are not charging into them at all...Not an easy route though...I am having to think very quickly...The only way to go is the opposite direction to the way I need to go to return to Luiz and Aline's apartment...I head in the direction of Leme rather than Ipanema and turn up the next road on to Rua Duvivier...I slip into a bar and order a beer to let things quieten down a little.

There is a very drunk English woman in the bar in a West Ham shirt...She is obnoxious even before she learns that I am a Spurs fan... I don't mind West Ham but this lady could change that very quickly! Her Chelsea boyfriend is a decent guy and is out here working on the technical production side of the media...She is complaining at the waiters as in her opinion, they haven't delivered her pizza... Her boyfriend is trying to tell her that she has already eaten it...She is having none of that though... The staff are getting a foul mouth tirade, her boyfriend is getting a foul mouthed tirade and now I am getting one too...I am debating whether running the gauntlet with the Police is preferable to listening to her...

I finish my drink, pay and leave, walking up Rua Duvivier away from the beach for a couple of blocks or so before turning left onto Rua Barata Ribeiro. There are lots of little bars full of genuine Argentine and Brazilian football fans having a post-match drink or a bite to eat. I walk passed Cardeal Arcoverde metro station and already fans are returning from the Maracana clutching their souvenir drinking cups.

On turning on to Cinco de Julio, I say hello to a guy in a Spurs shirt. He is an Australian from Sydney with his father at the World Cup. It is amazing how people from the other side of the World follow English teams so passionately. To think, people think I am crazy driving to games just over two hours away!

I walk into the apartment to see the happy smiling faces of Luiz and Aline who are delighted with the result!

Aline tells me the reworded song of Argentina...By Brazilians of course...

Argentina tell me how you feel now
Losing in your father's house,
I promise in the years to come,
We will never doubt that,
You will suffer the misery,
Schurrle dribbles, Goetze scores,
You are crying since 1990 and now

EL GRINGO'S ONCE IN A LIFETIME

You see Messi lose the World Cup
And Pelé is better than Maradona

It is 9.35pm and I realise I haven't eaten yet today.

Luiz and Aline give me some titbits of information:

After the game, Christ the Redeemer was lit in the red and yellow colours of Germany... Mischievously, I wonder what would have happened if Argentina had won!

The closing ceremony was received better than the opening ceremony...Shakira and Santana were apparently very good.

Messi was voted player of the tournament... Hmmm...By his comments Schweinsteiger certainly didn't seem to agree.

The Germans built their training centre in Bahia. They used local workers creating employment and after the tournament have donated the facilities which will be used as a school.

The German manager, Joachim Loew was very pleasantly surprised by the reaction of the Brazilian people after the defeat of Brazil.

Podolski is the most popular German player in Brazil. He has been tweeting regularly in Portuguese.

After winning the World Cup, the German players wore shirts which said thank you for a great World Cup Brazil and two of their four World Cup winning stars were in the green and yellow colours of Brazil.

The behaviour of the Germans throughout the whole tournament seems to have been not only exemplary but also managed to capture the hearts and minds of the Brazilian public.

The 171 goals total in the 64 games levelled the 1998 record.

Argentina were only behind a total of seven minutes in the entire World Cup which were the last seven minutes of extra time tonight after Goetze's goal.

It seems Luciano Huck, a popular Brazilian TV presenter, is in a bit of PR trouble as he compared the German defeat with the 9/11 terrorist attack...I understand what he is saying to say from a shock perspective but not quite the best comparison to make #easytomisconstrue

As an aside Luiz says his sister Beatrice (Tiza) was in a hotel near Central Park in New York when the 9/11 attack happened. Tiza woke up and looked out of her hotel window to be surprised that there weren't any cars driving up one of the main avenues...Instead people were walking on the road. A work colleague then rang her to suggest turning the TV on...

With it being World Cup Final night, it is a bit of a struggle but eventually we manage to find a taxi to take us to Restaurant Meza Bar in Botofogo...The restaurant has a wonderful ambience...A high ceiling, soft lights, dark wooden tables, comfy sofas as well as upright chairs...Huge paintings of the various bays of Rio de Janeiro decorate the walls. It is very art deco #coolandtrendy

Finally I eat my first food of the day...It is 10.40pm...Almost 24 hours since my last meal... I swear this is not deliberate and the worst is that because of the time of day I am eating...I feel as if I am putting on weight #sumowrestler

We share a starter and I have a sirloin steak cheeseburger with chips...Yes I know it isn't ideal at this time of night...

Aline and Luiz give me a few more pieces of information which are not known through the fan fest...

FIFA allowed the families to come onto the pitch at the end.

Another version of the Italia 90 song was sung by Brazilians in the stadium...

Leaflets with the words were distributed to fans at the metro stations on the way to the stadium:

Argentina tell me how you feel,
See from a long distance,
5 stars shining,
I swear from the years to come,
You will never reach me,
We have won 5 World Cups,
Without cheating,
My father didn't take drugs to play (son of a bitch),
One more thing to say,
So you will never forget,
Pelé alone has won more World Cups than you.

I pick up the bill by way of a thank you for offering to let me stay in their apartment tonight. We jump in a taxi and arrive back at the apartment around 00.15.

After minimal sleep last night, I do feel very tired.

An Argentine had said after the game that most cars will set off back on their 3000 Kms, 2200 miles drive around midnight once the affects of the alcohol wear off... Sounds like they will looking to drive in convoy on the circa two day return drive. The night will be very different to what it might have been and the journey back will also be very different to what it might have been had Messi and co taken their chances. What a difference a single goal makes to so many people...To Germans, Argentines and as well Brazilians!

We set up the sofa bed in the lounge.

It is 00.56...Time to sleep!

EL GRINGO'S ONCE IN A LIFETIME

The World Cup in Brazil meant the possibility of ending our historical rivalry, because if we won at their home it would be enough...We were sure this would happen.

Also we were hoping Messi to explode, and personally end the discussion between Maradona or him, a much better person and example for everybody in Argentina.

We didn't win, but it was an incredible month, living it as champions till the 113th minute of the final.

Before the World Cup nobody believed in the team because we didn't have any defence but great strikers, and in the end it was the other way around! In the final we had three clear chances and they missed them.

Carlos Maria Araujo, Buenos Aires, Argentina

It was about time that the football world returned to South America. With Brazil, Argentina, Uruguay, Chile and Colombia a huge reservoir of young players deserved the attention of the football community and despite the criticism prior to the event the whole organisation went well.

My team, Germany measured up with their fan's expectations and they won the title in an impressive manner. A young team which will bring a lot of joy for their supporters in the future. Obrigado Brazil!!

Jürgen Brandt, Stuttgart, Germany

For me it was a surprise in fact not exactly in terms of football but because we used to be very critical with ourselves, we used not to trust in our infrastructure, organization, etc... In the end things worked, and we have some pride about it. Talking about football, remains the feeling that we have lots of things to do and more than this, a team is not done just with one player.

Jamile Aun, Sao Paulo, Brazil

MONDAY 14TH JULY 2014

I wake at 8.42am having slept straight through the whole night on Luiz and Aline's sofa bed.

Today is a non-football day. Tomorrow is a non-football day as is the day after and the day after that...In fact every day is a non-football day for me now until the Premier League season begins on the 15th August when I go to Upton Park or as it is called these days...The Boleyn Ground for West Ham United v Tottenham Hotspur...The first Premier League game of the new season.

The sun is shining through the blinds...Fresh air is circulating through the open windows. It is a real glad to be alive day!

I have a shower...There is plenty of room to step in to the shower and turn on the taps without being scolded or turned to ice, a shelf for shampoo and body wash...It is perfect...The hot water feels fantastic...Running through my hair, down my face... I luxuriate in it...Never again will I have to face the morning challenge of Mr Cantankerous!!

To think...I would have stayed there through to Friday...Just because it was the easy thing to do....The moral of this story...

If you are not happy in your shower...Be brave, leave it...Move on...There will a better shower somewhere out there for you!! You may have to try a few others before you settle down with the right one...And who wouldn't want to try a few showers in the beautiful city of Rio de Janeiro...! Tonight I will try my sixth at the hotel where I am staying for the rest of my time in Rio...Umm didn't I say something along those lines when moving into Prado Junior!

The sofa bed is in the lounge so I quickly fold everything away and have everything back to normal.

Luiz heads off to work. He starts at 10am...It feels a very civilised time to start the day.

The newspaper headlines are "Germany Four Times Champions; Argentina are Runners Up."

The Government say they want to bury the World Cup, put it behind them and turn over a new page. A letter was sent to the players yesterday saying they wouldn't be invited to meet the President. It seems the Government do not want the disappointment of the World Cup and the fans reaction and downbeat mood to spill over into the elections. Who can blame them!

The opposition however are having none of it and are comparing the president to Scolari!

President Dilma handed the trophy to Germany...But every time she came up on the screen inside the stadium...She was booed... I ask why... It seems to quite a few Brazilians that corruption has increased during the four years of her leadership ...Legislation has been passed which seems to benefit the ministers and mayors. The poor people like her... Families receive money when breadwinners are in prison...A couple of years ago during the floods a huge part of a favela slid down a hill in Niteroi and lots of people died...Instead of moving people to safer areas she gives them money... Her party, PT hard workers party, has been in power twelve years...Lola was the president for eight years and was very popular...He doesn't have a little finger... The popular story is that he cut it off himself for an insurance claim!

The papers also report on the fighting after the game yesterday...It seems there were more incidents than just the one I saw...There is a picture of an Argentine burning the Brazilian flag on Copacabana beach in the O Globo newspaper.

There is talk in the paper of some Argentines staying on in Rio for a vacation...I wonder just how many were here in Rio yesterday.

The papers report that from the World Cup ending there are 754 days, 2 years and 23 days, until the Olympic Games start in Rio...And that about 25% of construction is completed!

A headline in Saturday's newspaper catches my eye... Aline translates the article which says Nigeria have been suspended from all competitive matches by FIFA. It seems the Nigerian Government have arrested the head of its football association and fired all the senior members for poor performance! I thought they generally played well in the Group and also in their last 16 game versus France...I am just a football supporter though...What do I know...FIFA are not happy with Government interference which is why the country has been banned from competitive matches.

So that is that then...The 2014 World Cup in Brazil is over... Some seven years of planning over and done with. Everyone I have spoken with, even those who have been robbed, have spoken in glowing terms of their time in Brazil.

After a ham and cheese crepe with grapefruit juice and coffee...Fit and raring to go...Seize the day John!

Aline has an hour CrossFit class at 11am and offers to let me stay in the apartment while she has her class...Considering we hardly know each other it is a lovely gesture but the sun is shining and not having had an opportunity to sunbathe for a few days I would like to go down to the beach.

I leave their apartment at 11am on Cinco de Julho and walk a block to pick up a taxi on Rua Barata Ribeiro...I give the taxi driver the hotel business card picked up during my reconnaissance visit with Luiz and Aline last Saturday night. The taxi driver feigns a "no se" don't know the address expression... Basically the fare is of no interest. A local says Rua Xavier da Silvieri, Hotel Atlantico's road, is two to three blocks in the direction of Ipanema...I have a large suitcase, a carry bag and a rucksack. The paths are narrow and uneven. This is going to be fun! Four blocks later I turn right and up to the hotel arriving by 11.30...This is the thing with time...Some half an hour's can pass by in the blink of an eye...If your team are one down with half an hour to go... Where did that go...Bloody hell only two minutes added time...Now if you were Sir Alex of course...Minimum of four minutes...It even became known as Fergie time!

Equally in enjoying pleasant company...Half an hour is nothing...But...When your team are a goal up and defending for their lives...Each minute feels like five minutes...Sometimes I swear the clock stops altogether! Equally when lugging my suitcase, carry bag and rucksack through the streets of Rio...It feels like forever!!

Bad news...The room won't be ready until 2pm earliest or at best 1pm. I complete all of my registration details and ask for the Wi-Fi code...The code cannot be given until I have checked in...But I have checked in and prepaid my room until Friday! Yes but you need to be allocated a room number as Wi-Fi is chargeable...This is the first hotel or apartment I have stayed in which charges Wi-Fi in my more than four weeks in Brazil.

I decide to get changed and head down to the beach... On a sun bed opposite the Budweiser hotel by 12 noon...Not a bad effort! My concern for Rob is growing...Despite sending a daily message to Rob, I have not heard back from him. I think of contacting friends in the UK or maybe going to the Marriott where he likes to go for lunch.

I am keen to speak with people who went to the Final to learn of their experience. I walk over to a group of guys and ask if they speak English...

Julio and Edwardo are from Buenos Aires...They work for a subsidiary of Budweiser who fly their senior management to the football and rugby World Cup Finals...Julio also went to the Liverpool v Chelsea FA Cup Final. What a great company to work for!!

They were at the World Cup Final yesterday and said it was a fantastic experience. The split of support felt around 50/50 with the fans mingled in together. The 50:50 split being due to the Brazilian fans supporting Germany. Although there were one or two one to one arguments and stand offs, it felt very safe inside and outside the stadium.

They were behind the goal Argentina were defending in the first half which had mainly German support. Every time they tried to sing for Argentina they were drowned out by whistling!

At the end of the game they applauded the Germans lifting the trophy. Very sporting!

Julio is originally from Uruguay and would support his own country versus Argentina but is also a supporter of his adopted country. He has five sons...Two support Uruguay and three support Argentina...

He is coming over to the 2015 Rugby World Cup in England and as a River Plate fan would like to see Lamela playing for Spurs. He gives me his contact details and asks me to get in touch.

A Dutch guy Harry from Groningen sits nearby me on the beach. He came out for the first week of the tournament with a friend. They saw the 5-1 victory over Spain and spent a number of days in Salvador...I say from what I hear it must have been dangerous...Harry said not for him. Along with a friend they hired a local heavy at 400 reals for an 18 hour day. Over seven days they were taken to places no tourists would ever be able to frequent...Local bars, street markets, favelas...They felt completely safe throughout their stay!! What a great idea!!

While they were in Salvador, they received a phone call from a friend staying in Rio. The friend took a prostitute back to his hotel room. When he woke up in the morning...The prostitute had gone...And so had all of his possessions... His wallet containing cash and credit cards, phone, passport, clothes out of the wardrobe, suitcase... Everything...Except the boxer shorts he was wearing in bed!!!

Harry flew back to Holland after his week in Salvador. As Holland progressed through the tournament, he was speaking with his son Anne (I will explain that one in a minute!) and they decided to fly out last Tuesday from Holland for the semi-final in São Paulo, hire a car and drive down to Rio to hopefully see Holland play Germany in the final. Harry says the support inside the stadium was

90% Argentine...Obviously a gut wrenching experience to lose on penalties...

They will make the six hour return drive to São Paulo in the morning. They had intended to set off at 6am but I show them photographs of the sun rise over Copacabana which convinces them to delay their departure by an hour or so. They say the drive from São Paulo has fabulous scenery so it won't feel a hardship.

Harry said the name Anne originated as a boy's name in the northern part of Holland called Friesland. It later spread as a girl's name.

I leave the beach to try to find Rob in the Marriott. The beauty of trying to find Rob is that because of his height he is easily described to the staff...Grande Inglese hombre with my arm stretching above my head. Yes they know of him so I handwrite a message to be passed on to him.

On my way back I stop off at the California Othon Hotel...Very handy to have stayed there one night as I have in the past 2-1/2 weeks nipped in frequently to log on for the free Wi-Fi.

I have received a message from Rob through WhatsApp:

The message says he changed his flight after the Brazil game, and returned back to the UK. His phone had been cut off as the bill had gone above £600. He had no means of contacting me...On his first day back he was hit by a taxi... Nothing serious just badly bruised and shaken...

Bloody hell...Poor Rob!! So it sounds like he is back in the UK...I will miss him this week...

I want to meet up with authentic Germans to hear of their excitement...

As I come out of the hotel, there is a feeling of a max exodus...Luggage, minibuses, taxis everywhere...All heading towards the airport...

On the way back to the beach I see a couple in a Germany shirt carrying a flag. I ask them if they speak English and they do... And they were in the Maracana for the final!

I ask them what it was like inside the stadium...They say it was amazing, a "once in a life time" experience!! Perfecto!!

They sat next to an Englishman in the stadium and joked that it must be difficult for him to know who to support in this game! In their opinion Germany were the best team in the tournament but Argentina probably deserved to win the final. They said there were a couple of fights after the game but nothing like on Copacabana...They ask my name and they introduce themselves as Kia and Sylvie...I say to Kia you speak English with an American accent...He says it is because he is from America and lives in Rio with his carioca partner! My search for an authentic German continues!

Back on the beach, there are still a lot of Argentines here but in relation to how many were here yesterday...Well it is all relative!

It starts to get a little chillier around 3.30... After 4pm Harry says goodbye to walk down to the murals and see the sunset over Ipanema.

The sun disappears behind the Budweiser Hotel as it does towards the end of the day and I decide to head back to the hotel to check in.

I cross the road and all the Budweiser signs are being taken or I might say torn down.

I arrive back at the hotel to find an enormous queue at check in...

Damian is in the queue in front of me. He is an Argentine living in Zurich, used to work for FIFA and his colleagues managed to get him a corporate final ticket. He said that although there was free food and drink and putting aside the result...He didn't enjoy the experience...To Damian it felt more of a social gathering than a football match. There were Malaysian, Polish, Chinese, corporates who were there for the occasion more than having a passion for football...Interesting perspective which I can understand. Most fans want to be amongst their own fans at games. Damian is another one forming a part of the exodus... He is checking in for the night and flying back tomorrow...Flight costs are prohibitive today...As I know only too well!

Another Argentine in the queue said there were a lot of problems in Buenos Aires after the game last night...Office windows and cars were smashed up... Recall when England lost to Germany in the 1990 World Cup...There were similar problems...Mercedes Benz and BMW cars were particularly targeted... Even though the cars had British registered number plates...Seemed bizarre at the time and 24 years later ridiculous...Just like smashing up your own country offices and cars because a few guys from your country lost a World Cup Final.

Any single rooms is shouted out from behind reception...That will be me then! It still takes another 10 minutes or so...Having completed the registration form this morning...I have no clue as to why it needs to take so long.

I get talking with a Parisian guy while waiting for my room key...No not in Paris... But the length of time of the wait...It could be!

He stood a few metres away from his friend who had two spare tickets for the Spain versus Chile game he was selling outside the stadium before the game.

A guy comes up to his friend and asks how much he wants. He says $800 USD. The guy starts to negotiate and then suddenly pulls a huge gun out on him. His friend panics and thinks it's a gangster...It is an undercover policeman!! It is illegal to sell tickets for a profit in Brazil. A prisonable offence...

His friend is escorted away and spends two days in a Brazilian prison cell. He has to employ a local lawyer to negotiate his release...

May be the story scared the reception as...Suddenly my room key is available!!!

There are others who were ahead of me in the queue still waiting...I seem to recall one of the feedback issues on one of the web sites being about the length of time taken by the reception staff...There is length of time and length of time and on top of those lengths of time...There is the reception desk at Hotel Atlantico!

I go to collect my suitcase...Thankfully there isn't a queue...Why would there be...releasing one room key every 15 minutes has some advantages!! But...The guy is shuffling papers and tells me...Wait...Oh right...Good afternoon to you too!

Eventually I receive my suitcase and summon an elevator which works at a similar speed to the reception staff...

Eventually I open the door to my room 614...It is a box...No not quite right...It is the minutest of small boxes...Just about enough room to swing the proverbial cat around in...A single bed. Might accept it if for one night only in central London...But for four nights in a Rio de Janeiro...While waiting at the reception a guy said that a room cost 3000 reals on Cup Final night... Surely not this room!!!!

It then hits me why even as a box it feels dingy...What doesn't a box have... Yes that's right...No windows...It is a prison cell...There is a dirty towel from the previous inmate by the sink... I can hear every noise in the corridor...No sound proofing at all.

I leave my luggage in the box and drop my key off at reception requesting a change of room.

I go for a walk along Copacabana and stop off at the California Savoy Othon to use the Wi-Fi and catch up with emails, twitter, WhatsApp etc. Very comfy chairs and time passes quickly in this chilled environment.

It is now 10pm and I realise yet again that I have not eaten since Aline's breakfast crepe...Being on my own, I decide to go the BBQ on Rua Duvivier... Always busy and easy to get talking with people

There are a couple of guys from New York but they are busy chatting up some girls who it seems don't live too far away from them.

I order the steak mignon...£10 for a steak mignon #bargain!

I ask a couple of English guys if they have any stories for my book...They say...Yes but not suitable for the book...I say...Don't be so sure!

They are reticent to tell me as it is about a mate who is sat at the far end of the BBQ. The guy is a big guy...Bulging biceps, covered in tattoos, beard...A biker type who you perhaps wouldn't want to argue with...What the hell...Anything for a story!

I shout down to ask his mate if it is OK to tell me the story on a no names basis...He says yes OK...So by now all the English speaking people in the BBQ are engaged in this!

His friend shouts to his mate...Are you sure?? Yep!!

So the biker type, Steve Porter...oops his name slipped out there!! Only joking...A totally made up name and if there was a Steve Porter in Rio on this date in the BBQ...It is a miraculous coincidence...Isn't it Steve haha...

So "Steve" pulled this girl in a bar and took her back to his apartment... She was very responsive and...How, shall we say, proactive...

Everyone's ears in the BBQ are pricked to attention...Some of the ladies are trying to pretend they are not listening...But everyone knows they are!!

She took the lead and took the lead a long way...He had had a drink and was happy for her to do as she pleased...And she did a lot!!!

Eventually he felt he should reciprocate a little and while kissing his hand started to wander...And found three things he wasn't expecting to find!!!!!

The guests in the BBQ let out a collective gasp...Then howls of laughter!!

No one can believe he allowed the story to be told. Everyone wants a copy of the book! The guy stands up... Puts his right arm across his tummy and performs an extravagant bow to loud applause! Well maybe not...But he might as well have done! I love this BBQ. If anyone ever watched the American sitcom Cheers... That is the kind of feeling it engenders within me!

I walk back along the promenade...It is busy with all sorts of activities taking place. A guy has put two skittles on the ground...Literally a football width apart. The ball is placed on the ground about three metres away. People, mostly drunken foreigners are constantly giving 2 reals to try to kick the ball through the skittles. If there is an easier way to make money...I have not seen it!!

I walk along to Rua Bolivar which is usually quite lively. Stopping off at a bar with a caipirinha in hand I get talking with four well to do guys from Argentina...They are great company...One of the guys is absolutely hilarious and causing belly aches through laughter...

They spot the ex-coach of the Argentina Pumas rugby team Santiago Phalan who kindly stands with me for a photograph.

The caipirinhas are taking affect... The Argentines want to meet again tomorrow and give me their business cards.

I stop writing at some point... The night starts to get a little fuzzy...I remember saying to the waiter that more cachaça is needed in the caipirinha...I now vaguely remember not having enough cash on me for the bill and having to run a good 10 minutes or so each way to my hotel room... Very trusting of the Argentine guys to trust me to come back!!!

No idea what time I fell into my single bed in my cell...Well after lights out though...probably closer to morning daybreak...Again...

EL GRINGO'S ONCE IN A LIFETIME

The World Cup is a great event where you can get involved and excited even though "your team" is not there. The most memorable march was the semifinal between Germany and Brazil! It was crazy!! The whole family watched the match and we went bananas as the goals kept coming. The "mannschaft" was a great winner of the championship this year.

Christine Bennborn, Stockholm, Sweden

I enjoyed very much being in Brazil to go to the final game. People on the streets singing and dancing before the game was an added bonus to an incredible event as a World Cup Final is and what it represents to football lovers.

The beaches in Rio were the perfect spot for such an amazing event. Being a Uruguayan living in Argentina for a long time, I had two teams that I was rooting for.

Uruguay did pretty well considering that the team is going through a process of replacing its main players from the South Africa tournament four years ago. It was a real treat to leave behind both Italy and England. Did not expect it before the tournament began... A big surprise in the group was the performance of Costa Rica. Didn't expect that either!! In my personal view, it was correct to sanction Suarez for biting and Italian player, but I think the punishment was too harsh on him. He was treated by FIFA as if he was a criminal. A couple games of suspension seemed more reasonable.

With respect to Argentina, I think they did very well. I was personally disappointed at Messi. Didn't play as a champion! Nevertheless, Argentina was very close to winning the final game, although I believe Germany was the right winner. It's details in play and execution that make the difference between a champion and a runner up. And Germany was flawless in that respect.

Aside from the game, my work colleagues and I spent three incredible days in Rio enjoying the atmosphere and the beautiful beaches.

Julio Freyre, a Uruguayan living in Buenos Aires, Argentina

TUESDAY 15TH JULY 2014

Wake up...Not sure whether daylight or dark...No window!! It is 9.15am... I am still drunk from last night...This is not good!!

I take the couple of paces across my room to the shower. Wow it is very good...Hot water...Strong flow and very spacious...! And especially in relation to the tiny room which still houses my unpacked bags...I can't stay in this room... It is not good for my soul...

Oh dear...The lifts are still as slow as ever!

I am in the restaurant now...Staggering round in a daze looking for something to eat... Milk and cereal on top of last night's caipirinha...I don't think so!! A few glasses of orange juice later...I see bread cheese and ham...Perfecto!! Everything feels off centre...Dear me...How can I still be so drunk!!!!!!!!!!!

Come out of the restaurant to try and have a coherent conversation with the guy on the front desk about my room. He must think I have been drinking this morning, technically he would be correct (but that was before I slept!) and am an alcoholic...Perhaps I have become one...Joking aside if I stayed out here much longer it would be very easy to slip into bad habits...What do you mean I already have them...What's wrong with being drunk at 10 in the morning!!!!

The gist of the conversation is that I got what I paid for...A single economy room for four nights with a total cost of 960 reals including breakfast...About £65 per night. I can upgrade for £22.50 per night. I would like to see the upgrade before committing but none available until later in the day.

I can get Wi-Fi in the lobby and time as ever slips by very quickly.

There are three guys with German shirts speaking German...May be they are German??? Authentic Germans!!! I ask if they went to the final and they did and...They actually live in Germany...And they are Germans!!! Never before have I been so happy to meet Germans!!!

They are Dieter, Pieter and Walter from Monchengladbach. They arrived in Recife in time for the Germany v USA game and have followed the team all the way through to becoming World Champions. The USA v Germany game was the last one for Paul and Ian before returning to the UK... Does that say something about the German psyche in comparison to ours?

They have been writing a blog for their local German newspaper and ask for my email address as they are interested in my book...It will be hugely embarrassing writing to tell everyone...Actually the book didn't get published... It simply has to be!!

The guys said it was an amazing night in the Maracana...To be there to see your team, your country lift the World Cup!!!

I asked them when they started to believe. One of them showed me his T-shirt which they had had printed for their trip...It said

"One team...One dream...One destiny"

Before the tournament they felt the loss of Reus would be too big a blow. They likened him as being as important to Germany as Messi is to Argentina. Imagine the hysteria in England if we were to lose someone of that quality in an easy warm up game just before the tournament started...Imagine to have someone of that quality in the first place!!

Once the tournament started and they saw the quality of their play and that the team was showing tremendous form...They thought Germany had a chance. I guess they were saying that Germany could be in the shake-up. Then when they flew out and the shape of the route to the final was unfolding...They started to believe...Obviously playing Brazil in Brazil looked a challenge but Brazil didn't look overly convincing...then the loss of Neymar and Silva for the semi-final gave them real cause for optimism.

They said the final was just an amazing experience in the Maracana...A chance in a life time...Then they said it...Once in a life time...And when I told them that will be the name of my book.. They laughed and agreed!!

In terms of the final, they felt Argentina played well and particularly in the first half. Throughout the game Argentina seemed to be creating the better chances but...As the game wore on they felt Germany looked the fitter and stronger side and...The goal was wunderbar! Sehr schoen...They waxed lyrical about Schurlle's run and the quality of the chipped pass into Goetze...Using their hands to emphasise the chip...And just how well Goetze took the pass and finished.

Their taxi then arrived to take them to the airport...Mission accomplished... Job done...World conquered!!!Destiny fulfilled!!! I congratulated them, shook hands and wished them a good journey home.

Aline sends me a WhatsApp to offer to take me out for the day tomorrow and to also invite me for dinner on my final night in Rio on Thursday evening.

Rob sends me a photograph of his bashed up knee and the taxi which hit him...Bloody hell...His knee is in a mess...Let's hope the scans show no long term damage....How could the taxi driver not see Rob on a pedestrian crossing... Ffs...He is 6'11" (2.11m)... Rob said the driver was driving too fast to stop in time...

On another subject...WhatsApp is a worldwide phenomenon now...At this World Cup, people from all over the world are using it...In fact they don't even ask for my number...They ask for my WhatsApp!!! In case any readers are not aware...Provided you are connected to Wi-Fi...It is possible to telephone, text and send photographs free of charge anywhere in the World...Don't ask me what the commercial logic is for WhatsApp...I have no idea...But it is incredibly useful!!!

I finally set off with the intention of being on the beach by noon.

I look along the beach to see that the second fan fest has now gone completely and that the main fan fest is being taken down.

I decide to walk down to have a look...Once I am down there...The cabins used by the authorities which have felt a permanent part of the Copacabana landscape are being lifted onto wagons.

The crew must have worked throughout the night... Substantial chunks of the main fan fest have already been dismantled...I take some photographs and wonder if it is the President or just Rio wanting normality back as quickly as possible...

I feel a sense of sadness well over me...All the high drama, the memories, the crowds, the fun, the optimism, the ecstasy, the agonies, the frustrations that have been shared in the fan fest and replicated throughout all the other fan fests across Brazil..

And then further afield in bars and shops and houses across the world...

I think of all the people from around the world I have met...Shared a drink or a photograph with...Some for just the course of a match...Others like Aline and Jessica who have become such good friends.

Maybe some people will have met in the fan fest and will go on to develop much deeper relationships...Then of course there was the not so good aspects... Stories of money and phones being stolen...The occasional fights...For the most part restricted to Brazil and Argentine fall outs but nevertheless a part of the history...

Fan fests have though been a huge success...And to be honest the atmosphere is in some ways better than being in a stadium. All walks of life and cultures are mingled together...Standing anyway always feels better to me and you can even get a drink without missing any of the action...There is an electricity amongst the fans which is often not there these days inside the corporate modern football stadiums...

Yes there is a sense of sadness at seeing the ripped FIFA sheeting, the half dismantled towers etc...The vast majority of the fans will have now returned home...To work and back to a sense of normality...And from my conversations the vast majority have thoroughly enjoyed their Brazil 2014 experience...In fact other than the results of their teams I am struggling to remember a single person I have spoken with who has not enjoyed it.

Bueno!! Life moves on!! While down here I decide to take the opportunity to go in the FIFA fan shop...Finally!! The shop will close for the last time tonight.

No queues to get in but it is incredibly busy inside. The queues to pay stretch across the entire shop which has a 1300 capacity.

I scout around for stuff to buy...I confess here and now...I don't like the World Cup mascot...It looks ugly to me...So that reduces a lot of my options! As to be expected a lot of the good stuff has sold out...The shop sells footballs but does not seem to sell the official match ball. There are drinking mugs but they don't seem particularly appealing...Quite an array of key rings, bottle holders, ruck sacks which are a little too bright yellow to take back to the UK...Umbrellas which are a little too long to fit in my suitcase, face paint, temporary arm tattoos with the name of your country...Little late for those! I wander around desperately wanting a few mementoes to remind me of this fabulous World Cup but can't seem to find anything worth queuing for...Well...To queue for over an hour for...

I then see a much smaller cash only queue which has staff in the centre of a square of display cabinets. There are some pens on display...Yes...And I have sufficient cash to join the relatively small queue.

While queuing I catch sight of a small replica World Cup on a plinth which says Brazil. It is around £30 and the perfect memento to take back with me... But I don't have sufficient cash...Hmmm...I ask a member of staff organising the queue who tells me that as long as my credit card is Visa...Which it is...Although the sign says cash only...The staff will take Visa...Good news!!

As is my way...I get talking with a guy behind me...Perg from New Zealand...

Liverpool born who moved out with his parents as a child.

He came via England...Went to the fateful Liverpool v Chelsea and was held responsible for the defeat by his friends!! Perg arrived in Brazil 10 June and initially stayed in Manaus for two weeks.

Perg said the England manager, Roy Hodgson, had apparently said something along the lines of not being overly keen to play in Manaus because of the heat...

This got lost in translation in Manaus and seemingly the local Mayor responded by saying he didn't want England in Manaus either! Perg said when England had the ball a number of locals booed...

It seems not only are Germany light years ahead of us on the pitch but also off the pitch in the way they wooed and won over the Brazilian people.

Other than the Premier League, in terms of football and as a nation, England feels to be a bit of an irrelevance in Brazil...We seem to have a far greater affinity and affection for Brazil than they do for us...A little like the words of the song... Girl from Ipanema...She looks straight ahead and not at me...

Perg tells me of being mugged in the tunnel between Ipanema and Copacabana...

Perg had been told never to go through the tunnel as it was infamous for muggings. Late at night, he was walking back to his hostel on Copacabana from a night out in Leblon. In his own words, he was tired and the thought of walking the long way round felt too much of an effort. He walked into the tunnel and two guys approached him and ever so politely asked him to hand over his money. He took out his wallet and gave them the 50 reals he had and his gold credit card.... Which made their eyes light up...What they didn't realise though was that it had expired some time ago! They let Perg keep his wallet and then... Bizarrely shook his hand and walked off!! The whole episode was very polite and respectful... Well other than for the fact that it was a theft by mugging!!!

The tunnel is not very far at all from Hotel Atlantico where I am staying... Mental note to take care...

Perg told me a funny story of a Canadian lady who was about to be mugged but whacked her assailant with her umbrella and he ran off...When she left home complaining about the rain this morning...!

When he was in Manaus there was an issue over accommodation and a local Brazilian guy on hearing of the problem kindly took Perg from the airport to stay and sleep at his house. When they arrived at the house it was in an incredibly poor area...Perg was given the guy's hammock in the kitchen and the guy slept on a mattress on the floor beneath the hammock! The mother, step father and three brothers also lived in the house.

A day or so later there was a Brazil match on the television and by way of a thank you for their hospitality, Perg bought them loads of beer and a massive piece of beef for a BBQ...They invited the whole neighbourhood round for the BBQ and match!! Lovely story of those who don't have very much sharing what little they have...

Through the tournament Perg has stayed in hostels but now his father is here has gone from a hammock to the luxurious splendour of Copacabana Palace!! Even saw Sepp Blatter in the lobby! He said at 40 he had previously done the whole hostel thing and probably feels a little long in the tooth for it now... He has had such a good time at the World Cup, I am not so sure!

His father bought a pair of World Cup Final tickets...Fantastic experience for him. Seems there is still good money in the Christmas Hamper business!!

Perg isn't exactly sure of where he is going after the World Cup. His whole adventure had been planned up to the World Cup Final. He has a vague idea of touring South America and returning to New Zealand in the New Year... Blimey!! I ask him about his job...He owns three properties in Queens Town which he rents out to tourists...They generate sufficient monies for him to enjoy his life...Wow...I rent a couple of properties out in England and they have been a bottomless pit...Issues of boilers, electrical problems...You name it...One is in negative equity and the other has been funding the shortfall in the gap between the rental income and the endowment payment...Anyway I digress!

As I stand in the queue I look across this massive FIFA shop...Thronged with people buying their last minute mementoes...About ten yards away I see a guy who looks remarkably like "Ted" Finch...The guy is wearing a white England shirt...It can't be Ted... I look more closely...Bloody hell...It might just be you know...Ted I shout...He turns round... It is Ted...Incredible!

Ted is Lincoln born and bred...Met him 40 years ago...We are both Spurs fans and as a 15 year old kid I used to travel down from Lincoln on the train to Kings Cross, take the 259 or 279 bus or underground to Seven Sisters to watch the games...Hard to believe in this day and age...After Spurs beat Newcastle 3-0...Two Cyril Knowles goals...One if not both were free kicks...This being written as I think it without access to the internet... I have a memory for this kind of stuff...I will check the date on line when I have Wi-Fi access...Anyway I go back to Kings Cross and am getting something to eat in the buffet which those of you old used to remember will recall it was located on the left hand side of the platforms as you looked at the track...In those days...Going to football matches was a dangerous hobby...Showing colours was not always a good idea...Railway stations were always hazardous as fans from different clubs ran into each other and fights would often break out in stations and even on trains. Travelling across London to an away game with your fans on the underground was always "interesting"...Another club say for example Millwall could be waiting on any platform to ambush...The fans by the tube train doors were always vulnerable to attack when the train stopped and the doors opened...Away games were a nightmare. I can remember going to grounds like Manchester United, Manchester City, Liverpool, Everton, Middlesbrough, Sunderland, Newcastle where Spurs didn't even have their own section in the stadium...In those days travel to away games that far north from London was not for the masses.

Hooligans in these cities would wait for away fans at train stations to attack them...The way the people dressed in each city was even different...So even without colours you could be picked out...Fans used to stuff their silk scarves down their trousers or jeans to hide them.

Once the waiting hooligans identified a "foreigner" like me they would ask me the time...Having a Midlands rather than a London accent saved me from many a beating...There were stories of leather coats and jackets being taken in those days!! I remember seeing a Manchester United supporter from London - they were called Cockney Reds - being held up against a wall struggling to meet the request of naming the Spurs team and suffering the consequences...

In my life time Spurs have played one season outside of the top league in 1977/78. The day we played Mansfield Town at home...I paid cash at the turnstiles...Wasn't all ticket in those days...And walked on to the Paxton Road terrace ahead of my London based Spurs mates...Being from the Midlands was nearly a problem for me that day...Spurs lads who I didn't know congregated round me...My accent was much more Mansfield than London...I was asked to name the team...Easy enough...I was then asked to say the scores of some of that season's fixtures... I had been to every game and was not only giving the results but also who scored our goals... It was the closest I ever came to a beating from my own fans...By the end they were in admiration of me being a Spurs fan from the Midlands...Strange but true...The Americans would call it friendly fire...Not sure how being killed by your own people can be called friendly.....

So anyway...I am in the buffet and see this lad with a silk scarf round his neck...As we had played Newcastle whose fans would also travel back from Kings Cross I was a little wary...The dark navy blue of Spurs was not always easy to distinguish on a silk scarf between the black of say Newcastle or Derby... Even in those days...I would like now in Brazil go up and speak with people...I didn't have colours showing or a London accent so felt relatively safe...And that was the day I met Peter "Ted" Finch!!

We took the same train back to Lincoln and he said to come to the YMCA on a Monday and Wednesday night to play 5 a side...There were usually around 20 guys playing football taking turns on the pitch and chatting football stuff off it...

As a wide eyed 15 year old it was a fascinating world. I think the film Green Street could have been based on these guys in those days... Watching football has changed so much since the early 70's....

Looking back 40 years and it is hard to believe that on a Monday night... They held a kind of feedback and lessons learnt discussion as to what happened with rivals at the Lincoln game...Who stayed, who ran etc. On a Wednesday night, attention would turn to finalising arrangements and tactics for the next Saturday's game...They had a points system and a league table for taking the colours of other teams...1 point for a hat, 2 points for a scarf and 5 points for a flag...It was amazing...They even had rules and points were only awarded if witnessed and they would congregate in The Red Lion on Lincoln High Street after a game proudly wearing an away teams scarf knotted around their necks... I imagine these types of gatherings were replicated across inner cities throughout the UK in the early 70's. Thankfully, in today's world, I have felt comfortable in taking my two boys since the age of four years old. I imagine it would have been nigh on impossible to take boys so young in those days. Fast forward 40 years and there is Ted stood in front of me grinning away ...Really unbelievable!!

After about 45 minutes of queuing...Finally I pay for my replica World Cup and pens, say goodbye to Perg and am out into the Copacabana sun with Ted.

I ask how long he has been out here...And as he starts to tell me his World Cup story...I am in awe!! I want to capture this it's amazing!!

Ted flew out to Buenos Aires on 5th June on his own. The whole time travelling across South America, Ted has been on his own and returns to the UK on Thursday 17th July...The day before me...six weeks of travelling on his own!

He had a flight booked to Buenos Aires and a flight booked home from Rio and that was it... No match tickets...No transport across South America and no accommodation. He is 56 years old and 18 months ago had pneumonia...It was like me a last minute decision to come...The illness having played a major part in Ted's decision...He only booked his flight two weeks before the World Cup started and one week ahead of actually flying out to Buenos Aires.

Almost every room was found by walking into a hotel and asking if a room was available! On arrival into a new city, he would ask at the Tourist Information centre for advice and whilst language was often an issue Ted has visited three countries and visited seven World Cup cities...He had seen seven World Cup stadiums and visited seven fan fests...But not actually been able to see a game or even go inside a stadium...

This is an overview of his remarkable story...

On arrival at Buenos Aires airport, he was told which bus to catch into the centre and where to get off to find a hotel... Walking through the streets, he was enjoying the lovely weather in a T-shirt but was shocked to see the locals in hats coats gloves and ear muffs!

While in Buenos Aires he visited and was allowed in to see the stadiums of Boca Juniors and River Plate.

During the guided tour of Boca Juniors stadium, the guide said that in the summer months, away fans are allocated the hottest part of the stadium...And in the winter... The coldest part where the wind is the most biting!

The guide said that they don't like the away fans to have a good choice or quality of refreshments so there is only a selection on a wooden table.

There is paint on one section of the terrace. This shows that the away dressing room is beneath. The Boca hooligans stamp on the ground above to try to intimidate the away team.

Maradona has been allocated a free corporate box for life at Boca. Ironically the one person who can truly afford to pay...Doesn't need to!

Ted left Buenos Aires by ferry on the 9th June to Montevideo in Uruguay, a journey I did many years ago and watched Brazil v Croatia there on television. He also watched Spain v Holland after which he took an overnight 12 hour bus ride to Porto Alegre...

Her asked for a hotel but was given a hostel and as he refused to share a room, the cost for his single room was extortionate. Each consecutive day stayed the price reduced but it was nevertheless still expensive and more than would have been paid for a hotel room.

He watched England v Italy in the fan fest at Porto Alegre. It was very cold and there were only about 200 people towards the back and nobody at all at the front except him...It was so absurd; he regrets not taking a photograph!!

On visiting the stadium, he was surprised to see the car park still being built!!

The next day the weather was much better and with the fan fest being only 30 minutes' walk from the stadium where the actual match was being played, it was full for France v Nigeria.

He then took a bus from Porto Alegre to Curitiba where he saw Brazil v Mexico in the fan fest which was five miles out of the city!! Imagine...Let's just pop along to see the match...ten mile return journey to watch a match on a TV screen!

It was though in a beautiful wooded area at an outdoor arena which is used by theatre companies for plays. In spite of the journey, Ted was charmed by the arena and the city itself.

The day of England v Uruguay was a Bank Holiday and everywhere was closed!! It was too cold to go back out to the fan fest so he ended up watching the game in a shopping mall!!

After the game he took an overnight bus to Sao Paulo which was a 6 hour ride and arrived at 4.30am...He had to wait until 6am for the information centre to open by which time he was feeling very ill...Ted blamed the cold in Porte Alegre! He booked into an Ibis Hotel but had to wait until 11am for his room so went for a walk and felt really sick...Shaking and shivering...All sorts of dark thoughts went through his head including Malaria.

He ended up staying in his hotel room for 21 hours...Recovering and watching games on television. Eventually he felt well enough to go to the fan fest to watch Brazil v Cameroon.

When leaving São Paulo, he had to walk a mile to the metro with all of his bags...The area didn't feel that safe but fortunately there were Military police on every corner. He took the metro to the bus station to catch the overnight bus to Belo Horizonte...

In Belo Horizonte the information centre gave him a map and he walked to the hotels to find a room...Booked in the Ibis but had to leave on the fourth night as Brazil were playing there and the price went up to 500 reals.

He went to the indoor fan fest which was again about five miles out of the city but was this time in a soulless exhibition centre... It felt like an aircraft hangar... Very dark inside but outside it was a glorious sunny day...Seemed to be more staff there than fans! He had to walk a long way across the exhibition centre to buy vouchers to then walk a long way to get a drink. It was the first really warm day he had had in Brazil and the first time he was able to wear shorts...And there he was stuck in an indoor fan fest!

By this time he still hadn't seen a Brazilian beach!

In the fan fest, the big screen was showing Uruguay v Italy with England v

Costa Rica being on a small screen.

Needless to say but Ted didn't go back to the fan fest and instead watched other games in city centre bars. On his final day he looked in a bar and there were four mates from Lincoln...One of whom was my cousin Steve Clucas! They were flying to Rio that day though and Ted was anyway going to Brasilia...

He watched the Brazil match in a shopping mall. Everyone from babies to grandmothers were decked out in the colours of Brazil watching their team... Ted was amazed by the passion, fervour and colour...And in a shopping mall... Beyond anything he had ever seen! Ted was the lone exception in his England shirt!

He caught the overnight bus to Brasilia...Being a relatively new city...Ted described it as a cross between Canary Wharf and Milton Keynes...It felt a little American in style with the residents living outside the centre and everyone needing a car to get around...Which Ted didn't have!

Ironically the Brasilia stadium car park was empty on match day while the match was taking place...People had taken buses from the metro station!

The good news was that the hotel was only a 15 minute walk from the stadium...Well it would have been good news had Ted got a match ticket...But sadly this didn't seem to be an option. The fan fest however was a long way out of the City...A 45 minute walk from the metro station...Very good fan fest...Lots of screens and very busy.

The day Ted wanted to take the metro to the bus station to move on to his next city...The metro had broken down for the first time in two years! Instead he had to take a taxi for the five mile journey.

From Brasilia he took the overnight bus to Salvador...A 24 hour bus journey!!!! Yes 24 hours!!! The bus broke down after 22 hours in the middle of nowhere!!! Nothing...Just wilderness...Are you thinking what I am thinking... Ted didn't have a lot of luck...He had to wait an hour and a half for another bus to came along...Rather quaintly it was women and children first but Ted managed to board the bus...

On these bus journeys people carried all of their belongings...It felt to Ted as if for many local people the long arduous bus journeys were the only way to get across the country...to visit friends or relatives...Even to move city. They take their own food and drinks on the journeys to keep the cost down...

Finally he arrived in Salvador! Now being a bit of a connoisseur on Brazilian fan fests, Ted says Salvador's was the best. It was on the sea front in a fortress type environment and as well on a slope so that everyone could comfortably see the screen. Ted saw the Brazil v Colombia match there and it helped that his hotel was nearby!

Ted has seen seven stadiums from the outside but as said earlier he didn't get in any matches live or even enter inside a stadium.

The final bus journey was of course the longest!! A grand finale!! It took 29 hours on the bus from Salvador to Rio...I can't begin to imagine...

I ask Ted whether he had enjoyed his travels...

Ted was very honest in his response...

Not surprisingly he felt long periods of isolation and loneliness...From a security perspective, he decided against bringing his telephone with him which meant he didn't have access to the internet to even know what was going on in the outside world.

Before leaving the UK, Ted thought he would be able see a game or two and be able to have a look inside the stadiums on non-match days...

The cost of the match tickets on the black market was just too high so any chance of seeing a game was soon ruled out.

He was though very disappointed not to be able to enter a stadium on a non-match day.

A lot of investment has been made in building these stadiums...Fans travelled from all over the world for, in many cases a one off visit, to many of these cities. Demand for tickets exceeded supply.

As well, there are the local people who have seen these stadiums being built...May be they might want to see them decked out in the World Cup colours and logos.

Ted questioned...Would it have been that difficult on non-match days to allow admission for a charge, even if restricted for an hour a day and to one particular section?

Thinking about it...I heard similar stories of people taking the metro to the Maracana on non-match days to be told they could not enter...Saying how disappointed they were...Coming all this way and not be able to see inside the iconic World Cup Final stadium...

The authorities could have made a lot of money and satisfied the desire of people to see inside the stadiums...#crazy

Ted also experienced a lot of frustration. For such a large international event, there was a lack of English speaking people in areas where international people needed them to speak English.

Ted says he would never do this type of trip again. He would plan it in advance.

He would log on to the FIFA web site and try to book tickets as soon as they are available, understand how easy it is to travel between cities...Whether for example trains are available...As well he wouldn't want to travel on his own again....

My trip has been very different to Ted's but I understand all that he says and for my part would prefer to plan future tournaments.

We talk about the Euros in France in 2016...Thousands upon thousands from England let alone all over Europe will travel there. Booking up on a camp site in the South of France and using it as a base to go to matches would be a great way of spending a couple of weeks or more!

World Cup programs are sealed up and sold at newsagent booths. Not publicised...I had no idea...Strange as not seen any programmes at the stadium... Will definitely be trying for a final programme!

EL GRINGO'S ONCE IN A LIFETIME

Finally I make it to the beach in my usual position opposite the Pestana hotel...Must get used to saying Pestana rather than Budweiser Hotel! I take a reclining chair rather than a sun bed.

It is 2.45...Some 2 3/4 hours later than planned...And I am so pleased it is... Isn't fate amazing...It was pure chance that I took the spontaneous decision to walk down to see the fan fest being dismantled. I had no intention of doing so when I reached the beach. Then... When down there to go in the shop for the first time...

Ted joins me on the beach and we reminisce over old times for an enjoyable couple of hours...Comfortable in each other's company, the way old friends can be. I have often joined up with Alan "Tanner" Corton and Graham "Beryl" Berry from Lincolnshire to go to Spurs games. There is that same comfortable feeling which many people all over the world may well relate to. Friends made by people during this World Cup may well develop into these relationships. This is the real "beautiful game" not the PR marketed vision of the "beautiful game".

As the sun begins to say it's farewell for the day, we walk back up on to the promenade...A juggler is doing keepie uppies with an egg...How an earth does he do that!!

I meet Ted at 8pm outside the Marriott Hotel and walk down to Segura Campos metro to Cinelandia station. We walk up to Lapa to the famous Arabic steps for a photo opportunity. There are still people about but it feels a different atmosphere...Still safe but not quite as relaxed as it was before...

Ted tastes his first ever caipirinha off a street vendor. My first caipirinha too... Of the day!

We walk passed the famous and enormous multi arched viaduct and turn a corner on to the Main Street.

I am shocked...There is a restaurant with street art above it. Last week not only was the restaurant full but the huge area in front of it was teeming with people sitting at tables and chairs...Tonight...Not only is the area in front empty but...The restaurant is all locked up...Closed...The owners no doubt having a well-earned holiday!

We walk down to the four bars crossroads...A little busier and still quite early...We walk on to Rio Scenarium...The 500 or 600 metre queues have gone. It is possible to walk straight in...Well it is if you are prepared to pay the 285 reals, nearly £80 entrance fee on a Tuesday night! I look inside and it is almost empty...Price elasticity and supply and demand comes to mind!

Sitting across the street opposite Rio Scenarium, enjoying the live music coming from inside...The lady singing is really very good...but for that money... It would be possible to see Kylie Minogue, have a meal and a couple of beers!

I order a beer...Ted is still drinking his caipirinha. Not sure how keen he is...I have noticed this about caipirinha...It is not a middle of the road drink...Seems a bit like marmite...People either love it or hate it.

It is still quiet here so we head back up to four bars crossroads, we turn right and go into my favourite small live bar, Boemia da Lapa...Tonight 70s rock music is being played...As ever the bar is rocking and we enjoy a couple of beers listening to classics such as Led Zeppelins Stairway to Heaven and Whisky in a Jar by Thin Lizzy.

Sitting outside the bar we get talking to a few of the locals who try to give us instructions to the bus stop...They are very helpful and even draw a map to basically walk down the street opposite and turn right...However the minutes we lost led to us missing the bus and waiting 30 minutes...What is c'est la vie in Portuguese?

As the bus approaches Copacabana on Roberto Ribeiro it branches to the right away from the beach. Ribeiro is already three or four blocks from the front...Could be dangerous to be too much further from the front so we jump off the bus and walk up Prado Junior, yes the road where I had an apartment and walk up to the front. We turn right at Mabbs and walk along Atlantique.

On reaching the square there are quite a lot of guys out drinking...It occurs to me...I haven't eaten since breakfast! We buy a beer for Ted and I have a caipirinha off one street vendor and a kebab stick for Ted and a sausage on a stick for me...

On ordering a second drink we get talking with a guy from Leeds who emigrated to Canada who is in Brazil with his two sons.

He tells me of meeting a lady in a bar in Salvador and being invited back to her house. When he got in the house she locked the door with padlocks which was a little unnerving...But security is security in Brazil... They are in the living area when down the stairs comes a very tall guy of a similar age to him about 45...Wtf!! She introduces him as her son!! This of course must make her about 65!!!!

He also told us of an issue at the open fan fest...About 1000 people had paid

20 reals for a deckchair to watch a match. The screen didn't come on and the vendors refused to repay the 20 reals...Their view being they had rented the chairs out...Not their fault the screen didn't work!

We said our goodbyes to Mr Anglo-Canadian and walk along the front to our accommodation. There are still Argentines sleeping in cars along the front.

We say goodnight and arrange to meet at the Marriott tomorrow night at 8pm.

As I walk back to my hotel, I really feel for Ted...He has done so much travelling and on his own... I am not sure I could have done what he did...In fact I know I couldn't...

I get into bed around 2am...Another superb day and the old adage...You never know what's ahead of you when you get out of bed in the morning comes to mind!

In Austria, we are normally a nation were skiing is the national sport, but big tournaments and our own national team are also very important. So of course the World Cup in Brazil was a big thing for us.

I think the World Cup in general was very good, the group stages in particular were filled with great matches. When it came to the knock-out rounds the tactics became more important, which is always the case when everything is on the line. The 7-1 was of course the most talked about game of the tournament.

As a host, Brazil was as far as I can see special. Football is ingrained in their culture and that was there for everyone to see. Our broadcasting also did a good job in showing other aspects of the World Cup aside from football.

Of course with Germany winning, we all had mixed feelings, because Germany are seen as our big brothers and the relationship between the countries is very competitive especially in sports.

Thomas Dolenc, Vienna, Austria

We in Germany really have been standing behind the German team and there has always been excitement and a good portion of hope in the air and on the streets around.

Even the businesses have changed their working shifts, so that the people could anticipate. The first matches have been really emotional to us, because we have not been sure to win the group games. But after this we have been more confident and looking forward to the playoffs. The greatest surprise was the game against Brazil. From that moment we have had a party in Germany. After we won the World Cup there were people around on the streets the whole night and cars around with flags to celebrate.

Dirk Brakemeier, Hannover, Germany

It was a great experience for me at the World Cup! I met lots of people from many different parts of the world, and shared many experiences and stories with them. It was great to see all the people together in a great atmosphere.

My team Argentina did well to make the final but just couldn't find a goal versus Germany. There were thousands of people from my country singing and cheering in Rio de Janeiro, it was amazing!

Beyond the results obtained by my dear Argentina, I've made good friends and it was good to take lots of souvenirs and gifts home to my family and friends in Santa Fe.

Santiago Buchini, Santa Fe, Argentina

EL GRINGO'S ONCE IN A LIFETIME

WEDNESDAY 16TH JULY 2014

After an early breakfast I head down it the beach. The weather is absolutely glorious. I want to make the most of my last few days in Rio de Janeiro.

On the way down to the beach, I follow Ted's advice and stop to buy World Cup magazines from the news stands. It seems that there aren't match programmes printed ahead of the games but a match report programme dedicated to each match after the game has been played. I buy some and the guy looks after them whilst I am at the beach.

Down on the beach by 10am...Must almost be a record time!

I take a reclining chair rather than a sun bed...It is the usual game of trying to adjust the recliner without falling head over heels on to the beach...The degree of recline is determined by lifting each arm of the chair and moving the arms backwards and catching the metal teeth in the hold at the level of recline you wish to have. Easy eh?

Well I push back...The teeth in the arms don't lock with the mouths in the chair and suddenly I am thrown forward back into an upright position! I look round to see how many people are falling off their own chairs in laughter...Hard to look cool in one of these!!

Eventually I am sorted...

Local lady turns up on the beach with her own chair. Pitches up and reclines smoothly into her preferred position with the day's newspaper to read. What a pleasant way to start the day. Imagine being in your own home...Looking out the window to a blue sky and thinking... Think I will just walk over to Copacabana beach this morning to read the newspaper for a couple of hours!!

There are three young Argentine girls nearby who I learn are from Rosario. If I had my life again...My holidays would definitely be in South America!!

A vendor comes along carrying a huge contraption in the shape of a parasol with loads and loads of bikinis hanging off it. The girls are trying a number of bikinis on and not really paying attention to their bags. Bearing in mind Doug's loss I tell them to take care with their bags...They have been here 12 days and had a great time. They are quite philosophical about the final and having really enjoyed Rio are so glad they came. Later they say goodbye and are heading off to the airport to fly home.

My ears prick up...A Geordie accent nearby talking to another English guy about something that has happened to him.

I walk over and John Paul who has a bandage around his wrist and dreadful skin burns tells me of what happened to him the night Argentina beat Holland on penalties...

Argentina fans were out in force celebrating in Lapa. People spilling out on to the roads...Sounded even crazier than usual...If that is possible!!

The fans were in high spirits and slapping on the windows of cars as they passed along the street. John Paul was crossing the street as the fans slapped the window of a taxi. The driver slammed his foot on the accelerator and hit John

Paul tossing him on to the bonnet. John Paul grabbed hold of the windscreen.

The driver doesn't stop. He is clinging on literally for dear life. His friends and others on the street are chasing the car... He is driving quite quickly and what felt to John Paul a hell of a lot quicker.

After about 50 metres, the driver slammed his breaks on which threw John Paul off the bonnet onto the road. He banged his head but remarkably only suffered a sprained wrist, a stinking headache and severe skin burns on a foot, his lower back and a few other places. The driver then completely panicked and sped off at high speed, mounting pavements in his haste to get away. Fortunately the crowd managed to scatter without any other injuries.

The guy he is talking with who is from Bristol tells a story of an English lad called Sam in a hostel in Brasilia. He woke up in the middle of the night to find a guy in full throttle pleasuring him...The alarm clock is a big enough shock to wake up to...Imagine...Actually I would prefer not to...

John Paul is in full flow now...In Nicaragua, they stayed in a hostel which had a pet female monkey attached to it. The monkey would embrace male guests but wouldn't go near female guests!

One night a guy was making love with his girlfriend and looked up...The monkey had come in through the window and was sat there watching them make love!!

Another night, he woke up to find the monkey pleasuring him!! John Paul says there is a picture on Facebook...The story is bad enough without the visuals!!!

The stories are coming thick and fast now!

With his friends they took a party boat down the Amazon from Colombia. Great experience sleeping on hammocks at night!

The boat in front however was boarded by Police who arrested a guy with five kilos of cocaine. The passengers on both boats felt it was a stitch up...The Police didn't search the boat but went straight to the guy and arrested him. The view was that there is a type of scam whereby a person called a "mule" working on behalf of drug gangs was on the party boat to tip off the Police.

This apparently then diverts attention and allows organised crime gangs to push through much bigger shipments...Not sure whether the view is in collusion with the Police or not...John Paul said many people he had come across on his travels felt that a similar situation had arisen with the girls in Peru...Yes of course they were stupid but that may be they were pawns in a much bigger chess game... Interesting perspective...

John Paul heard of two guys, in separate incidents being robbed at gun point in Manaus...It seems these were related to going off the tourist tracks in search of drugs...

On the way to Recife, they had to stop off in a place called Belem...The third most dangerous city in the world...They were going to walk out on the street.. The receptionist came running out to stop them saying it is not safe... Nobody walks on the streets of Belem! John Paul felt fortunate to come away from Belem only having had his phone stolen!

EL GRINGO'S ONCE IN A LIFETIME

Not related to the World Cup but nevertheless a funny story about a Danish guy in Thailand. He meets an absolutely stunningly beautiful lady. She is very feminine and he feels so proud to have her on his arm. There is a great chemistry between them and they spend the whole day together. During the course of the evening, they have a quite a few to drink and he can't believe his luck when she agrees to come back to his hotel. On the way back to the hotel... She says there is something I must tell you and drops the bombshell that she is a "ladyboy". He had had a drink and when telling the story to John Paul in English but with a very thick Danish accent was making him laugh out loud. The Dane then shocked John Paul by saying... I thought I have come this far I may as well continue! As John Paul said...Some people aren't too fussy!

Bringing the conversation back to the World Cup. We talk of the England legends being seen on and around the beaches. A few lads had a game of beach football with Glenn Hoddle and Alan Shearer!

The Bristol guy says he got to know the guys from the BBC Radio 1 Newsbeat show and he ends up interviewing Alan Shearer for the show!

Postscript to meeting with John Paul...On my return to the UK, I went to the Notts v Hants T20 Quarter Final cricket match at Trent Bridge. I am telling John Paul's Lapa story to a team mate of my son's cricket team Simon Pickerell who is also a Geordie, living in Nottingham, and he says I know a John Paul from Newcastle. I used to go out with his sister...We check on surnames...It is the same John Paul and Simon sends him a message!

I give my chair a pleading look...Please be kind to me on this busy beach... Sadly the chair does not seem to understand a word of English...

I receive a text from Phil in the UK who organises our tickets for Spurs games...Do I want to order a ticket for our first game West Ham United away on 16 August? And so planet football continues to turn.

The sun slips behind the Hotel Pestana ex Budweiser Hotel. It is doing this earlier and earlier as we move deeper into winter. My iPhone battery is down to 8%. It is 4pm and time to leave the beach.

I go to pay the beach chair vendor the 5 reals for my chair and another 5 reals for a coke zero...the drink that is!

For the most part I have coped with the currency fairly well. Coins are in denominations of 5, 10, 25, 50 cents plus 1 real coins.

The notes are in denominations of 2 reals, 5, 10, 20, 50 and 100 notes.

The notes are easy to distinguish except the 2 and 100 real notes which are a similar colour blue... Would be much easier if they made one of them a unique green colour! I do wonder how many times I may have made this mistake during my stay...Just as I nearly did now in paying for the beach chair and drink!!

On the way back I pick up my already paid for World Cup magazines and return to the hotel feeling quite chilled.

It is 4.30 Shower...No hot water...There is cold water but as I turn the mixer tap towards hot...The shower starts to splutter and eventually the flow stops altogether...It gives off the feeling of a horse refusing a fence...Stubborn as a mule...Cold water shower it is...Again...

I come out of the hotel and turn right away from the beach to head up to the lake for sunset. The Fire station is next door to the hotel...I wonder how they would cope with a fire on the 15th floor...And then wish I hadn't seen the Fire station to put the thought in my head!!

It is a good 10 minutes walk to the lake...I go up a hill and down the other side. The hill is notable as it makes me realise how flat Ipanema and Copacabana are! It isn't a particularly pleasant walk with a myriad of busy roads to cross #needyourwitssboutyou.

Eventually I am by the side of the lake.

There is dual pathway round the edge of the lake which is being used by runners, cyclists, walkers, mothers pushing prams etc

Pedalos are on the lake in the shape of large white swans which give off a feeling of serenity.

To my right high up above is a side profile of Christ the Redeemer sitting atop Corcovado. Red tail lights of the many vehicles start to appear around the lake as the sun sets on yet another brilliant day.

People are receiving exercise classes on the grassy verge...All around the lake; there is greenery in the water and on the water's edge... A few ducks are gliding close to the water's edge.

I go out onto a small jetty for photographs. There is a very relaxed feel to being around the lake...I can feel it enveloping me.

Looking around the edge of the lake, there are numerous sporting options available including tennis courts and a five a side pitch. There is also a park, an open air bar with red awnings which contrasts with the white apartments on all sides of this massive lake. The walk around the entire lake would be more than seven km!

There is a helicopter launch pad on the opposite side of the lake and helicopters are occasionally passing by overhead.

Behind the launch pad, jagged dark mountains form a magnificent backdrop behind which there is a pink milky sunset forming through fluffy light clouds...

As the sun sets, lights from the lakeside apartments begin to reflect off the water's surface as do the orange glow of the street lamps. It creates a fabulous view for photographs.

Favela lights begin to twinkle on the lower reaches of the mountain slopes... Particularly the mountain which is a much much smaller version of Vesuvius ...Gentle slopes rising up both sides but with the last third much steeper to the summit.

Right now, it really feels an "in the moment" place to be...

Well...Except for the incessant blaring of an emergency vehicle stuck in traffic somewhere behind me!

People are out walking their dogs...It has an upmarket feel about it...The air is still...A lovely temperature...Not hot, not cold no wind...Just perfect...

I feel very relaxed and chilled...There is a lady sat on a small rectangular wooden jetty...Legs crossed looking out across the lake...It would make a wonderful place to meditate...

Now the night sky is closing in...The mountains look increasingly dark in contrast to the artificial lights which are increasing in brightness.

Christ is now floodlit in his more usual white lights rather than the red yellow and black of Germany ...The red and yellow looked to me as if Christ had been subsumed by the devil!!

Rio really is a most special beautiful city. In some ways I have found myself here. I don't feel the need to be with anyone. I have inner peace here...It's a lovely feeling.

It is 5.56...The Pedalos are starting to turn into shore...I assume for a 6pm closure...Must be so tranquil out there on the lake.

A helicopter comes into land across the lake almost directly opposite me.

It is just after 6pm and I turn to return back towards Copacabana. There are a myriad of lanes to cross. If ever bridges or a pedestrian underpass was ever needed it is here...The traffic is very busy and the cars and buses come speeding passed...

Safely across the roads I walk back up the hill and down the other sides.

Now I am crossing Roberto Ribeiro heading down Miguel Lemos...The tunnel where Perg was mugged is almost a stone's throw away to my right. The grey white and yellow omnibuses are out in force as are the bright yellow taxis, motorbikes and cars...It is rush hour... And the noise of the traffic is incessant.

I walk towards the beach to see if any more wall murals were painted since the final.

On reaching the front a large street market has been set up in the central reservation between the two dual carriageways!

I walk through the market and its good to see post World Cup prices are in place...The Television Centre at the end of Copacabana is being dismantled... There is traffic passing and pedestrians walking beneath...Surely the road will have to close at some point!

It is a worthwhile journey...After completing the Klose painting...Underneath the artist has painted two Brazilian players slumped to their knees...

Alongside, the artist had then drawn the flags showing Germany v Argentina. The paintings are showing an unfolding story of the World Cup. The next painting to the right on the wall heading towards the promenade is a group of five German players holding the World Cup aloft. The words Jambeiro 2014 written to the side with a trail of the Brazilian yellow and green to the right. It looks very impressive.

A mild form of anxiety is creeping in. I leave in 46 hours...Truthfully I don't want to...I am happy here...But also I feel a shortage of time pressure... There are a number of places still to visit and some shopping I need to do...Yes I know!!! I have been here almost five weeks!

As ever people are out walking...Any time of the day Copacabana is just the most vibrant place to be. If you don't have it on your bucket list...Put it on your list. If it is already on your list...Elevate it...Because it is a place you are more than likely to want to come back to!

I stop off at the Bradesco Bank to withdraw funds from my Post Office MasterCard. It only allows me to withdraw 500 reals...Cash is now tight...Any cash top up on the card will only be available from 10am on Friday which is the night I fly back to the UK...May be I will have to try to withdraw cash on the new credit card. If it works though...Will be expensive...

The phone won't charge at all...The battery is dead. I don't feel comfortable in just turning up at Aline's to use or borrow her charger. I go back down the 15 floors again and head out in search of a phone accessories shop.

After three attempts I find a shop and we test the charger cable to make sure it isn't a problem with the phone. All is good and for 20 reals...Problem solved!

Time is marching on...Back down in the lift and a jog to meet Ted...Arrive at 8.10pm and thankfully Ted is still waiting. I ask if he would like to have a look round the street market I saw earlier and he would. We buy quite a lot of stuff...I spend about 800 reals ...Two worries come to mind now...Cash...I only have about 500 reals...And secondly how will I get all of the stuff that I have bought back to the UK...Towels for example are heavy and bulky...Hmmm

After dropping stuff off at the hotel and finally getting some food as Ted has never had a drink at a beach promenade bar...We head there. It's as ever a lovely night to be sat outside at a beach bar at midnight with a caipirinha. Life can't get much better than this - except we can see the fan fest being dismantled.

After a couple of drinks we head back towards the busy Rua Bolivar to have a couple of drinks at a bar closer to Ted's apartment and my hotel.

On the way, a lady with a French accent starts talking with us. She asks if we mind her joining us for a drink... I ask if she is on the program and she doesn't have a clue what I am talking about.

She is called Alice, lives in Paris but is originally from Rio. She has come back for a couple of weeks to stay with her parents where she is walking back to having had dinner with friends in Leblon.

We order drinks in a bar...I can't stop drinking caipirinha at the moment!! Alice leads us into a heavyweight political discussion about Palestine and what is going on in Gaza. As important as it is...At this time of night on Teds last night, we are not really wanting to get into such a difficult debate.. We then move onto a debate about Brazil, the merits of having the World Cup here and her view that the economy is strong and in good order.

I write all this because then she outrageously offers sex for 50 reals about £14...Plus 20 reals for a taxi back to her parents!!! Jaw dropping!! I challenge her about being on the program and she says she isn't a prostitute...Ummm... What do you call someone who offers sex for money...Goodnight Alice...

I say my goodbyes to Ted, wish him a good journey home and look forward to meeting up for a beer in the UK.

EL GRINGO'S ONCE IN A LIFETIME

We were in Brazil from the last 16 through to the Final and stayed in Rio De Janeiro Centro so we always travelled from Rio to the others Cities. We had a subway just one block away that was perfect!!! We went from Rio to Sao Paulo by bus for the last 16 match of Argentina vs Switzerland.The journey took six hours through the night and the seats were very comfortable, like beds, but it was impossible to sleep because the driver was crazy...Speeding and the route was through the mountains...so scary!!

The night we arrived we went to a city called Villa Magdalena and it was one of the best nights ever!! We were thousands and thousands of Argentinians together, singing jumping drinking so crazy all night long. There were TV cameras and newspaper journalists...It was unbelievable!!!!!

The next day was the game and we won!!

We then went to Brasilia for the quarters Finals Argentina vs Belgica, we flew there took and it took one hour and half from Rio de Janeiro. This was the happiest moment I had. In 24 years Argentina doesn't pass to the semi-finals, so when we won it was unbelievable, everybody was crying and hugging together because finally we got through to the semis.

Another priceless moment was in the Rio fan fest Semi Final vs Holland for the penalty shoot-out. Everybody was on their knees, putting arms over each other's shoulders to watch...the screaming, praying to pass to the final. After the penalties everybody crying on the sand, don't even thinking getting dirty, just celebrating and celebrating.........

The scariest moment was when we were in the Rio fan fest for the Brazil vs Germany game. The first fan fest was full so we been in the second Fan Fest which was packed too!!! Amazing......after the fifth goal people started fighting each other Brazilian vs Brazilian, we were in the middle of the crowd... the people started running, then the police came wading in to try to stop the fighting so people scared and going in to the water. They makes a "stampede" that was scary because we didn't know what's going to happen. I think was my fastest 200 meters run ever.....! Nothing bad happened but watching all the people falling and running, jumping in the water I'll never forget the people stampede......

The saddest moment of the trip was when we had too many opportunities to score in the final game and then in the end Germany scored and we lost the FINAL of the WORLD CUP we were so close to be champions........so was the saddest moment!!!!!

Sebastian Fernandez, Temperley City, Buenos Aires
and Miguel Orona, La Ferrere City, Buenos Aires, Argentina

From a global point of view, the success of the competition was a great pleasure for me. So many people were predicting that the country would not be ready to welcome the cup.

From a French perspective, the first thing was (like all other French people) forget the 2010 disaster, which was a pain deep in our heart. In that area, I think Didier Deschamps managed his team in such a way that it was a success.

The second point was to create the basis for a new team with young talented players in the perspective of the 2016 European Cup in France and the 2018 World Cup in Russia. In this second area, I do believe Deschamps was successful as well.

Lastly, in terms of results, it was not so bad: we were defeated by Germany 1-0 in the Quarter Final, the winners and by the same score as the one Germany did against Argentina in the Final....

Jean-Luc Chantran, Paris, France.

THURSDAY 17TH JULY 2014

I wake at 9.40...There is a message from Aline to say picking me up at 9.30...Oh dear...But as I stumble to get ready, another text comes in...Fortunately Nikki the puppy has delayed her...Phew!

After just making breakfast, Aline picks me up just outside the hotel at Cantagalo station and we head off towards Pedra Bonita Mountain.

We drive up as far as we can before parking the car to walk the rest of the way.

Aline takes me up to the paragliding station first...Walking up I am thinking... This is steep and only the warm up to the hike...Perhaps last night's caipirinhas weren't such a good idea...

At the station we stand just behind a lady who attached to her guide effectively jumps off a mountain!

I get talking with a German guy, Wolfgang who is waiting for his turn to jump off a mountain...People actually pay to do this!

Wolfgang had managed to get to see all Germany's games but didn't have a ticket for a final...Then two hours before the game he receives an email from a friend in Africa saying that a friend in Rio has a spare ticket and does he want it!!! Wolfgang gets a final ticket for 2200 rials!

Amazingly, Wolfgang who has travelled across Brazil to see the games has only had to pay to stay in a hotel one night and stayed with friends on all other nights! It just goes to show...You can never have too big a network!

His travels have been relatively incident free but was taken aback in Salvador when seeing an argument between a bus driver and a guy on the street. The Bus driver couldn't get by the guy's car...The guy who was drunk pulled a gun... It turns out he is an off duty policeman and being drunk and pulling a gun on people is quite normal!!

We are required to sign in before starting our hike as people previously lost their way on a nearby hike and it took three days to find them...

The hike up Pedra Bonita, translation Beautiful Rock, is 1257m which is 693m above sea level.

The average hike time is 35 minutes...Fortunately; the trees and their branches shade most of the sunlight as we climb a kind of well-trodden path. There is a feeling of tranquillity and peacefulness amongst the trees in the forest. The silence is from time to time punctuated by the sounds of birds singing and the distant voices of fellow walkers muted by the dense undergrowth.

It is hot work though walking through the forest and my shirt is soon soaked. Further on, the trail steepens and becomes more uneven...And hard on the breathing...

Walking up through the denseness it is quite a contrast to walk out on to a panoramic vista, as in the words of the song, above us only sky...And gulp in the fresh air.

We are on a plateau on top of Pedra Bonita. Looking straight ahead of us is Pedra da Gavea, Rock of Gavea which is higher and where the walkers were lost for three days...

To our left, stretching out before us is the most fabulous panoramic view imaginable!

Working across from left to right is Christ the Redeemer sitting proudly on top of Corcovado then nearer in the foreground, the "Dois Irmaos Mountain..."Two Brothers" mountain with favelas nestling within its foothills, further behind is Botofogo and Copacabana, the lake, Ipanema and immediately below us is São Conrado bay, beyond which is the vast blue Atlantic Ocean. Below us, we see a paraglider begin its downward descent and out across the ocean, the bright colours of another paraglider working its way back in to land.

It is an absolutely breathtaking view...Just stunning...and that is before I look across to our right!!

We walk across the plateau...There is a breeze...No railings...Best not to get too close to the edge!! There are a few groups of people sitting down, having a beer and just taking in, absorbing the majesty of the 360 degrees panoramic views.

Across to our right the forest gives way to a number of lakes, some large and interspersed by clusters of apartment blocks. To the left of the lakes is downtown Barra Tijuca and smaller lakes and the white beach which stretches it out for as far as the eye can see. With a mountain range to the right which seems to bank around in the far distance, it makes for a quite stunning setting.

The walk down is much quicker...Fifteen minutes or so...Can't think why! The smell is of trees and soil... Of hundreds of years of history... Red and pink flowers decorate the dense greenery. Even allowing for the heat it feels a special experience to walk through the forest

We stop on the way down at a sightseeing point. For some reason, a man has chosen to shadow-box train here...It's one of those moments which makes you feel a little uncomfortable #isheacrank?

We go up some steps for a view out across the ocean and the islands. The brightness of hand gliders and paragliders decorate the view. We walk down a path alongside the road and have a view right up to where we have been including the paraglider station. It looks a long way up but Beautiful Rock is a very apt name.

As we drive along São Conrado beach, memories from many years ago flood back, when I stayed at the International Hotel and met the Boca Juniors team, Riquelme et al ahead of a Copa Libertadores match, I think against Vasco da Gama,

EL GRINGO'S ONCE IN A LIFETIME

We drive around the point and pass Vidigal favela on our left which, as has been said, must have a quite amazing view of the coastline on either side of the favela.

We stop for a drink at the start of Leblon, a view of Vidigal favela with the Sheraton on one side and Leblon on the other...Rio is just amazing...It doesn't have one or two special views, not even ten or twenty...just loads and loads and loads...

The waves are crashing upon the rocks in front of us...Leblon beach stretches out ahead of us... An electronic sign says the temperature is 27 degrees... The beach is busy...Parasols, flags fluttering in the breeze, beach chairs, sun beds...

Aline says that Leblon, the lake and Urca are where the rich tend to live... A house could cost up to 4m reals around Guanabara Bay, Urca where the Olympic water events will take place...Although the Rio Mayor, Perez has already said that the pollution will not be cleaned in time for the Games!

We pass the marina hotel which splits Leblon from Ipanema... I learn that the literal translation of Ipanema is "stinky lake"...No wonder they only translated half of the song title Garota de Ipanema...The Girl from the Stinky Lake wouldn't have quite caught on so well!

We are now driving along Rainha Elizabeth which is the corridor between Ipanema and Copacabana and then we are back onto the four kilometre beach of Copacabana Balneario, seaside resort.

Having learnt about Ipanema, we decide to check the heritage of Copacabana and are surprised to learn that until the mid-18th Century, the district was called "Sacopenapa" which means "the way of the socos" a type of bird... How appropriate...The way of the birds and types of birds....Copacabana today haha

The name Copacabana originally comes from the name of a Bolivian town on Lake Titicaca which had a chapel built in honour of a sculpture of the patron saint which was associated with a miracle.

A replica of the chapel was built in Rio on Sacopenapa and as a result it was decided to change the name to Copacabana...I had no idea and suspect not many of us visiting Copacabana for the World Cup did either!

As we pass Prado Junior, I think back to last night and recognise that I felt some sadness being back in the area...Trying to understand why...?

We are heading towards Vasco which is 25km away to visit the football stadium of Aline's favourite team...Vasco da Gama. On the way I mention seeing Brazilian league games on the television at nights this week and Aline says the league had a mid-season break for the World Cup and has restarted straight afterwards. Only two players from the Brazilian squad play in the League...One being Fred who not surprisingly has asked to miss a few games as he needs a rest and the other being a reserve goalkeeper.

We are in the north of the city here and I can feel Aline's excitement as we turn on to Rua São Januario where the Vasco São Januario stadium is. As with all football supporters she has a sense of pride at showing her club and stadium to someone for the first time. She is enjoying parking in her usual spot...The pre match rituals...No doubt memories of many matches coming back to her!

The outside of the stadium is like the front of a row of old stately houses...

EL GRINGO'S ONCE IN A LIFETIME

Almost presidential.

We go into the club shop to find that a sale is on...The queues are very long.

It is possible to enter the stadium through the club shop...No issues...People can come and go as they please...There are a number of fans scattered around in the seats...The club feels very much a part of the community. Behind one goal is a statue of Romario...There is a feeling of spaciousness in the stadium...The stadium holds around 20000 and there is a small section for the away fans. It costs around 20 reals to enter the stadium behind the goal and c40 reals on the side.

While we are taking photographs, amazingly, the players come out onto the pitch to train...

I see the trophy room but it is closed. Looking through the window, it is full and the size of some of the cups...Wouldn't want to be lifting one of those after extra time and penalties!

Opposite the trophy room there is a second shop and I buy a couple of shirts for my boys. Aline is delighted to imagine Vasco da Gama shirts being worn in England!

We jump back into the car to beat the rush hour traffic I look at her and say... You owe me...Aline laughs and says...Yes, yes, we will come to Tottenham!

On arriving back at Aline's at 4.40pm, agreeing it has been a truly amazing day, we say goodbye and I set off along Copacabana to Leme to see the bears at the far end.

I can't believe this is my last night...I don't want it to be my last night!

On reaching the fan fest area, with the entertainment centres having been removed, the site looks enormous...

By the main screen, which is in the process of being dismantled, I walk passed the security guard on to the site...No problem... I ask for a piece of sheeting with FIFA World Cup logo...The guy is very helpful and we try to reach in a skip. It is getting dark though and I would like to see the sunset over Copacabana. The guy says no problem and to call back in on the way back.

On passing the Windsor Hotel, I leave Copacabana and am now in Leme. It strikes me that I haven't walked along the front past the Windsor into Leme in all of my time in Rio! I walk up on to the rocks at Leme which as you look out to the Atlantic Ocean is on the far left of the four kilometre beach. Towards the furthest point on the rock there are a lot of fishermen.

I am running out of superlatives to describe a view...It is amazing... To the right high up above the hotels and apartments, Christ the Redeemer is looking down upon us.

The view is beyond Copacabana and even beyond Ipanema and Two Brothers Mountain. The sky is turning a mellow pink and beyond there is a tinge of orange as the last embers of the sun melt away.

The sunset is reflecting back off the ocean and water's edge, creating a shiny finish to the wet sand beneath.

Waves are crashing onto the rocks beneath me...Surfers, clutching their surf boards, are jumping off the rocks into the sea......

I walk down from the rock...There is a circle of bear statues ahead of me. They are about two metres high and each one is unique and representing each of the different countries within the United Nations.

There is a free open air gym. Fixed equipment such as cross trainers, bench presses...

The bears are quite a tourist attraction. Beyond the circle is a long line of bears along the promenade with their backs to the beach. They are in country alphabetical order. Not sure why countries are depicted as bears as opposed to people or other animals but the essence is "We need to get to know each other better to understand each other better, to trust each other and live together peacefully together".

The gathering of nations for the World Cup has certainly achieved this. The camaraderie amongst the fans, the party atmosphere has, for me, been one of the major plusses. I might even have hopefully changed the views of a few Argentines about the English!

As I walk along the line, the 141 bears are very colourful and each one is unique...Some are very funny such as the Cuban bear which has a cigar in its mouth and the Irish which has a pipe. The United States bear is mimicking the Statue of Liberty and even painted in the same dark green colour.

Back to the rock, the mountains now form a very dark backdrop...Night has fallen and the artificial lights shine brightly all the way around the crescent bay, bouncing off the water's edge, lighting up the white surf as it reaches the end of its journey and hits the shore...Talking of journeys, it hits me that the next sunset I will see...Will be from the airport....#sad

I walk back along the promenade to the fan fest, passed security and back into the darkened fan fest...In England, it would be impossible...Health and

Safety...Induction, PPE etc etc...Guys are still working but it must be an hour and a half since I was last here and I suspect the guy who was helping me has gone home for the day...

Suddenly the need for money hits me, as it does most of us for most of the time! In this regard though, it is the need to withdraw some cash...I am a little anxious...Will the bank machines still be working and if they are...Will the new credit card work...

I leave the promenade and turn up Rua Duvivier and remember where the

Bradesco Bank is...Turn right on to Nossa Senhora towards Prado junior and go into Bradesco.. All works perfectly...Relief!!

I walk back the way I came...Saw a Bossa Nova music shop on Duvivier and go in to buy a couple of CDs...Chill: Brazil which is an excellent CD and well chosen by Bruno behind the counter...It really captures the spirit of Rio de Janeiro! I also buy "Perfil", translated as "Profile" by the Daddy of Bossa Nova, the man who brought the girl of Ipanema to life, Tom Jobim.

As I am paying Bruno, I notice a stunning tattoo on his wrist...I am not really a tattoo fan but this is such a stunning work of art I ask to take a photograph.

Bruno says it is of his father who is delighted with it... If you are in the area, even if you don't wish to buy a CD, I urge you to visit the shop...The tattoo is a tourist attraction in its own right!

Walking back up the promenade I negotiate a replica World Cup from a vendor for 30 reals...Blimey three different ones bought now...Three stars for England... I wish!!

After the street market purchases of the last couple of nights, I am now very much in negotiate and buy mode...I buy an Argentina shirt for my youngest with Messi number 10 on the back...Feel it would be wrong not to take something of Argentina back...Their Italia 90 song still plays on a loop in my mind...Although I have to say that I am pleased not to have heard it on Copacabana for some days now...Would be great to create a Spurs song from the tune though!!

The guy I buy the shirt from is from Chile... He tells me that Pinilla who almost scored a last minute winner against Brazil has had a tattoo of the crossbar he hit on his back!

The World Cup may have finished but at 8pm the promenade is alive... Guitarists playing at the beach side cafés...Tourists are here but also, I have the feeling a lot of Carioca...Locals...May be returning to their apartments post World Cup...Enjoying their city again and what a wonderful city it is... Enjoying the normality without having thousands of football fans dominating their neighbourhood...

There is a guy on the promenade selling tours. He offers a four hour favela tour for the morning...I don't have four hours...Just want a couple of hours at most...After some discussion, I shake hands with Walter who will give me a personal two hour guided tour of Rosina favela 8.30 till 10.30 for 30 reals. Walter will meet me in my hotel lobby at 8.30...Wow that it is great news and at this stage, it feels somewhat fortuitous to have stumbled into Walter!

I can't resist one more visit to the street market and buy some jewellery for my daughter.

Back to the hotel, I jump into the shower...It is freezing cold...Again...Feels as if I have been having cold showers forever...Is it really so difficult?

Tonight I am invited for dinner at Luiz and Aline's with Jessica and am on way now for what is a lovely way to spend my last night in Rio.

I had asked my German friend, Florian Harnau, who I met whilst staying up to see the sunrise on Copacabana, if he would kindly send me a summary of his travels across Brazil in his camper van. At the time of course, I didn't know Germany would win the World Cup! His summary has arrived and I trust you agree is a quite fabulous read:

EL GRINGO'S ONCE IN A LIFETIME

A short summary of our trip to the World Cup in Brazil from 11th June until 14th July 2014:

We started our trip on 11th of June 2014, we took the plane from Zurich, Switzerland to Lisboa, Portugal, and then from Lisboa to Rio de Janeiro. It was great to see all the other fans with the shirts and flag of their country, such a nice atmosphere at the airport and inside the plane.

In Rio we checked in our hostel in Botofogo, and have a couple of drinks in bars.

At the next morning we started our trip from Rio to Salvador, the first station of the German team. We drove with our VW T2 bus name "Guenther", we decorated our bus with flags and stickers in the German colours, and it looked really nice.

In every town between Rio and Salvador the Brazilian people cheered us and they were really friendly and nice to us, for example in a small town they invited us for a spontaneous barbecue, and took a lot of pictures with us and our bus and flags.

In Salvador we had a really nice apartment directly on the beach, on an island before Salvador; to come to Salvador we took the ferry boat. Salvador was absolutely great, a really exotic city nice decorated with a lot of flags and a beautiful old town in the colonial style.

The stadium was also really nice a lot of German fans at the first match against Portugal and a fantastic start in the tournament for our team, 4-0 against Portugal! After the match we had a great party in the old town and market place of Salvador.

After four days in Salvador we drove with our Bus to Fortaleza, the next "match city" of the German team. On our way to Fortaleza it was the same, in every town the Brazilian people, cheered us, in a small town for example we changed our shirts with the Brazilians, we signed their shirts and caps because a few of them thought we are an official delegation of the German football association. Our decorated VW Bus and our self-designed flag became really attractions for the people in the small towns. They often said that we were the first tourists who stopped in their towns.

In Fortaleza we had a really nice apartment again, only for our group a house with pool big garden etc. The match against Ghana was really exciting, and ended 2-2 it was a fair result, the team of Ghana played really well. In Fortaleza the way to the stadium was really interesting, you're passed a favela, but the people were really friendly and sold beer, other drinks and snacks to the thousands of fans, who passed their street. It was really nice to see, that the poor people could earn a little money, so they had at least a bit profit from the World Cup, but I also understand the critic of the people, there were a lot of things which go wrong in Brazil.

In Fortaleza we watched also the game Greece vs. Ivory Coast, in the second half it was a really dramatic match, Greece won with a penalty in the last minute of the game and went to the next round. Our group stood between the Greece Fans, and we had a big party with them.

We took the plane from Fortaleza to Recife, the city of the next match against the USA. Our Brazilian friend Carla drove our bus from Fortaleza to Recife. The weather in Recife was really bad, a lot of rain and water in the city, we needed round about four hours for our way from the city to the stadium. It was such a chaos in the city, traffic breakdown. We entered the stadium in Recife while the teams came in; at the beginning of the match the stadium was almost half full. It was a really tough match against the US but Germany won 1-0! After the match we had a great party with the US Fans, because the US achieved the next round too! It was singing and cheering in the rain, but really funny!

After the match in Recife we took the plane to the water falls of Iguaçu, such an incredible wonder of nature, it was high water so it was really spectacular! We stayed three days in Iguaçu it was a really nice contrast to the world Cup.

After our days in Iguaçu we took the night bus to Porto Alegre, the next station of the German team against Algeria. Porto Alegre was a big contrast to the cities in the north of Brazil; it was much more like in Europe, because a lot of people in Porto Alegre have ancestors in Germany, Italy, and Poland etc. In Porto Alegre all the German fans met each other at the central market place and then we walked all together to the stadium with music and singing, it was really great, a lot of Brazilians in Porto Alegre supported Germany because their grandfathers immigrated from Germany to Brazil, so it was a good atmosphere for the German team in Porto Alegre!

The match against Algeria was really exciting, it was really tough and we have to play the overtime to beat Algeria 2-1! After the match we had also a nice party in Porto Alegre, a lot of great bars and night clubs! And the steaks are also really delicious!

While we stayed in Iguaçu and Porto Alegre our friend Carla drove our bus during one week from Recife to Rio de Janeiro.

After our match in Porto Alegre we took the night bus to Florianopolis, a nice city with beautiful beaches. We stayed there for one night and afterwards we took the plane to Rio de Janeiro our next station against France!

It was our first match in the Maracana stadium, for every football fan it is fantastic to be in this stadium, it is a really special place but the spirit of the old Maracana is gone, similar like in Wembley!

Against France it was also a really tough and exciting match, but a fantastic atmosphere in the stadium, there were a lot of German Fans and it was a "home match" for the German team! We won 1-0, our goalkeeper Neuer was so fantastic and saved the result for us!

After the match we watched together with thousands of Brazilians their match against Colombia a really nice experience!

During the following days we had a lot of sightseeing in Rio, such an unbelievable city!

And we also met our Brazilian friend Carla with our VW Bus again! On

our last day before Rio to Belo Horizonte for the next match we visited the famous "Sugar Mountain" in Rio, what an amazing view over the city! But we had a big problem, we parked our VW bus on a wrong place so the Police took our bus with a truck away to the central place in Rio were they take all the cars which are parking on a wrong place! It was near the Sambadrome of Rio! So we had a lot of discussions with officers to get our bus free, but after four hours and with the help of two young German journalists we got our bus back! Really exciting experience!

But during driving back to our hotel in Copacabana we had problems with our car and we had to stop at Avenida Atlantique near Copacabana, for the Brazilian people it was really funny to see how we had to leave our German bus with all the flags and put it on the side of the street, cause it was 2 days before the semi-final against Brazil!

But finally we were able to ask a mechanico to repair our bus; this was a really exciting day!

After the days in Rio we drove with our bus to Belo Horizonte, the next station of the German team against Brazil! On the way to Belo Horizonte we had another technical problem with our bus, but we were also able to find some Brazil mechanicos who helped us to repair the bus, really nice and friendly people!

The match against Brazil was unbelievable, at the beginning it was an overwhelming atmosphere, 55.000 Brazilian fans vs. 5.000 German fans, and we had no chance at the beginning to come through with our songs, because the Brazil fans were so loud!

But the first 30 minutes of that match were historic, five goals against Brazil in such a short time we couldn`t believe it, was really unreal! After that first half time you only hear the German fans singing! 7-1 the final result it was like a dream! But after the match we had no problems with the Brazil fans, we went also to the city and had a big party everything was peaceful, no problem!

After this unbelievable match we went back to Rio our final station, a dream became true to be in the final and support our German team against Argentina in the Maracana stadium! In the city there stayed so many Argentinian fans it was a fantastic atmosphere in the city! The night before the final I couldn`t sleep I was so excited! For our group who started 4 weeks ago in Rio it was like a dream to achieve the final!

The final match was really tough again, Argentina played very well and they had a really strong defence so it wasn`t easy for our team to score! But I will never forget this moment in the 113 minute! Mario Goetze scored the 1-0 for Germany, in our German fan sector it was unbelievable, great emotions between screaming cheering and crying, everything! You can also see a lot of older German Fans crying, because they travelled to every world Cup since our last title in 1990 so for them it was also a really great experience to achieve the title in Brazil after 24 years!

After the final we had a beach party at the Copacabana with a lot of German fans until the next morning!

For our group it was an unforgettable journey four and a half weeks in Brazil with a happy end for the German team, everything was great there! And with our bus we see so much more from the country!

On the next day the 14th of July we left Rio and Brazil, a fantastic journey ended!

I hope you can understand and like my small essay about our trip to Brazil! From Germany:

Florian Harnau (that's me) from Salem (near Lake Constance) in South Germany and the rest of our group! FC Bayern München fan!

Benjamin Moser, Thaddaeus Sitta, Dmitri Karpekin, also from Lake Constance in South Germany!

Michael Kunzman from Cologne

EL GRINGO'S ONCE IN A LIFETIME

Soren Peschke and Ralf Hausmann from Hannover
And our Brazilian friend Carla from Frankfurt am Main
And Guenther our great old VW bus

What an amazing story from Florian! I am completely in awe of how well planned the adventure was...Even down to having a Brazilian driver take the bus without them for certain parts of the journey. And for those guys what a finale...To see the Quarter Final in the Maracana versus France, the unforgettable semi-final versus Brazil and then... Topped off by beating Argentina in the Maracana in the World Cup Final in Brazil!! How many of us dare to dream such an experience!

A truly "Once in a Lifetime" experience!!

Having read Florian's adventure, and by the way how kind of him to write it for me and in English... What a guy! I set off from my hotel with a spring in my step to see my fabulous Brazilian friends Aline, Luiz and Jessica for dinner and what will be a lovely but sad last supper...

On arriving at the apartment, the first thing the guys do is help me with my KLM check in and print off the documents through their laptop. It should be easy but alas...

I am English, KLM is a Dutch airline, I am in Brazil.... So why have KLM written to me in Italian???

I book an upgrade to have more leg room...It is all very confusing...I end up with more leg room on the Amsterdam to Birmingham flight rather than Rio to Amsterdam! #notneeded...

Luiz tells me that Scolari resigned Tuesday...No interviews have been given since his interview on the day of the third place playoff when he intended to stay. The CBF announced that his contract would not be reviewed so it seems he effectively jumped before he was pushed. We talk of who might replace him and they would still prefer a foreign manager as there aren't really any outstanding Brazilian candidates...I ask about Dunga...They say absolutely no chance...Not liked at all...Looks like it will be a foreign manager #shame

The CBF have appointed a new coordinator, Gilmar Rinaldi, who will choose the manager. Earlier is his career he was the backup goalkeeper to Taffarel... Rinaldi has stated that he won't hire a foreign coach...Hmmm

People are criticising his appointment as he is an agent for football players. The view is that even though he has said he will stop being an agent, he will still look after his own players...

It could be worse for them...they could be English...England have dropped to 20th in the World rankings....

We talk about our visit to Vasco da Gama's stadium...There is some banter between Luiz who supports Flamengo and Aline! I am intrigued by the name Vasco da Gama and ask the origins of the name...After many others had failed, Vasco da Gama of Portugal became the first explorer to successfully pass round the Cape of Good and reach India...A ten month voyage which successfully finished in July 1497. He was therefore the first man to link Europe with Asia by sea...I didn't expect to learn so much history when setting off on my two week World Cup visit!! Hundreds of years later, on 21st August 1898, Portuguese immigrants settling in Brazil formed a football team in Rio de Janeiro and named the club in his honour! The club badge has a sailing ship on its crest and there is a bust of Vasco da Gama within the stadium. Great story!

After a delicious fish dinner, Luiz, Aline and Jessica give me a present of a framed photograph of us at Urca with some lovely words on the back which cause a wave of emotion...They have become very good friends and in such a short space of time.

They are now convincing me to come back for New Year's Eve...Two million attend the firework display on Copacabana beach...Wow!

Aline and Jessica are now looking at flights for me to return and have found some reasonably priced Boxing Day flights returning 4th January...Birmingham via Paris to Rio...I know that route! They are now looking for apartments!

Over a beer, Luiz tells me of an interview given a year ago by Paul Breitner, an ex-German full back. At the time the interview did not receive much publicity... The key points of the interview were that after being knocked out at the group stage of the 2000 to 2004 Euros, the whole organisation was changed. He thought that Brazil were similarly falling behind now and that Germany would win the World Cup. The interview is now being seen as very prophetic and is being widely discussed in Brazil.

I say how big the fan fest looked today and Luiz looks up some facts...42000 square meters, a 20000 capacity and the screen size was 150 square meters.

News is coming through of a Malaysian plane being shot down over Ukraine ...295 people suspected dead...Before the flight a Dutch guy who boarded the plane took a photograph and posted it on Facebook saying .. This is what the aircraft looks like in case it disappears...

Paul has sent me a WhatsApp with Bradders at Lords and India have taken the score from 145/7 to from 290/9...England just can't seem to finish teams off...I also hear that Ferdinand, who I met on Ipanema just six days ago has signed for QPR...No surprise there!

The night is drawing to an end...Aline and Jessica arrange to see me tomorrow afternoon on Copacabana beach after my favela visit. Luiz will be at work tomorrow so this is it...We say our goodbyes...Fabulous memories created and Luiz says they will definitely come to England next year...I say I will hold you to that!

Aline insists on her opening the door rather than me... It seems to be a custom to make sure that a person returns.

EL GRINGO'S ONCE IN A LIFETIME

I walk Jessica to Barata Ribeiro and wait for a taxi with her...It is 1.30am and I decide to walk the six blocks back to my hotel...

May be because I am sober, may be because there are hardly any people on the streets, may be because ordinarily I walk along Avenida Atlantique which is much more open, may be because it is my last night and it would be a sad way to end the holiday but...I feel uneasy walking back to my hotel.. There isn't a specific reason to feel this way... There isn't any one around who looks remotely interested in me...But maybe I too should have taken a taxi...

I arrive back at the hotel and ask reception to give me a wakeup call at 7.30 and as I finish my diary for the day...The time is 2.08am.

The World Cup in Brazil was the best we've seen in 20 odd years…Good goals from all the teams and the team that deserved it won the World Cup. Here in Cyprus we all love football and we really enjoyed it. Hope to see England do better in the Euro's!

Costa and Staso Ioannou, Cyprus

For New Zealand the World Cup exists as two separate things. For our national team and their supporters the qualifiers are our World Cup Finals. If we qualify, we've won, with no expectations beyond that. That's happened twice, gloriously back in 1982 when we defeated arch-rivals Australia along the way, and in 2010 when we had a much easier path. In 2010 we finished the World Cup as the only unbeaten team, but only by playing embarrassingly defensive football.

This time round we tried to play more attacking football in the qualifiers and were undone by Mexico. So there was some interest in how Mexico fared in the finals and some satisfaction that we were beaten by a team that went on and played well themselves. But other than that, without a national team to support we were neutral or adopted a team based on ancestral heritage or favourite league. Many followed England as they are fans of the Premier League but were unsurprisingly disappointed again.

Games were on at convenient times in the morning, so I watched most at home before work but several in city bars opened up for viewing over breakfast. The atmosphere at these was great, except for after the final whistle of the Netherlands v Argentina semi-final as the Dutch fans who had taken over the bar were gutted, especially since they had looked like they might go on and win the thing.

I picked Germany from the outset and was pleased when they won it with that style of football, but was shocked at their hammering of Brazil. I was disappointed for the Brazilians who had done so much to host a great tournament despite the odds and had expected so much from their team.

Steve Lowndes, Wellington, New Zealand

FRIDAY 18TH JULY 2014

I wake at 6.14am…I try to fall back to sleep but it isn't possible…Now it is 7.10am…My final day in Brazil.

Alarm call asked for at 7.30…It is now 7.33…No call… Good job I am awake. The call comes through at 7.35…I jumped the gun!

I call reception for maintenance to sort out the water. I can't face another cold shower and am told they start at 8. My room 1508 can be the first job.

I do some more packing…Too much stuff bought…This is the trouble with being away so long… I should have gone home earlier! I am though genuinely concerned as to whether everything will fit in the suitcase and hand luggage…

But also as to how much everything will weigh.. I try to put as much of the heavy stuff in the hand luggage as possible and hope to wing it...

Earlier in the week the weather forecast gave a 60% chance of rain today... Not the ideal way to end my stay...Well unless it starts when I am on the way to the airport... But it feels very hot this morning...Let's hope the rain keeps away... 31 degrees is forecast in London today! I imagine the misery of being on an underground train in a business suit...

This four star hotel gives off the appearance of being top notch...The lobby is modern, smart and spacious. Having moved out of the economic prison cell, my room is actually fabulous...Spacious, stylish, double bed and a single bed too.... The breakfast here, as in all the Brazilian hotels I have stayed, is very good and with lots of choice...

It's just a shame they can't get the basics right... Hot water, lifts that work as you would expect them to...Having paid for Wi-Fi to actually be able to access it in the room, reasonable queuing times at the reception desk. A lot of the guests are saying the same thing...The hotel only opened this year so hopefully these are just teething problems.

The reason for writing this is that having spent time packing and messing about with the plumbing...Time is as usual a bit of a scarce commodity ahead of meeting Walter in the hotel lobby at 8.30am for the favela tour...

Walter arrives at 8 40 to take bus number 308 for the 20 minute ride to the Rocinha favela.

Walter tells me that only Alemao, which even has a cable car, with a population of c300,000 is bigger than Rocinha which has 280,000 inhabitants. When I meet Aline later in the day, Aline views Rocinha as the largest with Alemao being a group of several individual favelas.

Walter says he is a 41 years old Argentinian, an Independiente supporter from Cordoba who moved to Rio 12 years ago, married a Brazilian lady which sadly ended in divorce two years ago and has one child. He now lives in an apartment in the Central part of the city.

We arrive at Rocinha and Walter takes me up onto a footbridge crossing the road below for photographs with the favela acting as a back drop. The favela which is set in the hills behind me has buildings painted in various warm pastel colours such as lilacs, yellows, light blues and greens...

In all honesty I don't know quite what to expect in visiting a favela. There had been a documentary on TV before the World Cup, I think with Rio Ferdinand visiting a favela but with all that was going on in organising my trip...I never had the chance to see the program. I am eager to learn as much as I can about favela life but also a little apprehensive. I guess going all the way back to my first visit to Brazil in around the millennium, I have kind of built up an image of poverty, crime, violence and a favela being a dangerous place to go anywhere near..

It is 9.15am and we are about to enter Rocinha favela...Just before we do I say to Walter that I am writing a book and ideally would like to walk around with my iPhone in my hand taking notes and photographs...Yes, yes no problem he says... But people have said even on Copacabana and Ipanema my iPhone could be snatched from me. I have heard numerous stories of phones having been stolen. My diary is backed up but my 3000+ photographs are not backed up... Walter assures me it will be safe!

Throughout my whole five weeks in Brazil, I have walked around with my iPhone in my hand writing this book, sat in football stadiums, been on metros, public buses, stood in fan fests, walked along Copacabana late at night capturing the moment... At no time have I ever felt in any immediate danger... At times I have gripped my phone a little more tightly...On other occasions I have held onto my phone in the pockets of my shorts...Sensible precautions...But on other occasions as you well know...I have had one or two drinks or more... The thought occurs to me that perhaps the bulkiness of the charger case may disguise the iPhone...Maybe potential thieves, who are after a sleek iPhone, have mistaken my phone for another model...Or maybe I have just been a combination of streetwise and lucky...

And now I am going to be wandering around a favela... iPhone in hand...It feels like I have been in training for five weeks...Now is the ultimate challenge... The grand finale!

We take our first steps into the favela which is built into the side of quite a steep hill. We are at the bottom of the hill which seems to be a town centre area. There are the usual assortment of restaurants, bars and shops you would expect to see in a bustling community...Food, clothing...Even an electronics store with an immaculate white tiled floor and containing an assortment of laptops on display microwaves, flat screen televisions with brand names such as LG etc.

There is even a bank...I didn't expect that! In fact Rocinha feels very similar to a normal lower end community which somewhat kind of takes me by surprise.

Overhead cables dominate the view... running across the streets, along the side of buildings, up and down wooden poles in what look like an unstructured haphazard confused state.

Up ahead to the left and behind the buildings there is a four legged electricity pylon which rises steeply above the houses. Beyond the hills is the dense green vegetation of the hills or are they mountains...I can never decide!

Walter tells me that a favela operates almost entirely independently from the councils and governments. Rocinha has its own Mayor and Government who are voted in by the population living in the favela.

Rio allocates money to the favela for the local administration to determine how the money is spent between the usual conflicting priorities of health, education, policing etc.

It is for the most part a self-sufficient community. The workers earn a maximum of around 800 reals a month and can be as a low as 500 to 600 reals so fall below the lower tax threshold.

The cost of living is cheaper though... A studio apartment costs around 350 reals a month and a good meal can be had for about 6 reals.

As we walk up the hill and go deeper into the favela, there are all manner of shops which you would expect to see in a normal thriving local community... Even a pet shop. I feel safe...Safe enough to feel that I could actually come back and walk around these streets on my own.

Looking down some of the side passages, the poverty is very visible...There are uneven steps down to walkways between the houses and more uneven steps rising up the other side, presumably back up to a road on the other side. No street lighting...Night time on these steps would be a quite challenge for an unfamiliar stranger.

Many of the windows and particularly those within reach of the stairs and walkways have been bricked up. Some of the lower rooftops are made of corrugated metal. Make shift washing lines are drying clothes, the green and yellow bunting and Brazilian flags are shown, cables everywhere. A little girl of say nine or ten years old is sat alone on a bottom step...Unwittingly creating a powerful and poignant image...

Walter tells me that some maybe many of the inhabitants will work and live here and possibly never leave Rocinha. There are others who venture out to work in the service industries of Rio be it manual labour, tourist or domestic sectors. Aline had previously told me that the security guy at her apartment lives in the nearby Cantagalo favela.

There are black and white civil police cars driving around the favela. These are managed by the administrators of the favela rather than the Rio police authorities.

There are also taxis and motor bike taxis on the streets which are dedicated to the Rocinha favela. They operate purely within the confines of the favela.

On a bend in the road, there is a very high wall perhaps seven or eight metres, over 20 feet, in height which is covered with street art...Paintings and written words.

One reads:

"Por consequencia da limpeza vem a saude" which translates to "In consequence of the cleaning comes to health"

A number of others begin with the word "Tagarela" which on later using a translator means "Chatterbox"

With headlines below such as "Vacine seu filho contra paralisa"...."Vaccinate your child against paralysis" with a painting of a lady in a nurses red cross hat.

It seems that graffiti is used in a more practical manner in the favela than may be seen outside of a favela.

The vast majority of the buildings would be regarded as dilapidated in the Western World and not fit to live in...

I notice the white Rio buses driving through the favela which Walter confirms is a part of the normal bus route.

We pass a number of skips overflowing with refuse to such an extent that rubbish has spilled on to the roads and by the side of the road. The stench is awful...The first really unpleasant experience in my time in the favela. I guess this a drop off point for people to dump their domestic waste for wagons to come and lift the skips to take away...

As we climb the hill, the streets continue to be covered with bunting in the green and yellow of Brazil. There are some much more affluent pastel coloured apartments to our right which have been well built and maintained. Many of them have satellite dishes and the road outside these apartments is tree lined.

I am stretching out a little ahead of Walter and jokingly turn round to say come on Walter keep up...Walter says he is surprised by my age because in his words I have a full head of hair, am fit and have a youthful outlook in my eyes.

I have heard it said on a number of occasions that the favelas have the best views of Rio and looking from the favela out to sea and up to the green hills I can understand why.

Walter takes a different route on our walk back down. We come across a school which is used throughout the day and the evenings.

I haven't been able to substantiate this but Walter believes the classes are split into the following relatively short three sessions:

8am to Noon: Five to eight year old children

1pm to 5pm: Nine to twelve year olds

7pm to 10pm: Thirteen to eighteen year olds

And outside of these hours kids are often seen working in shops etc to support their families. Some children take buses to more regular schools outside of the favela.

Postscript: In trying to substantiate the school hours, I found this blog by a person who grew up in Rocinha which talks of the prejudices faced by someone just because they were born in a favela...An interesting read:

http://lifeinrocinha.blogspot.co.uk/2012/04/random-stuff-to-think-about.html

In addition to the schools, Walter says there are facilities for other activities elsewhere in Rocinha which range from a samba school to football, swimming, volleyball et al.

The favela has its own hospital, dentists and doctors. A 24 hour medical centre is located next to the school and I walk inside to have a look round. There is a busy, brightly lit low ceilinged waiting area in the centre. Running off the centre are corridors to what appear to be waiting areas. Obviously I have no idea of the quality of service provided but from just standing inside the Medical Centre, the standard is far better than my preconceived idea of what a favela Medical Centre might look like.

Walter tells me that burials do not take place within the favela but within the regular Rio community.

I notice the street cleaners are in the orange outfits worn by those deployed elsewhere in Rio and Walter confirms the refuse collectors and street cleaners are from Rio and mainly from the Gavia district.

We walk down a side street and all the bars are closed with shutters down but Walter says at night they will all be open and it is a really good vibrant, community atmosphere.

We leave the favela and what a fascinating experience it has been. I give Walter a 10 reals tip on the agreed 30 reals fee which he is delighted by and promptly buys me a beer!

We take bus number 359 back to Copacabana at a cost of 3 reals each. The bus, as a part of its route, takes us on a complete but rickety tour of the favela before heading back towards Copacabana!

On the way back I learn a little about how the drug gangs operate...

It seems there are two drug gangs in Rocinha. One controls the upper area and the other controls the lower area. There is a lot of animosity which spills over into turf wars between the two gangs. There are armed fights between the gangs and also with the police. Walter says there was even a battle either just before or during the World Cup with deaths occurring...

Anyone buying drugs from one gang must take care to ensure any future purchases are from the same gang or they are likely to face retribution from the first gang...

Favela prisons are very small and generally used to house prisoners for short seven to ten day cooling off periods. Longer sentences would be determined by the usual Rio courthouses and the custodial sentences would be served in the mainstream Rio prisons.

Walter said that for the last five years or so, in preparation for the World Cup, the National Government has used "Pacification Units" to clamp down on the drug gangs and favela violence.

Eight gang leaders were captured in Rocinha and put behind bars. This meant that the police were able to analyse the movement of the drugs and agents. It sounds a complicated operation to manage the drugs which emanate from leaves grown in Bolivia and Colombia. Colombian technologies and laboratories, which Walter says are regarded as the most advanced, are then used prior to moving the drugs into Brazil including through favelas and finally to the tourists and locals in places such as Copacabana and Ipanema.

Pleased to be hearing this after rather than before my visit to the favela and just a few hours before I fly home! Imagine if it had been on my first day in Brazil!

There are three favelas on Copacabana...Cantagalo which is near my hotel which has a population of c20000; Pavao c15000 population and Tabajara c5000 population. Chapeu favela controls Leme which shares the same bay as Copacabana.

The gangs from the differing favelas tend to respect each other and their boundaries and clients. The gangs want to be allowed to sell drugs in the tourist areas of Copacabana and Ipanema but the authorities won't allow them to. Street trading is illegal. Instead it seems, informally, the hotel staff might have a contact number should any guest ask the question. Similarly locals wanting drugs will either have contact numbers or visit the favelas directly.

It seems that here is a feeling amongst the public that education is the main weapon to fight the perceived corruption at all levels within the authorities...

Walter surprises me by saying there are in the region of 50 favelas in the Rio area and that about a third of the six million plus population lives in a favela.

The most dangerous favelas are outside of Rio in the metropolis where there aren't any police and the people are very impoverished with poor schools, hospitals and transport.

Learning how many people live in favelas leads me to ask how many people live in the main Rio beach areas. Walter amazes me by knowing!

Copacabana 160000

Ipanema Leblon 140000

Flamengo 110000

Botofogo 110000

Walter said more than a million people visited Brazil for the World Cup and about 800000 of them visited Rio. It did seem that most fans tended to use Rio as a base or at the very least visit the city. The largest influx of fans was unsurprisingly the Argentines with an estimated 100, 000 being here for the final! Colombia and Chile were assessed to have also brought tens of thousands.

These numbers pale into insignificance as compared to the three million who attended the Papal visit on Copacabana!

Sadly the Pope's visit was a disaster for many tradesmen. The visit was originally scheduled to be three hours away in Guaratiba ...Local tradesmen invested in drink and food etc. but one week before, floods forced the event to be moved to Copacabana...Local tradesmen lost everything...One man alone 20,000 reals!

We arrive back on Copacabana for 11.30am and say our goodbyes after a really interesting and enjoyable three hours.

Even after being here five weeks, I am still not used to the cultural differences between Europeans and South Americans in terms of pavement etiquette.

Not a criticism just a difference in that in Europe we have a degree of compromise to avoid bumping into each other... Here, there isn't that little subtle movement by a pedestrian who may be stood blocking the path or walking towards to me. I sense that if I don't move, we will bump into each other... Something that happened a couple of times in my early days here but now whenever I think about it I try to anticipate...But in my haste not today #collision

On returning to the hotel, I take the lift up to the roof top...Good view over Copacabana beach from the 18th floor...I am fully packed and in the lobby to check out by 12.35...12.48 out of the hotel with a taxi arranged to go to the airport at 4.30.

On route to the fort, I finally buy some flip flops! Brazilian yellow with the number one on the left foot and nought on the right foot.

I walk down to the fort at the Ipanema end of Copacabana bay and the military kindly waive the entrance fee to let me in to take some photographs. I ask a guy to take one of me and return the compliment.

Walking along the promenade to meet Aline and Jessica, I order a caipirinha from a vendor by the beach...Five reals...Post WC prices!!

I watch how the vendor prepares a caipirinha. He cuts a lime into eight pieces, adds two table spoonfuls of sugar which are crushed together with the lime before adding ice. All are closed in the shaker, shaken and poured into a glass with cachaça, added and stirred... A straw is put into the glass and another caipirinha is ready to be drunk...Mmmm!!

I meet Aline and Jessica for a drink at a beach side bar in front of the Hotel Pestana for one last drink. I will never make the beach today! As they have never visited a favela, I give them a flavour of my visit to Rocinha and they are now sufficiently intrigued to ask for Walter's details.

In talking of favela crime, Aline says that in April, a dancer from a TV show called Douglas Rafael da Silva Pereira, nicknamed DG, went to see his child and ex-partner in the Cantagalo favela and was killed. The police pacification unit was carrying out an armed operation against drug gangs with shots being fired.

In the days after, the riots were so bad that the area including Nossa Senhora and Barata Ribeiro was closed. On the day of the funeral and the day after in the confusion, one of the protesters was shot dead by the police.

Gosh this is all very close to where I have been staying and feels very close to home so to speak.

An investigation of the police is still ongoing...

Aline then says that yesterday in the upmarket suburb of Gavia, a lady owner of a restaurant collected 13,000 reals from the bank to pay wages. Two motor cyclists tried to mug her. She resisted and was shot in the head and died. Such incidents are apparently very unusual and especially in such an area as Gavia...

Sometimes, the less you know...

We have a couple of final photographs, finish our drinks and I take one long last look along Copacabana beach...absorbing its beauty for one final time...

We walk up Santa Clara and I buy individual match magazines from a news kiosk...

I ask Aline to hold my magazines and nip across the road and surprise them with flowers as a thank you for their hospitality and friendship. They are very special people...We say our goodbyes.

I go in search of cachaça and a caipirinha shaker.

Three shops later, I give up and then realise Aline must have my World Cup magazines. Aline asks me to call in at her apartment to collect them. While there I charge my phone whilst using the bathroom. I send a couple of Wi-Fi messages and we need to leave as Aline has a hair appointment at 3.30 and I would like to take a taxi to the airport by 4.30 with a twenty minute buffer. My flight is 7.50pm and the taxi journey is about one hour which will mean arriving at the airport two hours before my flight...All good!

I see a store selling wines and spirits near Xavier da Silveira...I find a caipirinha shaker crusher and a bottle of cachaça All for 85 reals.

I run down to pick my flip flops up from the shop...All paid for earlier today at 1150 Nossa Senhora, nip into the Savoy Othon Hotel to back up my diary and contemplate buying some food at the corner cafe.. Not eaten since breakfast... Think better of it and arrive back at the hotel by 4.40pm.

After retrieving my two bags, I change in the restroom and come out to pick up a taxi...I am concerned about the weight of the suitcase...The time is 4.50pm... Oh no, no, nooo...When charging the phone for those few minutes at Aline's I had to remove a part of the charger case and in the rush didn't pick it up. It is laid on the arm of the sofa...Aline is at the hairdresser's...I text her...No answer...I try to call her but the phone system isn't working. I text Jessica who answers straight away to say she doesn't have a key. I will have to go without it...Aline texts back to say she has left it with the front desk at the hotel. I have no idea as to how she achieved this... We walked out the apartment together and up the road as Aline was on her way to the hairdressers?

The hotel staff summon a taxi...The driver puts the small bag in the boot and straps the large suitcase in the front seat.

I ask the driver to go to the airport via Cinco de Julho. To do this he can't turn left down Ribeiro but has to drive two blocks towards the beach and turn left onto Nossa Senhora... At my request he stops the car and opens the boot for me to check my sweat top is in my bag in the boot...

The traffic is heavy as we are moving into the rush hour period... At every opportunity he is adjusting the position of the suitcase on the front seat...

Eventually we end up on Cinco de Julio., Even allowing for the one way system, exasperatingly, the driver has gone a long way round... Time is ebbing away...I pick up the telephone cover and we set off for the airport. The driver is still fiddling with the suitcase on the front seat. At the next traffic lights, I offer to move the case into the back which he jumps at the chance of. I think he is worried about the case falling on him while driving which is why I made the offer...Still no idea why it isn't in the boot...Isn't that what boots are for?

It is a struggle to get the seat belt undone, the straps removed, pull the case out the front door, shove it through the back door and shuffle it on to the back seat...The traffic lights have turned green and there are a lot of cars behind our taxi...Car horns are honking... The weight of the case is bothering me...heard some horror stories of excessive baggage charges at airports lately...

Duran Duran on the radio...No not Rio haha

The traffic is very heavy...We are making slow progress...

At 5.30, the driver said we would be at the airport by 6pm. It is now 6pm and he is now saying 6.20pm...We are hardly moving...There is just a trail of red tail lights in front of us...I am starting to get a little anxious...

It is 6.09...My long haul international flight takes off in 1 hour, 41 minutes... The driver says we are 5kms away...5 minutes without traffic... But there is traffic and lots of it...We remain stationary...An ambulance with its sirens blaring passes us...

We are stopping and starting now...And stopping again now...I am gonna to write a classic, gonna write it in an attic is on the radio...I think...I am trying to write one in the back of a Rio de Janeiro taxi!

The driver is talking to me in Portuguese... Ian... Where are you ...Help!!

The sign is to turn right to the airport...The lane is very busy...Standing traffic... The driver is going straight on... Suddenly the roads are clear...But I have no clue where we are going... It is 6.20 now and time is now a very precious commodity...I look through the front window screen...Miraculously we are here...How did that happen!!

Taxi fare 80.80 reals...I count out 81 reals in cash..,. The driver makes his displeasure known...But he hadn't seen that I had another 7 reals for him...Then he is happy.

I have to confess though that before I found a 20 real note in my back pocket...I was worried that I wouldn't have enough for the fare...I was told to expect a fare of 50 reals and 70 absolute tops...The collection of a part of the charger case would have added a little and the traffic the rest...

I dash in to the check in...Unsurprisingly...No queue! Explain the issue of KLM writing in Italian re booking the extra leg room on the wrong leg of the flight...The guy is great...He says probably because I look Italian with my skin colour and hat!

It would be 130 Euros to upgrade to extra leg room...I decide not to. He asks me to put my suitcase onto the scales...32.1kgs...He says 23kgs is the maximum and that I am almost 10kgs over. I explain my two flight rebookings and the cost of changing. Then I add that I am writing a book. He asks if I am a writer...First book I reply but am hoping to become one. He does scripts too for short cinema films...He gives me his email address and I promise to write. He wants to read my book and has offered to help with any Portuguese translations and smiling says my luggage is checked all the way through to Birmingham...What a great guy and a great last memory of this wonderful country.

I haven't eaten since breakfast and commit to spending my last 12.25 reals on a snack!!

I give the lady behind the food counter my money and we somehow arrive at a mutual understanding that I want to spend it all on food

As I had another 30 minutes before the check in closes...Perhaps it would have been better to have taken the taxi 20 minutes later and had something to eat in Copacabana.... Joke!!

I am required to take my belt off through security...Shoes stay on...No queues! I then proceed to passport control and hand over the customs documents that I have somehow managed to keep safe during my five weeks of travelling around Brazil...Passport stamped.

Wait a minute, where is my belt? It didn't come through on the conveyor... Maybe it's in my hand luggage? Nope...Run back to security and a lady is waving it in the air... No not in a...I want to spank you way haha...

Funnily enough...Even with my belt on...My jeans feel as if they might fall down at any minute...I am constantly pulling them up...Strange as in my upper body I feel as if I have put weight on.

I must remind you guys and myself... I did have two caipirinhas this afternoon... And on an empty stomach!! Well if it's before 10pm...It will be on an empty stomach!!

Eating a fish dinner at close to midnight last night...Well that is close to 4am UK time... Almost breakfast...Jet lag could well be an issue after 5 weeks in Brazil...

I sit down to charge my phone on one of the handy towers the Brazilian airports provide... I receive a tap on the shoulder from behind... Uh huh...What now??? It is my new friend from check in saying hello!!

It is 7.22pm...My flight is in 28 minutes and the passengers are boarding. I will watch the queue and charge my phone for as long as possible...It is at 42% and I don't have the luxury of the charger case which hasn't worked for some days.

It is now 7.30pm...The queue has gone...Shall I board or give myself another five minutes? We don't need another Charles de Gaulle Air France adventure! I am up to 47%...Flight mode on, brightness dimmed and I am boarding the plane. My smiling friend from check in is waiting to check my boarding pass and passport. What a delightful charming man... Can we replicate for customer service with a smile all over the world!!!

Then it hits me...One of the reasons for loving Brazil so much...I am not just a number here...The old values we used to have are still upheld here. Service staff are not so bound by governance and rules. They don't get in to trouble if they don't strictly follow the rules... The computer says no approach so brilliantly depicted in a UK sketch show... People genuinely care and want to be nice... To help. The military guy at the fort today and the guy at the fan fest yesterday. The list is endless...It makes for a better society and the people in general don't always follow the less restrictive rules either!

I am in the queue waiting to board the plane and I am looking at the guy in front of me from behind so to speak. He looks vaguely familiar but not in a celebrity or friend way... Then it comes to me...At the fort today, I asked a guy if he would mind taking a photograph of me and then I returned the compliment... I have to ask if he was at the fort today...In a guarded Dutch accent, he says yes he was...I say...I don't believe it...We took a photograph of each of us there... And then he recognises me and says...What a small world...Not for the first time I have thought that during this adventure!

Chances of what just happened happening? At the very best...Once in a life time...Haha...And what an amazing way to step off Brazilian soil onto the aeroplane.

I go to my seat...37C and obviously...There is someone sat in it...Why wouldn't there be? The guy jumps up and starts babbling away very quickly in a foreign language... I am English...He then asks would I mind changing seats as it would be nice for him to sit with his two children.

He shows me his boarding pass seat of 34C...The seat is three rows in front of my seat...No problem but would you mind moving the person sat in your seat... Musical planes!!!

It is a Brazilian lady who is travelling with her friend to Dublin to learn English...She doesn't speak any English but her friend does.

In the first five minutes of being sat in my seat, I kid you not...I have had to move her elbows back to her side of the arm rest on three occasions...Now she has a carry-on bag in her hand...She is stood up leaning back into me craning her neck to see if she can put the bag in the overhead luggage compartment... From that angle...not a chance and it is anyway full...I offer to put it into the one in front which through translation is appreciated. I lift it into the compartment and of course the people in the row in front turn to face me with a look which says...I hope you haven't squashed my luggage....well two of them do as the third, who is sat in front of me, has his seat in the reclining position and, for some reason, is vigorously rocking backwards and forwards!

Now the lady sat next to me has tears in her eyes. The passing air stewardess stops and asks if everything is ok. Her friend says she is scared of flying and feeling very worried. The stewardess reaches across me and kindly holds her arm to ask if there is anything she can do. Through her friend translating ...A glass of water would be helpful. The stewardess is fantastic with her and saying if there is anything she needs or to discuss, to press the stewardess button immediately.

Now she is up on her feet, trying to impossibly reach the bag I put in the locker just a few minutes ago! A passing steward obliges and waits while she gets what she needs and he puts the bag back into the overhead...

This has all happened within the first ten minutes of me sitting in my seat...

Well not my seat...Hmm, how much did the guy pay those two children to be their father for a few minutes!

The captain announces that aboard this 777-200 as long as phones and iPads are on flight mode, they can be kept on gate to gate. I have never heard that said before.

The captain announces a flight time of 11 hours 5 minutes... It has all the ingredients for being a long night! Come back Mr Nigeria, all is forgiven!! From now on Ms Brazil will be Ms Nigeria in honour of my Ivory Coast man who I nicknamed Mr Nigeria... I wonder if all this makes sense!

Now the lady who is how can I tactfully put it...Let's say a little on the large rather than small side...It has been hot today...She is wearing a sweater...Luggage will have been lugged to the airport. She is scared of flying...Now she has her right arm in the air, bent at the elbow and her lower arm is behind her head...I think rubbing her left shoulder. I am to her right...Which means I am getting the full benefit of her open armpit...Lovely!

8.40pm KLM flight KL 0706 is heading down the runway...We are airborne...5 weeks, 2 hours and 47 minutes precisely after I first touched down at 5.53pm on Friday 13th June. The outside temperature on arrival was 23 degrees...On departure 24 degrees...Tough winter!!

EL GRINGO'S ONCE IN A LIFETIME

Mosquito bites I didn't know I had around my ankles are itching ...Great!!!

Yaay...Ms Nigeria has fallen asleep. I am thirsty and ask the stewardess for a drink of water...Nothing is too much trouble for the cabin crew...Early days but the service on this flight is top notch...It is a long time since I flew KLM and ponder whether it is always this good or have the staff been requested to be at their best following yesterday's appalling terrorist attack on the flight from Holland to Malaysia...

Turbulence is quite heavy...The captain asks for seatbelts to be fastened...Ms Nigeria is awake...Heightened senses...Red alert...Not for too long though...The turbulence subsides and Ms Nigeria is back in the land of nod. She has one of the neck supports on and her head is leaning my way...Bless...

The stewardess brings TUC biscuits around with drinks off the trolley...I am very dry...Three more glasses of water...I ask what drinks she has... And she names a few and says anything I want really...Great! Caipirinha please... With a smile...You have probably had enough during your time in Brazil. I take a Heineken...We exchange names and I comment to Kate on how warm and friendly the crew are. I ask if yesterday's events had led to a special effort being requested by Management.

Kate says no not at all...This is normal and that she is my princess for the flight! The crew were in Rio when the shocking news came through...With it happening to a sister airline, there are all sorts of rumours as to how many KLM crew were on board...There is a feeling of everyone either knowing someone on board or knowing someone who knows someone...

It makes me sick to the core...A plane flying from Holland to Malaysia... Shot down over the Ukraine...Not even remotely connected to the conflict... Senseless..

Ms Nigeria is snorting in her sleep ...Right in my ear...Charming...Her right elbow is also encroaching into my ribs... I haven't the heart to wake her.

The battery is down to 23%...The time is 10.05pm...1 hour 25 minutes into the flight.

I am laughing and sharing a private joke with the Irish guy in the seat in front of me... Like me he is in the aisle seat. Already his sleep has been disturbed twice by the middle and window seat passengers wanting to pass by him...He is quite a big chap and has had to stand up four times already to let them by!

I am also feeling very tired...Struggling to keep my eyes open...Ugh... Loudest snort to date. I wonder whether the cabin crew have a point to charge their phones and will ask at a convenient moment.

Kate points me in the direction of a socket to charge my phone...The sockets are in each galley for the vacuum cleaners...Useful to know! Even has a British as well as European charging point.

Kate should win stewardess of the year. She says if I am not able to sleep to come down to the back of the plane for a chat. I thank her as with Ms Snorter next to me it is highly likely I won't be having much sleep. She says to do what she does to her boyfriend and mimes an elbow to the ribs! She is bubbly and funny with it.

One steward comes to tell me the charger won't work. I show him it is working.

Then another steward is not happy that I am sat on the floor by an emergency door and sends me to the back of the plane to stand in front of a toilet door and an emergency door...

1.45am I wake up in my seat. Must have slept in a funny position...My right foot has rolled over and hurting...My neck is too and I am very dry...Economy class on long haul flights during the night, sure most of us know it feels.......five hours into the flight.. Not half way yet...

2.10 am I am woken by Ms Nigeria and her friend who wish to go to the rest room.

2.30 I am woken again by the ladies who wish to return to their seats...

4.28 tickly cough...

EL GRINGO'S ONCE IN A LIFETIME

In Brazil, before the World Cup starts, we all had these thoughts: will everything be ready on time? Will it be a shame for Brazil? Will my city, Rio de Janeiro be able to hold such a big event? Even with all the money spent, as this was the most expensive World Cup ever staged, we didn't deliver as we should.

We could feel the lack of enthusiasm, before the start, people didn't decorate the streets as I used to see every single year…they weren't that excited. The stadium for the opening match wasn't ready and the opening ceremony was almost a disaster in our point of view!

However, we must find something positive in everything, especially in those things that you cannot control or change and taking this thought I entered into the World Cup mood.

The foreigners started to arrive in Rio taking to the streets of Copacabana and bringing to life the feeling of holding a World Cup in my country: it is an experience that I will probably have once in a lifetime!

The truth is that the World Cup brought us hope! Brazilians are friendly people who are crazy about football! And even after we lost in a historical match against Germany, we didn't lose that feeling and didn't stop the party.

We had the opportunity to watch the best soccer players of the world playing in our stadiums, watch their people support them and share their passion! The matches were unforgettable, the goals and the defences! The emotion of a penalty kick decision and of sudden death penalty kicks!

People from everywhere all together by football and love for their country. That is something to remember forever! I am now really looking forward to the Olympics!

Aline Cortes, Copacabana, Rio de Janeiro, Brazil

SATURDAY 19TH JULY 2014

5.45am I wake to receive a hot flannel ahead of breakfast on board the flight from Rio de Janeiro to Amsterdam… Passengers are allowed to open the window screens and daylight is flooding in. It seems a natural point to click the diary over to Saturday 19th July… The final day of my World Cup diary… My 2014 once in a lifetime World Cup adventure in Brazil.

I go to the back of the plane to queue for the restroom and as is my way ask the lady in front of me in the queue if she is returning from the World Cup. We introduce ourselves and yes Margaret from Ireland was flown out by her company to the Argentina versus Holland semi-final as well as the World Cup Final itself… Germany versus Argentina. I must find a job in the right company!!

I mention that I am hoping to publish a World Cup diary and we talk of our experiences and those of a relative of hers who was there in the earlier part of the tournament.

Margaret said Argentinians were offering her $15,000 and even $20000 US Dollars for her World Cup Final ticket… Which she gratefully accepted and is now planning... Only joking!! What sums of money though... Around £14,000... The touts must have made an absolute killing....

Through conversations with friends and family who went out to South Africa for the 2010 World Cup as well as to Brazil... Margaret felt the organisation, logistics and infrastructure were not as good as in South Africa. I didn't go to South Africa so cannot comment although...This is something I heard a number of times during my time in Brazil from people who had been to both.

When I think back to South Africa, my first thoughts are half empty stadiums...

Especially for the Group games with a clamour for FIFA to do something about it as fans wanted to go to games but couldn't buy tickets. My next thought is of the blessed vuvuzelas... Driving everyone crazy watching on television from afar...The final itself...Holland's brutal anti football tactics... Almost but not quite feeling sorry for Howard Webb!! Lampard's goal that never was... And before the tournament the fear of crime against supporters and the difficulties expected in getting around South Africa. The crime and travelling issues never seemed to materialise and those that went thoroughly enjoyed all South Africa had to offer which was a lot and relatively cheap once out there.

With regards to Brazil we agree on the stadiums, surrounding areas and infrastructure not always be ready and especially in the early stages of the competition.

From my own experiences getting around Brazil was not always easy... My friend Ted's experiences which are graphically described in great detail earlier in the diary confirm just how difficult it was...

Margaret talks of the language barrier and how difficult, frustrating and time consuming it could be... Not just in relation to match days but also at major tourist attractions such as Sugar Loaf and trying to book a helicopter flight. I didn't really notice the language issue until after saying goodbye to Ian but after then it was at times difficult, frustrating and time consuming...

We were visitors to a Portuguese speaking country and if Brazilians were visiting England how many of our service staff could respond in Portuguese and our education system is for the most part vastly superior. All that being said, English is regarded as an international language... Could perhaps a little more have been done to make it slightly easier for non-speaking Portuguese visitors?

Margaret though fully enjoyed her World Cup experience and seeing videos of metro stations teeming with Brazilian yellow shirts on match days was a sight to live long in the memory...For her like for many of us seeing a World Cup in Brazil was a fantastic experience...

I look up at the screen... 59 minutes until landing... The second half of the flight seems to have been a lot quicker than the first five hours. Brazilian time is 6.49am...11.49am in Holland and 10.49am in the UK. Generally I adjust my watch to local landing time as soon as I board the plane... I haven't done that this time... My watch... Gosh my new watch which I bought on the outward flight... Not seen it since... It has been locked away in my suitcase for the whole time I was in Brazil.

An announcement by a member of the cabin staff announces over the loudspeaker...Flights close 15 minutes prior to take off in Amsterdam... it is therefore recommended to go straight to the gate... I have four hours in Amsterdam... Enough time to nip into town then... Haha. The temperature in Amsterdam is 30 degrees... Hotter than Rio de Janeiro!!

We land in Amsterdam at 7.50am Rio time and 12.50pm Dutch time. A flight time of 11 hours 30 minutes. A further 15 minutes and we park at the gate and I disembark at 1.13pm into Schipol airport, Amsterdam and boy does it feel hot... Always the same when you leave a winter destination for a summer one!! Even hotter after a 19 minute walk to Gate D53 with heavy hand luggage having landed at terminal F...

My onward departure time is 4.20pm which will give me just over 2-1/2 hours before the gate closes...plenty of time...famous last words!! My battery is at 29%... Continuous battery throughout the flight!! Planes of the future must surely provide charger points for passengers as a matter of course...

I go to the gate at the required time of 3.15pm and it is very busy... My phone has not noted that I am in a different time zone... So plus five hours for Central European time it is 3.58pm I am waiting to board the plane... Flight KL1431 from gate D53 at 4.20pm in the extra leg room seat 15C for the princely sum of an additional €20 to Birmingham. The two seats next to me are empty...No Mr or Ms Nigeria to elbow me on my final flight of Brazil2014 and at 4.35pm we take off...Homeward bound!

It is 5.09pm CET and 4.09pm BST... The cabin crew announce over the loudspeaker that we have started our descent and will land into Birmingham in 20 minutes. The temperature is 21 degrees... And it is raining...Thought Amsterdam was too good to be true!! A Chicken Tikka Madras with Vegetable Rice has been calling me for the last few hours... I note that I haven't eaten since breakfast... Now there's a surprise!

We land at 4.32pm BST... Looking out of the plane window there are very black clouds in the skies above... Good old Blighty! The grass looks sodden and there are pools of standing water on concreted areas... There has been one hell of a storm here... No wonder there was turbulence as we began our descent!!

We park up at 4.35pm...Back in the UK!!

To all the people who contributed towards the writing of this diary... I thank you from the bottom of my heart. Not just for the stories you shared... Even more for the friendship we shared... The memories we created and the experience of a life time that you helped give me.

Cocooned in my own Brazilian bubble, I have no idea how well Brazil2014 has been received around the World or even in my own country England. What I do know is that to a man, lady or child... Everyone I have come into contact with on my travels has thoroughly enjoyed their visit to Brazil.

Yes, we experienced frustrations along the way, some even crime, fear or shock but overwhelmingly Brazil2014 has been perceived by the fans I met as an enormous success.

Ultimately what made it such a success...?

The drama and theatre created by the players...Surprises came tumbling in from day two with that never to be forgotten score of Spain, the reigning World Champions 1-5 Holland..

All the way through to the jaw dropping semi-final result of Brazil 1-7 Germany...

Ordinarily even the third/fourth playoff result of Brazil 0-3 Holland would be perceived as sensational but I can't bring myself to write that in the context of the semi-final score..

Then there was the surprise team of the tournament... Costa Rica...what a marvellous journey they took us on... From their third day Group game shock 3-1 win over Uruguay which was followed up by a stunning 1-0 victory over Italy...The pace and passing interchanges... Given the size of their country...They effectively won their own World Cup by being penalty kicks away from a place in the semi-finals...

Germany, the 2014 World Champions who went about their business with ruthless efficiency...Who provided some master class team performances and individual brilliance from their goal keeper Neuer throughout the side to their record breaking goalscorer Miroslav Klose. Off the pitch too they were flawless... They wooed and won over the Brazilian public...And not just with their words but also with their actions...The way in which they humbly managed the semi-final victory of the host nation Brazil... No jingoism but instead...Actually apologising to the Brazilian people... The way they respected football in beating the USA in the final group game rather than the bad taste carve up of the Germany v Austria 1-0 win of all those years ago – the only result that would have meant both sides qualifying. Their master class performance off the pitch went all the way back to investing in facilities for the local area...leaving a legacy for many years to come. Words and actions befitting true World Champions.

The enigma that is my own country England which the rest of the world just cannot fathom...They look upon the Premiership with respect and adoration. They love our stars such as Gerrard, Rooney, Sturridge, and Lampard...And yet they cannot understand why such great players cannot form a half decent side... Why a proud powerhouse of a footballing nation can have such little impact... Not only on this World Cup but nearly all others too... Stretching back to 1990 which 24 years ago was the last time England were involved in the business end of the World Cup...As an England fan I felt genuine pity for us from all other fans.. well except the lone Scotsman! Can there be any worse feeling to experience than pity...

The rise of the USA into a true footballing nation... This almost felt like a breakthrough tournament for the USA...What an amazing job Jürgen Klinsmann did as manager to bring such excitement across a nation. Ultimately, they were a last minute tap in away from a place in the World Cup Quarter Finals. This tournament seemingly took football to the masses in the USA as well into the White House. The fans are realistic enough to know they are still a young and to some extent naive footballing nation but that they are on a journey... The country is big enough and rich enough for that journey to one day take them to the very pinnacle of the game.

What of Spain...They came into the tournament as reigning World and European champions... Their club sides dominated European competition in the season just ended... The winners of the Champions League and Europa League... Even had two of their sides from just one city contesting the Champions League... And yet there is a feeling that the Barcelona/Spain possession era might be coming to an end...Their stars of Xavi and Iniesta moving towards the twilight of their career...The team being overtaken by teams such as Germany and Holland who not only play with a Plan B but also with a much more direct breathtaking exhilarating attacking style.. What now for Spain... How can they... How will they respond?

Italy...Historically one of the elite World Cup performers...Went out with a whimper...Anyone choosing the four powerhouse domestic leagues of World football would surely choose in any order...England, Spain, Germany and Italy. Three of those countries were knocked out at the Group stages and the other won the World Cup...Takes some understanding!!

Holland had a great World Cup and as Van Gaal said...Excluding penalties, they never lost a game. They played some fabulous football at times and to beat Spain, Australia, Chile, Mexico and Brazil in one tournament whilst drawing with Argentina and Costa Rica over 120 minutes is some achievement. In any other tournament, that level of performance would arguably have been good enough to at least get to the final if not win it.

Hopping across to Central and South America...

Mexico looked very good but alas will feel robbed of the opportunity to understand how far they could have gone.

They looked strong in the group phase. Their keeper was heroic in the draw against Brazil and the team performance in crushing a good Croatia side was excellent. May be the momentum was anyway with Holland at the time in that ill-fated exit...But who knows...And that will be the everlasting takeaway memory for Mexico...A feeling of unfinished business...

Uruguay...Condensed into won two games with Suarez; Lost two games without

Suarez...And as a result were knocked out without Suarez.

Colombia at times lit up the World Cup with one of the outstanding players of the tournament, James Rodriguez, winning the Golden Boot with six goals and in so doing elevating himself to superstar status ... His goal in the Maracana will live long in the memory. There were concerns that without Falcao, they might not have enough firepower...But Rodriguez alone solved that issue and it wasn't a problem from the 3-0 win in their opening game. Given how poorly Brazil played...May be they could or even should have performed better in that knock out game?

Chile came into the World Cup as potential dark horses. Winning their first two group games and qualifying comfortably, knocking out Spain in the process only added to the feeling that Chile could go deep into the tournament.

The setback in the final group game against Holland did not seem to be too much of an issue...Qualification had after all already been secured. That defeat though did pit Chile against the hosts Brazil...And yet in that game, Chile looked the better side with Pinilla in the final minute of extra time almost putting his team through with a thunderous shot which bounced back off the crossbar. A defeat on penalties was a sad way for the team to go out...

Then onto Brazil...What more can I write of Brazil...Such a shame that having waited all these years to host a World Cup again...And for the most part, during those years, entertained the World with exhilarating, breathtaking, skilful football...That this was the tournament Brazil became an anaemic shadow of their former selves. A long ball team which relied on the individual brilliance of one or two players...Notably Neymar...A fortunate first win over Croatia, benefiting from a couple of at best marginal refereeing decisions...First night nerves was perceived as a viable explanation and so it seemed in their next 2 group games.

The warning signs were flashing in red against Chile...Against Colombia some improvement...But these were only cracks being papered over which were ruthlessly ripped apart by Germany and rubber stamped by Holland.

The psychological damage may last a lot longer than the emotional pain and injured pride of these defeats...

Finally to Argentina...They went into the tournament with people purring over their firepower going forwards but concerns over their defence. The Group phase seemed to confirm this view...Great goals, notably from Messi but also defensive lapses in all three games.

Ironically, the defence only conceded one goal in the whole of the knock out phase...And that was in the 113th minute of the World Cup Final.

The Cup was lost not because of the defence but because the forward line misfired. Messi, Higuain, Palacio all fluffed their lines in front of goal...Enough chances to have fulfilled what for so long seemed to be their destiny...To lift the World Cup in Brazil...

What made this such a good World Cup for me?

The Brazilian people... warm, friendly, helpful, colourful, vibrant, fun loving, nothing ever seemed too much trouble...

The climate....Great weather...Well for the most part!

The setting...Rio de Janeiro... The beaches

The location of the fan fest in Rio

Central and South American fans... They came in their thousands...Their heroes for the most part play in Europe...It was a rare chance for their fans to see their team...And especially in a World Cup Finals. Their passion, the effort they put in to dress up buses, cars, themselves... The effort they made, the sacrifices they made to see their team or to just be in Brazil with little chance of seeing their team...

EL GRINGO'S ONCE IN A LIFETIME

The party atmosphere between the fans...OK there were one or two incidents but only a small percentage and for a very small percentage of the time. Every fan seemed to regard a fellow football fan as a friend...It was a very special atmosphere...Photographs of fans together from different countries...

The drinks...Caipirinhas, fruit juices, Brahma beers etc... The food...The BBQ, the fish...All excellent quality...

Oh yes...And let's not forget the football itself! The tournament equalled the highest number of goals ever of France 98...The excitement, entertaining attacking football...Lots of drama...Last minute goals.....Jubilation and heartache in equal measure.

The goals total equalled the previous record of France '98. Drama a plenty... An excellent World Cup on the pitch!!

Yes it was some World Cup!

And here I am now on a Saturday night in my home... The Bossa Nova CD playing in the background, a homemade caipirinha in my hand... And a Chicken Tikka Madras with Vegetable Rice...Some things you just couldn't get in Brazil!

I pick up a couple of news stories from the World Cup in today's paper:

The Nigerian match ban has lifted and surprisingly Lahm retires from international football at the young age of 30 years old but at the pinnacle of his career.

Postscript: 22nd July...Dunga has been appointed as the new manager of Brazil...I can almost hear the groans of a nation from 9360kms, 5817 miles away in Rio de Janeiro...

I transfer the diary from email into Microsoft Word...Word count shows about 320 pages in font size 10 c170,000 words... Enough for a book with photographs to be added... Talking of photographs, I finally back up the 3000+ photographs on my laptop...Phew...Not being able to find a solution whilst away, with all the iPhones being stolen, was a major risk as well as a constant worry...

There is still a lot of work to be done to turn this into a publishable World Cup diary but at least everything is now in place to be able to have a good go at achieving it.

And to finish the circle...Paul Duncombe, a close friend of mine who is a Spurs season ticket holder living in Brussels, texts me from Seattle to call me a lightweight... Because I am not out there to watch tonight's first preseason game of the new season!

I watch Seattle 3-3 Tottenham Hotspur on a stuttering live stream on my laptop...

Off we go again!

Having the World Cup in Brazil was the opportunity to experience, right here at home, an event which I always believed that I could only watch on TV!!! Experiencing this World Cup means having lots of stories to tell my grandchildren in the future!

Luiz Rangel, Rio de Janeiro, Brazil

The 2018 World Cup is going to be a second championship for Russia in a row, well this time because we're hosting it. Suddenly this fact turned into a popular joke. The general expectations of the World Cup are great as this will mean the massive upgrade of existing venues and construction of the new ones. It will lead to the huge upgrade of the transport and customer services. I believe that besides the huge spending, which will lead to some difficulties for the people of Russia, but once again we would be able to cope with it. I am really sure, that once it's done, the whole world community would be satisfied as Russia is popular for its desire to astonish. Winter Olympics in Sochi is a great example of the possibilities of Russian (and not only the Russian) people.

Millions of people in Russia hope, that despite the well-known controversial issues included the level of racism in Russian football, and perceived discrimination against LGBT people in wider Russian society as well as the involvement in the conflict in Ukraine we, the people of Russia will be let to watch the football of the highest quality and show one more time that we are ready to host such major tournaments and events. We really hope that the whole world in the end will understand that sports and football in particular have nothing to do with politics.

Alexey Pivovarenko, Moscow, Russia

EL GRINGO'S ONCE IN A LIFETIME

EL GRINGO'S ONCE IN A LIFETIME

THE END

Lightning Source UK Ltd.
Milton Keynes UK
UKOW06f2055191014

240264UK00012B/87/P